WRITING HISTORY WITH LIGHTNING

WRITING HISTORY WITH LIGHTNING

CINEMATIC REPRESENTATIONS
OF NINETEENTH-CENTURY
AMERICA

Edited by Matthew Christopher Hulbert
and John C. Inscoe

LOUISIANA STATE UNIVERSITY PRESS   BATON ROUGE

Published by Louisiana State University Press
Copyright © 2019 by Louisiana State University Press
William L. Andrews's essay, "I Survive: Individual, Community, and Slavery
in Steve McQueen's *12 Years a Slave*," copyright © William L. Andrews
All rights reserved
Manufactured in the United States of America
First printing

Designer: Barbara Neely Bourgoyne
Typeface: Whitman
Printer and binder: Sheridan Books

Library of Congress Cataloging-in-Publication Data
Names: Hulbert, Matthew C., editor. | Inscoe, John C., 1951– editor.
Title: Writing history with lightning : cinematic representations of nineteenth-
    century America / edited by Matthew Christopher Hulbert and John C. Inscoe.
Description: Baton Rouge : Louisiana State University Press, [2019] | Includes
    bibliographical references and index.
Identifiers: LCCN 2018035867| ISBN 978-0-8071-7046-5 (cloth : alk. paper) |
    ISBN 978-0-8071-7089-2 (pdf) | ISBN 978-0-8071-7090-8 (epub)
Subjects: LCSH: History in motion pictures. | Historical films—United States—
    History and criticism.
Classification: LCC PN1995.2 .W75 2019 | DDC 791.43/658—dc23
LC record available at https://lccn.loc.gov/2018035867

CONTENTS

III. SECTIONAL CRISIS AND CIVIL WAR

IV. THE LOST CAUSE, RECONSTRUCTION, AND THE WEST

V. LATE-CENTURY ECONOMICS AND IMMIGRATION

ACKNOWLEDGMENTS

In the violent climax of *Unforgiven* (1992), an incredulous "Little Bill" (Gene Hackman) looks up at William Munny (Clint Eastwood)—the hired gun about to extinguish his life—and proclaims, "I don't deserve this." "Deserve's," Munny replies with a signature Eastwood squint, "got nothin' to do with it." Thinking back over the production of *Writing History with Lightning,* this specific scene comes repeatedly to mind. Because whatever I might have done to deserve such a fantastic coeditor, an absurdly talented cast of essayists, and such a supportive press eludes me. Which means, at least in my case, Will Munny was probably right.

The concept for this book grew out of encouraging conversations with two fellow historians and cinephiles, Katherine Charron and Matthew Stanley. When I approached John C. Inscoe about coediting the project, it was admittedly with a guilty conscience; he was in the middle of writing his own book about historical films. But I figured this would be an offer he couldn't refuse. Since nearly the moment John became my doctoral advisor at UGA, we were talking movies. When I left Athens, we kept talking movies. The opportunity to work with John—who is now also a treasured friend—on a book about history and film has been, and always will be, one of the great highlights of my academic career.

On behalf of John and myself, a great deal of thanks is directed to our anonymous reader, everyone at LSU Press, and specifically to James Long. James immediately "got" the project and has been an exemplary editor from start to finish. We'd also like to thank our contributors, not just for accepting our invitation (which sometimes meant writing about pictures outside of their initial comfort zones), but for penning such elegant, insightful, thought-provoking essays. And finally, both Kylie Hulbert and Jane Inscoe deserve more gratitude than space will allow for the untold hours they've endured our film nerdiness— and for the untold hours still hopefully to come.

WRITING HISTORY WITH LIGHTNING

Introduction

Reappraising a Century's Worth of Lightning

MATTHEW CHRISTOPHER HULBERT

In the spring of 1915 a small, rather select audience convened at 1600 Pennsylvania Avenue—then the residence of Woodrow Wilson—and enjoyed a private screening of D. W. Griffith's new film, *The Birth of a Nation*. It's not hyperbole to say that at more than three hours long, starring silent-era heavyweights like Lillian Gish and Henry Walthall and replete with revolutionary new camera angles, its likes had never been seen before. In terms of both technical innovation and directorial panache the film set new standards for America's nascent motion-picture industry; and it established Griffith, at just forty years old, as a titan of the silver screen. Unfortunately, having been adapted from Thomas Dixon Jr.'s 1905 novel, *The Clansman: An Historical Romance of the Ku Klux Klan* (and in part from Dixon's stage adaption of the novel), the movie also peddled the very worst exhibits of white supremacy the Jim Crow South, a place in time literally renowned for the virulence of its racism, had to offer.

The plot of the film involved the untimely collapse of the Confederate States of America; in its place, spectators—the vast majority of them white—watched in growing horror as an unholy alliance of avaricious, northern Republicans and newly enfranchised freedmen transformed the idyllic Old South into a postslavery hellscape. Black veterans prowl the street, bullying and humiliating their former masters. Black politicians run amok in the South Carolina statehouse, grinding serious business to a halt. Most egregious of all, black predators lust openly after virginal white women. One scene, perhaps the most sensational of the entire film, goes so far as to depict a southern damsel, hounded to the edge of a cliff by one of these would-be rapists, preserving her chastity by way of airborne suicide. Just when this carnival atmosphere appears

1

to become irreversible, a group of ex-Confederates founds the Ku Klux Klan, and the tables begin to turn back, one violent encounter at a time. The Klansmen ride onto the screen like white knights of medieval lore (quite literally, given their regalia), put the African Americans back in their rightful, inferior place, and ultimately restore "order" to southern society.

The Birth of a Nation trumpets a rendition of the Civil War and Reconstruction in keeping with a Lost Cause ideology—still very much alive and thriving in 1915—in which southern race relations functioned smoothest under slavery and in which Johnny Reb, not his Yank oppressor, was truly the best and wisest man all along. It isn't difficult to imagine Griffith, the son of a well-known Confederate colonel, promoting such views. More troubling, though, is that Woodrow Wilson—himself a southerner, a Democrat, and far from a trailblazer for civil rights—allegedly said after seeing Griffith's version of the story on screen that it was "like writing history with lightning." "My only regret," he purportedly added, "is that it is all so terribly true." If these pronouncements were authentic, President Wilson would hardly have been alone in his melodramatic assessment of the film's historical pedigree. *The Birth of a Nation* became an overnight sensation, adored by spectators on either side of the Mason-Dixon line. In turn, the "history" it dispersed to the mainstream masses galvanized white supremacists nationwide and helped justify the hamstringing of many an egalitarian reform enacted in the immediate aftermath of the Civil War.[1]

This influence over the public mind should not surprise us. Nor is the ability to perceive this power unique to us in the twenty-first century. Wilson clearly understood it in 1915, just as investigators for the House Un-American Activities Committee (HUAC) did during the Second Red Scare in the 1940s and 1950s. In 1947 HUAC anchored its effort to root out a communist infiltration of the United States not only in Washington, DC, or New York City but also in Hollywood and issued the following rationale for doing so:

> The motion-picture industry represents what is probably the largest single vehicle of entertainment for the American public—over 85,000,000 persons attend the movies each week. However, it is the very magnitude of the scope of the motion-picture industry which makes this investigation so necessary. We all recognize, certainly, the tremendous effect which moving pictures have on their mass audiences, far removed from the Hollywood sets. We all recognize that what the citizen sees and hears in his neighborhood movie house carries a powerful impact on his thoughts and behavior.[2]

In other words, as mediums for mass communication go, film resides in a class by itself. Like printed materials, films have the ability to reach colossal audiences. Unlike books, magazines, newspapers, or even film scripts themselves, however, films are not typically constrained by matters of literacy or intellectual accessibility. The ability to bypass literacy, to compress hundreds or even thousands of pages of narrative into an afternoon, and to remove much of the burden of imagining foreign places, costumes, and customs is what differentiates many films from their textual origins as projectors of popular history. Films have virtually unlimited power to share ideas and symbols; to praise and honor causes and characters; to endorse or attack political ideologies; to carve out and normalize legacies; and to regulate patterns of collective remembrance on a national scale. Even social-media platforms such as Facebook, Twitter, and Instagram, each with millions of registered members, cannot begin to rival film in its ability to tell a coherent, memorable story packed with propaganda. In this sense, movies are something akin to historical Trojan horses.

But not all historical movies are created equal. The race and gender of audience members, as well as a film's genre, are critical to whether it will be accepted as a legitimate visualization of history by the moviegoing public. Comedies, while frequently laden with relevant political satire and social commentary—*The Great Dictator* (1940), *Dr. Strangelove* (1964), *Blazing Saddles* (1974), and *Network* (1976) being prime examples—are generally not accepted as a genre capable of painting a historical picture of the American experience, either in the time period they depict on screen or in the one in which they are produced. It's no secret that drama is chief among the historical genres; better scripts, better thespians, better soundtracks, better costumes, better set locations, and better production values—or at least the presumption of "better" in all these categories—reassure viewers that they are seeing a *serious* interpretation of historical subject matter on film. Nor is it a secret that since its inception, the Hollywood film industry has been dominated by white men—as writers, producers, directors, as well as leading heroes and villains. As a result, Americans tend to imagine the past through the eyes and actions of white men and often view films centered on other perspectives with skepticism or, occasionally, as revisionist attempts to "erase history."[3]

We must also recall that such communicative power does not exist in an intellectual vacuum. When films function as pop histories of the American experience, they influence how audiences think about any range of topics or issues; dialectic exchange is ongoing. Movies are not conceived immaculately or divinely—despite what their directors might believe—or independently of their surroundings. It's just the opposite, in fact. Films are shaped directly by the political pulses, economic patterns, social evolutions and revolutions, and cultural mores of the places and the times in which they are produced. In still plainer terms, films perform two functions on an unremitting cycle: they influence how a society thinks, and they reflect what a society, or at least a significant segment of it, is actually thinking.[4]

The corpus of scholarship categorized loosely as "film history" is extensive but generally lacking in methodological or analytical uniformity. Some works, aimed at niche audiences, purport to tell the behind-the-scenes story of the making or production of a particular film. Much more common in academic circles are texts that attempt to explore the relationship between film and history by focusing on an event (such as the American Civil War or the Second Red Scare),[5] a cause (such as female suffrage),[6] an institution or group (such as slavery or the Ku Klux Klan),[7] a region (such as the South),[8] an individual (such as Wild Bill Hickok or Jesus Christ),[9] a theme (such as war),[10] a time period (such as the 1930s, the 1960s, or the 1970s),[11] or a concept (such as the legal system or "the Western Frontier").[12]

In this volume, we seek to merge these thematic, regional, and conceptual approaches and to employ them on a grander chronological scale. More specifically, our intent is to explore how America's love affair with cinema has shaped collective understandings of an entire century's worth of history. For any one-hundred-year span this would be a major undertaking. For one brimming with byzantine political and economic change, with social upheaval, and with noteworthy characters, it is colossal.[13]

The nineteenth century saw Lewis and Clark survey a nation that would eventually reach from sea to shining sea. It was molded by Andrew Jackson's meteoric rise to power and by the Market Revolution, which prepared the way for America's future ascent to global prominence. Sailors and mountain men ventured deeper into the wilds than ever before, subduing the natural world to fuel the advances of industrial capitalism, though occasionally the natural world, in the form of whales and bears, fought back ferociously. The American people themselves changed too. National demographics shifted considerably as immigrants from Europe and Asia arrived in droves, as slaves began to reproduce naturally at higher rates, and as the last of the founding generation died off.

On one side, the nineteenth was a century of violent dissent. Mende slaves rose up against their Spanish abductors and seized the slave ship *La Amistad*.

Nat Turner led a revolt against the slavers of Virginia. John Brown stormed a federal arsenal in the belief that he was on a mission from God to spark an antislavery revolution. Irish gangs in New York's Five Points spearheaded the bloodiest, most destructive draft riots in American history. Newt Knight oversaw a Unionist insurgency in the middle of Confederate Mississippi. The Lakota Sioux overwhelmed and butchered Custer's Seventh Cavalry at the Battle of the Little Bighorn.

On another side, it was a time of racial strife and white imperialism. Speculators and military officials looked to clear new lands for "settlement" regardless of whether the lands had long been occupied by Indians or Mexicans. The majority of white Americans, in both North and South, believed in the inferiority of black Americans. In turn, millions of African slaves labored, suffered, and died on southern plantations; unlike Solomon Northup, virtually none had their plight immortalized in print. Slaveowners and their allies in the North became increasingly creative in their defenses of the "peculiar institution," and when talk failed, they became increasingly bold in wielding violence against their ideological opposites.

Eventually, southern slavers shattered the Union itself in order to preserve their interest in human bondage. Seven hundred fifty thousand men would die—some in conventional battle at places like Gettysburg, some at the hands of guerrillas, and still more from disease—putting the pieces back together again; in the process, legal slavery was extinguished from the newly reunited states once and for all. Both the war and emancipation were biracial efforts. Slaves ran away, severely damaging the Confederate economy and homefront morale. Black men donned the Union blue for the first time and distinguished themselves in combat, only to see the president who had called them to serve felled by an assassin's bullet and, not long after his murder, to see many of their hardest-won gains washed away by Black Codes, sharecropping, the Ku Klux Klan, and Jim Crow segregation.

From all of this—and we've only scratched the surface of what the nineteenth century can offer—has come a trove of iconic moments, events, characters, personalities, concepts, and even phrases, some real, others fictional, that help define, for better or worse, what it means to be an American in the present: "Remember the Alamo"; Lee sitting down with Grant in Wilmer McLean's living room; "Sic Semper Tyrannis!"; "My God, Mr. Chase, what is the matter?"; the somber moment when a former slave learns the difference between citizenship rights on paper and true freedom; the internal anguish of an immigrant woman attempting to keep her Old World identity from the "melting pot"; Custer dividing his forces; John Brown marching to the gallows; the sobs of Mary Lincoln on April 14, 1865; Patsy's death wish. Hollywood has interpreted these raw elements of Americanness for the masses. Our goal is to scrutinize the movie-born visual narratives that undergird and trigger collective memories of American history and to grapple with how (and why) understandings of them have changed over time.[14]

Unlike many books on film history, this one does not focus solely on discerning fact from fiction. We asked each contributor to explore how their chosen film (or films) has shaped, correctly or not, the way Americans have perceived some aspect of nineteenth-century history, as well as whether that perception has changed over time. In addition, we asked each contributor to explore more critically the power of film as a medium for "picturing" or "screening" the past and whether professional historians, Hollywood, or the public ultimately bears the responsibility for shining light on that power as the so-called history wars unfold around us.[15]

Because this book covers the full span of the century (1800 to 1899), with the first and last decades being more difficult to cast than the elongated middle, the book's filmography includes more than thirty films with release dates ranging from 1915 to 2016. Classics like *Jezebel* (1938), *They Died with Their Boots On* (1941), *Little Big Man* (1970), and *Glory* (1989) all survived final casting. Yet to achieve a measure of topical, thematic, and chronological balance, some of what might be considered "the usual suspects" have been necessarily omitted. With this in mind, *Gone with the Wind* (1939) and its pseudo-offspring, *Raintree County* (1957), fell to the cutting-room floor. So too did *The Red Badge of Courage* (1951), *The Horse Soldiers* (1959), and *Shenandoah* (1965). Additionally, iconic westerns such as *She Wore a Yellow Ribbon* (1949), *The Searchers* (1956), and *How the West Was Won* (1962) had to be sacrificed to allow for blazing new trails. (For more scholarship on films not covered directly, see the list of suggested further readings toward the end of the volume.)

Treatments of more recent favorites or "new classics" such as *Gettysburg* (1992), *Amistad* (1997), and *Gangs of New York* (2002) are included, but others, such as *Ride with the Devil* (1999), *Cold Mountain* (2003), and *Django Unchained* (2012), have been left out; their absence allows for the inclusion of other, moderately well known but frequently overlooked pictures that touch on similar or overlapping motifs in very important ways, such as *Bright Leaf* (1950), *Sommersby* (1993), and *The Journey of August King* (1995), to name just a few.

And while there can be great value in analyzing "bad history" on film—as seen in essays on *Santa Fe Trail* (1940), *The Far Horizons* (1955), and *The Undefeated* (1969)—we have nixed some truly dreadful pictures, most notably *Gods and Generals* (2003), simply to avoid beating horses long (and very mercifully) dead.

For a pair of unabashed cinephiles, these decisions were painful to say the least. However, perhaps the greatest silver lining is that they allowed deep readings of relatively new films, such as *The Conspirator* (2010), *Lincoln* (2012), *12 Years a Slave* (2013), *The Hateful Eight* (2015), *In the Heart of the Sea* (2015), *The Revenant* (2015), *Free State of Jones* (2016), and *The Birth of a Nation* (2016), some of which are analyzed here for the first time by a professional historian. Other pictures, such as *The Birth of a Nation* (1915), *The Prisoner of Shark Island* (1936), *The Gorgeous Hussy* (1936), *Young Mr. Lincoln* (1939), *Abe Lincoln in Illinois* (1940), *The President's Lady* (1953), *The Alamo* (1960/2004), and *Jeremiah Johnson* (1972), are explored comparatively in ways that yield bold new conclusions about the environments that produced them. Still other films have not been taken seriously by previous historians or have flown under the radar of academics. By including *Mandingo* (1975), *Hester Street* (1975), *Daughters of the Dust* (1991), and *Far and Away* (1992), we aim to give these movies their long-awaited debuts on the stage of film scholarship.

In closing, the editors fully understand that some readers will disagree with the lineup of films we've constructed. In fact, we would be disappointed if the book's filmography *didn't* trigger debate: arguments about which films ought to represent the national past, which films are most accurate, or which films constitute important historical markers in the American experience only verify the enduring significance of the medium in everyday American life. Put another way, our collective history *has* been written with lightning, but to find out what's terrible or true or both about the nineteenth century, you'll just have to let us take you out to the movies.

NOTES

1. If Wilson's words were apocryphal, the fact that they have been attributed to him so frequently and gone relatively unquestioned for more than a century only underscores the extent to which Americans have believed in the narrative of the film as historical truth (and thus have seen no need to disagree and further scrutinize the quotation) and to which the sentiments reportedly expressed by the president fit snugly with how we conceptualize Wilson's own brand of racial politics. In other words, that virtually everyone believed that Wilson not only could have but *would have* reviewed *The Birth of a Nation* this way is arguably more important to our

understanding of how the film became a visualization of popular history than whether he actually did so. For perhaps the earliest example of the phrase *history written with lightning* being attached to Wilson, see the "The Birth of a Nation," *Atlanta Journal Constitution,* 5 December 1916.

2. *Hearings Regarding the Communist Infiltration of the Motion Picture Industry: Hearings before the Committee on Un-American Activities, House of Representatives,* 80th Cong., 1st sess., 1947; Pub. L. 601, sec. 121, subsec. Q(2).

3. Because of the farcical nature of comedies set in the nineteenth century, such as *Almost Heroes* (1998), *Shanghai Noon* (2000), and *A Million Ways to Die in the West* (2014), it is unlikely that Americans will begin taking films in the genre seriously as depictions of history, even when serious themes are addressed via satire and backhanded humor.

4. This explanation of the communicative power of films, particularly how they simultaneously influence and reflect a society's social, political, and economic expressions, is adapted from Matthew C. Hulbert, *The Ghosts of Guerrilla Memory: How Civil War Bushwhackers Became Gunslingers in the American West* (Athens: University of Georgia Press, 2016), 212–13.

5. Bruce Chadwick, *The Reel Civil War: Mythmaking in American Film* (New York: Vintage Books, 2009); Brian Wills, *Gone with the Glory: The Civil War in Cinema* (Lanham, MD: Rowman & Littlefield, 2011); Jim Cullen, *The Civil War in Popular Culture* (Washington, DC: Smithsonian Books, 1995); Gary Gallagher, *Causes Won, Lost, and Forgotten: How Hollywood and Popular Art Shaped What We Know about the Civil War* (Chapel Hill: University of North Carolina Press, 2008). On the Second Red Scare, see Larry Ceplair and Steven Englund, *The Inquisition in Hollywood: Politics in the Film Community, 1930–1960* (Urbana-Champaign: University of Illinois Press, 2003).

6. Amy Shore, *Suffrage and the Silver Screen* (New York: Peter Lang, 2014).

7. Natalie Zemon Davis, *Slaves on Screen: Film and Historical Vision* (Cambridge, MA: Harvard University Press, 2000); Donald Bogle, *Toms, Coons, Mulattoes, Mammies, and Bucks: An Interpretive History of Blacks in American Films,* rev. ed. (New York: Bloomsbury Academic, 2016); Tom Rice, *White Robes, Silver Screen: Movies and the Making of the Ku Klux Klan* (Bloomington: Indiana University Press, 2016).

8. Jack Temple Kirby, *Media-Made Dixie: The South in the American Imagination* (Athens: University of Georgia Press, 1986); Deborah E. Barker and Kathryn McKee, eds., *American Cinema and the Southern Imaginary* (Athens: University of Georgia Press, 2011).

9. Sandra Sagala, *Buffalo Bill on the Silver Screen* (Norman: University of Oklahoma Press, 2013); Richard Stern and Clayton Jefford, *Savior on the Silver Screen* (New York: Paulist Press, 1999); Adele Reinhartz, *Jesus of Hollywood* (New York: Oxford University Press, 2009).

10. Glen Jeansonne and David Luhrssen, *War on the Silver Screen: Shaping America's Perception of History* (Lincoln, NE: Potomac Books, 2014); Peter C. Collins and John E. O'Connor, *Why We Fought: America's Wars in Film and History* (Lexington: University Press of Kentucky, 2008).

11. J. E. Smyth, *Reconstructing American Historical Cinema: From "Cimarron" to "Citizen Kane"* (Lexington: University Press of Kentucky, 2006); Jonathan Kirshner, *Hollywood's Last Golden Age: Politics, Society, and the Seventies Film in America* (Ithaca, NY: Cornell University Press, 2012); Barry Grant, ed., *American Cinema of the 1960s* (New Brunswick, NJ: Rutgers University Press, 2008).

12. On the legal system, see Paul Bergman and Michael Asimow, *Reel Justice: The Courtroom Goes to the Movies* (Kansas City, MO: Andrews & McMeel, 1996); Anthony Chase, *Movies on Trial: The Legal System on the Silver Screen* (New York: New Press, 2002); Ross Levi, *The Celluloid Courtroom: A History of Legal Cinema* (Westport, CT: Praeger, 2005). On "the Western Frontier," see Matthew Carter, *Myth of the Western* (Edinburgh: University of Edinburgh Press, 2015).

13. An approach on this scale has been employed before for the twentieth century but never for the nineteenth century. Often books on twentieth-century film history are concerned with how films were used to shape the interpretations of events in their immediate past. For example, *All the President's Men* was meant to control the popular narrative of the Watergate scandal, and *Platoon* and *The Deer Hunter* were meant to shape American perceptions of the Vietnam War. By contrast, this volume travels much further back into the past to investigate how film interpretations of our national history are constantly contested—with social, political, and economic power in the present at stake. For an example of contemporary narrative control, see Douglas Kellner, *Cinema Wars: Hollywood Film and Politics in the Bush-Cheney Era* (Hoboken, NJ: Wiley-Blackwell, 2009). For examples of this elongated chronological approach in the twentieth century, see John Bodnar, *Blue-Collar Hollywood* (Baltimore: Johns Hopkins University Press, 2006); Steven Mintz and Randy Roberts, eds., *Hollywood's America: Twentieth-Century America through Film* (Chichester, UK: Wiley-Blackwell, 2010); and Steven J. Ross, ed., *Movies and American Society* (Hoboken, NJ: Wiley-Blackwell, 2014).

14. On collective memory and American identity, see Michael Kammen, *Mystic Chords of Memory: The Transformation of Tradition in American Culture* (New York: Vintage Books, 1993). See also John Bodnar, *Remaking America: Public Memory, Commemoration, and Patriotism in the Twentieth Century* (Princeton, NJ: Princeton University Press, 1994).

15. See Robert Brent Toplin, *Reel History: In Defense of Hollywood* (Lawrence: University Press of Kansas, 2002); and Jim Cullen, *Sensing the Past: Hollywood Stars and Historical Visions* (New York: Oxford University Press, 2013).

FRONTIERS, EMPIRE, AND THE EARLY NATION

1

The Far Horizons
The Lewis and Clark Saga as a Surfeit of Stereotypes

DONNA J. BARBIE

Despite a cast of high-powered stars, including Charlton Heston, Fred Mac-Murray, Barbara Hale, and Donna Reed, many critics panned *The Far Horizons,* a 1955 film that took in a somewhat disappointing $1.6 million at the box office. One reviewer declared it dull;[1] another called it "surprisingly dull."[2] A fanciful critic claimed that the film induced "torpor" that could be used to "train children to squirm or whisper."[3] How could a film about the Lewis and Clark Expedition, one of the most inspiring episodes of American exploration, possibly be boring? These and other critics objected to less than flattering portrayals of the captains, the casting of an obviously Caucasian Reed as the native woman who accompanied the Corps of Discovery, and an ahistorical plot that featured a romance between William Clark and Sacagawea.[4] One reviewer claimed that the story had been "Hollywoodized,"[5] but the film constituted more than simple-minded convention. Like so many other films about the American West, *The Far Horizons* contributed to perceptions about the wilderness and the peoples who originally occupied the land.

The nation has relished stories of intrepid explorers who penetrated the frontier, even after that period was long over. By the mid-twentieth century, America was "between" wars, business was thriving, and the civil rights movement was just coming to life. In spite of, or possibly because of, the Cold War, popular texts seemed preoccupied with the nation's frontier past. In 1955 alone, America spawned such works as *Oklahoma,* a film based on the Broadway hit; "The Ballad of Davy Crockett," a song that prompted the coonskin-cap craze; and the television hit *Gunsmoke.* As Philip Fisher discusses in *Hard Facts: Setting and Form in the American Novel,* cultural texts often retrace the past in an effort to perform valuable service for the present. By stabilizing, simplifying, and justifying past events and by repeating their culturally mandated meanings, these works install "habits of moral perception."[6] *The Far Horizons* did just that by vivifying and reinforcing common conceptions of the sacred mission into the wilderness, the dichotomy between civilization and savagery, and the heroic but hapless Indian princess.

American frontier myths made up a nexus of resilient constructs for more than two centuries, with cultural texts telling the story of the nation's true beginnings and purpose. Those works claimed that America had been born when Europeans secured land with the help of a beneficent God. Settlement became a sacred mission to carve out consecrated space for a new social order, an idea that eventually came to be known as "manifest destiny." The Lewis and Clark Expedition embodied and exemplified civilization's first step in settling the largest savage wilderness. Among other writers, Helen West dubbed the endeavor "America's national epic" and claimed that the expedition excited generations because it symbolized uniquely American qualities of strength and courage.[7] The director, Rudolf Maté, along with the screenwriters, Winston Miller and Edmund H. North, tapped into that symbolism in *The Far Horizons*. The film was based on Della Gould Emmons's novel *Sacajawea of the Shonshones*,[8] but the film's title emphasized the distance and difficulty of the sacred quest. In an overt pitch, the voiceover from the official trailer claims that the film captures the "mightiest of all frontier spectacles." The narrator also states that the corps "set out to cross a virgin continent and forge a new nation," with "immortal heroes" leading the "amazing expedition into the unknown."[9] Manifest destiny could hardly be more explicit.

Trailers are created to sell and are not subtle, but dialogue in the film also blatantly reflects frontier ideologies. Although the Louisiana Purchase would more than double the "healthy young country," that enormous addition is apparently was not sufficient for President Jefferson. As he explains to Meriwether Lewis, the expedition must go much farther because "the dream upon which this nation was built can never be secure until the United States stretches from the Atlantic to the Pacific." Jefferson all but uses the phrase *manifest destiny*. Much later in the film, Lewis employs similar rhetoric. Tired after eighteen months of exploration, the men of the corps declare that they will go no further because they are exhausted and have fulfilled their contractual obligation. Addressing the entire corps, Lewis responds, "If this river can be followed to the ocean, then the United States will be one nation, from the Atlantic to the Pacific. . . .

All I can promise is a chance to serve the country well." As he argues, the mission is far more significant than mere contracts; these men must help to shape a mighty nation. Lewis delivers the film's most explicit message of manifest destiny when the explorers arrive at the Pacific Ocean. The bugle sounds as they raise the flag, and he claims for America "all the land that we have traveled, from the Rocky Mountains to the Pacific Ocean." The music swells to an inspiring crescendo, and those who witness the speech, the men of the corps and moviegoers alike, are filled with national pride.

As Jefferson and Lewis note, land is an essential element of America's destiny, and Paramount and Maté do everything possible to capitalize on that connection. Touting the studio's new technology, the trailer opens with a giant scripted message, "Now the screen is BIG ENOUGH to tell The Greatest of all American Sagas. . . . Filmed by Paramount in Glorious VistaVision."[10] According to Martin Hart, curator of the American Widescreen Film Museum, in the early 1950s film studios were attempting to entice television audiences to return to the movies by leveraging new technologies. Paramount developed VistaVision to provide "vastly improved images" on wider screens.[11] *The Far Horizons,* filmed on location in Wyoming, seemed perfectly suited to that agenda. Many critics applauded the cinematography, including *New York Times* reviewer H. H. T., who noted that the scenery was "radiantly framed,"[12] and *Commonweal* film critic Philip Hartung, who declared that it "steals the show."[13]

Although VistaVision presented beautiful vistas, the land offered more than visual appeal. The film illustrated that the land must be penetrated, claimed, and tamed. Employing explicit rhetoric, the trailer's voiceover promises that audiences will "share the thrill of discovery and beauty of the untamed wilderness."[14] The film, however, generally relies on images to relay that message. When the explorers arrive at Woodriver, for example, cameras capture the stark contrast between a civilized Washington, DC, and the leading edge of the frontier. Primitive bridges and wooden structures are surrounded by the natural beauty of towering pines and a wide river, with snow-topped mountains in the distance. The expedition represents the spearhead of civilization. In another scene, the camera pans over waterfowl and land animals as the captains comment on the bounty that awaits settlement. The most stirring scenery appears when members of the expedition traverse Shoshone lands on horseback, venturing courageously into the rugged Tetons. This land is beautiful but also dangerous, and only with courage and fortitude was America able to fulfill its destiny.

Despite spectacular cinematography, the plot overshadows Wyoming land-scapes. Maté adopts a formula whereby characters experience high danger or explore titillating romance, and then the picture fades. Suddenly the audience witnesses amazing scenery, accompanied by stirring music. The vistas are short lived, however, because the plot must advance. In essence, the land seems to have been used as a transitional device. For example, as the expedition departs, Lewis orders Clark to leave Sacagawea behind with her people. The scenery is magnificent, but rapidly shifting camera shots draw attention away from nature and toward Sacagawea as she runs along the shoreline. The primary focus of the film is not the land but the characters and their stories.

One of the most important elements of the plot is the depiction of sav-ages who occupy the wilderness. Roy Harvey Pearce contends in *Savagism and Civilization* that myriad texts have portrayed America as civilized only when settlers rescued the land from profane contamination. Of course, fierce and unequivocally barbaric tribesmen perpetrated the adulteration.[15] According to Ralph and Natasha Friar, American films have played a prominent role in con-flating native existence into stereotypes of cruelty and treachery.[16] As a result, images of savage natives have become inseparable from portrayals of America's untamed landscape. In harmony with that tradition, *The Far Horizons* populates the land with scores of savages. Dialogue in the film emphasizes the dangers. When the expedition arrives at Woodriver, Sergeant Gass asks Lewis if he is ex-pecting trouble, and Clark answers, "They're Indians, aren't they?" Later, Clark declares that no Indian can be trusted. After avoiding an ambush, Clark says to Charbonneau, "I thought you said they wouldn't give us any trouble," and he responds, "They are savages, Captain." Ironically, this declaration comes from a despicable French fur trader, a man who is not quite civilized himself. After the corps finds overturned canoes and a group of dead men, obviously killed by savages, Gass warns the captains that the place is "crawling with Indians." Savages seem to be no more than viscous and potentially deadly insects.

Powerful images and sounds also relay the dangers. Like many Hollywood films prior to the 1960s, *The Far Horizons* employs withering visual stereotypes. The natives live in teepees and wear buckskins and beads, with the chiefs sporting full headdresses of feathers. Indian "braves" have a single feather, ride ponies, and use bows and arrows to wreak havoc on the intrepid explor-ers. When the savages are preparing for war, they are half-naked, their faces painted. They beat war drums and dance in a frenzy, whooping and ululating in anticipation of taking "many scalps." They are frighteningly and palpably dangerous. As if images were not sufficient, music reinforces and compounds messages of menace and treachery. In every scene that shows savages sneaking around or attacking, the music inevitably shifts from a major key to a dissonant, portentous minor.

Although the vast majority of natives in the film are undifferentiated, some have names, including the Chief of the Minatarees and Wild Eagle of the Shoshones. Deceitful and tricky, the chief plots with Charbonneau, yet he still accepts the medal that signifies American sovereignty. Once the expedition boat has launched, he pulls the medal off, throws it to the ground, and calls for war. Wild Eagle is even more savage, filled with lust, rage, and a thirst for blood. He is the only obviously disfigured character in the film, bearing a terrible scar down one side of his face. Fierce and powerful, he sneakily kills a member of his own nation to prevent the message of peace from reaching others along the route. Later, he leads a group of savages in an attempt to trap the explorers' canoes and massacre all the men of the corps. Increasing the suspense, the music is frenetic, with cinematographers using quick cuts from one location to another. In the midst of chaos and death, a daring captain frees the canoes from the nets, and they escape the deadly arrows. As this scene implies, civilization was hard fought, but wise and courageous men prevailed.

Films have supplied audiences with a glut of images portraying male savages, but they have generally provided only glimpses of the female counterpart. The "squaw" is sometimes the perpetrator of heathen viciousness, but more often she is portrayed as a victim of her primitive society. Maté offers a few examples. When the captains arrive, the native women remain inert and impassive, with doughy, indistinguishable faces. After Lewis gives them a trunk filled with presents, however, they become animated. They wrangle with one another, scrambling for their fair share of the booty. Their existence and circumstances are strong evidence of their savagery.

Although American films have never featured squaws, the opposite has been true of Indian princesses. Philip Young writes in "The Mother of Us All: Pocahontas Reconsidered" that the Pocahontas legend first captured the American imagination and then begot more stories of Indian princesses.[17] Indian princesses are irresistible, exuding youth, beauty, grace, kindness, gentleness, and self-sacrifice. Ralph and Natasha Friar contend that in the 1950s and 1960s Hollywood featured princesses in 65 percent of films portraying native women.[18] Although some people might doubt the stereotype's harm, Rayna Green claims in "The Pocahontas Perplex" that the Indian princess occupies an ambiguous position between savagery and civilization. She aids white men in the sacred mission and is heroic only because she fosters the penetration of the wilderness by a superior "civilization."[19] Indian princesses have not only been pervasive in American culture; they have also powerfully reinforced frontier myths.

Sacagawea, the Indian princess in *The Far Horizons,* arrived on screen through a circuitous route. She was not featured prominently in any of the Lewis and Clark journals, but Eva Emery Dye was determined to present a heroine in *The Conquest: The True Story of Lewis and Clark,* a novel published to mark the expedition's centennial.[20] As Dye writes in her journal, "Out of a few dry bones I found in the old tales of the trip, I created Sacajawea. . . . For months I dug and scraped for accurate information about this wonderful Indian Maid." Dye later notes that the "faithful Indian woman . . . appealed to the world."[21] Her Sacagawea became a template for other creators, including Della Gould Emmons, author of *Sacajawea of the Shoshones.*

Although the film's title does not bear Sacagawea's name, her story is one of the focal points of the work. From the moment she appears on screen, Sacagawea is clearly different from other native women. She is slender and beautiful, with well-defined, northern European features. Although Reed wears heavy brown makeup to signal her heritage, she is lighter than other natives. She wears beautifully tailored, form-fitting attire. She does not look like a typical Indian. More importantly, she does not think or act like a savage. When the rest of the women vie with one another for presents, she does not join the fray. When Clark states that she might be deceiving them, she states, "I do not lie." In one scene, she gives the captains a bag of seeds that she has secreted, asking them to teach her people how to plant so they will not starve in the winter. Even before she is part of the corps, Maté establishes that she is a superior being. Thereafter, the film offers many examples of her heroism. She observes the war dance and steals a horse to warn the explorers. She tells them which fork to take in the river, she rescues precious instruments and maps, and she saves Clark's life when he has a fever. Sacagawea is the indispensable Indian princess.

Faithful to Emmons's subplot, Maté includes a romantic entanglement between Sacagawea and Clark. He makes one significant change, however. The novel acknowledges that Sacagawea is one of Charbonneau's wives, that she bears him a son prior to their departure from the Mandans, and that she carries the baby on her back throughout the journey. Conversely, *The Far Horizons* features a lovely, virginal woman who is in danger of being despoiled by villainous men, first the contemptible French fur trader and later the horrifyingly savage

Wild Eagle. Apparently, images of a brutal husband and innocent child would have interfered too much with the plausibility, or acceptability, of a romance with the heroic Captain Clark.

Much to the chagrin of some critics, the love affair is a centerpiece of the film's plot. Even before the romance begins, the camera captures Sacagawea glancing at the captains in wonder and admiration. Clark at first seems unaware of her interest, but he eventually sees the signals, and he is obviously attracted to her. When they talk about the importance of the survey instruments, Sacagawea asks Clark if white women are beautiful, and he says, "Some of them, just like some Indian women." She preens, touching her hair, and then rewards him with a glorious smile. Of course, he inevitably succumbs to her allures. Dressed in a cloth "bag" while her buckskins dry, with her hair loosed from its braid, Sacagawea shyly approaches Clark, and he asks to call her "Janey," telling her it means beautiful. Even then, the love affair is not consummated with a kiss. Forced to leave her with the Shoshones, Clark is distraught when he sees her desperately attempting to follow them. At the climactic moment, he steers the canoe ashore, gathers her in his arms, and kisses her passionately.

These love scenes are far more than titillation, however. They also offer the culture an opportunity to examine miscegenation and native assimilation and acculturation. Interracial mixing has often been an important aspect of American discourse. In the 1870s, for example, the US Congress became disturbed by reports of miscegenation between Army officers and native women, reports Sherry Smith, and Congress convened the Banning Committee in 1876 to investigate sexual immorality occurring at frontier Army posts.[22] Although the men might have had liaisons with native women, restrictions against miscegenation were so forceful that the officers insisted in their diaries and letters that whites would be degraded by sexual relations with native women. Post records also reveal that almost no officers married native women.[23] As these and other sources indicate, even when adherence to social strictures lapsed, taboos against miscegenation functioned as a cultural reality.

According to Michael Hilger, a considerable percentage of celluloid Indian princesses of the 1950s and 1960s became entangled in doomed relationships with "civilized" men.[24] Participating in that tradition, Maté foreshadows that Sacagawea and Clark's love can never prevail. Although Maté confirms that Sacagawea is finer than other savages, the film constantly signals that she is uncivilized. The trailer declares that she "led the white strangers but followed

FRED **MacMURRAY** · CHARLTON **HESTON** · DONNA **REED** · BARBARA **HALE**

WILLIAM DEMAREST
ALAN REED
EDUARDO NORIEGA
PINE & THOMAS — MATE
MILLER & NORTH
A DELLA GOULD EMMONS
A PARAMOUNT PICTURE
COLOR BY
TECHNICOLOR

VISTA VISION

THE **FAR HORIZONS**

Fred MacMurray as Captain Meriwether Lewis, Charlton Heston as Captain
William Clark, and Donna Reed as Sacagawea in *The Far Horizons*.

the primitive code of her own people."[25] At one point, Gass calls her a "squaw."
She claims that she belonged to Clark when he fought Charbonneau because
"it is the custom." Throughout the film, Sacagawea and Clark consistently
differentiate "your people" from "my people." The chasm between the two
would-be lovers is most blatant when they bury the dead men. Everyone in the
corps but Sacagawea recites the Lord's Prayer. She remains mute, a considerable distance away. The film leaves no doubt that Sacagawea is "other" despite
her heroism.

A legitimate examination of miscegenation hinges on the characters' acknowledgment of the barriers to assimilation. As can be seen in a lobby card,
the ill-fated love story is visually telegraphed. Sacagawea gazes adoringly at
Clark, apparently oblivious of any tensions. Lewis and Clark meanwhile stare
at each other, Clark stiff jawed in defiance of Lewis's disapproval. Sacagawea
comes to understand the obstacles, however. When she declares that she will
wait for him to ask her to marry him, Clark tells her, "It's not that simple."
He knows that pursuing their love is more than a personal decision. Such

relationships constitute a cultural act. Later in the film, Clark is wary of returning to Washington. He seems worried that wilderness love will not be acceptable in civilization. The most dramatic moments of the film focus on Sacagawea's inexorable discovery that she can never fit into Clark's world. Accompanying him to Washington, DC, she ends up in his other fiancé's bedroom. Sacagawea is awed by the White House and amazed that Julia has so many clothes. When Julia asks if she would like to wear one of her dresses, Sacagawea declines. She knows she cannot be Clark's wife. In a painfully long scene, Julia reads Sacagawea's parting words to Clark as the scene flashes to a carriage. A single tear slides down Sacagawea's impassive face as she makes her escape. She understands that the chasm between savagery and civilization cannot be breached. She is a noble Indian princess, and her wisdom and superiority ironically cause her to reinforce strictures against miscegenation.

As Fisher argues, "Habits of moral perception" remain potent because condoned images are manifold.[26] Part of that tradition, *The Far Horizons* did not allow frontier myths to fade from individual or collective memory. Fulfilling the nation's need to celebrate America's beginnings, the film offered a sentimental look at the expedition and the conquest of the wilderness. *The Far Horizons* illustrated the rectitude of manifest destiny, conflated native groups and declared them all savage, and exhibited a noble but unfortunate Indian princess. A great deal has changed since 1955, however. By the 1960s people had begun to question and reject received knowledge of the frontier mission. Successes in civil rights spawned the Red Power movement, and many Americans, some sports fans notwithstanding, have begun to understand that *savage* and *Indian* are inappropriate and reductive signifiers for diverse native peoples. Although America has abandoned some elements of frontier myths, stories of Indian princesses seem to thrive. When Walt Disney marketed the animated film *Pocahontas* in 1995,[27] for example, the studio did not simply create a product but rekindled and fed long-held fascinations with Indian princesses. Perhaps the world's most successful corporate mythmaker, Disney exploited a story that has struck a chord for more than three centuries. Perhaps Disney's princess will be the last.

NOTES

1. Moira Walsh, review of *The Far Horizons,* directed by Rudolf Maté, *America* 93 (1955): 339.

2. H. H. T., review of *The Far Horizons,* directed by Rudolf Maté, *New York Times,* 21 May 1955, in *The New York Times Film Reviews, 1913–1968,* vol. 4 (1949–58) (New York: Arno, 1970), 154.

3. "Fair Warning," review of *The Far Horizons*, directed by Rudolf Maté, *Newsweek*, 2 June 1955, 98.

4. Scholars have long contested the spelling and pronunciation of the native woman's name, variously recorded as *Sacajawea, Sacagawea,* or *Sakakawea*. The US Bureau of Ethnicity has endorsed *Sacagawea*, which is the spelling we use except in quotations.

5. Review of *The Far Horizons*, *Time*, 6 June 1955, 56.

6. Philip Fisher, *Hard Facts: Setting and Form in the American Novel* (New York: Oxford University Press, 1987), 3–5.

7. Helen B. West, "The Lewis and Clark Expedition: Our National Epic," *Montana: The Magazine of Western History* 16, no. 3 (July 1966): 2–5.

8. Della Gould Emmons, *Sacajawea of the Shoshones* (Portland, OR: Binfords & Mort, 1943).

9. "*The Far Horizons* Official Trailer," YouTube, accessed 3 January 2017, https://www.you tube.com/watch?v=WMEwhTOss2c.

10. "*The Far Horizons* Official Trailer."

11. Martin Hart, "The Development of VistaVision: Paramount Marches to a Different Drummer," The American WideScreen Museum, last modified 2006, http://www.widescreen museum.com/widescreen/vvstory.htm.

12. H. H. T., review of *The Far Horizons*.

13. Philip T. Hartung, "The Screen," review of *The Far Horizons*, by Rudolf Maté, *Commonweal* 62 (1955): 256.

14. "*Far Horizons* Official Trailer."

15. Roy Harvey Pearce, *Savagism and Civilization: A Study of the Indian and the American Mind* (Berkeley: University of California Press, 1988).

16. Ralph E. Friar and Natasha A. Friar, *The Only Good Indian . . . : The Hollywood Gospel* (New York: Drama Book Specialists, 1972).

17. Philip Young, "The Mother of Us All: Pocahontas Reconsidered." *Kenyon Review* 24, no. 3 (1962): 391–414.

18. Friar and Friar, *Only Good Indian.*

19. Rayna Green, "The Pocahontas Perplex: The Image of Indian Women in American Culture," *Massachusetts Review* 16, no. 4 (1975): 698–714.

20. Eva Emery Dye, *The Conquest: The True Story of Lewis and Clark* (Chicago: A. C. McClurg, 1902).

21. Alfred Powers, *History of Oregon Literature* (Portland, OR: Metropolitan, 1935), 93, 410.

22. Sherry L. Smith, "Beyond Princess and Squaw: Army Officers' Perceptions of Indian Women," in *The Women's West*, ed. Susan Armitage and Elizabeth Jameson (Norman: University of Oklahoma Press, 1987), 63–65.

23. Smith, "Beyond Princess and Squaw," 69–72.

24. Michael Hilger, *The American Indian in Film* (Metuchen, NJ: Scarecrow, 1986).

25. "*The Far Horizons* Official Trailer."

26. Fisher, *Hard Facts*, 3–5.

27. *Pocahontas*, directed by Mike Gabriel and Eric Goldberg (Burbank, CA: Walt Disney Pictures, 1995), film.

2

We Are Melville's Monsters

In the Heart of the Sea as Eco-Horror in the Age of Climate Change

BRIAN ROULEAU

In the first few frames of *In the Heart of the Sea* we see a watchman lighting streetlamps throughout the port of Nantucket, off the southern coast of Massachusetts. Fueled by whale oil harvested from the bodies of some of the world's largest mammals, these beacons in the night began to burn bright in cities and towns throughout the Atlantic world beginning in the eighteenth century. The blubber and bones of whales served many purposes, from illuminating thoroughfares as part of broader crime-fighting initiatives to lubricating the machinery that made up the nascent industrial revolution, as well as fastening the corsets, stays, and hoops with which Victorian women adorned themselves. And it was the United States—principally through the ports of Nantucket and New Bedford—that stood at the center of the business in whale products. From the end of the War of 1812 to the beginning of the Civil War, more than three-quarters of the world's whaling voyages departed American ports. The industry sent tens of thousands of young men to sea aboard some of the most complex and capital-intensive investments then in existence, and those whalemen commenced a wholesale slaughter of cetaceans wherever they could be found. America, now a signatory to several treaties outlawing whale fishery, once led the world in the harvest of deepwater animal life, and that reaping remained a crucial sector within the broader national economy.[1]

In other words, whale oil, directly or indirectly, had become a fixed staple in nineteenth-century life. And the film *In the Heart of the Sea,* one of the whaling industry's very few cinematic treatments, does that fact some justice in having the famed author Herman Melville (Ben Whishaw)—wandering 1850s Nantucket in search of material for a new novel about a "monster" whale—

muse to himself that "since it was discovered that whale oil could light our cities in ways never achieved before, it created global demand. It has pushed man to venture further and further into the deep blue unknown." But this is also the moment when the film stakes one of its philosophical signposts. For as Melville continues to reflect, the ceaseless quest for natural resources has led humanity to ends of the earth shrouded in mystery. "How does one come to know the unknowable," he wonders. "What faculties must a man possess? We know not [the ocean's] depths, nor the host of creatures that live there. Monsters. Are they real? Or do the stories exist only to make us respect the sea's dark secrets?" Whaleships, which overhunted America's coastal waters, next chased disappearing stocks of whales across the Atlantic. But when that vast field of enterprise was depleted by the 1820s, the Pacific became the industry's next frontier. Implicit in Melville's voiceover, however, is a query that has animated ecologically inclined filmmaking since the 1960s: at what point does nature begin to push back against the intrusive and destructive instincts of humankind? Enter the whaleship *Essex*, rammed and sunk by an enraged sperm whale in the central Pacific on November 20, 1820.[2]

Melville has arrived in Nantucket in 1850 to meet with Thomas Nickerson (Brendan Gleeson). Former greenhand aboard that ill-fated vessel, Nickerson was one of the few to survive a harrowing ordeal of months adrift atop the Pacific Ocean in a small boat, short of food, short of water, and reduced to cannibalism. And yet, within the first few minutes the movie has opted to betray the historical record in the service of storytelling. We know of no such meeting between Melville and Nickerson. More problematically, the film treats the crew's resorting to cannibalism as a very closely guarded secret, one that Melville himself is unaware of until a dramatic revelation toward the film's conclusion. Indeed, the entire story of the *Essex* appears, in the world of this movie, as something about which very few people had knowledge. Nothing could be further from the truth. Both the ship's captain, George Pollard (Benjamin Walker), and first mate, Owen Chase (Chris Hemsworth), published narrative accounts of their sufferings at sea. Sadly, no surviving copy of Pollard's story has yet surfaced, but Chase's 1821 book, *Narrative of the Most Extraordinary and Distressing Shipwreck of the Whale-Ship Essex*, was quite forthcoming about the men's need to consume human flesh for sustenance. Chase's *Narrative*, meant as a self-serving testimonial to his own leadership skills, not to mention an exculpatory exercise designed to deflect blame for the incident, acted to preserve his career and reputation as an officer. But more to the point, it went through multiple printings during the nineteenth century. It was widely circulated and eagerly read by a public hungry for tales of adventure at sea and titillated by cannibalistic transgression. A young Melville read Chase's account during his own stint at sea, and it became the basis for his classic 1851 novel *Moby-Dick*. Nickerson himself, it should be noted, much later in life wrote an account of his experiences titled *The Loss of the Ship "Essex" Sunk by a Whale*. Set aside before it could be published, the manuscript lay undisturbed in an attic for nearly one hundred years before it was rediscovered, authenticated, and posthumously published. The former cabin boy's narrative is a fascinating contrast to Chase's account and an important document for historians.[3]

And so the film begins with a series of contrivances theoretically meant to elevate the dramatic stakes. Nickerson appears as something of a tortured hermit unable to transcend his youthful trauma—an odd choice, given that it was in fact Captain George Pollard whose post-traumatic stress quite infamously caused him to live a cloistered and "unbalanced" life of obsessive food hoarding. Melville, meanwhile, is the down-and-out author who's spent his last dime to travel to Nantucket in search of inspiration for what the viewer knows will become perhaps the quintessential American novel. After some cajoling and prodding, Nickerson begins to unburden himself. The action unfolds in the form of a flashback, even as we are periodically pulled into the "present" when Melville asks questions and presses for detail. By the end, the telling of the tale (and the "shocking" reveal of his "shameful" cannibalism) has earned the narrator absolution and gifted the author a timeless tale about monomania, greed, and a vengeful whale.

But therein lies the problem, at least regarding the film's "faithfulness" to the historical record. The writers, along with the director, Ron Howard, clearly decided that the actual story of the *Essex* was not, in and of itself, sufficiently interesting or poignant for contemporary moviegoers. And so they decided to graft the famed "white whale" from the novel *Moby-Dick* (in no surviving account was the whale that rammed the *Essex* described as an albino) onto the historical experiences of Pollard, Chase, and Nickerson. Our best guess is that the actual whale in 1820 mistook the ship's keel for a rival bull and attacked. In the film, the "white whale" is referred to and anthropomorphized as a "demon," driven by vengeance against those humans who have harassed and killed his fellow creatures. And so even as the *Essex* sank and her real-life castaways spent months in several small boats before the rescue of a fortunate few, the cinematic castaways are hunted and harassed across the Pacific by their sperm whale "nemesis." In an entirely fabricated series of episodes, the "white whale" destroys the crew's lifeboats off the coast of a deserted island, forcing them ashore in order to rebuild the craft. Convinced that they are the victims of a vendetta—that the whale will not stop until they are dead—the men also begin to improvise a large harpoon so that they might strike first. With food on the island becoming scarce and water nonexistent, most of the crew take to the sea once again in their reconstructed boats. We do see vivid depictions of the ensuing suffering. The film's makeup artists spared no expense in depicting the ravages of extreme thirst and hunger on the human body. We also see, very briefly, the decision made to begin consuming the dead so that the living might endure, a choice that culminates in a drawing of lots and the butchery (as did actually occur) of Captain Pollard's own nephew. But the whale continues to stalk the men, and the climactic scene seems to be not the cannibalism but rather a moment when their blubbery antagonist surfaces to gaze upon the survivors. First mate Owen Chase raises his weapon to kill the beast, but his eyes meet with the whale's, and in a moment of awareness, some spiritual truce between the two, Chase allows the animal to depart. Captain Pollard chastises his mate for a missed opportunity, but the viewer is led to sympathize with Chase's act of mercy. Very soon after this transpires, the men are rescued and returned to Nantucket. Some debate ensues about what the men should divulge and what they should keep secret. But the film ends with Nickerson having finally cleared his conscience by confessing his sins and Melville inspired to tell the tale of a monster whale, not to mention those monstrous impulses that lay just beneath the surface of "civilized" man.

In one sense, then, the film comprises a series of betrayals of the historical record. To be fair, it *does* get many of the smaller details correct: the tensions between Captain Pollard and his first mate, Owen Chase, as well as their (ultimately disastrously) conflicting leadership styles; the acrimonious rivalry between Nantucket-born seamen and those they demeaned as "coofs," or off-islanders; the incredible complexity of sailing ships and the skilled knowledge required to operate them (scenes portraying men buzzing around the ship and high atop the yards amidst surging seas never fail to thrill); the immensely messy and arduous task of capturing, butchering, and processing whale carcasses; and, finally, the diversity of a typical whaleman's crew. Nearly half the crew of the *Essex* was black (hardly a rare thing within the maritime trades more generally), though the film, much like the historical record, gives African American sailors, despite their numbers, very little voice or agency. Indeed, the director and writers very neatly sidestep a troubling fact to emerge out of the *Essex* disaster, namely, that the first men to die and be eaten were black. The historian Nathaniel Philbrick posits that the endemic poverty of Nantucket's black residents (itself a product of segregation and their failure to be promoted through the ranks) doomed those men to an early death in any crisis situation. Because of their poorer diet and thus lack of stored fat and nutrients, the impact of the era's widespread racism became in some literal sense inscribed on their bodies, and so they more quickly succumbed to deprivation and exhaustion. But again, such complexities are perhaps beyond commercial filmmaking's praxis, and the movie does get certain details right. The problems arise when we recognize that those details are put in service of a story demonstrably at odds with the lived experience of the men aboard the *Essex*.[4]

What happens, however, when we move beyond the relatively narrow question of "accuracy"? True, in several crucial ways the film lacks it. But to subject screenplays and cinema to the same standards as academic scholarship is to conflate two divergent modes of storytelling, one dependent upon verifiable evidentiary streams and the other totally unmoored from any real need to demonstrate the veracity of its claims. The gap between the "truth" of painstaking archival research conducted by trained historians and Hollywood's addiction to that shiftiest of claims, "based on a true story," is an epistemologically significant one. Even so, the gap is not nearly as wide as we might like to think. Most twenty-first-century scholars seem willing to concede that narrative history is itself a deeply "loaded" enterprise. Fraught with biases embedded in our evidence, scholarly work is refracted yet again through the filters and interpretive lenses authors themselves choose to impose upon the past.

The actual story of what transpired aboard the *Essex* is an ideal example of the ways in which a certain measure of "creative license" must be utilized by scholars to close gaps and mitigate shortcomings in the evidence. We have two surviving accounts of events on the ship, written by the officer Owen Chase and the cabin boy Thomas Nickerson. Those two accounts were written with very different agendas in mind, at two very different points in history, and while they agree in certain key respects, they disagree in others. Scholars use their best judgment—judiciously weighing conflicting data, searching for corroborating evidence—in order to tell what is by their own reckoning the most accurate version of events. But it's an imperfect and imprecise science at best, and one that produces analyses of events riddled with shortcomings and silences. Call it the fragility and frailty of human memory—the human capacity to selectively forget or, worse, deliberately misremember—embedded indelibly within the deep structures of our investigation of the past. In this sense, historians tend to see their stories about particular events as one (and perhaps the most) plausible interpretation among many, not a definitive judgment. Those tentative conclusions, moreover, always reflect the priorities and problems of the society within which the scholar lives. "There is no history," the famed philosopher G. K. Chesterton once said, "only historians." History, in other words, is not an investigation into bygone eras frozen in time and awaiting discovery and definitive designation as "fact." Rather, it is an evolving conversation between scholars and sources, subject to constant reevaluation and revision.[5]

On that level, what if we thought about *In the Heart of the Sea* not as a film that was supposed to obey the conventions and rigorousness of formal historical practice (again, few films are) but rather as yet another version of a story many people have tried to tell since the *Essex* sank in 1820. Director Ron Howard, then, joins the ranks of eyewitnesses like Chase and Nickerson, novelists like Melville, and historians like Nathaniel Philbrick. Storytellers all, they emphasized certain pieces of information, discarded others, and reinvented still more in the service of their respective missions. They all steered their narratives of that ill-fated whaleship toward some larger lesson to be taught to their respective audiences. Some of the earliest accounts—if not nakedly opportunistic attempts to shift or deflect blame for the disaster—attempted to divine some providential purpose behind the ordeal. God, they imagined, had sent the whale as an instrument meant to test the faith of both those unfortunate souls aboard the vessel and the community from which they had departed. Melville, meanwhile, used Chase's narrative to sow a veritable thicket of symbolisms, themes, and implications. We are *still* debating the "meaning" of *Moby-Dick*, but at the very least it seems to fit into the author's oeuvre, characterized as it was by a healthy skepticism regarding the verities and pieties of nineteenth-century American civilization, not to mention a wariness concerning the moral, spiritual, and practical costs of his fellow citizens' self-destructive and single-minded pursuit of wealth. But the question becomes, what then might Ron Howard have had in mind when he joined an already long line of storytellers seizing upon the *Essex* to speak their own truths?

It might be argued that the thematic core of the movie emerges out of a conversation between Captain George Pollard and mate Owen Chase on the rocky shore of Henderson Island as they debate departing a precarious situation on the island for an equally perilous future at sea. The two men, antagonists at this point in the movie (and indeed, there is evidence to suggest that they did not see each other as allies aboard the actual *Essex*), evince in just a few moments very different understandings of their trials at sea thus far. Chase asks Pollard to speculate concerning what offense they have committed against God that might explain their current predicament. Pollard replies in a matter-of-fact tone: "The only creature to have offended God here is the whale." "Not us?" asks Chase. "In our arrogance, our greed?" Pollard soliloquizes in rejoinder that "we are supreme creatures made in God's own likeness. Earthly kings, whose business it is to circumnavigate the planet bestowed to us. To bend nature to our will." To which Chase bitterly retorts, "You really feel like an earthly king after everything that we've been through? We're nothing. We're . . . we're specks. Dust." But Pollard does not hear the wisdom in Chase's words. Instead, he resolves only that "we sail into the sun at dawn. If we are to die, then with God's grace let us die as men." And with that the exchange ends. The men once again head out to sea to face their fate. Cannibalism, Chase's act of mercy toward the whale, and the surviving crew's eventual rescue all unfold in short order.

It's a brief bit of dialogue, one without any basis whatsoever in the historical record, and yet it's exactly the entirely fabricated nature of the scene that seems to suggest its importance to the film's interpretation of events surrounding the *Essex* disaster. Here is the moment when characters based on historical personages are most obviously asked to channel twenty-first-century sensibilities. In this case the conduit is Owen Chase, whose epiphany regarding the cruelty of whaling, his conviction that humankind's relentless and selfish ravaging of the environment could be construed as a kind of "crime against nature," does not square much with nineteenth-century sensibilities. It is Pollard who sounds closer to an "actual" early American in explaining that God gave humankind dominion over the earth, which was to be exploited in whatever way the dominant species, made in "his" image, saw fit. Hence the captain's verdict that, if anything, it was the whale who had sinned. Chase, however, appears humbled. He now sees humankind as insignificant "specks," not clay shaped by a "Creator" and granted suzerainty over nature but rather animals who ought to live *in* or *alongside* nature. Pretending otherwise, as Chase expresses, seems a hollow fantasy that only leads to ruin. Evidence of such sensibilities—the "ethic of the environmentalist"—would have been exceptionally hard to find in 1820 Nantucket.[6]

But that's the point. Chase has, by the movie's end, departed the realm of the nineteenth century and come to channel a distinct strain of late-twentieth- and

In making the protagonist appear microscopic, this promotional poster for *In the Heart of the Sea* helps reinforce Owen Chase's (and the film's) philosophical perspective: human beings are hardly "masters" of the earth but instead remain easily overawed by nature.

early-twenty-first-century thought regarding the importance of environmental stewardship and human humility. Those who would, in Pollard's words, "bend nature to [their] will" are regularly exposed as frauds threatening to upset the fragile but meaningful kinship between the planet's living creatures. It is dangerous, the movie implies, to treat the earth so callously and carelessly. It is folly, we come to understand, to assume that we are anything but one species among many, interconnected with the natural world, subject to its whims, sharing in a planet's collective fate, and worthy of condign punishment when we violate collective norms. In that sense, *In the Heart of the Sea,* as a text, seems less closely connected to the nineteenth-century archive it claims as its inspiration and more powerfully aligned with a movement within contemporary Hollywood culture toward environmental conscientiousness. Indeed, it hardly seems an accident that these men meet their gruesome doom in search of oil meant to meet the energy needs of nineteenth-century America. The disaster at sea acts as a thinly veiled parable for our own oil-addicted civilization and its heedless quest, never mind the consequences, to pull petroleum out of the earth and spew pollutants into the air. Such thematics constitute what we might call filmmaking calibrated to the Age of Global Warming.

In 2018 it is, of course, exceedingly difficult to assess the impact or durability of a film released only three years prior. One suspects, however, that as an individual product, *In the Heart of the Sea* will not achieve much critical interest among future scholars or cineastes. The consensus today seems to be that the film was too uneven an exercise, at times exciting and poignant, while at other times muddled and tedious. Audiences, moreover, did not flock to theaters to see it. Some of the subject matter—whaling and cannibalism—seemed an odd fit for a December "holiday season" release. Meanwhile, the demographically limited audience (overwhelmingly fifty years old and over) did not seem to connect with the film's young star, Chris Hemsworth. As a result, its $100 million budget, subject to significant cost overruns (attributed to the difficulties of shooting on water) and a late conversion to 3-D, was not recouped. One imagines that it will stand as a "lesser" Ron Howard vehicle, a relatively "forgettable" film, and a cautionary tale for future studio executives contemplating big-budget maritime-historical films.

But if we look beyond this movie as a discrete product and situate it within a broader constellation of thematically similar films, its star might shine a bit brighter. The environmental movement, from the 1960s onward, has inspired a number of movies that speak to questions raised by *In the Heart of the Sea.* Summarized succinctly, these ecologically inclined disaster films ask the viewer to reconsider whether human beings are the dominant species on earth and whether that belief itself might be considered more pathology than paradigm. As Chase quite openly states to Pollard, it is a useless delusion to imagine that human beings could do as they pleased with the natural world without expecting consequences. Disaster epics of the twenty-first century, such as *The Day after Tomorrow* (2004), *2012* (2009), and *The Happening* (2008), portray worlds in which a criminally abused nature strikes back. Quieter exercises in independent filmmaking, like *Take Shelter* (2011), *The Last Winter* (2006), or *The Bay* (2012), as well as international cinema, exemplified by *Snowpiercer* (2013), take up similar themes of a planet dangerously changed by humanity's thoughtless exploitation. These are not new ideas or questions, of course. One is tempted to draw a straight line connecting *In the Heart of the Sea* with the underrated 1977 eco-horror movie *Orca*. In both films, a vengeful whale enacts bloody vengeance against its human adversaries. In both, the viewer is asked to sympathize with and "root for," to some extent, a whale that has been "wronged."[7]

The very idea that animals might possess some essence or spirit worthy of human respect, that a whale could be considered a "victim" rather than a "resource," is a fairly modern concept. It was virtually absent in the historical record on the nineteenth-century Nantucket whaling industry, thus making *In the Heart of the Sea* a product very much of its own time and place in history. And yet, this should not necessarily be seen as a flaw. Rather, the film is its own interpretation of humanity's long record of rationalizing profit-driven (mis) use of the world's plant and animal life. The past is, as we have discussed, an unstable construct subject to constant reevaluation. More than a century ago, the famed historian Frederick Jackson Turner observed that "each age writes the history of the past anew with reference to the conditions uppermost in its own time." It is a good thing that this is so, for such an impulse provides the wellspring from which the discipline renews, refreshes, and reinvigorates itself. And so while Ron Howard might not have much to teach us about the nineteenth-century whaling industry, we do learn a great deal from his representation of the past about the changing politics and preoccupations of our own time and place. In this sense, *In the Heart of the Sea,* even if it is contrary to the historical *record,* still stands as an embodiment of history's *philosophy:* dialogue between past and present that often has as much, if not more, to teach about where we are as a society as about where we have been.[8]

NOTES

1. An excellent overview of the American whaling industry is Eric J. Dolin, *Leviathan: A History of Whaling in America* (New York: Norton, 2007). See also Margaret Creighton, *Rites and Passages: The Experience of American Whaling, 1830–1870* (Cambridge: Cambridge University Press, 1995).

2. David Ingram, *Green Screen: Environmentalism and Hollywood Cinema* (Exeter, UK: University of Exeter Press, 2004).

3. By far the most thorough account of events aboard the *Essex* is Nathaniel Philbrick's *In the Heart of the Sea: The Tragedy of the Whaleship "Essex"* (New York: Viking, 2000). Philbrick himself is credited as a screenwriter for the film, though it appears as though the book only loosely guided the film's narrative.

4. These issues are covered in Philbrick, *In the Heart of the Sea*. The best treatment of black sailors is W. Jeffrey Bolster, *Black Jacks: African American Seamen in the Age of Sail* (Cambridge, MA: Harvard University Press, 1997).

5. G. K. Chesterton, "History versus the Historians," in *Lunacy and Letters* (London: Sheed & Ward, 1958).

6. A brief overview of humanity's supposedly unimpeachable "usufruct rights" to the natural world, at least according to a "Western" and "proto-capitalist" or "capitalistic" purview, is contained in William Cronon, *Changes in the Land: Indians, Colonists, and the Ecology of New England* (New York: Hill & Wang, 1983).

7. See Joseph J. Foy, "It Came from Planet Earth: Eco-Horror and the Politics of Postenvironmentalism in M. Night Shyamalan's *The Happening*," in *Homer Simpson Marches on Washington: Dissent through American Popular Culture*, ed. Timothy Dale and Joseph Foy (Lexington: University Press of Kentucky, 2010), 167–90.

8. Frederick Jackson Turner, "The Significance of History," in *Rereading Frederick Jackson Turner: "The Significance of the Frontier in American History" and Other Essays*, ed. John Mack Faragher (New Haven, CT: Yale University Press, 1999), 11–30. It should also be noted that what exactly the whale *could* be considered—whether fish or "something else"—became in the early nineteenth century quite a contentious point between scientists, insisting upon new classificatory schemes, and "traditionalists," insisting on the Bible's authority in referring to the whale as a "fish." See D. Graham Burnett, *Trying Leviathan: The Nineteenth-Century New York Court Case That Put the Whale on Trial and Challenged the Order of Nature* (Princeton, NJ: Princeton University Press, 2007).

3

"Some Say He's Dead, Some Say He Never Will Be"

Mountain Men and the Frontier-Hero Myth in
Jeremiah Johnson and *The Revenant*

JACOB F. LEE

A riverboat glides up to the docks of a bustling frontier outpost. A lone soldier steps onto the planks and navigates his way through the crowd of boatmen, stevedores, and passengers. "His name was Jeremiah Johnson," a narrator begins, "and they say he wanted to be a mountain man." As Johnson (Robert Redford) walks through the dirt streets, the voice continues, "The story goes that he was a man of proper wit and adventurous spirit suited to the mountains. Nobody knows whereabouts he come from and don't seem to matter much. He was a young man, and the ghosty stories about the tall hills didn't scare him none." A quick cut, and Johnson is mounted on horseback, leading a packhorse loaded down with traps and other gear. He inquires of the sutler, "Just where is it I could find bear, beaver, and other critters worth cash money when skinned?" Pointed to the Rocky Mountains, Johnson rides off, saying "goodbye to whatever life was down there below."

As Johnson heads out of town, the narrator begins to sing, "Jeremiah Johnson made his way into the mountains, bettin' on forgettin' all the troubles that he knew." Johnson follows the path of "the eagle or the sparrow" across prairies, rivers, and deserts and eventually into the Rockies. As he stands on a peak—a lone figure gazing across a vast, empty wilderness—the narrator sings of the solitude of the mountain man, who "leaves a life behind." For Johnson, that isolation is the appeal of his chosen path. Alone except for the birds that guide him and the fur-bearing critters he hopes to trap and skin, Johnson intends to escape the turmoil of life on the flats.

In its characterization of Johnson as a disaffected young man seeking refuge in the solace of the mountains, the film bearing his name builds on the long tradition of the mythology of the "frontier hero," a trope reinvented, generation after generation, to speak to changing anxieties, concerns, and ambitions. From the earliest descriptions of frontiersmen and mountain men, writers disagreed on whether they represented the vanguard of "civilization," men who used the skills required to survive in the woods to conquer the wilderness, or, alternately, wild men always searching for independence and freedom.[1] Writing about Daniel Boone in *The Discovery, Settlement and Present State of Kentucke* (1784), the author and land speculator John Filson cast the frontiersman as "an instrument ordained by God to settle the wilderness."[2] Yet, during the first decades of the nineteenth century another image of Boone appeared, one of "a fugitive from civilization who could not endure the encroachments of civilization upon his beloved wilderness."[3] The mythic Boone became the basis for written accounts of subsequent frontier heroes—real, exaggerated, and fictitious—including James Fennimore Cooper's Leatherstocking, the Tennessee frontiersman Davy Crockett, the river boatman Mike Fink, and Kit Carson, the first mountain man to enter the pantheon of western heroes.

The Rocky Mountain fur trade thrived for less than twenty years between the initial foray of a St. Louis fur brigade up the Missouri River in 1822 and the last rendezvous, the famed annual gatherings of trappers, in 1840. Between 1810 and 1845, perhaps as many as three thousand men entered the Rocky Mountain fur trade, although more conservative estimates put the total at only a third of that number. Often from poor or middling backgrounds, mountain men headed up the Missouri River seeking money in the form of beaver pelts, which, once processed and made into hats, decorated the heads of stylish men and women across eastern North American and Europe. Although more than half of all trappers were Anglo-American, a quarter were French American or French Canadian, and Francophone capital, labor, and knowledge buttressed the fur trade of the Far West. Far from operating in isolation, mountain men usually hunted in groups, and for pay and supplies they depended on economic networks that stretched from the Rockies to St. Louis, Montreal, New York, New Orleans, London, and places beyond. The work of trapping and hunting in the Rockies was brutal and dangerous. The trappers posed an economic threat to native peoples, who risked losing their place as the principal suppliers in the fur trade, and as a result, Indians often attacked mountain men, driving them away from rich sources of beaver. The trappers worked in extreme climates. As a result, a mountain man's life could be hard and short. Of a sample of 446 trappers, 182 (40 percent) of them are known to have died in the mountains and deserts of the Far West. Like other laborers in antebellum America, trappers depended upon capital and markets and often worked as wage laborers. But the danger of their trade and the exoticism of their environment gave their work a sheen of adventure absent from that of a millworker or farmer.[4]

The image of the mountain man, like that of the trans-Appalachian frontiersman or the Texas cowboy, has a resonance in American culture that far outweighs his brief period of historical significance. In the 1830s and 1840s, when Washington Irving, John C. Frémont, and other writers and travelers published tales of their encounters with mountain men, the trappers of the Rocky Mountain fur trade became western legends, the cultural descendants of Daniel Boone.[5] Mountain men have represented both absolute freedom from the restrictions of American society *and* the front line of "civilization" spreading into the Far West, but these competing analyses share common ground. At root, they highlight the skill, bravery, and toughness—in short, the masculinity—of their heroes. The films *Jeremiah Johnson* (1972) and *The Revenant* (2015) bring these narrative traditions into the late-twentieth and twenty-first centuries as they explore the complicated relationship between the supposed freedom of the "wilderness" and encroaching "civilization" and revel in the masculinity of their protagonists. They also participate in the storytelling devices of frontier mythology as they spin the lives of historical figures into epic stories based only partially in the world of fact.

Each film tell the story of a historical figures about whom we know little. Upon the release of *The Revenant*, the historian Jon T. Coleman, the leading scholar of the mountain man Hugh Glass and the legend surrounding him, summarized verifiable knowledge about the trapper as follows: "We know Hugh Glass existed and we're pretty sure he got mauled by a grizzly bear."[6] He left behind one letter, secondhand accounts of campfire stories, and many rumors. His origins are shrouded in mystery. Perhaps he was a sailor, once captured by the famous Gulf Coast pirate Jean Lafitte. Perhaps he was a runaway apprentice from Pennsylvania. Regardless, by 1823 he was unemployed in St. Louis, where he answered General William H. Ashley and Captain Andrew Henry's advertisement calling for men to enter the Rocky Mountain fur trade. Ashley and Henry hoped to recover their losses from 1822, their first season on the Upper Missouri, when a tree had caught and sank a keelboat carrying ten thousand dollars' worth of supplies. The second try met with its own parade of hardships and violence. Arikara Indians, whom the Americans threatened to cut out of the Missouri trade, attacked the party, killed seventeen hunters, and closed the river. Glass escaped with a leg wound. Later that summer he survived his near-fatal bear attack. Two of his comrades, paid by Henry to watch over Glass until he expired, left him for dead. He crawled and hobbled a reported two hundred miles to catch the men who had abandoned him. He survived another Arikara attack before reaching his destination late in 1823. At the company fort, Glass lectured James Bridger, later a famous mountain man but then an inexperienced tenderfoot, on the impropriety of deserting one's fellow trapper. He then followed Fitzpatrick, the other man who had left him, downriver to Fort Atkinson, in present-day Nebraska. There Glass chewed out Fitzpatrick as well and considered the matter finished. He returned to the fur trade and died at the hands of Arikaras in 1833. Writers and filmmakers have turned the raw bones of this story into epic poems, novels, short stories, and two feature films.[7]

Like Hugh Glass, John Johnston—better known by the sobriquet "Liver-Eating" Johnson, *sans* the *t*—is an enigmatic figure. Of a generation later than Glass, Johnson is described in legend as a deserter from the US Army during the Mexican-American War who became a mountain man. In the Rockies, Johnson married a Flathead woman named Swan and then launched a one-man war against the Crow Nation after they murdered her. While carrying out his vendetta, Johnson earned a reputation for eating the livers of his slain enemies. Although frequently repeated—and the inspiration for *Jeremiah Johnson*—this story rests on little evidence beyond the questionable statements made decades later by dubious informants. If in fact Johnson worked as a mountain man in the late 1840s, he would have been an anomaly. Born circa 1824, Johnson was younger than most trappers by a decade or more and would have entered the fur trade at the moment it collapsed as a result of overhunting, changing fashions, and cheaper alternatives, such as South American nutria.

In reality, Johnston seems to have entered the West in the 1860s. He served in the Colorado militia during the Civil War. He earned the handle "Liver Eating" in 1869 on the Missouri River during a fight between white woodcutters, who provided fuel for steamboats, and Lakota Indians, whose lands they trespassed and whose resources they stole. After the battle, Johnston reportedly decapitated one Lakota corpse before disemboweling him "and taking a piece of the liver to put a taste in his mouth." Some suggest that this may have

Jeremiah Johnson (Robert Redford) travels alone through the deserts of western Utah. Building on the frontier-hero myth, *Jeremiah Johnson* depicts mountain men as solitary figures and ignores their place in social and economic networks that linked them to families, corporations, and global markets.

been a gruesome joke rather than actual cannibalism, but if it was mockery, Johnston fooled the witnesses. In the aftermath of this event, Johnson gained some notoriety, at least locally. In 1876–77 he served as a scout for General Nelson E. Miles in the US wars against Native Americans on the northern plains. During the 1880s he served as a lawman in Montana and also dabbled in the entertainment business, traveling with a Wild West show. As a performer, he spread legends about his life in the mountains, claiming to have killed 1,299 Indians. He died in a veterans' home in Santa Monica, California, in 1900.[8]

The film *Jeremiah Johnson* fits neatly into the tradition of the frontier hero. Entering the "tall hills" as a greenhorn, Johnson meets the experienced bear hunter Bear Claw Chris Lapp (Will Geer), who takes the younger man under his wing. When Johnson has gained the skills necessary for survival, he sets off on his own. He travels with little sense of purpose. For a man ostensibly searching for "bear, beaver, and other critters worth cash money when skinned,"

Johnson spends precious little screen time either trapping or trading. Although he is intent on solitude, events force Johnson to adopt a mute orphan boy (Josh Albee), whom Johnson names Caleb, and to marry Swan (Delle Bolton), the daughter of a Flathead chief. Johnson and his family briefly enjoy happiness before the outside world intrudes. US soldiers appear at their home seeking a guide through the mountains to rescue a wagon train of settlers stranded in the snow. Against his better judgment, Johnson leads the soldiers through a Crow burial ground. In response, Crows kill Swan and Caleb, and Johnson spends the rest of the movie trapped in a cycle of vengeance. As this private war continues, Johnson becomes a legend. When he encounters a new family squatting in the house where Johnson had met Caleb, the man of the family leads Johnson to a shrine Crows have erected in his honor, telling him, "Some say you're dead—on account of this. Some say you never will be—on account of this." In the film's last scene, Johnson makes peace with the Crow leader, Paints His Shirt Red. In the end, the film suggests, Johnson finds his long-sought peaceful solitude. "And," according to the narrator, "some folks say he's up there still."

Jeremiah Johnson reinvented the myth of the mountain man to reflect the values of the counterculture of the 1960s and 1970s. According to Robert Redford, it's the story of "a man who decides he doesn't want to live by someone else's code. He wants to create his own. . . . He just wanted to go off by himself."[9] To Redford, Johnson's story was not unlike that of untold numbers of young people who embraced the counterculture as an alternative to the rigid, oppressive mainstream of American society.[10] In the words of one reviewer, echoing the LSD guru Timothy Leary's famous dictum, Johnson was "an 1848 dropout."[11] Audiences also recognized the environmental themes of the film, with one critic calling it "the first ecological Western," a film that emphasized living with, instead of against, nature.[12] A less generous voice deemed it "a long-winded plea for ecology."[13] Such a message mirrored the concerns of the era that saw the celebration of the first Earth Day, the founding of the Environmental Protection Agency, and a revitalized back-to-the-land movement, whose members sought a sustainable lifestyle free from the "smog" and "pollution" of the city and the "rat race" of corporate careers.[14]

Where *Jeremiah Johnson* builds on the image of the lone trapper in search of freedom, *The Revenant* twists the mountain-man-as-civilizer narrative into a tragedy. As the film opens, Hugh Glass (Leonardo DiCaprio) and his son, Hawk (Forrest Goodluck), are hunting elk to feed the trappers of Ashley and Henry's Rocky Mountain Fur Company. The action shifts to the chaotic, gory work of skinning and tanning on the banks of the Missouri, an image that contrasts sharply with the peaceful scene of the hunt. From that moment, Glass and his son are marked as outsiders. When asked why he "came out to the edge of the world," Glass responds, "I do like the quiet." A fellow trapper, who seems to have known Glass for some time, later remarks, "He keeps to hisself." For reasons left vague, Glass aids the trappers with the knowledge drawn from his years of experience, but as DiCaprio later stated, Glass is "always within and without. He's there, . . . he's a scout, but he's trying to remain detached from this whole wave of capitalism surging towards the wilderness."[15]

The Revenant juxtaposes the knowledgeable, tolerant, and family-minded Glass with the greedy, racist, and violent John Fitzgerald (Tom Hardy). The film quickly establishes their contrasting characters. During the film's initial battle scene, Glass urges his son and the other trappers to flee—"Get to the boat!"—emphasizing survival over protecting their furs. In contrast, even while he's fighting off Arikara attackers with gun and knife, Fitzgerald implores the men around him, "Grab the pelts!" As they descend the river, Glass urges abandoning the boat, which Arikara will easily spot and attack, in favor of an overland route back to their fort. When Henry (Domhnall Gleeson) agrees with Glass, Fitzgerald grumbles about leaving the season's work secreted under some rocks, complaining, "This ain't right. We all know that these furs ain't gonna be here by the time we get back." Fitzgerald then turns his attention to Glass and Hawk, questioning their loyalty to the party and repeatedly using slurs to describe Hawk, his Pawnee mother, and all Indians. As far as Fitzgerald is concerned, any show of friendship or affinity to any Indians, even Pawnees, enemies to the Arikaras, makes a person suspect.

Fitzgerald's animosity toward Glass reaches its apex after a bear nearly kills Glass, who had again ventured off on his own to hunt. As Henry, Hawk, and Jim Bridger (Will Poulter) try to save Glass, Fitzgerald recommends, "The proper thing to do would be to finish him off quick." Glass survives the night, but he is immobile and unfit to travel with the men still desperate to reach the safety of their fort. After dragging Glass miles through woods and across rivers, Fitzgerald once again advocates killing him, as keeping him alive—in Fitzgerald's words, "lettin' him go on sufferin'"—"ain't doin' us, nor him, no favors." The two teenagers, Hawk and Bridger, refuse to abandon Glass, and Henry offers seventy dollars to any man who will stay behind with them and give Glass a proper burial after his imminent death. Fitzgerald negotiates for one hundred dollars and then finally agrees to stay after Bridger offers him

The battered Hugh Glass (Leonardo DiCaprio) treks across the frozen landscapes of the Rocky Mountain West. Despite its critiques of colonialism and capitalism, *The Revenant* clings to the image of rugged masculinity central to the "frontier hero" myth.

his share as well. After a week of waiting, with Bridger at the creek gathering water, Fitzgerald murders Hawk, who finds him on the verge of killing Glass. He then buries Glass alive before persuading Bridger that Arikaras will soon attack and they should flee. When Glass pulls himself out of his shallow grave, he discovers his son's body. For the remainder of the film he pursues Fitzgerald, determined to overcome his wounds and the elements to avenge Hawk's death.

Imbedded in *The Revenant* is an implicit critique of both colonialism and capitalism. Rather than celebrating the hunter and mountain man as the first line of colonization, the film casts its hero as a reluctant participant in the conquest of North America. Released amid fears about global climate change, *The Revenant* highlights the environmental destruction wrought by colonialism and extractive capitalism. For example, in a vision induced by his severe wounds, Glass sees a mountain of bison skulls, an anachronistic scene that hints at later devastation wrought by the fur trade and other industries in the American West. In contrasting Glass and Fitzgerald, the filmmakers cast the trappers, with few exceptions, as vulgarians, while the hero remains unsullied by the desire for profit. Leonardo DiCaprio made the film's environmentalist message more explicit during his promotional appearances, drawing a direct line between the early capitalism of the fur trade and contemporary environmental issues, including global climate change. In one interview he stated, "Historically, we look back at human nature and . . . what we've done to the natural world. And we say, *God, how ignorant we must have been, how short-sighted.*" People, DiCaprio continued, like to believe that they have improved since earlier generations "carved up nature for our own comfort." Instead, DiCaprio saw the fur trade as "this first wave, this first influx of capitalism" that led to contemporary environmental crises.[16]

Yet, for their reinventions of the mythic mountain man as environmentalist or hesitant capitalist, *Jeremiah Johnson* and *The Revenant* both highlight the masculinity of their protagonists in ways that have been central to western myths since the days of Filson and Boone. Both films glorify men for their strength, skill, and refusal to surrender, while rendering women invisible or in need of protection. Johnson enters the mountains "a man of wit and adventurous spirit" but with no experience in trapping, hunting, or surviving in the harsh climate. Yet, in the elderly hunter Bear Claw, Johnson finds both a mentor and an example of how to lead an independent life. Early in the film, Johnson asks Bear Claw if he ever gets lonesome. Initially shocked at the suggestion, Bear Claw tells him that he did have a Cheyenne wife for a decade but then, with a laugh, reveals that he later "traded her for a Hawken gun." With his natural abilities, Johnson is a quick study under Bear Claw's tutelage, and soon he is prepared to set off on his own. As he packs to leave, Bear Claw tells him, "You've learned well, pilgrim, and you'll go far." Like Bear Claw, Johnson is a reluctant husband, accepting Swan as his wife only when Del Gue informs him that a rejection would insult her father and lead to their deaths. The film contrasts Johnson's masculine education under Bear Claw with his marriage to Swan. As Swan prepares a meal shortly after their wedding, Johnson laments, "Cookin' sure don't smell like Bear Claw's." After tasting the corn cake she prepares, Johnson walks back to his horse, where he spits it out and sneaks a piece of jerky. In Johnson's world, even domestic tasks are best done with a masculine hand. Over time, Johnson grows fonder of his family, but he still envies the freedom of a hawk flying overhead.

In the opening voiceover to *The Revenant*, DiCaprio intones what amounts to the film's thesis statement: "As long as you can still grab a breath, you fight." In his struggle with the grizzly bear, Glass enacts this mantra, killing the bear with his knife after it has already slashed, bitten, squashed, and thrown him.

Upon finding the near-dead Glass, a fellow trapper comments, "Gotta give him credit for taking that griz down with him." (In reality, Glass's comrades shot and killed the bear.)[17] The imperative to fight then drives Glass as he claws and crawls across the frozen West. Predicted to die "inside an hour" after the bear attack, he survives because of his grit and determination. (The film's title means one who returns from the dead, from the French verb *revenir*.) One historian stated that the actual Glass's "major talent" was "accident proneness," but in *The Revenant,* Glass performs a series of superhuman feats, including riding a horse off a cliff to escape pursuers.[18] According to DiCaprio, the film valorizes "every character," even the bear, as a survivor.[19]

In both films the emphasis on masculinity obscures the crucial roles of women in the fur trade and reduces female characters to victims whose suffering spurs men to action. Johnson's war of vengeance against the Crows stems from the death of his wife. In *The Revenant,* Glass kills a US soldier for murdering his wife, an event possibly leading Glass to enter the mountains. The Arikara leader Elk Dog attacks the trappers after the kidnapping of his daughter. In reality, the fur trade depended upon Indian and Mexican women, who often married mountain men. Indian women acted as cultural brokers, mediating between their husbands and their nations and working as translators and go-betweens. They also performed domestic duties and provided much of the labor required to prepare furs for shipment. As the fur trade shifted southward into northern Mexico during the 1830s and 1840s, Mexican women offered access to the social networks that ruled the New Mexican trade. Trappers, in the words of historian Richard White, "were men who needed women."[20]

As they promoted their films, the casts and crews of *Jeremiah Johnson* and *The Revenant* noted that the actors' bravery and toughness matched that of the men they portrayed. Verisimilitude became a keystone of their marketing campaigns. In 1972 the director Sydney Pollack stated: "I think Redford might well have been a mountain man if he lived at that particular time. He is a man who places a great deal of value on solitude, and he's terribly concerned with ecology." An "avid skier and horseback rider," Redford "spends hours off alone just wandering in the back areas of unexplored places." Confusing leisure activities with work, Pollack believed Redford "would have sought out nature in its most virgin, pristine sense had he lived at that time."[21] That the film was shot, in part, on property Redford owned in Utah further linked actor and character.[22] At the Boston premiere of the film, Pollack noted that a blizzard had pummeled the cast and crew while filming in the Wasatch Mountains.[23]

Other accounts noted that "much" of the film had been shot "in twenty-five-below-zero weather."[24]

Nearly forty-five years later, stories accompanying the release of *The Revenant* repeatedly reminded readers that the vegetarian DiCaprio had *actually* eaten a raw bison liver during filming or that he had braved subfreezing temperatures to *actually* crawl naked into the carcass of a dead horse—later revealed to have been a latex and hair mock-up. He had *actually* waded through icy streams, "enduring freezing cold and possible hypothermia constantly."[25] DiCaprio remarked, "Every single day of this movie was difficult. It was the most difficult film I've ever done."[26] The director, Alejandro G. Iñárittu, said of his cast, "They were miserable! And they really feel the fucking cold in their ass! They were not acting at all!"[27] The repeated lamentations of hardship became so overwrought that the satirical publication *The Onion* reported that DiCaprio was a strong contender for an Academy Award for his performance (which he ultimately won), because "in addition to stumbling and falling a bunch of times in the snow, there were some scenes where he shouted so loud it made his throat hurt."[28]

Before the release of *The Revenant*, DiCaprio acknowledged that Glass's story contained few historical details, remarking, "I took that opportunity to create my own Hugh Glass: my interpretation of *who he could have been*."[29] In that moment, DiCaprio hit at a core truth about mountain men—far more so than Redford had when he insisted that *Jeremiah Johnson* "was an education as to what mountain men were really like."[30] The trappers of the Rocky Mountain fur trade have long existed on the edge of fact and myth, of who they were and who they "could have been." As storytellers and memoirists, mountain men mixed their own experiences with tall tales, folklore, and outright lies, and other writers and filmmakers followed suit, often romanticizing their subjects to bask in their legendary independence or to praise the westward march of "civilization."[31] During the late twentieth century many Americans grew skeptical of their nation's founding myth of manifest destiny, and they recognized the devastation wrought by colonialism and capitalism. As they reevaluated the nation's history, they produced art, especially films, that inverted myths into critiques.[32] *Jeremiah Johnson* and *The Revenant* condemn the destruction wrought by colonialism and urge viewers to live sustainably. Yet, while they revise some western myths, they perpetuate visions of the West that center on rugged individualism and masculinity, shrouding the role of women, families, and corporations in the history of the fur trade and the American West.

NOTES

1. Henry Nash Smith, *Virgin Land: The American West as Symbol and Myth* (1950; reprint, Cambridge, MA: Harvard University Press, 1970), 51–58, 81–89; Richard Slotkin, *The Fatal Environment: The Myth of the Frontier in the Age of Industrialization, 1800–1890* (New York: Atheneum, 1985), 198–207.

2. John Filson, *The Discovery, Settlement, and Present State of Kentucke: And, An Essay towards the Topography and Natural History of that important Country* (Wilmington, DE: James Adams, 1784), 81; Richard Slotkin, *Regeneration through Violence: The Mythology of the American Frontier, 1600–1860* (1973; reprint, Norman: University of Oklahoma Press, 2000), 268–312.

3. Smith, *Virgin Land*, 54.

4. This overview is based on Richard J. Fehrman, "The Mountain Men—A Statistical View," in *The Mountain Men and the Fur Trade of the Far West*, ed. LeRoy R. Hafen, 10 vols. (Glendale, CA: A. H. Clark, 1965–72), 10:9–15; William H. Goetzmann, "The Mountain Man as Jacksonian Man," *American Quarterly* 15 (Autumn 1963): 402–15 (409 for mountain-man deaths); Goetzmann, *Exploration and Empire: The Explorer and the Scientist in the Winning of the American West* (1966; reprint, New York: History Book Club, 1993), 105–80; David J. Wishart, *The Fur Trade of the American West, 1807–1840* (Lincoln: University of Nebraska Press, 1979); William R. Swagerty, "Marriage and Settlement Patterns of Rocky Mountain Trappers and Traders," *Western Historical Quarterly* 11 (April 1980): 159–80 (for number of mountain men, see 159n1); Robert M. Utley, *A Life Wild and Perilous: Mountain Men and the Paths to the Pacific* (New York: Henry Holt, 1997); Jay Gitlin, *The Bourgeois Frontier: French Towns, French Traders, and American Expansion* (New Haven, CT: Yale University Press, 2010), esp. 83–138; Eric Jay Dolin, *Fur, Fortune, and Empire: The Epic History of the Fur Trade in America* (New York: Norton, 2011), 223–54.

5. Smith, *Virgin Land*, 81–89; Slotkin, *Fatal Environment*, 121–22, 198–207.

6. Michael Miller, "The Real Grizzly Man: The Amazing True Story behind Leonardo DiCaprio's Character in *The Revenant*," *People*, 6 January 2016, http://people.com/movies/leonardo-dicaprio-s-revenant-character-the-true-story-of-hugh-glass.

7. Jon T. Coleman, *Here Lies Hugh Glass: A Mountain Man, a Bear, and the Rise of the American Nation* (New York: Hill & Wang, 2012).

8. Nathan E. Bender, introduction to *Crow Killer: The Saga of Liver-Eating Johnson*, by Raymond W. Thorp and Robert Bunker, new ed. (Bloomington: Indiana University Press, 2015), ix–xiii; Bender, "The Abandoned Scout's Revenge: Origins of the Crow Killer Saga of Liver-Eating Johnson," *Annals of Wyoming* 78 (Summer 2006): 2–17; Fehrman, "Mountain Men," 9; Swagerty, "Marriage and Settlement Patterns," 161–62; Utley, *Life Wild and Perilous*, 174–75; Dolin, *Fur, Fortune, and Empire*, 280–89; Greg Gordon, "Steamboats, Woodhawks, and War on the Upper Missouri," *Montana: The Magazine of Western History* 61 (Summer 2011): 30–46 (quote on 44).

9. "Robert Redford on Sydney Pollack," sidebar to "Sydney Pollack: The Way We Are," interview by Patricia Erens, *Film Comment* 11 (September–October 1975): 24–29.

10. Richard Aquila, *The Sagebrush Trail: Western Movies and Twentieth-Century America* (Tucson: University of Arizona Press, 2015), 246, 251–53.

11. Milton Krims, "Jeremiah Johnson: Mountain Man," *Saturday Evening Post*, no. 244 (Winter 1972–73): 128.

12. Ralph Brauer, "Who Are Those Guys? The Movie Western during the TV Era," *Journal of Popular Film* 2 (Fall 1973): 403–4 (quote on 403).

13. Rex Reed, "Rex Reed Reports: The Chaos of Cannes Can Match Marx Bros. Madness," *Chicago Tribune*, 21 May 1972, http://archives.chicagotribune.com/1972/05/21/page/461/article/rex-reed-reports.

14. Dona Brown, *Back to the Land: The Enduring Dream of Self-Sufficiency in Modern America* (Madison: University of Wisconsin Press, 2011), 202–26, esp. 209–10.

15. John Horn and Robert Garrova, "Leonardo DiCaprio on the Environmentalist Undertones in 'The Revenant,'" *Frame*, 24 February 2016, http://www.scpr.org/programs/the-frame/2016/02/24/46632/leonardo-dicaprio-on-the-environmentalist-underton.

16. Horn and Garrova, "Leonardo DiCaprio on the Environmentalist Undertones," emphasis in the original.

17. Coleman, *Here Lies Hugh Glass*, 3.

18. Coleman, *Here Lies Hugh Glass*, ix.

19. Horn and Garrova, "Leonardo DiCaprio on the Environmentalist Undertones."

20. For the extensive literature on women and intermarriage in the North American fur trade, see Sylvia Van Kirk, *"Many Tender Ties": Women in Fur Trade Society in Western Canada, 1670–1870* (Winnipeg, MB: Watson & Dwyer, 1980); Jennifer S. H. Brown, *Strangers in Blood: Fur Trade Company Families in Indian Country* (Vancouver: University of British Columbia Press, 1980); Jacqueline Peterson, "The People in Between: Indian-White Marriage and the Genesis of a Métis Society and Culture in the Great Lakes Region, 1680–1830Đ (PhD diss., University of Illinois at Chicago Circle, 1981); Tanis C. Thorne, *The Many Hands of My Relations: French and Indians on the Lower Missouri* (Columbia: University of Missouri Press, 1996); and Anne Hyde, *Empires, Nations, and Families: A History of the North American West, 1800–1860* (Lincoln: University of Nebraska Press, 2011). On the marriages of mountain men, see Swagerty, "Marriage and Settlement Patterns," 164–69; and Richard White, *"It's Your Misfortune and None of My Own": A New History of the American West* (Norman: University of Oklahoma Press, 1991), 46–47 (quote on 46).

21. Sidney Pollack, quoted in "The Saga of Jeremiah Johnson," directed by Elliot P. Geisinger, on *Jeremiah Johnson* (1972; Burbank, CA: Warner Home Video, 1997), DVD.

22. Robert Redford, "Combining Entertainment and Education: An Interview with Robert Redford," by Mikelle Cosandaey, *Cinéaste* 16 (1987–88): 8.

23. Pril Patton, "Sydney Pollack: Mountains and the Man," *Harvard Crimson*, 11 January 1973, http://www.thecrimson.com/article/1973/1/11/sydney-pollack-mountains-and-the-man.

24. See, e.g., Krims, "Jeremiah Johnson," 131.

25. Leonardo DiCaprio, "Leonardo DiCaprio on Fighting a Bear in 'The Revenant' and Film vs. TV," interview by Jordan Zakarin, *Yahoo! News*, 19 October 2015, https://www.yahoo.com/movies/leonardo-dicaprio-on-fighting-a-1281529422913590.html; Jason Guerrasio, "How That Infamous Bear-Attack Scene in 'The Revenant' Was Made, and Other Secrets of the Movie Revealed," *Business Insider*, 26 December 2015, http://www.businessinsider.com/the-revenant-filming-secrets-2015–12.

26. Robert Capps, "The Nine Lives of Leonardo DiCaprio," *Wired*, January 2016, https://www.wired.com/2015/12/leonardo-dicaprio-interview-revenant-climate-change.

27. Chris Connelly, "Exclusive: Leonardo DiCaprio and Alejandro G. Iñárittu on 'The Revenant,'" *Grantland*, 15 July 2015, http://grantland.com/features/exclusive-leonardo-dicaprio-and-alejandro-g-inarritu-on-the-revenant.

28. "Leonardo DiCaprio Hopes He Screamed and Cried Good Enough in 'THE REVENANT' to Win Oscar," *Onion,* 14 January 2016, http://www.theonion.com/article/leonardo-dicaprio-hopes-he-screamed-and-cried-good-52170.

29. Connelly, "Leonardo DiCaprio and Alejandro G. Iñárittu," emphasis in the original.

30. Redford, "Combining Entertainment and Education," 12.

31. Coleman, *Here Lies Hugh Glass,* 10–11, 79–88; Slotkin, *Fatal Environment,* 198–207.

32. Richard Slotkin, *Gunfighter Nation: The Myth of the Frontier in Twentieth-Century America* (1992; reprint, Norman: University of Oklahoma Press, 1998), 578–660.

4

Andrew Jackson and the Ladies
The Gorgeous Hussy and *The President's Lady*

JOHN F. MARSZALEK

If there ever was a historical figure meant to be portrayed in film, that person was Andrew Jackson. Tall, thin, gruff, bigger than life, frontiersman, military officer, and president, Jackson spoke his mind and lived a life that was full of controversy and excitement. He had all the attributes that Hollywood looks for in a leading man: he was the kind of individual who could dominate the silver screen as he dominated the age in which he lived. While his career was certainly one of the best documented among those of nineteenth-century Americans, cinematic treatments of Jackson have not been particularly conscientious in terms of historical accuracy.[1] This is particularly true of the two films considered here.

In the mid-1930s, when Jackson was already an American icon, the motion-picture industry was undergoing tremendous expansion and important innovation in terms of historical and biographical storytelling. This included perhaps the most sensational motion picture about Andrew Jackson that ever appeared. As its title suggests, *The Gorgeous Hussy* (1936) did not center on Jackson but rather on the subject of a political scandal of sorts during the early years of his presidency: Margaret (Peggy) O'Neill Timberlake Eaton. Nearly two decades later, *The President's Lady* (1953) employed a broader chronology to tell the story of Andrew and Rachel Jackson's courtship and marriage and of yet another scandal that resulted from both.

It should come as no surprise that both these motion pictures were adapted from novels. *The Gorgeous Hussy* is based on a tale of the same title by Samuel Hopkins Adams, published in 1934. In his frontispiece, "A Letter to the Meticulous Reader," Adams writes that no one should "attempt to reconcile my story with the accepted data of history."[2] *The President's Lady* is taken from a book that calls itself a novel in the very title: *The President's Lady: A Novel about Rachel and Andrew Jackson* (1951), by Irving Stone, the author of several fictional biographies that were adapted to film. Like Adams, Stone opens with a note to readers in which he assures them that what follows is "authentic and documented"; he says he did a great deal of research in a wide variety of primary and secondary sources and relied heavily on historians and librarians for help.[3]

The screenwriter for *The Gorgeous Hussy* was Stephen Morehouse Avery, who had begun his career as a Hollywood writer only three years earlier. Clarence Brown, who directed the film, was one of the major directors of that era. His films won thirty-eight Academy Awards, and he himself was nominated five times as director.[4]

Those who made *The President's Lady* were equally prolific. The screenwriter was John Patrick, best known for his play and later motion picture *Teahouse of the August Moon,* for which he won a Pulitzer Prize and a host of other awards.[5] The director was Henry Levin, who had more than fifty feature films to his credit, averaging more than one motion picture a year from 1944 to 1980, though many of them were what Hollywood called "B" movies.[6]

These two Andrew Jackson films each had a famous leading lady. The earliest plan for *The Gorgeous Hussy* called for Jean Harlow and then Katharine Hepburn to play the female lead. Ultimately, Joan Crawford, already a major star, won the part of Margaret O'Neill. Her supporting cast was similarly distinguished. Robert Taylor played John "Bow" Timberlake, Margaret's first husband; Lionel Barrymore was Andrew Jackson; Franchot Tone (Crawford's husband at the time) played her second husband, John Eaton; Melvyn Douglas was John Randolph; and Jimmy Stewart was Margaret's fictitious friend "Rowdy" Dow. The well-known character actress Beulah Bondi played Rachel Jackson, winning a supporting-actress Oscar nomination for her performance.[7]

The President's Lady also had major male and female leads. The role of Rachel Jackson was played by the glamorous Susan Hayward, whom one book on Hollywood women accurately described as follows: "Susan Hayward was more the actress and less the sex symbol, and her female audiences could relate to her portrayals of women who overcame great obstacles and survived." This was clearly a description of Rachel Jackson.[8] However, Hayward received mixed reviews for her portrayal, and some critics believed that more of the movie centered on her apparel than on the story. Playing Andrew Jackson was a young

Charlton Heston, who very much looked the part. It was the first of many roles in which Heston was cast as a larger-than-life historical figure. In addition to a second performance as General Jackson in *The Buccaneer* (1958), Heston also played Moses in *The Ten Commandments*; Michelangelo in *The Agony and the Ecstasy*; and the title character in *El Cid*. Both Heston and Hayward faced the challenge of aging over three decades on screen, which both manage to do fairly convincingly.

Despite attractive stars, lavish productions by first-rate directors, excellent screenwriters, and popular books to draw on, *The Gorgeous Hussy* and *The President's Lady* had only limited box-office success and garnered only mixed reactions from critics and audiences. Simply because of the title and recognizing that the film dealt with an alleged sexual reprobate named Margaret O'Neill Timberlake Eaton (more commonly known as Peggy Eaton), many theatergoers would no doubt have been attracted to *The Gorgeous Hussy*. However, the 1930s were a time of censorship (with the Hays Code having gone into effect in 1930 but only seriously enforced from 1934 on), so there was little chance that this motion picture would be very risqué. Because of the new restrictions, filmmakers had to tell any story dealing with love, sex, and marriage in the most delicate, sexless way. An early script of *The Gorgeous Hussy*, for example, was even cited for having too many "hells" and "damns" coming from Andrew Jackson.[9]

Historical accuracy was hardly the primary consideration in *The Gorgeous Hussy*. The first scene itself shows Senators Daniel Webster and John Randolph of Roanoke debating states' rights on the floor of Congress in 1823. This scene is jolting, since neither man played a significant role in Andrew Jackson's interaction with Margaret, the daughter of a Washington taverner (Gene Lockhart) whose inn was frequented by politicians. Only later does its relevance become apparent when she becomes infatuated with Randolph. While in reality Randolph was unable to function sexually and had a high-pitched voice, in the film he has a deep voice and is distinguished and serious looking. Despite his misrepresentation on screen, the film puts a great deal of misplaced emphasis on Margaret's alleged infatuation with him. She reluctantly marries Bow Timberlake because Randolph thinks she is much too young for him and puts her off.

On the night of the young couple's wedding, Andrew and Rachel Jackson, then an elderly couple whom Margaret affectionately calls Uncle Andy and Aunt Rachel, arrive in town and come to the inn. When Jackson hears some noises coming from the room next to theirs, he and Rachel rush into the newlyweds' room and Jackson demands their wedding license. Timberlake cannot find it and instead shows the Jacksons his orders for a three-month tour on a naval ship. Without their glasses, the Jacksons cannot read the orders and accept them as a wedding license. Margaret can read the print, however, and is shocked at what she sees. Hardly the usual wedding-night scenario.

Adding to the confusion, the film has Randolph return from a diplomatic tour in Russia in 1828, when he actually died there in 1830 after a residence of only a few months. Meanwhile, Jackson is elected president in 1828. Shockingly, Rachel dies, the film insists, because of the accusations against her, mostly about bigamy but also about her being an uncouth western woman. On her deathbed, she supposedly makes Margaret promise to take care of Jackson in Washington; according to the film, Margaret becomes the White House hostess and Jackson's closest friend. In fact she was neither.

Back and forth the motion picture lurches. Timberlake dies at sea, but John Randolph reenters the scene, this time to lead the southern opposition to Jackson over states' rights. Such politics play out further at a grand ball where Margaret prevents her alleged longtime friend "Rowdy" Dow (played by a very young Jimmy Stewart, not yet a star) from attacking John C. Calhoun, who has apparently insulted her. Randolph is shocked to see Rowdy and Margaret dancing, though she is quick to tell him that she still loves him. This time Randolph accepts her affections, and a marriage is planned. But when Margaret realizes that Randolph is a states' righter, while she agrees with Andrew Jackson's nationalist views, she breaks off the engagement. Fascinating scenes, but none of this ever happened.

Despite her young widowhood, Margaret is suspected of being a scarlet woman. The film provides no information about accusations against her, although it does her to be a flirt. Finally, Jackson's secretary of war, John Eaton, enters the film's romantic interplay. He expresses his longtime love for Margaret; she admits some affection for him and is persuaded by the president that marriage would stop all the accusations of unladylike behavior on her part. She agrees to marry Eaton but does so unhappily. (Once again, none of this is accurate.)

A year later the fictitious Rowdy Dow returns to Washington for a visit and creates further fictional complications. He tells Margaret that Randolph is dying from a bullet wound inflicted on him by a southern states' righter. Margaret rushes to Randolph's side, and he dies happily, knowing that she is with him. On the way back to the nation's capital, however, Rowdy and Margaret are

Joan Crawford as Peggy O'Neal in *The Gorgeous Hussy*, surrounded by the men in her life, including Senator John Randolph (Franchot Tone), *far left*, and her true love in the film, the fictional Bow Timberlake (Robert Taylor), *behind her.*

attacked by the same man who had allegedly just shot Randolph. He threatens to tell the world about what he perceives as their secret rendezvous, and Rowdy throws him out of the coach.

Still, the film insists that news of Margaret's visit to Randolph becomes the talk of Washington, and members of the cabinet and their wives demand that Jackson force Margaret out of his White House. He does, but in the film this happens much earlier than it really did, and certainly it was not done because of any visit to Randolph. Meeting with his cabinet, which Jackson actually did (although he never met with their wives), Jackson lies that he had told Margaret to go to see Randolph and that John Eaton had given Rowdy Dow permission to accompany her. Angry at the response from cabinet members and their wives, the president demands the resignation of his entire cabinet except Eaton. Jackson did, in fact, break up his cabinet but not until 1831. Actually, the first to offer their resignations were Eaton and Secretary of State Martin Van Buren, who is mentioned only vaguely in the film, although he was a major figure in the controversy. Despite Jackson's attempt to protect Margaret's reputation, she can see no hope for the future. She asks Jackson to make Eaton a special envoy to Spain, where she thinks she and Eaton can live in peace. In fact, Jackson sends the Eatons to Florida before they go to Spain. At this point the motion picture ends, with the audience exposed to more erroneous than accurate information.

Nearly twenty years later a very different treatment of Jackson appeared on film: *The President's Lady,* a reference to Rachel, although, ironically, she dies before he takes office as president. This 1953 motion picture traces the full arc of Andrew and Rachel's relationship, from their turbulent courtship in the 1790s to her death in 1828, just after his election as president. It repeats mistakes in the earlier movie but is at least a more appealing representation of the Jacksons. Charlton Heston and Susan Hayward present a much younger and more glamorous couple than the elderly twosome depicted in *The Gorgeous Hussy.*

The President's Lady opens in 1789, with Andrew meeting Rachel for the first time when he arrives at her mother's home just outside Nashville, Tennessee, as a new lawyer seeking accommodations in a cabin on her property. Rachel's mother, Mrs. Donelson (Fay Bainter), agrees to let him live there. At a social gathering that evening, Andrew and Rachel are dancing together when Rachel's estranged husband, Lewis Robards, walks in. He cuts in but apologizes to Rachel for ever doubting her. When Jackson goes to the Donelson home for breakfast the next morning, he learns that Robards has taken Rachel back to his Kentucky home.

In a fully fictionalized scenario based on Irving Stone's novel (Robards and Jackson never actually met), Jackson pursues the couple and tells Robards, who's engaged in an open affair with a black servant, that Mrs. Donelson has sent him to retrieve her daughter. Robards is furious, and the two men get into a fight. Jackson escorts Rachel back to Nashville, but because of threats from Indians en route, they take a room in an inn (in separate beds, of course, although viewers can use their imagination). The next morning they arrive at a fort, where they find Mrs. Donelson waiting with the news that Robards is determined to take Rachel back. She refuses to go, and Robards accuses her of loving Jackson instead, which she vehemently denies.

Rachel then decides to go to Natchez to get away from Robards. She stows away on a river raft, where, coincidentally, Jackson is already present. He single-handedly defends the vessel and its passengers during an Indian attack, which ultimately sparks the first kiss between the two, bringing their romance into the open.

The motion picture shifts to Natchez, where the couple, obviously in love, have temporarily settled. They talk about an annulment for Rachel, and soon afterward Jackson receives a letter informing him that Robards has filed for divorce. Andrew says that he and Rachel can now get married, but she is not sure. Jackson reminds her that Robards is claiming her adultery with Jackson as the reason for his divorce proceedings. Marked for life, she asks Jackson, "How could he be so spiteful?" Again, there is no evidence that such a scene ever took place, although the uncertainty about the divorce is accurate.

Andrew and Rachel decide to return to Nashville as husband and wife. Several years pass, and Andrew begins to show an interest in politics, while Rachel broods about the lack of any children in their marriage. Jackson's law partner, John Overton, arrives to inform them that Robards had not processed the divorce papers as they had assumed, so his divorce from Rachel had not been legalized until recently. Rachel immediately wants to get married again in order to make sure that future children are fully legitimate. Jackson reluctantly agrees, and a wedding takes place in the Donelson home. None of this, other than the uncertainty about the timing of the divorce, can be verified.

Soon thereafter the controversy about Rachel's first marriage explodes. The film shows the couple traveling by buggy to a nearby store, where a bystander makes a remark about Rachel's lack of purity and Jackson immediately attacks him to defend her honor, which leads to an all-out brawl. On the way home, they discover that Rachel's brother has been killed by Creek Indians, and for the first of many times Jackson leaves her to go to war. He is gone a long time, and when he returns, he brings with him a Creek Indian baby named Lyncoya for Rachel.

Jackson continues to leave Rachel for long periods of time, usually to fight Indians. At home, Rachel is prevented from joining a local woman's group, some of whose members accuse her of being a bigamist. Returning home upset, she finds Lyncoya, by then an adolescent, dead. She now asks herself and the slave woman, Molly, her one constant companion, what she had she done to deserve having no children and then losing Lyncoya? Molly responds that the early Christians did not doubt God even when they were thrown to the lions. All this is a touching story, but blacks did not have such elevated status at that time, and there is no proof of any of this except Jackson's bringing Lyncoya home from an Alabama battlefield.

When next Jackson comes home (which had expanded over the years from a log cabin to the white-columned Hermitage), a party is held in his honor, but something is clearly wrong. Only men attend. Women refuse to come because of Rachel's low-down reputation. At this social function there is a horse race, and Jackson bets five thousand dollars that his horse will win. Allegedly, he does not have any money to make such a bet, having spent it all on his men during the latest war. Fortunately, his horse does win, and Rachel demonstrates her superiority to the snubbing women by forgiving their bet against the Jackson horse. Once again, this is a good story but one without any factual basis.

After learning that he is the new head of the state militia, Jackson hears yet another personal insult against his wife. He tells Rachel that he must fight a duel with the person who made the insult so that he can lead his militia men into battle with honor. Rachel says that she will leave him if he duels, but he says he has no choice. Despite opposing this duel, Rachel still wakes Jackson in time for the encounter. Jackson returns with a gunshot wound, and his antagonist, John Dickenson, is dead. Rachel is upset, but Jackson says it has to be.

The War of 1812 then erupts on the screen and forces Jackson back into the fray as troop commander. (There's only brief reference to the Battle of New Orleans.) The film's narrative focuses on Rachel waiting at home, where she is forced, unbeknownst to Andrew, to work in the fields alongside their slaves, often with only Molly at her side. Later, although he is opposed to the Tennessee governor's appointing him to the US Senate, he accepts the appointment and travels with Rachel to Washington.

In 1828—no mention is made of his 1824 run for the White House—Jackson is nominated to be president of the United States, and he tells Rachel to go to nearby Nashville to buy an inauguration gown. Molly warns her not to travel because of her poor health, but she goes anyway. From her carriage she witnesses a parade with people carrying signs saying that they do not want a prostitute in the White House. Rachel breaks down in tears. The next scene in this chronologically confused narrative shows Rachel confined to bed. Word arrives that Andrew has won the presidential election. She tells him that she will never make it to Washington, but he disagrees. To Jackson's shock, and the tears of the loyal Molly, Rachel dies.

The film's final scene shows Jackson walking to the podium to deliver his inaugural address. He stops, takes out his pocket watch, and looks at Rachel's picture. He remembers all their wonderful days together. He knows that some people will feel sorry for him, but he tells himself that he has enough good memories to last him the rest of his life.

In both motion pictures historical fact is lost in the clutter of inaccurate information, but that was not often the primary criterion by which critics or audiences judged a movie. A typical review of *The Gorgeous Hussy* praised its "many fine qualities" and in passing seemed to accept as accurate everything in the film, stating merely that "there is evidence everywhere of authenticity of preproduction and it is a well-rounded entertainment by an excellent cast."[10] Another reviewer gushed that it "can be sold to the patrons who go for big names, to those who seek entertainment, and to those who love romance. The ladies will love it—but so will the rest of the family."[11] Only a few took on its historical inaccuracies, including one critic who called the film "as tiresome [a] distortion of history facts as I've ever seen." Joan Crawford, the review says, plays Margaret Eaton only "as a vehicle for wearing about two hundred of the fetching velvet sunbonnet hats of the period."[12]

By the same token, *The President's Lady* garnered mixed reactions. *Time* magazine incorrectly declared that it "hews fairly closely to historical fact," while another review avoided such judgment, insisting only that "the picture is neatly put together with direct appeal to the human sentiments and broad spates of melodramatic excitement."[13] But in fact most reviews were critical. The *New York Times* criticized the film for its "unimaginative direction, the generally wooden dialogue," and "the redundancy of the Jacksons' tearful re-unions." Perhaps the *Nation* puts it most succinctly of all, calling the film "a studiously dull picture."[14]

Yet, a film can be lacking in historical accuracy and still have a major impact if it draws large audiences and much attention from the media. Such was not the case with these two films. Neither appeared among the top box-office attractions in the year it was produced. (In 1936 the most popular film was *Modern Times,* Charlie Chaplin's last silent movie and his protest against rapidly changing society. In 1953 the Walt Disney cartoon *Peter Pan* and *The Robe,* a religious spectacular based on a bestselling novel, led the way.)[15]

The two films on Andrew Jackson fail the test of historical accuracy and insight into his era. They present confused stories that do little to inform viewers about who Jackson was and what his age was really like. The films take a flippant view of the history of the people of the time and of the era itself. Had the filmmakers adhered to more historically based plots and characters, they might well have offered better and more interesting tales than they actually do.

NOTES

1. The earliest well-known book about Andrew Jackson is James Parton, *Life of Andrew Jackson* (Boston: Osgood, 1876). Other important biographies and collected papers include Robert V. Remini, *Andrew Jackson,* 3 vols. (Baltimore: Johns Hopkins University Press, 1998); Jon Meacham, *American Lion: Andrew Jackson in the White House* (New York: Random House, 2008); Mark Cheathem, *Andrew Jackson, Southerner* (Baton Rouge: Louisiana State University Press, 2013); and *The Papers of Andrew Jackson,* ed. Sam B. Smith, Harriet C. Owsley, Harold D. Moser, and Daniel Feller, 9 vols. to date (Knoxville: University of Tennessee Press, 1980–).

2. Samuel Hopkins Adams, *The Gorgeous Hussy* (Boston: Houghton Mifflin, 1933), v–vi. The factual account is John F. Marszalek, *The Petticoat Affair: Manners, Mutiny, and Sex in Andrew Jackson's White House* (New York: Free Press, 1997).

3. Irving Stone, *The President's Lady: A Novel about Rachel and Andrew Jackson* (Garden City, NY: Doubleday, 1951), frontispiece. Other biographical novels by Stone made into films include *Lust for Life* (Van Gogh) and *The Agony and the Ecstasy* (Michelangelo).

4. "Stephen Morehouse Avery" and "Clarence Brown," Internet Movie Database, www:IMDb.com.

5. Myrna Oliver, "John Patrick, Playwright, Screenwriter, Won Pulitzer," *Los Angeles Times,* 10 November 1995, obituary.

6. "Henry Levin," Internet Movie Database, www.IMDb.com.

7. *The Gorgeous Hussy,* in "AFI Catalog of Feature Films," American Film Institute, www.afi.com.

8. Dawn B. Sova, *Women in Hollywood: From Vamp to Studio Head* (New York: Fromm International, 1998), 118, 299.

9. *The Gorgeous Hussy,* in "AFI Catalog."

10. Review of *The Gorgeous Hussy,* in *Commonweal,* 18 September 1936, 487.

11. Review of *The Gorgeous Hussy,* in *Film Daily,* 1 September 1936, 7.

12. "The Movies," review of *The Gorgeous Hussy,* in *Judge,* 26 November 1936, 12, 22.

13. Review of *The President's Lady,* in *Time,* 4 May 1953, 102–3; "A Dance, a Dream and a Flying Trapeze," review of *The President's Lady,* in *Theater Arts* 37 (May 1953): 83.

14. Reviews of *The Gorgeous Hussy,* in The Current Cinema, *New Yorker,* 30 May 1953, 60; "Tribute to Jackson and His Wife," *New York Times,* 22 May 1953, 31; and Films, *Nation,* 11 April 1953, 314.

15. On motion-picture box-office success, see, e.g., www.filsite.org/boxoffice.

5

Delineating Davy, Defining Ourselves
The Alamo in 1960 and in 2004

JAMES E. CRISP

In the predawn darkness of March 6, 1836, after a siege of thirteen days, a motley crew of two hundred–odd Texan rebels who had tried to turn a dilapidated Spanish mission at San Antonio—the Alamo—into a genuine fortress were overwhelmed by a Mexican force far superior in both number and arms. Every last defender died, either in combat or by execution immediately following the battle. Within weeks the doomed men were being celebrated by the English-language press in Texas and the United States as heroic martyrs, and their sacrifice compared to that of the Greeks at Thermopylae. Less than seven weeks later, near the San Jacinto River, the victorious Mexican general Santa Anna's forces were surprised by the ferocity of a Texan force under General Sam Houston that overran their camp with the cry, "Remember the Alamo!" Santa Anna was captured, the vanguard of his army killed or captured, and the independence of Texas won.[1]

For more than a century, Alamo movies have been made in Texas, Hollywood, and elsewhere—most often claiming historical authenticity and most often falling far short of that noble dream. The first, *The Immortal Alamo,* came in 1911, filmed in the actual "Alamo city" of San Antonio by the Frenchman Gaston Méliès, one of cinema's founding fathers. Only still images from this lost work now survive, but these show the swarthy Mexican enemies of the Alamo's defenders as harboring lust for both blood and white women. Moreover, the presence of Texans with carbines and cowboy hats confirms a certain lack of historical awareness in terms of both fashion and weaponry.[2]

The earliest surviving Alamo movie is *The Martyrs of the Alamo, or The Birth of Texas,* filmed in the same year (1915) and in the same D. W. Griffith studio as its more famous twin, *The Birth of a Nation.* Both films render their villains in stark, racialized terms as dark, oversexed tyrants. It is no accident that the actor Walter Long, who plays the Mexican dictator Santa Anna in the Texas film, appears as the sinister rapist "Negro Gus" in *The Birth of a Nation.*[3]

The blatant racism of the early years was muted in the half dozen rather forgettable cinematic efforts to "Remember the Alamo" that followed over the next four decades. In more recent years, the medium of television has attempted several times to bring the story of the Alamo to American audiences, with occasional attempts at even-handedness, but with generally disappointing results. Some of these small-screen epics were truly dreadful, most notably *James Michener's Texas* (ABC television, 1994) and the History Channel's wildly inaccurate 2015 miniseries *Texas Rising.*

Since 1988 the IMAX theater near the Alamo in San Antonio has been daily screening *Alamo . . . The Price of Freedom,* a very short (shown in 39- and 48-minute versions) but respectable attempt to convey the basics of the battle and its context, but in terms of "major motion pictures" the two most recent and most ambitious works have been titled simply *The Alamo.* John Wayne produced, directed, and starred in the 1960 release; the 2004 Disney feature was directed by John Lee Hancock and starred, most notably, Billy Bob Thornton, who, like Wayne, was cast as Davy Crockett.[4]

In terms of historical authenticity, the two films are like night and day—or rather, day and night, as the Wayne version shows separate massive Mexican attacks on the Alamo occurring in broad daylight, while Hancock's ostentatiously "authentic" movie correctly portrays the Alamo falling to a furious assault in the darkness just before dawn. Neither the 1960 nor the 2004 version conveys the overtly racialized and sexualized plots and images of the early-twentieth-century films, but both have been criticized for their portrayal of Mexicans. While Wayne's 1960 film reverses the sexual gaze by making the many busty Hispanic women inhabiting San Antonio's oddly commercialized "cantina" the targets of Davy Crockett's lusty coterie of Tennesseans, Wayne cast an elegant Mexican politician (and personal friend), Ruben Padilla, as a very gentlemanly Generalissimo Santa Anna.[5] Conversely, the 2004 Disney version shows Santa Anna (played by the Mexican actor Emilio Echevarría) as a cartoonish, oily, lustful and bloody martinet who browbeats his own officers, while the Mexican women who are featured are tender and chaste caregivers to the sick and wounded.

Staging the fall of the Alamo in bright sunlight was by no means the Wayne film's worst sin against the historical record. One could be forgiven for thinking that Wayne and his chief scriptwriter, James Edward Grant, were determined to *avoid* any factual relation to the actual past. As a result of their erroneously placing the Alamo (and therefore San Antonio) on the Rio Grande (which was completely outside the boundaries of Mexican Texas) and their using fictitious place names for most other sites, any sense of the strategic importance of the battle is hopelessly lost. Moreover, the opening scenes of the film, in which General Sam Houston (played in a cameo role by Richard Boone) orders the Texan cavalry officer William Barret Travis (played with an inconsistent accent by British actor Laurence Harvey) to hold the Alamo at all costs, contradict Houston's actual wish that the old mission turned fortress be abandoned and destroyed, its numerous cannon brought eastward to buttress his outnumbered Texas "army" (made up predominantly of undisciplined volunteers).

The largest segment of the Texan army was actually ninety miles downstream on the San Antonio River, *southeast* of the Alamo at the old Spanish fortress of Goliad, under the hapless command of James W. Fannin. In Wayne's counter-factual version of history, Fannin and his men are "ambushed" and killed on their way *south* to relieve the Alamo. In reality, Fannin's rickety "relief column" foundered barely two miles upriver from the Goliad fortress. Then, three weeks *after* the fall of the Alamo, Fannin's botched effort to retreat and join Houston's small force was intercepted by the intrepid Mexican General José Urrea. A week later, against Urrea's wishes but on the direct orders of Santa Anna, Fannin and more than four hundred of his men were executed as "pirates."[6]

Within the besieged Alamo itself, in Wayne's version as in virtually all Alamo films, the chief tension (other than the nervous wait for relief that never comes) derives from the clash of personalities between the two would-be commanders of the garrison: the stiffly officious regular-army officer Travis and James Bowie, legendary knife-fighter and leader of the rowdy Texan volunteers. The historical Bowie, who had close ties by marriage and friendship to the Hispanic residents of San Antonio, had actually defied Houston's wishes by deciding to defend the Alamo. Inexplicably, the Bowie character (played by Richard Widmark) under John Wayne's direction fiercely argues through most of the film for leaving the Alamo behind and fighting the Mexican army using hit-and-run guerrilla warfare. In fact, the argument between the two men was over *who should command the garrison,* not over tactics.

Wayne had hired two famed Texan writers, J. Frank Dobie and Lon Tinkle, as his "historical consultants" (though neither was a professional historian).

But James Grant's script drove both men to leave the movie set in disgust and to order Wayne to remove their names from the credits.[7] Wayne and his art director, Al Ybarra, also claimed (falsely) to have consulted the "original plans" of the Alamo in Spain, and at least their version of the old mission bore a strong resemblance to the original.[8] The same could not be said for their re-creation of the municipality of San Antonio, which appears as a one-street "western" town, complete with commercial storefronts, rather than the typical Mexican town, oriented around a series of plazas.[9] Indeed, the Wayne film has the look and feel of a traditional American "western," even without the ahistorical presence of the carbines and cowboy hats of *The Immortal Alamo*.

In stark contrast, *The Alamo* of 2004 was conceived, and in large part executed, as a project devoted to historical accuracy—in plot, set design, costume and weapons, language, and virtually every possible detail. The production designer, Michael Corenblith, and the initial director, Ron Howard (who was replaced by Hancock after clashing with the Disney studio over his plan to make a gritty, bloody, and very expensive R-rated film), built a set in central Texas that matched in all but a few technical details what is known of the Alamo and San Antonio in 1836.[10] The well-known face of the Alamo chapel (virtually all that remains of the fortress today) was turned ninety degrees to face the southern sun for more even and efficient lighting, the chapel was moved forward by several dozen yards to make its familiar face more visible in outdoor scenes, and the distance between the city (held during the siege by the Mexicans) and the Alamo (held by the Texans) was reduced for dramatic effect.[11]

Extraordinary efforts were made by Corenblith, Howard, and Hancock to re-create the clothing, weapons, and even the speech heard in the Texas of 1836. Mexican uniforms were deemed correct only if the very buttons were authentic; many of the Texans (who had no uniforms) looked more like Early Victorian characters from *A Christmas Carol* than the virtual cowboys of previous Alamo films. Director Hancock referred to the desired sartorial effect as "Dirty Dickens."[12] Remarkably, large sums of money were paid to language consultants, who coached the actors in period-perfect Spanish, English, and even Cherokee. Sam Houston (played by Dennis Quaid) spoke Cherokee fluently, but the "Indian Village" scenes featuring Quaid and the Native American actor Wes Studi ended up on the cutting-room floor.[13] Some compromises with language, despite the heavy use of English subtitles, were made for dramatic effect: the Mexican women tending James Bowie when he is unconscious on his deathbed implausibly speak English to each other rather than Spanish, and

The classic "western" look of the 1960 *Alamo* is clearly shown in the apparel of,
left to right, Richard Widmark as James Bowie, John Wayne as Davy Crockett,
and Laurence Harvey as William Barret Travis.

the important Texas Mexican character Juan Seguín (played by the Spanish actor Jordi Mollà) is portrayed as being fluent in English, though in reality he was not.[14]

The Seguín character is important in this film, as his presence among the Texas rebels fighting against the Mexican government indicates the complexity of the political situation in Texas in the 1830s. The Texas Revolution began as an outgrowth of a Mexican civil war, and the two sides were not, as so often portrayed in the early Alamo films, cleanly divided along ethnic lines. John Wayne in his 1960 film gave only very brief (and factually incorrect) attention to Seguín, but the 2004 Disney version puts him front and center as a close friend and confidant of Sam Houston. The Seguín character had an even greater role in the script for *The Alamo* prepared by John Sayles in 2002, which was the one being used by Ron Howard as he began casting the film in that year.[15]

The problem with the Sayles script, and the reason it was so thoroughly rewritten by Leslie Bohem, Stephen Gaghan, and John Lee Hancock that Sayles was not listed in the movie's final credits, is that Sayles attempted to capture the entire Texas Revolution in snippets of the dozens of battles, incidents, and confrontations (social, political, and military) that constitute this complex and generally little-understood conflict.[16] An audience of Texas historians would understand what was going on, but for the general public the result would have been severe confusion, if not cognitive whiplash!

John Wayne approached this dilemma by keeping things simple: the Texans, mostly settlers from the United States, were revolting because they were being threatened by a centralized dictatorship, and his Wayne-like Davy Crockett was ready to stop Santa Anna in Mexico so that he would not be a threat to the United States. Focusing strictly on the Battle of the Alamo, Wayne did not even bother to include the ultimate Texan victory over Santa Anna at the Battle of San Jacinto, perhaps leaving some in his audiences to wonder who had actually won the war!

As Ron Howard grappled with the complexities of the Texas Revolution (and of the Sayles script) in 2002, he privately voiced the wish that the project had been conceived as a miniseries, and indeed that might have been the only way to encompass the multiple, intersecting "plots" the revolution represents.[17] After Howard was replaced by Hancock as director, the emphasis shifted from re-creating the entire conflict among nations and interests in Texas to examining the conflicts (and their ultimate resolutions) among the Alamo's leading personalities: Travis, Bowie, Crockett, and, in the wings (but never arriving at the Alamo), Sam Houston. Hancock purposely portrays each of these men as "fallible"—a failure in his previous life who found a "second chance" in Texas.[18] Indeed, Hancock makes this notion the theme of Travis's dramatic appeal to all the men of the Alamo to remain with him and face almost certain death. Rather than drawing a heroic line in the sand, Travis (as played by Patrick Wilson) admits that "Texas has been a second chance for me. I expect that might be true for many of you men. It has been a chance not only for land and riches, but also to be a different man, I hope a better man. . . . I'd like each of you men to think of what it is you value so highly that you are willing to fight and possibly die for it. We will call that Texas."[19]

Sean Means, a movie critic for the *Salt Lake Tribune*, argues that there are basically only two ways to deal with the Alamo story on film: "historic or heroic—and both lead to trouble." According to Means, full faithfulness to history would bring down the wrath of Texans for denigrating their heroes; mythologizing the event, in his opinion, leads to "John Wayne's cheeseball flag-waving version," with simplistic "comic-book heroes." As for the 2004 film, Means ac-

John Lee Hancock, the director of the 2004 version of *The Alamo,* strove to emulate the genuine look of ordinary Americans of the 1830s. Modeling the outfits that he labeled "Dirty Dickens" are Billy Bob Thornton as Davy Crockett, Patrick Wilson as William Barret Travis, and Kevin Page as the Tennessee lawyer Micajah Autry.

cuses director Hancock of trying to "split the difference," with the result being "an aimless epic that's long on production design and short on substance."[20] Other reviewers echoed this criticism of the 2004 *Alamo,* with Martin Hoyle, of the London-based *Financial Times,* suggesting that the film had fared poorly in the United States because it fell somewhere "between pro- and anti-war factions."[21]

This reference to attitudes about war brings up an oft-forgotten fact about the 2004 film's production: it was the 9/11 attack on the United States in 2001 that prompted the Disney head, Michael Eisner, to put what had been a dormant project on the fast track to completion.[22] Yet rather than ride the expected wave of patriotism, after several delays the film opened in 2004 on Easter weekend, during some of the "worst fighting in Iraq since the overthrow of Saddam Hussein." The author of a British film review even suggested that in this movie "Santa Anna is thoroughly Saddamised—degenerate, sadistic, megalomaniac bon vivant surrounded by foppishly epicene officers."[23] Even with such villains in life and on the screen, by 2004 very many Americans were beginning to have their doubts about the mission that seemed not to have been accomplished in Iraq.

As for the America of 1960, no film critic or film historian fails to note that John Wayne's *Alamo* is a product and lasting artifact of the Cold War. He fiercely believed that his story of the Alamo would "shake hell out of people all over the world."[24] "These are perilous times," Wayne told the Hollywood columnist Louella Parsons. "The eyes of the world are on us. We must sell America to countries threatened with Communist domination."[25] The circumstances surrounding Wayne's film were as important as the movie's actual content in establishing this connection. An over-the-top publicity campaign by the Texan native Russell Birdwell arguing that a failure to give *The Alamo* the Oscar for Best Picture would be a failure of patriotism hugely backfired. Moreover, the message Wayne delivered in his role as Davy Crockett, about meeting a dangerous foreign enemy head-on in Texas, was used by Wayne himself to emphasize the "domino theory" in relation to Vietnam as he sought to gain the support of President Lyndon B. Johnson for his next Cold War epic, *The Green Berets*. As he wrote to Johnson,

> Perhaps you remember the scene from *The Alamo,* when one of Davy Crockett's Tennesseans said: "What are we doing here in Texas fighting—it ain't our ox that's getting gored." Crockett replied: "Talkin' about whose ox gets gored, figure this: a fella gets in the habit of gorin' oxes, it whets his appetite. May gore yours next." Unquote. And we don't want people like Kosygin, Mao Tse-tung, or the like, "gorin our oxes."[26]

John Wayne's version of Davy Crockett, as many observers have noted, was essentially John Wayne playing himself. Ironically, the same could be said for Davy Crockett as portrayed by Billy Bob Thornton in 2004, who admitted that "honest to God, I played him kind of like myself."[27] Director Hancock agreed. He told Thornton that the actor and Crockett were "the same guy, really."[28] Or as Thornton's costar Dennis Quaid put it, "It's really weird, because you have a hillbilly star playing a hillbilly star."[29] But there was an important difference. Thornton's Crockett, who in the minds of most critics was the best feature of an otherwise forgettable movie, was a man who was very aware of the power of a myth to encircle and even destroy a man, just as surely as could a Mexican army.

Holed up in the Alamo and wishing he were somewhere else, Thornton's Crockett tells Jim Bowie (played by Jason Patric): "If it was just simple old me,

David, from Tennessee, I might drop over the wall some night and take my chances." And then after skipping a beat: "But this Davy Crockett feller, they're all watching him. He's been fightin' on this wall every day of his life."[30] The closest Thornton's Crockett comes to a Vietnam reference is his chilling and decidedly unheroic story told during a campfire meal in the Alamo, of burning a cabin full of Indians alive during the "Redstick War" and then eating the potatoes found under the house, which had "been cooked by the grease that run off them Indians." He added: "Since then, you pass me the taters, I'll pass 'em right back."[31]

On the controversial subject of the manner of Davy Crockett's death at the Alamo, Hancock's film again attempts to split the difference between the historical and the heroic. There is ample evidence that Crockett was among the half dozen defenders who were taken prisoner by General Manuel Castrillón as the battle ended and then slaughtered by sword thrust at the behest of Santa Anna. Thornton's Crockett is indeed captured and killed, but not before engaging in a (purely Hollywood) verbal confrontation with Santa Anna. After seeing one of the victorious Mexican soldiers wearing *his* coonskin cap, a thoroughly trussed Thornton mutters to himself, "Davy Crockett!" and then offers to accept the Mexican general's surrender. We hear Crockett's defiant yell as (beyond a wide camera shot from outside the Alamo) the bayonets are thrust into him on Santa Anna's orders.[32] At least this Crockett's death makes more sense than John Wayne's version, in which the hero, already mortally wounded by a Mexican lance, blows himself up in the Alamo's powder magazine—which, as Garry Wills points out in his biography of Wayne, is located in the chapel, where the women and children had been placed for their safety![33]

The America of the Iraq War of 2004 was far less sure of itself and its mission in the world than the America of John Wayne's *Alamo* (or of John F. Kennedy's inaugural address, which followed in 1961), and this ambivalence is clearly reflected in the Disney/Hancock film. Second thoughts about America's present may perhaps best be inferred from the movie's second thoughts about America's past. These are most clearly revealed in the comments of the "minorities," who are given a limited but far stronger voice here than in any previous *Alamo* release. In an early scene, one of Juan Seguín's men questions his alliance with the rude and bumptious Anglos who now seem to dominate Texas by asking, "Why are you fighting for these scum?" When Seguín answers that both he and they are opposed to a murderous Santa Anna, his companion responds: "But Santa Anna only wants to rule Mexico. These . . . these want the world."[34] The next sentence from the John Sayles script was dropped from the final cut: "They talk about freedom, but it's the freedom to own slaves."[35]

Slavery as a part of Anglo-Texan life is not ignored in either Alamo film, but the 1960 John Wayne film simply gives Bowie a slave named Jethro, who is tolerant of Bowie's constant drunkenness and treats his master with respectful obedience. When given his freedom in time to leave the Alamo, Jethro exercises his new rights by deciding to stay. In fact, Bowie did not have a slave with him in the Alamo. Travis *did* have a slave by the name of Joe in the historical Alamo, and Hancock adds another, allegedly owned by Bowie, named Sam. Dialogue between these two is used to critique the Texans' "peculiar institution." As they talk between themselves, the older and wiser Sam tells the young Joe not to sacrifice his life for his master: "You clean up they shit, take care of they horses, wash 'em, feed 'em. Damn if you ain't gonna die for 'em, too."[36] Hancock's Bowie allows Sam to leave the Alamo but promises to hunt him down after the battle. Joe, in history and in this film, survived the battle and lived to tell the tale.[37]

Corenblith and Hancock set out to make their Alamo story a "multicultural and multidimensional" one, one that would represent their world as opposed to the Cold War environment that had so shaped Wayne's.[38] That they succeeded has been judged by countless critics as both their film's greatest strength and its greatest weakness. Pure history does not always make great drama, and even in the aftermath of 9/11, good and evil are not strictly relegated to opposing sides in real-life conflicts. We live today in a world, and in an America, that is even less sure of itself and its future than either of the Americas that produced these two films. In glorifying the collective, voluntary decision of a diverse group of men to risk their lives for a cause greater than themselves, virtually every Alamo film has, in some way, glorified democracy itself.[39] The question we must ask ourselves is whether that form of government, and that way of life, is still viable in our own troubled world.

NOTES

1. For an excellent introduction to the "mythic Alamo," see Paul Andrew Hutton, "The Alamo as Icon," in *The Texas Military Experience: From the Texas Revolution through World War II*, ed. Joseph G. Dawson III (College Station: Texas A&M University Press, 1995), 14–31. For the historic Battle of the Alamo, see Stephen L. Hardin, *Texian Iliad: A Military History of the Texas Revolution* (Austin: University of Texas Press, 1994), 123–49.

2. Frank Thompson, *Alamo Movies*, 2nd ed. (Plano, TX: Wordware, 1991), 17–23.

3. Thompson, *Alamo Movies,* 24–30.

4. Thompson, *Alamo Movies,* 67–84, 100–109; see also Frank Thompson, *The Alamo: The Illustrated Story of the Epic Film* (New York: Newmarket, 2004).

5. For the hiring of Padilla, see Donald Clark and Christopher Andersen, *John Wayne's "The Alamo": The Making of the Epic Film,* Carol Publishing Group Edition (New York: Citadel, 1995), 57. For a critique of Wayne's sexualized portrayal of the Mexican women of the "cantina," see Richard R. Flores, *Remembering the Alamo: Memory, Modernity, and the Master Symbol* (Austin: University of Texas Press, 2002), 123.

6. See Craig H. Roell, *Remember Goliad! A History of La Bahía* (Austin: Texas State Historical Association,, 1994).

7. Frank Thompson, "Reprinting the Legend: The Alamo on Film," *Film & History* 36, no. 1 (2006): 22.

8. Thompson, *Alamo Movies,* 72.

9. Frank Thompson, *"The Alamo:* Wayne's Reel Heroes," *American Cinematographer* 71, no. 7 (July 1999): 37.

10. Josh Young, "Texas Two-Step," *Entertainment Weekly,* 23/30 August 2002, 8–9.

11. Allen Barra, "Trying for the Truth about the Alamo," *American Heritage* 54, no. 6 (December 2003): 54.

12. Thompson, "Reprinting the Legend," 24.

13. The "Cherokee" scenes that were cut from the film may be read in the complete script provided in Thompson, *Alamo: The Illustrated Story,* 100–102.

14. The best available work on Juan Seguín is *A Revolution Remembered: The Memoirs and Selected Correspondence of Juan N. Seguín,* ed. Jesús F. de la Teja, 2nd ed. (Austin: Texas State Historical Association, 2002).

15. "THE ALAMO by Leslie Bohem, Current Rewrite by John Sayles, First Rewrite January 13, 2002" (hereinafter cited as Sayles script). The typescript is stamped "Received FEB 15 2002 Imagine Story Department." My thanks to the Alamo movie historian Frank Thompson for providing a copy of this document.

16. The final credits are listed in Thompson, *Alamo: The Illustrated Story,* 158.

17. Ron Howard, telephone conversation with the author, May 2002.

18. For Hancock's comments in this regard, see Bronson Tate, "Remembering the Alamo," *Smithsonian* 35, no. 1 (April 2004): 64–72; and Eric Hoover, "Myth Understood," *Chronicle of Higher Education* 50, no. 32 (16 April 2004): A16–A20.

19. The official working script had used the word *hopefully,* but the film adviser Frank Thompson warned the director that this was not a nineteenth-century usage. See Thompson, *Alamo: The Illustrated Story,* 134. Thanks to Frank Thompson for bringing this change to my attention.

20. Sean Means, "'The Alamo' Is an Aimless Epic," *Salt Lake Tribune,* 9 April 2004, E1.

21. Martin Hoyle, "Houston, We Have a Problem," *Financial Times,* 2 September 2004, 13.

22. Thompson, "Reprinting the Legend," 23. See also Barra, "Trying for the Truth," 55.

23. J. Hoberman, "Desert Storm," *Sight and Sound* 14, no. 2 (July 2004): 32–34.

24. Clark and Andersen, *John Wayne's "The Alamo,"* 3.

25. Thompson, *Alamo Movies,* 80.

26. John Wayne to President Lyndon Johnson, 28 December 1965, quoted in *John Wayne's America: The Politics of Celebrity,* by Garry Wills (New York: Simon & Schuster, 1997), 228.

27. Jane Sumner, "'Alamo' Stirs Hearts, Souls of Stars," *Reno Gazette-Journal*, 6 April 2004, www.newspapers.com/image/150988261/.

28. "The Killer Moment," *Entertainment Weekly*, 22/29 August 2003, 84.

29. Bill Muller, "Cooking Up Crockett: Independent-Minded Thornton Meshes Man, Myth for *The Alamo*," *Arizona Republic* (Phoenix), 8 April 2004, 5

30. Thompson, *Alamo: The Illustrated Story*, 123.

31. Thompson, *Alamo: The Illustrated Story*, 129. The story is taken from *A Narrative of the Life of David Crockett, by Himself*, intro. Paul Andrew Hutton (Lincoln: University of Nebraska Press, 1987), 88–89.

32. Thompson, *Alamo: The Illustrated Story*, 146. The circumstances of Crockett's death are explored in my introduction to the expanded edition of José Enrique de la Peña, *With Santa Anna in Texas: A Personal Narrative of the Revolution*, trans. and ed. Carmen Perry (College Station: Texas A&M University Press, 1997), xi–xxv; and, in greater depth, in James E. Crisp, *Sleuthing the Alamo: Davy Crockett's Last Stand and Other Mysteries of the Texas Revolution* (New York: Oxford University Press, 2004), 61–138. See also Crisp, "Documenting Davy's Death: The Problematic 'Dolson Letter' from Texas, 1836," *Journal of the West* 46, no. 2 (Spring 2007): 22–28; and Dan Kilgore and James E. Crisp, *How Did Davy Die? And Why Do We Care So Much?* (College Station: Texas A&M University Press, 2010).

33. Wills, *John Wayne's America*, 215.

34. Thompson, *Alamo: The Illustrated Story*, 106–8.

35. Sayles script, 38–39.

36. Thompson, *Alamo: The Illustrated Story*, 128. Jethro was played by Jester Hairston, Joe by Edwin Hodge, and Sam by Afemo Omilami. See Thompson, *Alamo: The Illustrated Story*, 50–51.

37. The two best works on slavery in Texas at the time of the revolution are Randolph B. Campbell, *An Empire for Slavery: The Peculiar Institution in Texas, 1821–1865* (Baton Rouge: Louisiana State University Press, 1989); and Andrew J. Torget, *Seeds of Empire: Cotton, Slavery, and the Transformation of the Texas Borderlands, 1800–1850* (Chapel Hill: University of North Carolina Press, 2015). Campbell does not see slavery as an immediate cause of the revolution; Torget argues that the expansion of cotton and slavery into Mexican Texas made the revolution virtually inevitable. Joe's identity has been discovered and his life before and after the Alamo explored in a remarkable new book: Ron J. Jackson Jr. and Lee Spencer White's *Joe: The Slave Who Became an Alamo Legend* (Norman: University of Oklahoma Press, 2015).

38. Thompson, *Alamo: The Illustrated Story*, 12 (quoting Michael Corenblith).

39. See Don Graham, review of Frank Thompson, *Alamo Movies*, in *Southwestern Historical Quarterly* 98, no. 2 (October 1994): 354–55; see also Brian Huberman and Ed Hugetz, "Fabled Façade: Filmic Treatments of the Battle of the Alamo," *Southwest Media Review*, Spring 1985, 30–41.

SLAVERY AND THE ANTEBELLUM SOUTH

6

A Fugitive Slave in Southern Appalachia

The Journey of August King

JOHN C. INSCOE

Given the range of ways in which Hollywood has depicted American slaves and slavery over the past century, *The Journey of August King* (1995) is exceptional in both its content and its approach. Curiously, it is the only feature film that makes an escape story its centerpiece and one of a few in which a female slave is the protagonist.[1] Equally as distinctive is its setting. It is the only substantive treatment of southern slavery on film without a stereotypical plantation backdrop. It plays out instead in the heart of Southern Appalachia in the early nineteenth century (1815 to be precise), when the region was still very much in its frontier stage of development.

The credit for these distinctions, of course, lies not with Hollywood producers alone. First and foremost, the 1971 novel of John Ehle, a native of Asheville, North Carolina, provided the basis for the film, and Ehle himself wrote its screenplay.[2] Ehle's literary career consisted, in part, of a vast fictional output, with eleven novels to date, seven of which are deeply researched historical treatments of various stages of western North Carolina's early settlement and subsequent development.[3] His seventh novel, *The Journey of August King,* is one of the most notable of the series simply because it embraces the subject of slavery in a highland setting. The book confronts in both subtle and not so subtle ways themes of both race and class, which historians have only more recently tackled in regard to the mountain South.[4] The film adaptation, like the novel, not only explores the ways in which slaveholding, racism, abolitionist sentiment, and class distinctions played out in the mountain South; it also conveys the realities of isolationism and connectedness, of subsistence and market economies, in that still formative society early in the nineteenth century. And all this is reflected in a deceptively simple escape story.

Returning home from a biannual, week-long trip to a bustling market town (identified in the novel as Old Fort, North Carolina), August King, a recently widowed farmer, discovers in hiding an adolescent slave girl named Annalees. After fleeting encounters with the fugitive along his route through a rugged and sparsely settled wilderness, King reluctantly befriends the starving, foot-sore, and desperate young woman. Over the course of three days of trekking back to his farm in a remote cove community, he conceals her with great difficulty, shunning acquaintances and sacrificing his own newly acquired stock and supplies in order to protect her from her ruthless master and the eager, if bungling, search party hired by her master to retrieve her. In the process, King falls in love.

Unlike more typical commercial Hollywood productions, the love story between King and Annalees remains, as it was in Ehle's novel, underplayed and ultimately unconsummated. In the novel, King is a somewhat older man, which likely lowered readers' expectations of romance between the two protagonists. Yet it is obvious that the filmmakers sought to forefront the attraction between the two, simply by the casting of the youthful actors Jason Patric and Thandie Newton. (Newton had already scored on screen in another strong role as a slave. As Thomas Jefferson's Sally Hemings, she was the most compelling character in *Jefferson in Paris*, an otherwise disappointing Merchant-Ivory production, two years earlier.) The love story in *August King* amounts to a tentative "brief encounter" that propels the narrative forward as this white man and black woman climb toward home and freedom, respectively. It is also a tale of personal rejuvenation and even spiritual redemption for August King, though the terms of his psychological "journey" are not nearly as well developed in the film as they are in the novel.[5]

Particularly noteworthy is the specificity of time and place in both the novel and the film. The movie's opening credits appear as the camera sweeps from east to west over an early-nineteenth-century map of North Carolina, from the Atlantic coast to the sketchily delineated mountains, lingering only as we see the names of the last settlements, Wilkes and Morgantown, and not much beyond. The date too is revealed early on. When he makes a final mortgage payment on his small farm, August King's deed is marked paid and dated April 27, 1815.

The filmmakers are equally conscientious in their careful re-creation of a still remote but thriving frontier society. Stunningly photographed, the movie was filmed almost entirely on location in scenic Transylvania County, North Carolina. The Carolina highlanders depicted in the film are neither backwoods hillbillies nor "coonskin cap boys."[6] They are hunters and farmers, most of them family men eking out a modest living on small landholdings. But they do not do so alone. Far from enduring isolated existences in the midst of a still vast wilderness, these early highlanders make up an interactive society driven by trade and commerce. There is a constant sense of movement throughout the film, as livestock and poultry crowd the roads along with people and wagons. Far more of the story plays out at trading posts and drover stands, as well as along roads and at fords and campsites, rather than on farms or in cabins. A major achievement, in fact, of both Ehle and the Australian director John Duigan is that while the film vividly conveys settlers' interpersonal bonds as part of a greater connectedness inherent in this frontier society, it also conveys, through the character of August King in particular, the loneliness and isolation that was also integral to highland life at the time.[7]

This carefully constructed sense of time, place, and socioeconomic development serves as the backdrop to a story that is at heart a saga of slavery. Slavery in the mountains was well established by 1815, but few historians had acknowledged this basic fact at the time when Ehle wrote his book.[8] There is no sign of slavery in the vast array of images, assumptions, and stereotypes on which popular or even scholarly understandings of Southern Appalachia were based. But slaves there were: according to census analysis, roughly 15 percent of the Appalachian populace in 1820 was enslaved, though only 10 percent of highland households held slave property.[9] By coincidence, possibly the first slave in western North Carolina was a young girl named Liza, brought into the area of Old Fort where August and Annalees first cross paths. According to a long oral tradition among her descendants in the Asheville area, she accompanied Samuel Davidson, generally regarded as the "first white settler west of the Blue Ridge."[10] But although slaves were certainly present in the mountains from an early time, they were a limited presence, a demographic reality made fully apparent in the film. Besides Annalees and Sims—a fellow fugitive from whom she has become separated, who is never shown (alive) on screen—the only other African American characters are three or four servants who make up a silent, grudging entourage of their owner, Olaf Singletary.

From beginning to end, this is a story of escape and pursuit, and in that respect the setting is most appropriate. The idea of the southern highlands as a refuge for fugitives of various sorts has long been an integral part of the higher moral ground many have attributed to the region. The abolitionist John Brown was by no means the first to acknowledge that the mountains of western Virginia, so central to his Harpers Ferry scheme in 1859, "were intended by the Almighty for a refuge for the slave and a defense against the oppressor."[11] Another observer noted simply that "the hills, in their exquisite isolation, became havens for the disenchanted black and white, who needed to escape burdensome drudgery and slavery."[12]

Yet Annalees is not a lowland fugitive who has lifted her eyes unto the hills. She is owned locally. Her master is well known to both August King and the others in the area, and she is merely moving deeper into the wilderness when she encounters King. Neither novel nor screenplay specifies where she is heading or *thinks* she is heading. On their first encounter, August King simply directs her to follow a stream headed north. At the film's end, he escorts her to a high ridge above his farm and points her to a "trail to the North." Whether the Underground Railroad ever moved through the southern highlands is open to debate. I have argued elsewhere that there is no real evidence of its presence in the region.[13] Even if some regularized escape route developed later, it is highly improbable that it would have been established as early as 1815. But such a system is obviously what Ehle had in mind when he had King send his fugitive charge off with no reference at all to a final destination. "The trail has been used for years. It's marked," he tells her vaguely. "People will show you kindness on the way." (The film's final and most striking, if unlikely, shot is an aerial view of the young slave girl, decked out in a bright red dress, marching northward on a path that follows the meadowed ridgeline of the Appalachian Trail, as if she no longer has any need to move undetected.)

The pursuers are as vital as the pursued in demonstrating the complexities and contradictions that characterized highland attitudes toward slavery. Olaf Singletary is the story's sole slaveholder, referred to early in the film as "the wealthiest man in the mountains." When he tries to rally a search party to look for his two runaways, Singletary at first finds few willing volunteers, which forces him to offer rewards and payment for their services and those of their dogs. For some, the idea of the search itself is troublesome. One man states that it "hurts my conscience to set dogs on people," while another wonders about offering a horse as a reward for a human being. Such sentiments suggest a genuine moral resentment at the dehumanization the "peculiar institution" imposed upon its victims. For earlier regional chroniclers, such qualms typified the views of freedom-loving southern highlanders. It fueled the image of

"Holy Appalachia," where, according to one turn-of-the-century writer, those in the mountains "cherish liberty as a priceless heritage. They would never hold slaves and we may almost say they will never be enslaved. They are true democrats, holding all men to be equals in society, as they are taught that all of us are before God." Or as Harry Caudill once put it, "These poorer mountaineers, fiercely independent as they were, found something abhorrent in the ownership of one person by another."[14]

Yet such idealized characterizations of antebellum Appalachians fail to acknowledge other, less noble factors that fueled their resentment toward both the enslaved and those who enslaved them. Ehle also stresses the class-based contempt toward the sole beneficiary of slave ownership in their midst. While his nonslaveholding neighbors fear Singletary and his power, they also see him as an object of derision and resentment. In this respect, they conform to what the historian Carter Woodson once referred to as a "liberty-loving and tyrant-hating race," which exhibited "more prejudice against the slave holder than against the Negro."[15] It was often assumed that the first generations of southern highlanders, in particular, were driven from the more desirable lowlands, resulting in a resentment of the planter class, which had driven them away. According to one version of this premise, "The aristocratic slaveholder from his river-bottom plantation looked with scorn on the slaveless dweller among the hills; while the highlander repaid his scorn with high disdain and even hate."[16]

Though hardly "aristocratic," Olaf Singletary provides a ready target for such resentment on the part of his nonslaveholding neighbors. And yet in characterizing the film's single slaveholder, Ehle has stacked the deck. Certainly the least subtle aspect of the film is that Singletary emerges as a rather one-dimensional villain. As portrayed by Larry Drake, he is the least attractive character on screen, fat and scowling, brutish and violent. His arrogant contempt for both his slaves and his poorer white neighbors is made abundantly clear. From a dramatic standpoint, one can understand the need for a clear-cut villain, and who better than the man in pursuit of the film's heroine, the man who's driven her to flee in the first place? It is evident that having to share Singletary's bed was what the seventeen-year-old Annalees found most unbearable; further complications not fully explored are suggested by her revelation that Singletary is her father as well. When King asks her outright why she ran away, her response is simple but profound: "To keep him from taking my soul." With Singletary as the sole embodiment of highland slaveholding, it is hard to distinguish between

Farmer August King (Jason Patric) worries about his role in abetting the escape of the slave girl Annalees (Thandie Newton) in the mountains of North Carolina in *The Journey of August King*.

the personal hatred of so despicable a character by those who know him and a broader condemnation of the system and class he represents.

Yet, to Ehle and Duigan's credit, the villainy of the film hardly rests solely on the shoulders of the loathsome Singletary; his nonslaveholding neighbors can claim few moral exemptions, as they reveal their own shades of racial bias. Once recruited to pursue Annalees and her fellow fugitive (and presumed lover) Sims, Singletary's henchmen are fully contemptuous of their prey. Even though they are motivated by promises of material rewards, they are fully committed to seeing the system restored and those rebelling against it punished.

Only in its final segment does the film present any sense of a communal abolitionist spirit within the region. King brings Annalees to his cabin in the remote cove settlement of Harristown, and after putting her up for a night, he sends her off fortified with food and dressed in his dead wife's clothing. It is only after her departure that neighbors gather, and August must finally account for his actions. King had told Annalees earlier that "they don't allow slaves in the community I live in," and when his neighbors confront him, it becomes apparent that they are sympathetic toward his actions but apprehensive about the consequences he soon must face from Singletary. Led by Mooney Wright (Sam Waterston), they urge King to lie in defending himself, and they offer to help explain away the circumstantial evidence linking him with Annalees. Yet in an informal trial staged inside his own cabin, King stands firm in declaring the truth before the man whose enslaved property he helped escape, so that his neighbors can only watch as Singletary and his men inflict a costly retribution by burning King's house to the ground, thus completing his economic ruin. August himself seems content with that harsh judgment. His final words reflect his lack of remorse at what he's done for Annalees. As he watches his house burn, he states simply to himself: "I was right well-to-do. Only in a day or two, I lost everything. But I've never been so proud." So his journey is completed, and his conscience clear.

If the extent of that retribution is historically dubious, the antislavery sentiments that bound this community together are somewhat more credible. There were indeed pockets of highland settlement in which a black presence was unknown and unwelcome, though such bans were more often motivated by antiblack prejudices than by antislavery sentiments. As Frederick Law Olmsted noted in moving through this very region several decades after the film's time period, many highlanders found both the presence of blacks and the privileges that ownership of them bequeathed to other whites to be the worst features of a slaveholding society, and they fought to maintain their distance from both.[17]

Yet true antislavery activity spurred by humanitarian motives, such as those evident early in the film and embodied in Mooney Wright at the film's end, also found a place in the southern highlands. Sporadic efforts emerged and then faded out at Wheeling, Virginia; Berea, Kentucky; and Maryville, Tennessee, during the antebellum era. Yet it was in an area much closer to Ehle's fictional Harristown settlement, both geographically and chronologically, that Appalachian abolitionism most flourished. In the second and third decades of the nineteenth century, fledgling organizations, instigated by New Light Presbyterians and Quakers from Pennsylvania and Ohio, emerged in Jonesboro and other northeastern Tennessee communities (just across the state line from Harristown).[18] Mooney Wright makes clear that he is acting from a sense of decency that opposes anyone's enslavement and that he silently applauds Annalees's triumph over the system. But it is never clear whether the same higher ground lies behind the other neighbors' willingness to stand by August King. The basis for their opposition to Singletary and their sympathy for Annalees is, perhaps fittingly, left ambivalent.

Part of the power of both the film and the novel lies in the fact that Ehle sets his story so early in the nineteenth century and thus so early in the development of Appalachian society. These western Carolinians—and August King in particular—are forced to deal with a moral dilemma that has not yet been fully articulated. This escape story is set well before the Underground Railroad was in place, and its characters wrestle with the wrongs of slavery well before a full-fledged abolition movement emerged to do so. It is a relatively spontaneous situation with two opponents—one fighting for her freedom, the other fighting for the recovery of his legally owned property—that forces this community of white highlanders to confront the legitimacy of the institution for the first time. They are well aware of the legalities of slavery. King's initial reaction to Annalees's request for help is, "You know I can't do that. It's against the law." When King's complicity in her escape is revealed and he must face Singletary's retribution, Mooney Wright—in typical Sam Waterston deadpan—states simply why such punishment must be accepted: "Laws have been broken, property rights violated."

August King seems to have had little reason to question that truth until he makes this fateful journey. As played by Jason Patric, he is a simple farmer, an everyman whose quiet strength and moral resolve audiences are meant to identify with. Neither he nor his neighbors own slaves, but nor have they taken any stand against a system that allowed "a horse in exchange for a man." Yet when the opportunity to fight that system presents itself in the form of this beautiful and vulnerable young woman, King rises to the challenge and in his small way helps to undermine the institution that has so victimized her.

Perhaps Ehle and the movie's casting director stacked the deck here as well. Given the obvious charms of Thandie Newton as Annalees, one wonders whether King's moral courage has been truly tested. August's explanation for his actions suggests his own ambivalence about his motives. "A spell came over me," he tells Mooney Wright and other neighbors. "I did a hundred things strange, nothing customary." Would he have pushed as hard or risked as much if he had first encountered Sims (Annalees's male companion) or if Annalees had been an old or even middle-aged woman? As things are, his libido never seems far from his conscience.

Yet the power of the story derives in no small part from the sexual tensions that drive it, and it seems unfair to suggest that those dynamics in some way compromise the strong moral fiber that is evident not only in the film's title character but also in its overall tone. The film works on a variety of levels, historical context being only one. Portraying such a compelling, if relatively unexplored, aspect of the southern slave experience, and one so shaped by its setting, with as much talent, sensitivity, and integrity as is evident in *The Journey of August King* is commendable, particularly in light of how rarely Hollywood filmmakers have sought to explore these issues as seriously and as ably as those here have done.

NOTES

1. Various film versions of *Uncle Tom's Cabin* feature the iconic escape across the icy Ohio River of Eliza and her young son. The film adaptations of Ernest Gaines's *The Autobiography of Miss Jane Pittman* (1974) and Toni Morrison's *Beloved* (1998) center on black women, though they focus more on their characters' postemancipation lives than on their early years as slaves. *12 Years a Slave* (2013) and *Django Unchained* (2012), while vastly different in scope, tone, and historical grounding, both give serious attention to the plight of female slaves. Colson Whitehead's recent bestselling novel, *The Underground Railroad* (2015), currently in development as a film, features a fugitive female protagonist.

For treatments of slavery on film, see Thomas Cripps, *Slow Fade to Black: The Negro in American Film* (New York: Oxford University Press, 1977); Edward D. C. Campbell Jr., *The Celluloid South: Hollywood and the Southern Myth* (Knoxville: University of Tennessee Press, 1981); Jack Temple Kirby, *Media-Made Dixie: The South in the American Imagination*, rev. ed. (Athens: University of Georgia Press, 1986); and Natalie Zemon Davis, *Slaves on Screen: Film and Historical Vision* (Cambridge, MA: Harvard University Press, 2000). The only book-length treatment of Appalachia on film is J. W. Williamson, *Hillbillyland: What the Movies Did to the Mountains and What the Mountains Did to the Movies* (Chapel Hill: University of North Carolina Press, 1995).

2. John Ehle, *The Journey of August King* (New York: Harper & Row, 1971). This essay is a modified version of "Slavery, Freedom, and Frontier: A Historical Perspective," which appeared in *Appalachian Journal* 24 (Winter 1997): 204–15, as half of a "debate" with Jack Wright over the film's merits. For a far more critical assessment of the film, see Wright's essay, "How Monochrome Was Their Valley," in the same issue, pp. 193–204.

3. Borden Mace, interview by Steve Ward, *Appalachian Journal* 23 (Fall 1995): 51. Much of this interview focuses on the production of *The Journey of August King*. See also Carol Boggess, "Interview with John Ehle," *Appalachian Journal* 31 (Fall 2006): 32–51.

4. Carter G. Woodson's seminal essay "Freedom and Slavery in Appalachian America," *Journal of Negro History* 1 (April 1916), 132–50, stood alone on the subject for several decades. More recent treatments of the topic include Richard B. Drake, "Slavery and Antislavery in Appalachia," *Appalachian Heritage* 14 (Winter 1986): 25–33; John C. Inscoe, *Mountain Masters: Slavery and the Sectional Crisis in Western North Carolina* (Knoxville: University of Tennessee Press, 1989); Kenneth W. Noe, *Southwest Virginia's Railroad: Modernization and the Sectional Crisis* (Urbana: University of Illinois Press, 1994), esp. chap. 4; Wilma A. Dunaway, *Slavery in the American Mountain South* (Cambridge: Cambridge University Press, 2003); Dunaway, *The African American Family in Slavery and Emancipation* (Cambridge: Cambridge University Press, 2003); and several essays in *Blacks in Appalachia*, ed. Edward J. Cabbell and William H. Turner (Lexington: University Press of Kentucky, 1985), and in *Appalachians and Race: From Slavery to Segregation in the Mountain South*, ed. John C. Inscoe (Lexington: University Press of Kentucky, 2001).

5. The relationship between August King and Annalees fits a pattern film scholars have termed the *mockingbird syndrome,* after the Atticus Finch character in *To Kill a Mockingbird* (1962), in which a white protagonist serves to "save" one or more black victims. See Hernan Vera and Andrew M. Gordon, *Screen Saviors: Hollywood Fictions of Whiteness* (Lanham, MD: Rowman & Littlefield, 2003); and Matthew W. Hughey, *The White Savior Film: Content, Critics, and Consumption* (Philadelphia: Temple University Press, 2014), neither of which makes reference to *The Journey of August King.*

6. The latter term was coined by Jerry Williamson to denote one of the stereotypical categories into which Appalachian men are often relegated in film. Williamson, *Hillbillyland,* 70–78.

7. A number of historians have wrestled with issues of connectedness and isolation and the dynamics of localism in early settlement patterns, with most of them confirming realities that John Ehle much earlier had conveyed with such insight in his novel. See Robert D. Mitchell, *Commercialism and Frontier: Perspectives on the Early Shenandoah Valley* (Charlottesville: University Press of Virginia, 1977); David Hsiung, *Two Worlds in the Tennessee Mountains: Exploring the Origins of Appalachian Stereotypes* (Lexington: University Press of Kentucky, 1997); Paul Salstrom, *Appalachia's Path to Dependency: Rethinking a Region's Economic History, 1730–1940* (Lexington: University Press of Kentucky, 1994); and Wilma A. Dunaway, *The First American Frontier: Transition to Capitalism in Southern Appalachia, 1700–1860* (Chapel Hill: University of North Carolina Press, 1996).

8. See the works cited in n. 4 above, all of which, other than Woodson's essay, appeared after Ehle published his novel in 1971.

9. William H. Turner, "The Demography of Black Appalachia: Past and Present," in Cabbell and Turner, *Blacks in Appalachia,* 237–38.

10. John Baxter, interview by Maggie Lauterer, quoted by Patricia D. Beaver in "African-American and Jewish Relations in Early Twentieth Century Asheville, North Carolina" (paper, Appalachian Studies Conference, Unicoi State Park, GA, March 1996).

11. John Brown and John Kagin, interview by Richard Hinton, August 1858, reprinted in *John Brown,* ed. Richard Warch and Jonathan F. Fauton (Englewood Cliffs, NJ: Prentice-Hall, 1973), 54.

12. Leon F. Williams, "The Vanishing Appalachian: How to 'Whiten' the Problem," in Turner and Cabbell, *Blacks in Appalachia,* 201. See also John C. Inscoe, "The Strength of the Hills: Representations of Appalachian Wilderness as Civil War Refuge," in *The Blue, the Gray, and the Green: Toward an Environmental History of the Civil War,* ed. Brian D. Drake (Athens: University of Georgia Press, 2015), 113–43.

13. See John Inscoe, "Race and Racism in Nineteenth Century Appalachia: Myths, Realities, and Ambiguities," in *Appalachia in the Making: The Mountain South in the Nineteenth Century,* ed. Mary Beth Pudup, Dwight B. Billings, and Altina Waller (Chapel Hill: University of North Carolina Press, 1996), 108–10. The whole notion of Appalachia as a center of Underground Railroad activity is suspect. Most major treatments of the Underground Railroad make no reference to routes in the southern highlands. See Larry Gara, *The Liberty Line: The Legend of the Underground Railroad* (Lexington: University Press of Kentucky, 1961); and William Still, *The Underground Railroad* (Philadelphia: Porter & Coates, 1872). The only such account to refer to even the possibility that Appalachians provided regular routes is Wilbur H. Siebert, *The Underground Railroad from Slavery to Freedom* (New York: Macmillan, 1899), 118–19, but the accompanying map (facing p. 113) indicates no routes anywhere in the region.

14. Julian Ralph, "Our Appalachian Americans," *Harper's Monthly*, June 1903, 37. The term *Holy Appalachia* comes from both Allen Batteau, *The Invention of Appalachia* (Tucson: University of Arizona Press, 1992); and Harry M. Caudill, *Night Comes to the Cumberlands: A Biography of a Depressed Region* (Boston: Little, Brown, 1962), 38–39.

15. Woodson, "Freedom and Slavery in Appalachian America," 147.

16. Samuel Tyndale Wilson, *The Southern Mountaineers* (New York: Little & Ives, 1914), 57.

17. Frederick Law Olmsted, *A Journey through the Back Country in the Winter of 1853–54* (New York: Mission Brothers, 1860), 237–39. See also Inscoe, "Olmsted in Appalachia: A Connecticut Yankee Encounters Slavery and Racism in the Southern Highlands, 1854," *Slavery & Abolition* 9 (September 1988): 65–79.

18. On abolitionist activity in Southern Appalachia, see Woodson, "Freedom and Slavery in Appalachian America"; Drake, "Slavery and Antislavery in Appalachia"; Asa Earl Martin, "The Anti-Slavery Societies of Tennessee," *Tennessee Historical Magazine* 1 (1915): 261–81; Gordon E. Finnie, "The Antislavery Movement in the Upper South before 1840," *Journal of Southern History* 35 (1969): 319–42; and Durwood Dunn, *An Abolitionist in the Appalachian South: Ezekiel Birdseye on Slavery, Capitalism, and Separate Statehood in East Tennessee, 1841–1846* (Knoxville: University of Tennessee Press, 1997).

7

Birth and Rebirth
Filming Nat Turner in the Age of Fake News

KENNETH S. GREENBERG

When Nate Parker appropriated the title of D. W. Griffith's 1915 epic *The Birth of a Nation* for his 2016 film, he firmly linked his work to the larger story of race and imagery in American culture. In its modern form, involving photography and film, this was a story that began in the 1840s, when Frederick Douglass first distributed daguerreotypes of himself as part of his battle against slavery and racism. It continues to the present and includes conflicts over a vast array of racist and antiracist images extending over a period of more than 170 years.[1]

One of the most shameful moments in the history of our nation's battle over racial imagery involved the production of the original *Birth of a Nation*, the film that historians generally credit with creating Hollywood. *The Birth of a Nation* introduced many of the innovations that became standard features of American film. Perhaps most significantly, the film moved decisively away from attempting to duplicate live theatrical experience. Instead of filming with one camera from a static location, D. W. Griffith set many cameras in motion and filmed from a variety of angles. Ultimately, he pieced together the finished product in the editing room, creating a story and adding drama by cutting together images taken from multiple perspectives.

In addition, Griffith introduced significant innovations in presentation and marketing. As a result, *The Birth of a Nation* was a spectacular box-office success. During the period before its release, Griffith saturated the nation with full-page newspaper advertisements and large billboard signs. Theaters sold reserved tickets weeks in advance. In southern states, marketers ran special trains to theaters. Inside, usherettes in period costumes greeted patrons, who then watched a three-hour extravaganza that was accompanied in many locations by a full symphony orchestra.

At the same time, the content of this first major American film was deeply racist, with especially pernicious consequences during the era of segregation and lynching. Every attempt by African Americans and their allies to modify its disturbing images or to prevent its release proved a failure. It was a film that offered a view of the Civil War and Reconstruction that was sympathetic to the Confederacy and to white southerners. It portrayed newly freed people as savages who took over the South after the Union victory. African American men appeared as inferior beasts who could neither govern the nation nor govern themselves and who lusted after white women. The great heroes of the film were members of the Ku Klux Klan, who rode to the rescue of white women threatened by rape from black men. Within the logic of the film, and consistent with the dominant scholarly interpretations of the period, the Klan redeemed the South at its moment of greatest peril.[2]

This was the target the black filmmaker Nate Parker had in mind when he wrote, produced, directed, and starred in his own *Birth of a Nation*. We must begin by recognizing the extraordinary ambition and nobility of his goals. Before examining the content or the consequences of the film, we must understand that Parker intended to work within the tradition established by Frederick Douglass, fighting racism and moving people to action by photographing himself as a dignified African American hero (Nat Turner) and then widely disseminating the images. For seven years Parker gave up work on other projects to work on this independent film; he partially funded it with his own money and raised the rest through the force of his own commitment and personality. He convinced others, both investors and everyone hired to create the film, that they were involved in a righteous enterprise, an enterprise that directly challenged the original sin of racism so centrally present at the birth of American film.

During the period leading up to the release of Parker's film at the Sundance Film Festival in 2016, there were strong indicators that it would be a successful project. The subject matter of Parker's film was not the same as that of Griffith's 1915 film. It was not the story of the Civil War and Reconstruction. But it did address some of the central themes of the earlier film. Parker's film told the story of Nat Turner, the man who in 1831 led the most important rebellion of enslaved people in American history. While the 1915 film told the story of the birth of a white nation, Parker's film told the story of the birth of a black nation. Since Parker had successfully appropriated the title of the movie that invented Hollywood, and since his film would be released one hundred years after Griffith's film, film critics and others seemed compelled to discuss the two films together. Parker's *Birth* and Griffith's *Birth* seemed destined to be linked in ways that would strikingly expose the racism of the earlier film in contrast to the racial progressivism of the latter.

This seemed even more likely when, shortly before the premiere of Parker's film at Sundance, the Academy of Motion Picture Arts and Sciences released the 2015 Oscar nominations. For the second year in a row, no African American actor had been nominated for an Academy Award in a major category. As a result, critics from inside and outside Hollywood attacked the film industry for its continuing racism. Many envisioned Parker's likely success as a way for the industry to begin to atone for its continuing failure to acknowledge the achievements of African Americans, as a way to begin to erase the sin of the founding moment. Even before the public screening of Parker's film, many in the industry singled it out as a front-runner to win an Academy Award. At Sundance, *The Birth of a Nation* sold out the first day tickets became available. After it screened, the audience rose in multiple standing ovations. It won the Audience Award and the Grand Jury Prize for the best domestic dramatic film, then was quickly sold to Fox Searchlight Pictures for the highest price ever paid for a Sundance film.

It seems clear in hindsight that by the time the film premiered at Sundance, excitement about it was so elevated that it had become nearly impossible for it to achieve all that some supporters envisioned. It may have taken the earlier film's title, but it could not reasonably be expected to replace that film in the history of American cinema. At best, it could call attention to the long and brutal history of the killing of African Americans at the hands of whites in authority, as well as to the past and present racism of the film industry. It could also move and inspire audiences to admire a heroic African American who died fighting for the cause of liberty. But it could not be expected to create or transform an industry. At its core, it was an independent, relatively low-budget movie. It was a powerful work of art dealing with a significant subject, but it contained no grand film innovations. Nor, unlike its namesake, was it destined for great box-office success. In recent years, most films about slavery had had mixed ticket sales domestically and even less success in the world market. *The Birth of a Nation* would prove no exception to this pattern.

In the end, it was the public discussion of Parker's rape trial fifteen years earlier that further undermined the box-office and critical success of the film. In 1999 Parker and his roommate, Jean McGianni Celestin (who received a film credit for working with Parker to develop the *Birth of a Nation* story), had been students at Pennsylvania State University and members of the wrestling team. After an evening of partying, a fellow student had accused Parker and Celestin of sexually assaulting her while she was drunk and unconscious. At a three-day trial in 2001 Celestin had been convicted, but Parker had not; Celestin's conviction had later been overturned.

Several factors added fuel to the explosive 2016 public conversation about this rape case. In addition to the rape charges, the victim had also accused Parker and Celestin of harassing her after the incident, and she had accepted a monetary settlement from Penn State after claiming that the university had not adequately protect her. Moreover, after the rape accusations became generally known in 2016, the public and Parker learned for the first time that the victim had committed suicide in 2012 and that some family members believed her death had been linked to the events of 1999. Most significantly, Parker's first 2016 public comments about the rape seemed self-centered and insensitive. Instead of expressing sympathy or understanding for the woman, Parker described the incident as "a very painful moment in my life."[3] He seemed to think of himself as the victim. Parker's public reputation never recovered from this statement. By the time *The Birth of a Nation* was released in October 2016, the character of the artist and the character of the work of art had become inseparable. How could anyone separate Parker as a person from the film in which he was the star, the writer, the producer, and the director?[4]

What about the film as a work of history? It is best to begin this discussion by recognizing that presenting history on film and presenting history in writing are two very different activities. Woodrow Wilson may have told D. W. Griffith that *The Birth of a Nation* was "history written in lightning," but we should not forget that at its core, film is not written at all. Of course, films have scripts, but they primarily tell their stories through images. And feature films have other imperatives that differentiate them from histories produced in articles and books. History on film and history in writing are both constructions, but they are constructions shaped by radically different imperatives. A feature film must appeal to a mass audience since production costs are high and investors expect profits. Only certain types of stories are likely to sell to a mass audience.

Moreover, history in writing can more easily describe different possible inter-pretations. The bias in a feature film (with few exceptions) is to tell a story a single way, without hesitation and with certainty. Finally, when historians do not know something about an event, they can just leave out those details or note their lack of understanding. A feature film cannot sustain the luxury of blank spaces. To describe the situation metaphorically, if a director presents a house in a feature film, it must have a door, even if no one has any idea what the actual door might have looked like.[5]

Clearly, filling in blank spaces from no solid base of knowledge cannot typi-cally be counted on to enhance our knowledge of the past. Yet sometimes it can be helpful. While we are now well into an age when the distinction between fiction and nonfiction is collapsing, most professionally trained historians still try to maintain the difference. Usually, they do not invent dialogue, or characters, or events, and they support their analyses with footnotes pointing to original sources. These are practices that we can only treasure and admire, especially in a culture increasingly less sure of the distinction between "news" and "fake news," during an era that has been labeled by some as "post-truth." Yet these conventions of written history do not serve us well under all circum-stances. Nonliterate populations, for example, do not leave written records, and under certain circumstances we must depend on novelists and filmmakers to imagine their world. This can sometimes best be accomplished by abandon-ing the conventions followed by professional historians. Otherwise we would always only reproduce the silence left by past oppression. Sometimes nonfic-tion requires fiction to re-create the full truth of the past. Sometimes we need Toni Morrison to help us better understand Margaret Garner.[6]

For these and other reasons, it is pointless to judge the success of a historical film solely on the basis of how closely it conforms to written history. By that standard, virtually all historical films, including both *Birth of a Nation* films, fail. We must be open to the possibility that sometimes a filmmaker's different approach will enhances our understanding of the past. With this in mind, it is possible to discuss Nate Parker's *Birth of a Nation* in a way that takes seriously the work of both the filmmaker and historians.

Consider Nat Turner's wife, Cherry, who plays a central role in Nate Parker's film. Cherry first encounters Turner as she is about to be sold to a master who clearly intends to sexually assault her. Turner witnesses the impending sale, fully understands the danger to Cherry, and persuades his master, a man he believes to be kind and humane, to purchase her. We then watch Turner and

Cherry fall in love and ultimately achieve union in a moving marriage ceremony. Cherry is central to the action of the film because it is her gang rape
by brutal patrollers that triggers Nat Turner's decision to rebel. Turner had
already witnessed many atrocities associated with slavery, but it is this assault
on Cherry that moves him to action. In a brilliant decision that links the Nat
Turner story to the larger story of black oppression, Parker films the brutalized
Cherry in bed with a swollen face, a face bearing a remarkable resemblance to
the face of Emmett Till as he lay in an open casket after being lynched in 1955.

What do we know from historical sources about Nat Turner's wife? There is
good evidence that Nat Turner had a wife, but we know very little about her.
She is mentioned, but not by name, only in a single letter dated September 17,
1831, written by a resident of Southampton County and published in Richmond's *Constitutional Whig* on September 26. The writer notes, "I have in my
possession, some papers given up by his [Nat Turner's] wife, under the lash."
Aside from this reference, both the folk tradition and some public records
mention a woman named Cherry or Chary who lived at least a dozen years on
the same farm as Turner.[7]

One of the puzzles associated with Nat Turner's wife is that she did not
appear at all in Turner's *Confessions* of 1831. *The Confessions of Nat Turner* is
a fascinating and mystifying document. After the rebellion, Turner eluded
capture for two months, hiding in a variety of locations near his home farm.
After he was captured and while he sat in jail, he agreed to speak to the local
lawyer Thomas R. Gray. Shortly after Turner's execution, Gray published a
document based on those conversations under the title *The Confessions of Nat
Turner*. It is a document that must be read carefully by modern historians. It
both Gray's and Turner's voices, and any reader must consider carefully which
parts of the document must have been shaped by Gray and which by Turner.

In any case, neither Gray nor Turner refers to Turner's wife in the *Confessions*. One portion that seems to be in Turner's voice mentions the influence
of other family members but not of his wife. The meaning of Cherry's absence
in the *Confessions* is unclear. Perhaps Nat Turner did not mention her because
he wished to spare her from possible implication in the collapsed rebellion or
because she was not important to him. The *Confessions* contains many references to Turner as a man who felt close to God and who distanced himself from
other people.

Once Nate Parker decided to include Cherry as a central character, he had
to invent her in every way. He invented her personality, her beauty, her dia-

logue, her relationship with Nat Turner, and her rape. All this invention should make historians uneasy, but we should not dismiss it. The sources do not permit a sketch of the real Cherry, because slavery destroyed the evidence. If we condemn her invention, then we allow the masters of the Old South to continue to shape our memory. This becomes especially evident in the invention of her rape. We have no direct evidence that white men raped black women in the area of the Nat Turner rebellion and certainly no evidence of the rape of Nat Turner's wife. Yet we know from other sources that in slave society white men frequently raped black women. So, paradoxically, the invented rape of Nat Turner's wife and others in Nate Parker's film may offer a truer picture of slavery than the absence of rape in the work of historians who write about the Nat Turner rebellion.

The film also contains other inventions that help us understand the past. In Parker's film, Nat experiences and witnesses many acts of brutality perpetrated by masters. While we know violence was central to the everyday functioning of the institution of slavery, there is no particular evidence for this in relation to Nat Turner. Hence, Nate Parker invents the illustrations. Similarly, while we have some evidence that many among the enslaved community deeply respected Nat, Nate Parker visualizes this through a dramatically powerful invention. After Turner is whipped in the film (an invented scene), he is left at the whipping post overnight. At first the camera focuses on his face, but we can see in the background out-of-focus points of light appearing on the ground. As the camera refocuses, we realize that the points of light are candles left by other enslaved people. As with his depiction of violence toward enslaved people, Parker creates a specific fiction in order to illustrate a general point. The candles tell us about support from the black community. This is what we should expect from the best historical films.

But not all fictions created in this film enlighten us about the past or even serve the purposes of the filmmaker. Many of these fictions seem intended to capture the patronage and approbation of a modern audience. Others seem to be arbitrary insertions that serve no discernible purpose. Consider a few examples. Nate Parker sets the rebellion in a physical landscape that resembles the Old South portrayed in *Gone with the Wind*—with large plantations surrounded by vast cotton fields. Nat Turner's actual owner in 1831 lived in a single-story two-room house with a separate kitchen, a barn, and probably two or three slave cabins. It was a modest farm that produced some cotton but also cattle, hogs, fodder, corn, and cider.[8] By setting his film on a large plantation

Nate Parker as Nat Turner, *center,* in *The Birth of a Nation* leads the charge
as his slave uprising reaches full momentum.

in the cotton South and filming it in Savannah, Georgia, rather than in Southampton County, Virginia, Parker distorts the past for no apparent purpose and reinforces modern viewers' stereotypes of the Old South.

Parker also presents Samuel Turner as Nat Turner's master at the time of the rebellion. In fact, Samuel had died in 1822 and in 1831 nine-year-old Putnam Moore was Nat Turner's owner. This invention relates to the larger treatment of white women and children in the film. In *The Birth of a Nation* Nat and the rebels kill only adult white men, while in actuality a majority of the victims were women and children.[9] Nat Turner's young master was among the first victims, as was an infant. These deaths cannot simply be dismissed as the invention of racist white witnesses. Evidence of the deaths of women and children comes from multiple sources that are mutually consistent. It is easy to see why Parker left out the killing of women and children: he wanted modern audiences to regard Nat Turner as an inspiring heroic leader who fought against a brutally oppressive institution. If Parker had included the death of even a single woman or child, he would have had to rewrite his script to explain why Turner should still be considered a hero. This would not have been easy.

But this decision, while understandable, had some important negative consequences. The killing of women and children tells us a great deal about the character of Nat Turner and the nature of his world. To leave it out is to impoverish a heroic figure. Turner was inspired foremost by the Bible, which contains the justified deaths of many women and children, including the deaths of the firstborn sons of the Egyptians, who enslaved the Jews. Turner was also committed to spreading "terror" as a tactic, and the killings served that purpose. In addition, the structure of slavery led to the deaths of many African American children, and Parker missed the opportunity to present the deaths of white children in that context. Parker could have shown that slavery was so brutal that the rebellion against it could only take the most brutal form.

Less easy to understand is Parker's portrayal of how Nat Turner learned to read. In the film, the plantation mistress, Elizabeth Turner, teaches him to read. The historical record contains two other descriptions of Turner's path to literacy, neither of which involves a white woman. Early in the *Confessions*, Turner tells us that no one taught him, that he learned spontaneously as if it were a miraculous gift from heaven. Later in the document, Thomas Gray tells us that Turner was taught to read by his parents. In light of this evidence, it is difficult to understand Parker's decision to invent a white plantation mistress as teacher. Certainly this did occasionally happen in the South, as in the case of Frederick Douglass, but there is no evidence that it happened in Turner's case. It would have been perfectly consistent with Nate Parker's vision of Turner as creator of a black nation to have him taught by his parents or by a miracle and not by a benevolent plantation mistress.

This decision had other negative consequences. I attended the opening screening of *The Birth of a Nation* at the Sundance Film Festival in 2016. After the applause died down, the cast and crew came onto the stage to answer questions from the audience. One audience member directed a question to Penelope Ann Miller, the actress who played Elizabeth Turner, asking her how it felt to portray the woman who taught Nat Turner to read. Miller replied that "being a woman in those days and teaching a young African American slave to read was not only unheard of but it was illegal. And so this was a pretty, to me, courageous woman to take this young boy under her wing and she believed he had a gift and she believed that this was something she needed to do. . . . She felt it was a blessing. And he really became to her like a surrogate son." I found this exchange disturbing on several levels. If Nat Turner's parents really taught him to read, it was a great disservice to replace them with a plantation mistress. Moreover, it was painful to watch Penelope Ann Miller build on Parker's invention and take pride in portraying a fictional character while assuming she had portrayed a historical one.[10]

Perhaps the most problematic invention in Nate Parker's *Birth of a Nation* is the structure of the story itself. In a film in which every character, all the dialogue, and the setting are fictional creations, it should come as no surprise that major elements of the plot are also fictional. *The Birth of a Nation* bears an uncanny resemblance to Mel Gibson's *Braveheart* (1995), the story of the Scottish rebel William Wallace. Parker had long admired Gibson's work and even consulted him during the production of his own film. Parker's Turner and Gibson's Wallace share many of the same heroic qualities. They begin as peace-loving men who live in communities dominated by rapacious and vicious occupiers. Despite repeatedly witnessing violence and injustices perpetrated by their oppressors, neither protagonist is moved to rebellion. It is only when their wives are attacked that they rise up to lead their people in revolt. In the end, both heroes are executed, but in a way that suggests their deaths mark the first step toward the future liberation of their people.

Nat Turner was a hero who died for the cause of liberty. Nate Parker produced a moving film that, appropriately, presents him as a hero to be admired by a nation that has never adequately honored its enslaved rebels. But we must wonder whether we might better honor him by rooting his story more firmly in the historical record. Since it is a record largely generated by whites who hated Turner, we must use it with great care. But we should not dismiss it. As Parker's film demonstrates, sometimes we need to turn to fiction in order to imagine parts of the story not contained in the documents, but we also need to turn to the documents when they can help us understand a man who can no longer speak for himself. We should admire Nate Parker for what he accomplished but at the same time remain aware that more needs to be done.

NOTES

1. On Frederick Douglass and photography, see John Stauffer, Zoe Trodd, and Celeste-Marie Bernier, *Picturing Frederick: An Illustrated Biography of the Nineteenth Century's Most Photographed American* (New York: Liveright, 2015). On the larger battle over race and visual images in American history, see, e.g., Deborah Willis, *Reflections in Black: A History of Black Photographers, 1840 to the Present* (New York: Norton, 2000); Maurice Berger, *For All the World to See: Visual Culture and the Struggle for Civil Rights* (New Haven, CT: Yale University Press, 2010); and Molly Rogers, *Delia's Tears: Race, Science, and Photography in Nineteenth-Century America* (New Haven, CT: Yale University Press, 2010).

2. The best description of the controversy surrounding the 1915 *Birth of a Nation* can be found in Dick Lehr, *"The Birth of a Nation": How a Legendary Filmmaker and a Crusading Editor Reignited America's Civil War* (New York: Public Affairs, 2014).

3. Background and the Nate Parker quotation can be found in "The Nate Parker Interview: What's Next for *The Birth of a Nation*," *Variety*, 23 August 2016.

4. The full story of the rise and fall of Nate Parker's film—from the triumph at the Sundance Film Festival, to the public discussion of the rape issue, to the collapse of the film at the box office—can be found in dozens of newspaper, magazine, online, radio, and television stories throughout 2016. Some samples include "Inside the Nate Parker Rape Case," *Daily Beast*, www.thedailybeast.com/articles/2016/08/16/inside-the-nate-parker-rape-case.html; and Anderson Cooper's interview with Nate Parker, *60 Minutes*, 3 October 2016,www.cbsnews/news/60-minutes-nate-parker-birth-of-a-nation-anderson-cooper. See also several articles in the *New York Times*: "Nate Parker and the Limits of Empathy," 19 August 2016; "Nate Parker Deflects Questions," 12 September 2016; "Review: In Nate Parker's 'The Birth of a Nation,' Must-See and Won't See Collide," 6 October 2016; and "How 'The Birth of a Nation' Silences Black Women," 12 October 2016.

5. On history, film, and Nat Turner with reference to the documentary film *Nat Turner: A Troublesome Property* (a film created in collaboration by Charles Burnett, Frank Christopher, and Kenneth S. Greenberg), nationally broadcast on PBS in 2004, see Kenneth S. Greenberg, "Nat Turner in Print and on Film," in *New Directions in Slavery Studies: Commodification, Community, and Comparison*, ed. Jeff Forret and Christine Sears (Baton Rouge: Louisiana State University Press, 2015), 72–90.

6. See Toni Morrison, *Beloved* (New York: Knopf, 1987).

7. The quotation in the 26 September *Constitutional Whig* can be found in Nat Turner, "*The Confessions of Nat Turner" and Related Documents*, ed. Kenneth S. Greenberg (Boston: Bedford/St. Martin's, 2017), 79. On the historical Cherry, see David F. Allmendinger Jr., *Nat Turner and the Rising in Southampton County* (Baltimore: Johns Hopkins University Press, 2014), 63–67. For other recent important work by historians on the Nat Turner story, see Patrick H. Breen, *The Land Shall Be Deluged in Blood: A New History of the Nat Turner Revolt* (New York: Oxford University Press, 2015); and Kenneth S. Greenberg, *Nat Turner: A Slave Rebellion in History and Memory* (New York: Oxford University Press, 2003).

8. Allmendinger, *Nat Turner and the Rising*, 80–81.

9. For a list of the men, women, and children killed by the rebels, see Allmendinger, *Nat Turner and the Rising*, 286–88.

10. A video of the question-and-answer session at the Sundance Film Festival premiere, including the Penelope Ann Miller comments, can be found at "The Birth of a Nation" Premiere—Complete, Uncut Q&A @ The Sundance Film Fest 1-25-16, www.youtube.com/watch?v=SM3BDY_bwUQ.

8

History White-Washed
Reflections on Steven Spielberg's *Amistad*

MARCUS REDIKER

During the moonless early hours of July 2, 1839, several captive Africans quietly slipped out of their chains in the hold of the slave schooner *La Amistad*, bound from Havana for the burgeoning sugar-plantation region around Puerto Príncipe, Cuba. The Africans had broken a padlock and removed the chain that bound them down in the hold of the vessel. A Mende man named Sengbe (later to be known as Cinqué) led the way as a gang of warriors climbed out of the hatchway onto the main deck. They killed the ship's cook and captain and in a matter of minutes captured the vessel, making prisoners of their so-called owners, José Ruiz and Pedro Montes. The rebels wanted to return to their homes in Sierra Leone, but none of them knew how to navigate the schooner. They decided to keep the surviving Spaniards alive to help them sail the vessel eastward, toward the rising sun, which had been at their backs as they made the Middle Passage on a different slave ship, the *Teçora*, two weeks earlier.[1]

Montes, formerly a merchant-ship captain, used his specialized knowledge to deceive his new masters. During the day, he sailed east, sails loose and flapping in the wind to limit the *Amistad*'s progress. By night he steered back to the west and north, picking up speed and staying in busier sea-lanes in hopes of being intercepted and saved. After eight weeks a US Navy vessel made good his plan, capturing the *Amistad* off the northern tip of Long Island, New York, and carrying the Africans, the Spaniards, the cargo, and the schooner to New London, Connecticut.

The African rebels were then jailed in one of the world's leading slave societies. Would they be returned to Cuba to be tried—and surely executed—for the crimes of mutiny, murder, and piracy as the governments of Spain and the

Congressman and past president John Quincy Adams (Anthony Hopkins)
talking with the leader of the slave uprising at sea, Joseph Cinqué (Djimon Hounsou),
through his American interpreter (Chiwetel Ejiofor), a meeting featured in
Amistad that historically never occurred.

United States demanded? Or would they, as Lewis Tappan and other abolitionists insisted, be allowed to go free? Now that the slave trade had been abolished
(in 1808), had they not merely defended their own natural rights by killing the
tyrant who had illegally enslaved them? An epic struggle ensued. Assisted in
their legal battles by the distinguished attorneys Roger S. Baldwin and former
president John Quincy Adams, who made dramatic speeches before the US
Supreme Court in March 1841, Sengbe/Cinqué and the other *Amistad* rebels
won their freedom. A few months later they would return, in triumph, to their
African homelands. The abolitionist movement claimed a great, historic, and
altogether unlikely victory.

This, in brief, is the history as told in director Steven Spielberg's epic film
Amistad, which appeared in 1997 to great acclaim and some controversy. The
all-star cast included Anthony Hopkins as Adams, Djimon Hounsou as Cinqué,
Matthew McConaughey as Baldwin, Morgan Freeman as Theodore Joadson, a
fictional African American abolitionist, and Stellan Skarsgård as Tappan. The

film was nominated for many awards, including four Oscars, but won few. It grossed more the $58 million at the box office worldwide ($44 million in the United States) but fell short of the estimated $75 million spent in production. (Its original budget had been $40 million.) The film nonetheless had a broad impact, inspiring public history projects, children's books, school lessons, and a host of other initiatives. It was widely regarded in its time as the best film to date on slavery, and it enhanced public consciousness of the history of bondage in America.[2]

Several features of the film were unprecedented, even shocking. The depictions of the Middle Passage aboard the slave ship *Teçora* and the revolt itself aboard the *Amistad* broke cinematic taboos, bringing painful, violent images rarely seen on the big screen to popular audiences. Spielberg depicted the cramped, squalid, deadly conditions Africans faced below decks during the Atlantic crossing. He showed a young mother choose suicide over slavery for herself and her child as she slipped backward over the ship's rail into the high seas and a watery grave. Spielberg also demonstrated the violence of the crew as they cast a long, weighted, chained coffle of living Africans overboard to their death at the bottom of the sea. The film also included a flashback to Sierra Leone in which a group of raiders threw a net over Cinqué and quickly spirited him away from his village and family toward a slave ship waiting on the coast. At the end of the film, Spielberg shows the *Amistad* Africans as they reverse the Middle Passage, sailing solemnly toward the rising sun as they had tried to do three years earlier after the revolt. Their repatriation was an unusual event at the time and a powerful symbol of abolitionist victory.

Spielberg offered an interpretation of the "*Amistad* affair," as it was called, and an entire moment of American history. Historians predictably complained. Spielberg employed the distinguished Sierra Leonean historian Arthur Abraham as an adviser and brought the *Amistad* expert Howard Jones onto the set for consultation; nonetheless the filmmaker got many facts wrong, distorted others, and took numerous liberties with the story. Characters in the film speak about the coming civil war, even though the cataclysmic event was foreseen by no one in 1839, more than two decades before it broke out at Fort Sumter, South Carolina. The historian Eric Foner voiced the concerns of many of his colleagues when he wrote of the film and its official study guide, "Most galling, however, is the assumption that a subject does not exist until it is discovered by Hollywood. The guide ends with a quote from Debbie Allen, *Amistad*'s producer, castigating historians for suppressing the 'real history' of African-Americans and slavery. Historians may be guilty of many sins, but ignoring slavery is not one of them."[3]

Jesse Lemisch, a pioneer of "history from the bottom up," wrote a blistering critique entitled "Black Agency in the *Amistad* Uprising: Or, You've Taken our Cinqué and Gone," in which he lambasted Spielberg for a multitude of ideologically driven misrepresentations and omissions. The *Amistad* Africans were stripped of agency and treated as "bystanders" as "great white men" argued "among themselves about whether or not to make them free," said Lemisch. This elite white paternalism expressed toward the Africans is complemented by ridicule for the abolitionists, who are treated as "fanatics." The entire interpretation offered by Spielberg struck Lemisch as redolent of 1950s conservativism.[4]

As Lemisch made clear, *Amistad* is in many ways a classic example of "top-down" or "great man" history, but with a twist. The "great men" in this case are five in number, in roughly the following order of significance: Adams, Cinqué, Baldwin, Joadson, and Tappan. Three are white and two are black, which is itself a departure from the usual top-down format. Let us treat these characters in turn to show how Spielberg uses them to spin his version of the *Amistad* tale.

Adams is clearly the greatest of the great men. He appears about a quarter of the way through the film and thereafter grows ever larger, delivering in the film's climax a personal and highly sentimental argument that wins the day with the Supreme Court. Based on advice he gets from Cinqué, he makes an appeal to "the ancestors"—America's Founding Fathers, whose marble busts solemnly decorate the courtroom. (One of them was John Adams, John Quincy's biological father.) John Quincy Adams appears in the film as a fully formed historical figure. The eminent former president and current member of Congress commands reverence, even awe, from all other characters. Almost every time he appears on screen the musical score becomes soft and nostalgic as if to encourage a mawkish adoration from the viewer. Adams is a not-so-subtle embodiment of American national spirit.

Cinqué also looms large in the film but in an entirely different way. The leader of the rebellion and subsequently of the entire group of *Amistad* Africans, he is depicted as a great man, always sympathetically but superficially. He is essentially a noble savage who stands outside history and culture, particularly his own Mende culture of southern Sierra Leone. The film begins with a solitary Cinqué using his bloodied fingertips to pry a nail from a block of wood. He then uses the nail to pick a padlock and secure freedom for all his fellow Af-

ricans. Yet according to the *Amistad* Africans, they achieved their liberation after someone "broke" the padlock. That someone was in all likelihood one of the
two blacksmiths who were among the enslaved aboard the schooner. Communal knowledge is thus suppressed in order to emphasize the role of the heroic
savior. The film's condescending disregard for African culture is also clear when
the speech of the Africans, so crucial to the uprising, is not awarded the common decency of subtitles, whereas the Spanish of Ruiz and Montes is always
translated for the viewer. Cinqué is a great man of a distinctly lower order.

Perhaps the oddest—and most revealing—move in the film is Spielberg's
wildly inaccurate representation of Roger S. Baldwin, the attorney who represented the *Amistad* Africans throughout the case and whose patient, careful
legal work—much more than the speechifying of John Quincy Adams—actually won them their freedom. Spielberg uses Matthew McConaughey to depict
Baldwin as a country bumpkin of a lawyer, and no abolitionist, who insinuates
himself into the case by a series of shrewd moves designed to endear him to
the wealthy and ardent abolitionist Lewis Tappan. In actual history Baldwin
was very nearly the opposite: a committed abolitionist and an urbane, sophisti-
cated attorney descended from a distinguished and wealthy Connecticut family
whose maternal grandfather, Roger Sherman, had signed the Declaration of
Independence. Part of the reason for presenting Baldwin this way is to embed
inner drama within his character as he is transformed over time from a naive,
opportunistic pragmatist into an emotionally involved defender of human
rights and values. Baldwin is presented as an object of strong identification
for the audience. The white characters Adams and Baldwin carry the main
action-point message of the film.

In creating the fictional character of Theodore Joadson, a black abolitionist,
Spielberg went beyond the scholarship of his time and indeed anticipated future developments. He presented an African American modeled on the figure
of the well-to-do sailmaker and antislavery activist James Forten of Philadelphia playing a significant role in the abolition movement. Recent scholarship
on the abolitionist Vigilance Committees, formed in the 1830s to assist runaways and fight against "blackbirding" (the capture of free blacks and their
sale into the illegal slave trade), emphasizes the role of African Americans in
direct-action, cutting-edge opposition to slavery. Joadson, himself formerly a
slave in Georgia, manifests a dignified and purposeful presence throughout the
film. He plays a significantly lesser part than Adams and Baldwin, but he does
implicitly provide a perspective from below.[5]

The least significant of the five great men, Lewis Tappan, is nonetheless revealing of Spielberg's deeper purposes. More than any other character, Tappan represents the abolitionist movement, for better and for worse. As Jesse Lemisch has pointed out, Spielberg takes a dim view of the movement, representing abolitionists as "fanatics," just as many of their nineteenth-century opponents did. Tappan is aloof, condescending, and to some extent inhuman. Unlike Adams and Baldwin, he does not regard the *Amistad* Africans as real people, but rather as pawns in a larger game of power. Indeed, he shocks Joadson when he explains that he might prefer that the *Amistad* Africans be executed because they would be more useful to the cause of abolition as martyrs. That invented speech would also shock anyone who knows the actual Tappan, who was self-righteous but not murderously so. At the same time, Spielberg's broader vision of abolitionism is conveyed when Cinqué and his fellow African Yamba watch a group of men and women abolitionists, all dressed in black, kneel before the jail to sing the hymn *Amazing Grace*. Cinqué and Yamba note that "they look like they are going to be sick" and ask, "Why do they look so miserable?" The abolitionists definitely are not sympathetic characters, to the Africans or anyone else.

It is important to note that the original actors, context, and consequences of the *Amistad* rebellion were profoundly multicultural and transnational. The rebels themselves came from a dozen different nations and cultures in Sierra Leone. The motley crew of slavers they met at Lomboko were led by a Cuban, Pedro Blanco. The first slave ship on which they sailed, the *Teçora*, was Brazilian or Portuguese. They sailed to Havana, then after the revolt to the Bahamas and the United States, ending up first in New York and finally in Connecticut. The governments of Spain, Great Britain, and the United States played important roles in the trials. The ripple effects of the successful rising were transatlantic, flowing from the United States to Europe, Africa, the Caribbean, and Latin America. Some of these elements appear, at least fleetingly, in Spielberg's film.

Yet the film as a whole is guided in its interpretation by what we might call a sentimental American nationalism. Adams is of course the primary purveyor of this theme. The speech by the beloved, eccentric former president to the Supreme Court is an appeal to early American ancestors, six of whom he names: James Madison, Alexander Hamilton, Thomas Jefferson, Benjamin Franklin, George Washington, and, of course, his own father, John Adams. Their example and wisdom, Adams suggests, will guide the court to make the right decision in the *Amistad* case, in full accordance with America's highest ideals.

The problem with this appeal is that *five of the six Founding Fathers he appealed to owned slaves*. (The only one who did not was his father.) Three of them, Washington, Jefferson, and Madison, represented the savvy slaveowning ruling class of Virginia, where the "peculiar institution" first took root in American soil. What might these Founding Fathers have said to the Supreme Court justices? It would have depended on when they were asked. Franklin and Hamilton owned slaves but ended up joining antislavery societies later in life. Washington, in his old age, was profoundly troubled by slavery. Jefferson, on the other hand, was not only a leading slaveholder but one of the preeminent racists of his age. It simply will not do to search for virtue regarding slavery among the Virginia aristocracy. But Spielberg was trying to create a feel-good story about American history. The white marble busts to which Adams appeals speak a terrible, unacknowledged truth.

In order to make possible this nationalist interpretation, Spielberg is forced to hide what abolitionists called the American "Slave Power." No American slaveowners appear in the film as slaveowners, and American slavery itself is rendered almost entirely invisible. True, John C. Calhoun, the firebrand southern nationalist from South Carolina, makes an appearance, but only as the political representative of his class, to make a threatening (anachronistic) speech about the looming civil war to a large dinner party in Washington, DC, hosted by the embattled president, Martin van Buren. More tellingly still, Spielberg actually makes the American legal system a hero of the *Amistad* story. After all, at the end of the day the legal system crafted by the Founding Fathers works: the Supreme Court humanely sets the "poor Africans" free. But against Spielberg's celebration of American virtue we must ask, are we talking about the same legal system that was, in 1839, holding two and half million African Americans in bondage? We are. The American legal system is not the hero of the story.

The most fundamental point—and one hidden by the film, as Spielberg speaks primarily through his liberal, paternalistic, nationalist white characters—is that the *Amistad* Africans were the heroes of their own story. As Lemisch pointed out, the film marginalizes the successful revolt at sea and hence those who successfully made it, against all odds. Of the film's 154 minutes, only 4.5 are devoted to the uprising, while another 5.5 show a flashback to Sierra Leone depicting enslavement and the Middle Passage. The remaining 144 minutes—93.5 percent of the film—are devoted entirely to the legal battle. This is, as the old saying goes, to put the cart in front of the horse. Without the daring, unlikely successful revolt carried out by a small group of West African warriors off the north coast of Cuba in 1839, John Quincy Adams would have had no one to defend before the Supreme Court.

NOTES

1. This essay draws on evidence and conclusions I presented in *The Amistad Rebellion: An Atlantic Odyssey of Slavery and Freedom* (New York: Viking, 2012).

2. The four Academy Award nominations were for Best Actor in a Supporting Role (Anthony Hopkins), Best Cinematography (Janusz Kaminski), Best Costume Design (Ruth E. Carter), and Best Music, Original Dramatic Score (John Williams). For a good critical summary of the film by a historian, see Julie Roy Jeffrey, "*Amistad* (1997): Steven Spielberg's 'True Story,'" *Historical Journal of Film, Radio, and Television* 21 (2001): 77–96.

3. Eric Foner, "The Amistad Case in Fact and Film," *History Matters* (1998), available at http://historymatters.gmu.edu/d/74.

4. Jesse Lemisch, "Black Agency in the Amistad Uprising: Or, You've Taken Our Cinqué and Gone," *Souls: A Critical Journal of Black Politics, Culture, and Society* 1 (1999): 57–70, available at http://www.columbia.edu/cu/ccbh/souls/vol1no1/vol1num1art6.pdf.

5. Graham Russell Gao Hodges, *David Ruggles: A Radical Black Abolitionist and the Underground Railroad in New York City* (Chapel Hill: University of North Carolina Press, 2010); Eric Foner, *Gateway to Freedom: The Hidden History of the Underground Railroad* (New York: Norton, 2016); Manisha Sinha, *The Slave's Cause: A History of Abolition* (New Haven, CT: Yale University Press, 2016); Jesse Olsavsky, "'Fire and Sword Will Do More Good': Fugitives, Vigilance Committees, and the Making of Revolutionary Abolitionism" (PhD diss., University of Pittsburgh, in progress).

9

"I Survive"
Individual, Community, and Slavery in
Steve McQueen's *12 Years a Slave*

WILLIAM L. ANDREWS

On the heels of the unprecedented sales of Harriet Beecher Stowe's novel *Uncle Tom's Cabin* (1852), Solomon Northup's bestselling autobiography, *Twelve Years a Slave* (1853), captured a large readership by portraying slavery from an extraordinary point of view. Previous narratives by African American anti-slavery activists such as Frederick Douglass (1845), Lewis and Milton Clarke (1846), William Wells Brown (1847), Josiah Henson (1849), and Sojourner Truth (1850) had testified, as did Northup, in graphic, unsparing detail to the gross inhumanity of slavery.[1] But if the sales of Northup's book are any indication—thirty thousand copies sold between 1853 and 1855, a record not even Douglass's 1845 *Narrative* could match[2]—*Twelve Years a Slave* evoked a degree of empathy from white northern readers that the narratives of even the most famous fugitives from the South did not.

A probable reason for the strong appeal of Northup's narrative is that like his antebellum white readers, and unlike the celebrated fugitive slaves before him, Solomon Northup was born into freedom, not bondage. A native of Saratoga, New York, Northup informed his reader that as a young family man he had pursued "his humble progress in the world" spurred by "the common hopes, and loves, and labors" that made his life "nothing whatever unusual" until he was kidnapped and sold into slavery.[3] Like the majority of his white readers, the young Northup had been no abolitionist. Before the turning point in his life, Northup thought little, and knew less, about the enslaved of the South. "I was too ignorant, perhaps too independent, to conceive how any one could

be content to live in the abject condition of a slave" (20). In this rueful remark, Northup implicitly admitted that his "independent" life in the North,
distanced and disconnected from slavery in the South, had instilled in him a
complacency about his own personal freedom, as well as a sense of dismissive
superiority to those who could somehow "be content" with a life of bondage.

Steve McQueen's Oscar-winning movie, *12 Years a Slave,* chronicles the
same journey through the antebellum United States, at once geographical and
psychological, that made Northup's autobiography such a rare and engrossing
text in its own time. Northup's story (in both print and film) reverses the
typical "narrative of ascent" for escaped slaves running from South to North.[4]
Northup's twelve-year ordeal begins with the free black family man prosper-
ing in small-town New York, descending into Dantesque depths of terror and
desperation in slavery-ridden rural Louisiana, and finally being restored to his
loving family in his New York hometown. Reviewers in 1853 and 2013 rightly
applauded Northup's heroic faith, resilience, and perseverance in the face
of innumerable forms of violence spawned by chattel slavery, ranging from
outright combat between slave and enslaver to beatings, rape, slaps, kicks,
verbal threats, and casual insults. Through a free black everyman with little
knowledge of slavery and no discernible commitment to antislavery before
he is thrust into bondage, readers of the original narrative and viewers of the
2013 film experience Northup's shock, horror, and daily struggle to survive
the "peculiar institution" that dominated US political, economic, and social
institutions for the first ninety years of the country's existence.

During his twelve years of bondage Northup (Chiwetel Etiofor) was a man
with a foot in two worlds, neither freeman nor slave but both simultaneously,
an emotionally riven man whose original narrative reads much like the work
of a participant-observer in the ruthless mechanisms of chattel slavery. The
opening scenes of the film portray a day in Northup's life as a slave: cutting
sugar cane in a gang of slaves; silently eating a meager supper; secretly whit-
tling a rude pen at nightfall and, by candlelight, futilely attempting to write
with it; and later impassively rebuffing the advances of a female slave as they
lie next to each other on the floor of a slave cabin crowded with about a dozen
male and female slaves trying to sleep. As yet unnamed in the film, the man
who is central in each of these snapshot scenes is distinguished by an aloof
detachment from the enslaved, both male and female, in his community. The
sugar-cane workers sing as they labor, but this man doesn't join in. He eats his
supper wordlessly, separate from his fellows. His efforts to write are private.

The pathos of the beautiful woman's needs in the night moves him to neither desire nor any expression of compassion.

As this silent man turns away from the weeping female slave, he drifts into a flashback to an intimate moment with another beautiful African American woman who represents an entirely different life, one characterized in subsequent scenes by evidence of economic prosperity, domestic tranquility, and social recognition that this man once enjoyed in Saratoga, New York. Enslaved and renamed Platt ("nothing but a Georgia runaway") by a savage Washington, DC, slave trader (Paul Giamatti) who sells him to the Deep South, Northup clings to the memory of who he once was—freeman, husband, and father in a faraway North. But with a pragmatism bordering on cynicism, a fellow slave, Clemons Ray, advises him on board a ship bound for New Orleans: "If you want to survive, do and say as little as possible. Tell no one who you really are and tell no one you can read and write. Unless you want to be a dead nigger." The only male slave in the film with whom Northup has a conversation, Ray counsels self-preservation, "keepin' your head down," as the key to survival. Northup objects. "Days ago I was with my family in my home. Now you tell me all is lost. Tell no one who I am? That's the way to survive? Well I don't want to survive. I want to live." How to survive as Platt in order to live again as Northup someday is the kidnapped freeman's challenge throughout the film.

Northup's career as Platt commences when a pious Louisiana slaveholder, William Ford (Benedict Cumberbatch), purchases him in New Orleans along with a female slave named Eliza, recently separated by force from her two children. Ford's approachability and relatively humane treatment of his slaves encourage his new acquisition to volunteer his ideas and skills to help the slaveholder transport his timber along the Red River to market. In addition to Ford's gratitude and respect, Northup gains an unexpected and much valued reward, a handsome violin. Possession of a fine musical instrument not only signals Northup's status as Ford's favorite slave. The slaveholder's largesse enables the talented slave to pursue a profitable sideline business as a fiddler at parties held by upper-crust whites. Although only in Ford's possession for a short time, Northup becomes locally celebrated, according to his autobiography, as the "smartest nigger in the Pine Woods" (61). This leads to his being assigned various skilled work that, while he is enslaved by Ford, keeps him from punishing agricultural labor in the cotton and sugar industries. Both book and film show that under Ford, Northup more than survived—he thrived, earning favors, opportunities, and rewards that placed him in the higher echelons of enslaved workers in the Red River environs of Louisiana. McQueen's film suggests that Ford's regime represented the best of all possible worlds in which Northup could have found himself after being reduced to slavery.

In one of the rare verbal exchanges between Northup and a fellow slave in McQueen's film, Eliza, Northup's confidante (Adepero Oduye), offers a less than congratulatory perspective on Platt's improving prospects under Ford. Severely depressed over the loss of her children, the perpetually grieving Eliza rejects Northup's warning about the danger of becoming "overcome by sorrow." "Do I upset the master and the mistress?" she asks sarcastically. "Do you care less about my loss than their wellbeing?" Eliza goes on to accuse Northup of being all too ready to "settle into your role as Platt." When Northup defends Ford as "a decent man under the circumstances," Eliza charges: "You luxuriate in his favor. You grovel at his boots." Incensed, Northup explodes: "I *survive!* I will not fall into despair. I will keep myself hearty till freedom is opportune." But is settling into a role, especially one that curries "favor" from the enslaver, justified on the grounds of keeping oneself "hearty" for freedom? Or do such favored roles lead to compromised principles and accommodation, albeit in the name of survival?

Viewers of 12 *Years a Slave* do not meet a single enslaved male in Louisiana who harbors the freedom agenda that motivates Northup. In his 1853 autobiography, however, Northup pays tribute to a number of enslaved male and female fugitives as well as insurrectionaries in the Red River environs of Louisiana, where he was held captive. *Twelve Years a Slave* identifies by name several male and female slaves with whom Northup worked and lived and whom he recalled fondly, but these people are absent from McQueen's film. The director's decision to focus so tightly on his protagonist enhances the heroic singularity of Northup, but at the expense of individualizing enslaved men other than the briefly appearing Clemons Ray. McQueen tries to compensate for allotting enslaved men (other than Northup) virtually no speaking parts in his film by dramatizing three significant conversations (none of which appears in the 1853 text) between Northup and enslaved women in Louisiana. In these exchanges McQueen explores the conflicted, sometimes excruciating social and psychological ramifications of the surviving-versus-living conundrum that shadows Northup during his years of bondage.

In addition to his already-noted argument with Eliza, Northup has a late-night verbal confrontation with Patsy, the persecuted and multiply violated slave of Edwin Epps (Michael Fassbender), a depraved and despicable planter into whose hands Northup falls after Ford's debts oblige him to sell his valuable slave.[5] The much-abused Patsy (Lupito Nyong'o in an Oscar-winning performance) begs Northup to drown her so that she can finally escape Epps's manifold depredations. Sternly refusing, Northup upbraids Patsy—"How can you fall into such despair?"—and assures her that she suffers from "melancholia, nothing more." He has no more patience with Patsy's "despair" than with Eliza's. Northup cannot see that Patsy's requested mercy killing and Eliza's persistent weeping for her lost children might well constitute desperate but purposeful forms of protest and resistance to a life of mere miserable survival. Patsy's plea adds further complexity to the film's interrogation of the complex bases on which survival might be morally justified for enslaved men or women. Although Northup is determined to "survive" until he can live again in the North, Patsy seems determined to claim her right to reject survival because, as a slave, she has so little to live for.

The gravest moral and social threat entailed by a code of survival appears in a third conversation that McQueen creates between Northup and an enslaved woman, this one occurring late in the film, when Northup is sent to fetch Patsy from a neighboring plantation, where she has gone to visit Charlotte Shaw (Alfre Woodard), the lady of the house. A former field slave who has installed herself in her enslaver's bedroom and parlor, the handsomely dressed, tea-sipping "Mistress Shaw," as Northup addresses her, reveals herself to be an unapologetic, opportunistic survivor. "I ain't felt the end of a lash in more years than I can recall," Shaw proudly informs the man she calls "Nigger Platt." "I ain't worked a field neither. Where once I served, now I have others servin' me. . . . If that what keep me from cotton-pickin' niggers, that what it be. A small and reasonable price to pay." Between the calculating self-aggrandizement of Shaw and the pathetic victimization of both Eliza and Patsy stands Northup, struggling to survive without succumbing to the despair of Eliza and Patsy or the cynicism of Shaw or any other slave who "luxuriates in his [enslaver's] favor."

Charlotte Shaw's indifference to her fellow slaves—she is attended by an enslaved waiting maid who waits on her during Northup's visit—represents an extreme of social alienation from an enslaved community that Northup never approaches. Nevertheless, in McQueen's film there is little sign of Northup's being markedly affected by any of his attenuated relationships to his fellow slaves. After helping to bury a male slave who has dropped dead in a sweltering cotton row on Epps's plantation, Northup appears in a rare group shot with Epps's slaves as they sing "Roll, Jordan, Roll" outside the slave graveyard. Initially Northup does not participate in the singing, suggesting, once again, that he does not feel a commonality with his fellow slaves. But gradually he joins in, perhaps because a line in the chorus, "My soul arise in heaven, Lord, for the year when Jordan roll," speaks movingly to his own struggles against the temptations to despair that beset him on Epps's plantation. But at the nadir of his fortunes after being sold to Epps, neither the slave community nor its religion offers Northup more than momentary solace.

McQueen's film strongly implies that survival is the best that Epps's slaves hope for or aspire to. Northup's solitary dedication to freedom, by contrast, elevates him in the latter half of *12 Years a Slave* into a stoic, staunchly undaunted figure. Northup's 1853 autobiography describes the almost ten years that Epps owned Northup as a sort of crucible in which the kidnapped freeman was finally and fully initiated into the horrors of slavery. Under Epps's reign of terror, according to McQueen's film and the 1853 text, the once-favored slave was demoted to the rank and file as an ordinary cotton picker. The film also mirrors the original autobiography in depicting the new slave as so inept at field work that he is flogged nightly for failing to meet the daily production quota that Epps demanded of all his cotton-field workers. However, McQueen's film omits a crucial fact about Northup's working life that his autobiography makes amply clear. According to McQueen, Northup must simply endure the deprivations and punishments meted out to every field worker subject to Epps's insatiable zest for whipping. But in Northup's original narrative, thoroughly disgusted with his new slave's unacceptable performance as a picker, Epps concludes that Platt will be more profitable in a different job—slave driver.

Northup worked as a driver, also known in various parts of the South as a "foreman" or "head man," for eight of the twelve years of his enslavement (172). As Epps's driver, Northup had the usual duties invested in his position throughout the slaveholding South. As "part of the coercion necessary to keep the plantation machinery humming," the driver, or foreman, was charged with working his fellow slaves to maximum efficiency, usually with a whip to enforce completion of each day's tasks to the master's or overseer's satisfaction.[6] The driver served as straw boss of enslaved rank-and-file agricultural workers, especially on plantations like Epps's, where the owner aimed to save money by promoting a slave to driver rather than hiring a white overseer. A driver who met his enslaver's expectations generally could expect various kinds of incentives, rewards, and privileges, not the least of which was supervision of rather than subjection to back-breaking, mind-numbing field work.

In most slave narratives contemporary with Northup's, drivers are portrayed as objects of their fellow slaves' fear and hatred. The former slave Lewis Clarke spoke for many when asked why a black slave-driver was worse than a white one. He replied, "He must be very strict and severe, or else he will be turned out [i.e., lose his position]. The master selects the hardest-hearted and most unprincipled slave upon the plantation [to serve as driver]."[7] Slaveholders generally picked their drivers from their most capable, loyal, and trustworthy slaves, which could easily arouse tensions between the master's "head nigger" and the slaves obliged to work under him.[8] Northup was not the only antebellum slave narrator to have worked as a driver and to comment on the conflicting allegiances and ethical dilemmas built into the job.[9] By glossing over this key feature of Northup's final eight years of slavery, McQueen's film further shrinks the web of social relationships Northup had to negotiate in bondage while also simplifying the moral problems Northup had to wrestle with. If we are to fully appreciate these complex dimensions of Northup's experience of slavery, we must refer to his original text.

In his autobiography Northup admits that he accepted the job as Epps's driver rather than risk the violent reprisals he believed would come should he refuse. Northup knew what was expected of him, having observed the behavior of his predecessor, a driver named Robert, who was "severe in the extreme" (128). Wearing "a whip about my neck in the field" each workday, Northup kept one eye on his master and the other on the workers under him. He "dared not show any lenity" to the enslaved workers as long as Epps was nearby (128). But as Northup's experience as a driver and his expertise with the whip progressed, he "learned to handle the whip with marvelous dexterity and precision, throwing the lash within a hair's breadth of the back, the ear, the nose, without, however, touching either of them. If Epps was observed at a distance, or we had reason to apprehend he was as sneaking somewhere in the vicinity, I would commence plying the lash vigorously, when, according to arrangement, they [Epps's slaves] would squirm and screech as if in agony, although not one of them had in fact been even grazed" (128).

Had the 2013 film delved into the effects of the power Northup as driver wielded over his fellow slaves, his compromised role as their boss, and his attempts to mitigate the harm that role did to himself and his fellow slaves, 12 Years a Slave would have been a much more searching and revealing portrayal of both Northup and his enslaved community. The film, however, dispenses with all these issues. Instead of a black driver, McQueen furnishes Epps a white overseer (Paul Dano). The most horrific scene in the autobiography depicts Epps ordering Northup the driver to use his whip to cut more than forty lashes into helpless Patsy's back before "my heart revolted at the inhuman scene" and he finally refused to continue the whipping (144). In the film version of the same scene, the director must rely on several contrivances to maneuver the whip into the unwilling hands of Northup, a convenient bystander, before Epps takes the whip and finishes the gory atrocity. McQueen's film enhances Northup's moral authority by having him outspokenly condemn his master's brutality at the conclusion of the whipping. However, what Northup speaks aloud to his fiendish enslaver in the film, he confines solely to his thoughts in the original autobiography (146).

It would be impossible in a feature film slightly more than two hours in length to convey anything like the thick description of slavery, not to mention the insights into the work, customs, mores, and outlook of the enslaved in their communities, that Northup recorded in his autobiography. McQueen's film must be credited with distilling from Northup's 1853 text one unforgettable image: an indomitable black man, bereft of his northern family, in but not of his southern black community, who endures, spirit unbent and conscience uncompromised, until he can finally regain his liberty. It is an inspiring story, evocatively and compellingly rendered. But as the film invites us to applaud Northup's heroic struggle and ultimate triumph, McQueen assigns the role of silent onlooker to practically all the enslaved men and women whom Northup encounters during his terrible sojourn in the South. Should the repulsive yet enthralling white sadist Edwin Epps be awarded such a commanding presence in a film about slavery, while the majority of enslaved persons (male especially) in the same film are granted no more than a phrase, a nod, or a tear? If popular media's accounts of slavery celebrate exceptional black individuals who resist soulless whites in life-and-death struggles to escape bondage, what of the vast majority of enslaved men and women and their families and communities who struggled not just to survive but to live with dignity and purpose despite all they were up against, despite the lack of opportunity or means to end their oppression short of death? Today's audiences have yet to see, hear, and fully appreciate the lives of these men and women. Fortunately, their stories still exist embedded in seldom read nineteenth- and early-twentieth-century African American autobiographies awaiting recovery and imaginative retelling by filmmakers as accomplished as Steve McQueen.

NOTES

1. *Narrative of the Life of Frederick Douglass, an American Slave, Written by Himself* (Boston: American Anti-Slavery Society, 1845); *Narratives of the Sufferings of Lewis and Milton Clarke, Sons of a Soldier of the Revolution, Dictated by Themselves*, ed. Joseph Cammet Lovejoy (Boston: Bela Marsh, 1846); *Narrative of William W. Brown, a Fugitive Slave, Written by Himself* (Boston: American Anti-Slavery Society, 1847); *The Life of Josiah Henson, Formerly a Slave, Now an Inhabitant of Canada, As Narrated by Himself*, ed. Samuel A. Eliot (Boston: A. D. Phelps, 1849); *Narrative of Sojourner Truth, a Northern Slave*, ed. Olive Gilbert (Boston: privately printed, 1850).

2. Scholars estimate that the *Narrative of the Life of Frederick Douglass, an American Slave* sold thirty thousand copies within five years, whereas *Twelve Years a Slave* sold that many copies in three. John W. Blassingame, "Introduction to Volume Two," in *The Frederick Douglass Papers, Series Two*, vol. 2, *My Bondage and My Freedom*, ed. John W. Blassingame, John R. McKivigan, and Peter P. Hinks (New Haven, CT: Yale University Press, 2003), xxx–xxxi; Solomon Northup, *Twelve Years a Slave*, ed. Sue Eakin and Joseph Logsdon (Baton Rouge: Louisiana State University Press, 1968), xiv.

3. Solomon Northrup, *Twelve Years a Slave*, ed. Henry Louis Gates Jr. and Kevin M. Burke (New York: Norton, 2017), 21. Subsequent quotations, from this most recent annotated edition, and cited parenthetically in the text.

4. Robert B. Stepto, *From Behind the Veil* (Urbana: University of Illinois Press, 1979), 167.

5. McQueen's film elides the fact that John M. Tibaut (referred to as Tibeats both in the book and in the film) purchased Platt from William Ford in the winter of 1842, about six months after Ford had bought him from a New Orleans slave trader. In April 1843 Tibaut sold Platt to Edwin Epps for fifteen hundred dollars. Northup remained enslaved by Epps until he was liberated in early January 1853. See Northrup, *Twelve Years a Slave*, ed. Eakin and Logsdon, 75, 120n8, 228.

6. John W. Blassingame, *The Slave Community* (New York: Oxford University Press, 1972), 161. The standard study of the slave driver is William L. Van DeBurg's *The Slave Drivers: Black Agricultural Labor Supervisors in the Antebellum South* (Westport, CT: Greenwood, 1979).

7. *Narratives of the Suffering of Lewis and Milton Clarke*, 122.

8. In his second autobiography, Josiah Henson acknowledged that during his early manhood in Montgomery County, Maryland, he had been "proud of my success" as his master's "head nigger," that is, his enslaved foreman and driver. *Father Henson's Story of His Own Life* (Boston: John P. Jewett, 1858), 66.

9. In addition to Henson and Northup, Jermain Loguen also worked as his enslaver's "head man," or driver, during the latter years of his Tennessee enslavement. Jermain Wesley Loguen, *The Rev. J. W. Loguen, as a Slave and a Freeman* (Syracuse, NY: privately printed, 1859), 226–27.

10

"Now You Are Ready for *Mandingo*"
Sex, Slavery, and Historical Realism

DIANE MILLER SOMMERVILLE

Years ago, my nonacademic husband was describing the subject of my first book, on rape and race in the South, to a professional colleague. Her reflexive response was, "Not that Mandingo crap?," though her language was a bit more colorful. For many, including this woman, the term *Mandingo* conjured the deep-seated racial stereotype about black men's sexuality built on myths about oversized genitalia, innate lustfulness, and especially the imagined sexual threat they posed to white women. These lurid associations with the term *Mandingo* continue today. A perusal of the online slang reference tool *Urban Dictionary* yields multiple crowd-sourced definitions, nearly all of which allude to a black man's large penis and/or sexual prowess.[1] While the etiology of the sexual connotation of *Mandingo* is not certain, the popular understanding of the term can most certainly be traced to the 1975 film *Mandingo*, directed by Richard Fleischer and produced by the legendary Dino De Laurentiis.

Based on the 1957 novel of the same name by Kyle Onstott, the film depicts a decrepit Mississippi plantation, Falconhurst, home to a father-son partnership overseeing a slave-breeding outfit. The setting is the backdrop for a searing critique of slavery and a patent rejection of the moonlight-and-magnolias depiction of the antebellum South that prevailed in many film and literary venues, the most influential of which was, of course, the classic novel, then movie *Gone with the Wind*, which stubbornly continued to shape many Americans' syrupy ideas about the slave South through much of the twentieth century.

Critically panned but popular among black audiences and widely denounced as both racist and exploitive, *Mandingo* emerged in the seventies as part of a genre called *blaxploitation*, movies targeting black audiences that featured African American actors and dealt with subjects from the perspective of African Americans, or at least sympathetic to blacks, all while appropriating white stereotypes of blacks. Oppressed blacks were heroes; whites, racist exploiters and villains.[2] The films were heavy on violence and sexuality. *Mandingo* adheres to most of the conventions associated with blaxploitation films, including graphic violence and the prominence of black male sexuality, which in most mainstream films before the seventies was muted.[3] The late film critic Roger Ebert condemned *Mandingo* as a "piece of manure," "racist trash," "obscene," and "excruciating to sit through." He punctuated his scathing review decrying, "This is a film I felt soiled by."[4] The film fared no better in a *New York Times* review that described the movie as "vapid" and dismissed it as "steamily melodramatic nonsense." In a final swipe, the reviewer slammed the actors for acting "with ludicrous intensity." "I assume," he snidely concluded, "they had no choice."[5]

Blaxploitation films like *Mandingo* deployed graphic depictions of violence, nudity, and sex in an effort to fully convey their messages to their audiences. Paradoxically, mainstream reviewers became so preoccupied with the brutally raw and, frankly, offensive representations that they often missed the powerful messages conveyed in the film. *Mandingo,* for instance, held little back in portraying the routine and callous degradation of slaves, a central theme of the movie. In one scene, the purchaser of a male slave orders him to drop his trousers so he can inspect him for hemorrhoids. In another, the patriarch Warren Maxwell (James Mason) sits with his feet on top of a prostrate slave child because he has been told this will drain the rheumatism from his body into the boy's. Film critics, who had never seen slavery depicted so starkly before, were so revolted by these degrading and dehumanizing representations that they were unable to consider the alternative, more realistic narrative of slavery the film offered.

Despite a poor reception among critics, the film subsequently has found a friendly audience among scholars who have reconsidered its cultural message, especially in the wake of recent releases that appear to have drawn inspiration from *Mandingo,* knowingly or not—*Django Unchained* (2011), *12 Years a Slave* (2013), *The Birth of a Nation* (2016)—notably for its no-holds-barred critique of the institution of slavery and the explicit depiction of violence and degradation in slave life. Film scholars now argue that *Mandingo* was ahead of its time in delivering a rendering of slavery that they had not encountered elsewhere in film, one that portrayed the slaves' conditions sympathetically and condemned the institution as evil while portraying its perpetrators and beneficiaries—white slaveowners—as morally bankrupt. One reassessment of the film's significance explains that *Mandingo* "presents and explores racism, depicting its cruelties inflicted on the slaves, the slaves' struggle to make the best of a horrifying situation, and the effect this system of ownership has on both black and white, man and woman."[6] Twenty-three years after *Mandingo's* release, the English film critic Robin Wood offered high praise, dubbing it "the greatest film about race ever made in Hollywood."[7] Robert Keser took the film seriously as a critique of the capitalist economic order that sustained slavery, asserting that it exposed "the social mechanisms that supported racial and patriarchal domination."[8]

Mandingo was the first film to take up a revisionist treatment of slavery. To this point, *Gone with the Wind* (1939), and *The Birth of a Nation* (1915) before it, had dominated celluloid representations of slavery. They had contributed mightily to the shaping of an antiblack national narrative about slavery and its demise, one that soft-pedaled human bondage and waxed nostalgic about an Old South dotted with majestic plantation homes adorned with inviting verandas and populated with doting Sambos and Mammys. *Mandingo* sought to counter the myths conveyed in those iconic films, which cast white southerners as victims and slaves as either inept or menacing, by presenting a more realistic version, one that laid bare slavery's inhumanity, brutality, and degrading, noxious impact on southern society. It did so most cuttingly by daring to broach the third rail of racial politics in America: interracial sex.

Sex, specifically across racial lines, is a central part of the slavery story in *Mandingo*, as it is historically. Through the interrogation of interracial sex we witness the best and the worst aspects of slavery, as well as all its contradictions and complexity. Ultimately, the film concludes that slavery is so insidious and miasmic that nothing good can be salvaged. Everything it touches withers. Thus, *Mandingo* emphatically rejects the innocuous, benign interpretations of slavery that had prevailed in American cinema and instead portrays the horror of slavery and the suffering of individual slaves, though with a paradoxical twist.

The sensational sexually and racially provocative *Mandingo* promotional poster brazenly mocked the iconic image of Clark Gable's seduction of Vivien Leigh taken from the *Gone with the Wind* poster, mimicking the pose while replicating the fiery orange-and-red background. It prominently featured the two main interracial couplings of the film: Mede, the "Mandingo buck," and Blanche, the master's wife; and Hammond, the master, and his "bed wench,"

Ellen. Mede (Ken Norton), nude from the waist up, baring sinewy biceps, embraces the white mistress, Blanche (Susan George), whose naked back is exposed in a precoital pose. The other image directly lampoons the famous depiction of Rhett Butler, down to the white shirt partially exposing his chest, and a submissive Scarlett O'Hara, bosom on full display. Hammond Maxwell (Perry King) looks longingly at Ellen (Brenda Sykes), his concubine, overcome, presumably in anticipation of torrid lovemaking. The poster reads, "Expect the savage. The sensual. The shocking. The powerful. The shameful. Expect all that the motion picture screen has never dared to show before. Expect the truth. Now you are ready for 'Mandingo.'"[9]

What exactly was so "shocking" about the film? While there is much in the movie that jarred its audiences—horrific violence, blatant racism—surely the major jolt to American moviegoers was the flagrant crossing of racial and sexual boundaries by the main characters, which was still very much a taboo in much of America in the 1970s. To that end, the film, through its exploration of interracial sex, was a nod as much to racism in twentieth-century American society as to a more honest historical narrative about slavery.

The sanctioning of marriage across racial lines had not yet become mainstream in America by the 1970s. The *Loving* decision, the Supreme Court ruling that declared unconstitutional Virginia's ban on interracial marriage, had been handed down in 1967. Until midcentury no fewer than thirty states had prohibited marriage across racial lines.[10] Despite the successful legal challenges to anti-miscegenation laws, the matter was far from settled in the minds of many Americans. Many southern states continued to contest the high court's decision into the 1970s and brought suit in an effort to retain bans against interracial marriage.[11] Moreover, the social and cultural taboo against cross-racial coupling remained robust, especially in the South.

In 1967, the same year the Supreme Court heard the *Loving* case, the film *Guess Who's Coming to Dinner* debuted. Audiences watched as a young white woman and her African American fiancé worked to overcome the resistance of both sets of parents to the news of their engagement, this at a time when only about 20 percent of Americans approved of marriage across the color line.[12] The following year, NBC executives expressed reservations about an episode of *Star Trek* in which Captain Kirk (William Shatner) was to kiss Uhura (Nichelle Nichols), an African American woman. Worried about how it would be received in the South, the network asked production to tape two versions, one with a kiss, one with an embrace but no kiss, and planned to distribute the episode with the embrace instead of the kiss to southern affiliates.[13] The first interracial couple in a television series did not appear until 1975 in *The Jeffersons*, in which friends of the title couple, both African American, included a black woman and her white Jewish husband. Many of the show's threads revolved around George Jefferson's discomfort with the neighbors' interracial relationship, then his own son's marriage to their daughter.[14] Uneasiness with or opposition to mixed-race relationships remains palpable in some pockets of America today. A poll conducted in 2011 among Mississippi Republicans found that 46 percent opposed interracial marriage.[15] *Mandingo*'s forceful and audacious engagement with the topic of interracial sex, especially the depiction of a black man having sex with a white woman, would have set tongues wagging in many sectors of America in 1975.[16]

The shock value of *Mandingo*, however, was not just that it openly and unapologetically broached the subject of interracial sex in slave times but that it did so graphically. Reviewers denounced the film as "soft porn" because of the torrid lovemaking between a black man and a white woman and scenes in which brutal, dehumanizing violence stood in for foreplay between a white man and a young female slave.[17] In fact, *Mandingo* was released in the wake of the collapse of the Motion Picture Production Code in 1968, which had provoked a critical discourse about the prevalence of sexually graphic and violent films.[18] The movie's producer appears to have aimed to exploit this censorship loophole.

It is also noteworthy that when *Mandingo* appeared, few historians had taken up the issue of interracial sexuality in slavery in a meaningful way, making the revisionist message of the film even more remarkable. Scholars of slavery rarely used the word *rape* in describing the sexual encounters between masters and their female slaves, opting for more sterile terms like *miscegenation, affairs, seduction,* and *interracial unions,* all of which effectively masked or downplayed coercion and violence.[19] (Male) historians also overtly subscribed to a narrative about interracial sex that naturalized white males' attraction to female slaves, assumed black women's promiscuous nature, and rarely acknowledged the coercive nature of master-slave sexual behavior. Kenneth Stampp, in *The Peculiar Institution: Slavery in the Antebellum South* (1956), for example, explained that white men and boys surrendered to "temptations found in female slaves in their own or neighbors' households" and conceded that "overseers often succumbed to the temptations surrounding them." White men's sexual encroachments of their female slaves, in Stampp's rendering, were unavoidable and natural. "Human behavior in the Old South was very human

In *Mandingo,* Hammond (Perry King) and his cousin Charles (Ben Masters) are presented with "bed wenches" for the night. (Courtesy George Eastman Museum)

indeed."[20] Eugene Genovese, whose monumental book *Roll, Jordan, Roll: The World the Slaves Made* (1974) was roughly contemporaneous with the film's release, similarly downplayed the coercive aspect of master-slave sexuality, ameliorated the sexual misdeeds of slave masters, and failed to consider that whites' sexual overtures to slaves might have been unwanted or predatory.[21] Not until the early 1980s, with the published works of the feminist historians Catherine Clinton and Deborah Gray White, did interracial sex in the slave South undergo sustained analysis.[22]

Nonconsensual sex between master and slave in *Mandingo* occurs along a continuum from sadistic and violent to tender and loving. The most startling portrayal of sexual assault of a female slave occurs when Hammond Maxwell and his cousin Charles are invited, in a gesture of southern hospitality, to bed two "wenches" while visiting a plantation. Charles roughly fondles the slaves' breasts, rejects the virgin of the two as being too much work, then throws his wench onto the bed facedown, rips off her clothes, and begins whacking her buttocks with his belt as a prelude to sex. The camerawork leaves no doubt in the viewer's mind that the slave is shocked, humiliated, and in pain. Hammond and his "wench," Ellen, are taken aback by the display of violence even though Charles assures his dubious cousin that the beating "makes a man feel good" and insists that "she likes it, too."

A less violent portrayal of a white master forcing himself on a slave occurs when "Big Pearl," a slave girl, is in bed sick. The attending physician diagnoses her as being in heat: "She cravin. In the bud of heat." The cure is for Hammond to have intercourse with her, as she is a virgin and it is the "master's duty to pleasure the wenches for the first time." Big Pearl cries at the pronouncement and runs off, but the matter is settled. Hammond will tend to the mundane "chore" after dinner. Big Pearl's mother and the plantation mammy bathe her and offer advice. When leaving Big Pearl upon Hammond's arrival in the cabin, her mother admonishes, "Don't forget to say thank you." Big Pearl is resigned and acquiesces without resistance; Hammond fulfills his obligation. The perfunctory act is devoid of warmth and intimacy, but neither is it rough or violent.

These examples of nonconsensual sexual relations between master and slave, though, are peripheral to the main relationship of the story, that between Hammond and Ellen. In myriad ways, this is the most normal relationship in the film, inverting the notion that intraracial relationships are the norm, perhaps a subversive tweak of contemporary attitudes toward sex and race. As recounted previously, Hammond first encounters Ellen when she is offered up as a sexual favor, a gesture of hospitality, by an overnight host. Hammond rejects his cousin's forceful approach to bedding his "wench" and says so to Ellen: "You don't like what Charles is doing? I don't like it either." This display of compassion by a white man both surprises and attracts Ellen and disarms her initial fear of him. "You's strange for a white man." In what amounts to the eroticization of racial subjugation, Hammond actively woos Ellen rather than forcing himself on her. He is tender and loving, insisting that she look at him. "You're looking away from me. . . . Put your eyes on me." The request flusters Ellen, who, mindful of her subordinate status, starts to explain, "Niggers don't . . ." "Look a white man in the eyes," Hammond finishes Ellen's sentence. Hammond broaches his desire to have sex with her but assures her that if "you don't like me you don't have to stay," providing at least the veneer of consent. Stay she does.

Then Hammond does the unthinkable. He kisses Ellen, something minutes earlier he had castigated Charles for doing. Kissing represented intimacy and an acknowledgment that sex had emotional meaning for Hammond, who treats Ellen with tenderness as he beds her. Even though custom (and his father) requires Hammond to secure a white wife, after he marries he returns to purchase Ellen and make her his "bed wench." This relationship, not his marriage to his white wife, is authentically affectionate and based on kindness. "Nobody, never, black or white, gonna take your place," he promises Ellen. But the futility of a viable, enduring relationship in slavery is exposed in one of the final scenes of the film, admittedly the most emotionally painful. Hammond, consumed by anger and frantically searching for his Mandingo slave Mede, whom he learns has impregnated his wife, knocks Ellen to the ground and out of his way while taunting, "Don't think because you get in my bed you're anything but a nigger." In an instant, the promising romance is dashed, and with it, the viewers' hopes that Hammond might rise above the system.[23]

Mandingo's structuring of a loving relationship between master and slave was made possible by inverting the sexual and temperamental attributes associated with black women. Ellen is demure, proper, submissive, and pure, a counter to the Jezebel stereotype that represented slave women as promiscuous.[24] Ellen and Hammond's romance is also predicated on Hammond's failed marriage to his cousin Blanche, whom he marries to satisfy his father's prodding for an heir. Hammond, though, discovers on his wedding night that she is not a virgin (later he will discover that Blanche's brother, Charles, had deflowered her) and so turns his back on Blanche while rededicating himself to Ellen, whom he purchases on his way home from his honeymoon. As a result of Hammond's withholding sex from Blanche, she devolves into a sex-starved, narcissistic alcoholic consumed by jealous rage over her husband's obvious affection for Ellen. Blanche becomes the antithesis of the plantation mistress, who was deemed to be chaste, sober, and asexual.[25] Deprived of her husband's attentions, she exhibits sexual frustration and grovels for his love. Their (intraracial) marriage is held up as the most dysfunctional, tortured relationship of all.

Motivated partly by revenge, partly by her unsated desire, Blanche coerces the prized Mandingo slave Mede into having sex with her by threatening to accuse him of rape. Mede is the quintessential Mandingo "buck": his physical prowess is unmatched, as shown by his skill as a fighter. His animalistic instincts are apparent when he rips open the jugular of a competitor in the ring, another slave, with his teeth. His physique, strong and toned, is regularly flaunted throughout the film in multiple scenes in which he is shirtless. Mede's sexual prowess is also readily apparent. When Hammond presents his father, Warren Maxwell, with the newly purchased Mede, a "pure" Mandingo, Warren questions him about the size of his new slave's genitalia. Hammond reassures him that Mede "is so big he tears the wenches." Curiously, despite the implications of Mede's ample libido, the only time the audience sees him act passionately is when he is *forced* to engage in sex with Blanche. Even then, he is reticent and visibly resists his carnal desire for Blanche. As Blanche taunts him—"Ain't you ever craved a white lady before?"—he sits impassively, frozen

Blanche (Susan George) blackmails Mede (Ken Norton) into having sex with her in *Mandingo*. (Courtesy George Eastman Museum)

with fear, one assumes. Blanche disrobes him, caresses his body, then disrobes herself. Only when she embraces him does he finally cave in to passion and engage in frenetic lovemaking.

Here again we see the inversion of sexual and racial stereotypes. Blanche, the white woman, is sexually aggressive, while the black man represses his sexual desires until they are extorted from him. In this way, the film exploits stereotypes about black men's hypersexuality by placing Mede in bed with a white woman and allowing him to pleasure her, while he is denied agency.

The director thus hints at but does not fully embrace the myth of the black beast rapist, so famously featured in *The Birth of a Nation*.[26] But neither does he possess or wield sexual agency, even though he is imbued with virility and (presumably) desire. To have acknowledged Mede's attraction to Blanche would have exposed the moviemakers to some risk. First, the portrayal of a "black buck" in a 1970s film came perilously close to the sexual stereotypes that had been perpetuated for nearly a hundred years and still resonated with many white Americans. Second, given that the intended audience of *Mandingo* was primarily African American, viewers steeped in the rhetoric and ideology of both black militantism and black feminism might not have been receptive to the depiction of a handsome black man being attracted to a white woman.[27]

In the decades following the release of *Mandingo*, scholars have come to understand the futility of studying American race relations or racism without the scaffolding of sexual dynamics. But in the early 1970s, historians viewed sexuality on the margins of the slave narrative. In many ways, then, *Mandingo* broke new ground for putting interracial sex center stage and for using sex as the vehicle through which to retell the slavery narrative while unmasking the system's most brutal features. Despite the stark visual representations of sexual exploitation and the corrupting influence of the slave system, *Mandingo* nonetheless offered the potential for empathy, desire, and warmth across racial boundaries. In doing so, the film foreshadowed later historical treatments of slavery that contemplate the paradoxical nature of cross-racial sexual encounters and that serve simultaneously as sites of both racial and gender subjugation as well as sexual liberation and fulfillment. Sex acts could serve both as a reprieve from the harshness of slavery and as a source of hedonistic indulgences and oppression.[28] *Mandingo*, visionary in its realistic portrayal of slavery, unmasked the complexities, ambiguities, and paradoxes of America's peculiar institution, largely through its attention to sex across the color line, an approach adopted only much later by professional historians, who came to understand that sex is central to unlocking a more complete understanding of the slave experience.[29]

NOTES

1. On contemporary usage of the word *Mandingo*, see Andrew DeVos, "'Expect the Truth': Exploiting History with *Mandingo*," *American Studies* 52, no. 2 (2013): 6.

2. Joe Meyers, "'Mandingo': They Don't Make Them Like This Anymore (Or Do They?)," *Joe's Views* (blog), 26 July 2012, http://blog.ctnews.com/meyers/2012/07/26/%E2%80%98mandingo%E2%80%99-they-don%E2%80%99t-make-them-like-this-anymore/.

3. Ed Guerro, *Framing Blackness: The African American Image in Film* (Philadelphia: Temple University Press, 1993), 69–111; DeVos, "Expect the Truth," 8–9; Novotny Lawrence, *Blaxploitation Films of the 1970s: Blackness and Genre* (New York: Routledge, 2008), 18–25. Notably, Novotny does not include *Mandingo* in his blaxploitation filmography. Film scholars disagree about whether *Mandingo* truly fit the category of blaxploitation. The filmologist Celine Parreñas Shimizu classifies Mandingo as "not quite Blaxploitation and not quite plantation-genre film." "Master-Slave Sex Acts: *Mandingo* and the Race/Sex Paradox," *Wide Angle* 21, no. 4 (October 1999): 42.

4. Roger Ebert, review of *Mandingo*, 25 July 1975, http://www.rogerebert.com/reviews/mandingo-1975.

5. Vincent Canby, "Film: Vapid 'Mandingo,'" *New York Times*, 8 May 1975. It is worth noting that even though the film was a critical disaster, it was very popular, especially with African American audiences. For an extended treatment of black and white press reviews of the film, as well as of the reception by black audiences, see DeVos, "Expect the Truth," 10–14.

6. Timothy Sun, "Mandingo," *Not Coming to a Theater Near You* (blog), 11 June 2008, http://www.notcoming.com/reviews/mandingo/.

7. Robin Wood, "'Mandingo': The Vindication of an Abused Masterpiece," in *Sexual Politics and Narrative Film: Hollywood and Beyond* (New York: Columbia University Press, 1998), 265.

8. Robert Keser, "'The Greatest Film about Race Ever Filmed in Hollywood': Richard Fleischer's *Mandingo*," *Bright Lights Film Journal*, 12 October 2015, http://brightlightsfilm.com/greatest-film-race-ever-filmed-hollywood-richard-fleischers-mandingo/#.WJOJffkrJPY. Other reassessments of Mandingo include James Kendrick, "Retrospective: *Mandingo* (1975)," [1998], https://groups.google.com/forum/#!topic/rec.arts.movies.reviews/puhJIYuHFLY; "Mandingo," accessed 27 December 2016, http://www.cliomuse.com/mandingo-1975-dir-richard-fleischer.html; Greg Klymkiw, "In Praise of Richard Fleischer & 'Mandingo,'" *Daily Film Dose* (blog), 6 July 2008, http://www.dailyfilmdose.com/2008/07/in-praise-of-richard-fleischer-mandingo.html; and Meyers, "Mandingo."

9. DeVos, "Expect the Truth," 5.

10. Peter Wallenstein, *Tell The Court I Love My Wife: Race, Marriage, and Law—An American History* (New York: Palgrave Macmillan, 2002), 173.

11. Wallenstein, *Tell The Court I Love My Wife*, 234–38.

12. Glen Anthony Harris and Robert Brent Toplin, "'Guess Who's Coming to Dinner': A Clash of Interpretations Regarding Stanley Kramer's Film on the Study of Interracial Marriage," *Journal of Popular Culture* 40, no. 4 (August 2007): 712. For an analysis of Sidney Poitier's character in *Guess Who's Coming to Dinner*, see Guerro, *Framing Blackness*, 71–78.

13. Stephanie Buck, "Star Trek's Interracial Kiss the Deep South Almost Never Saw," *Business Insider*, 22 July 2016, http://www.businessinsider.com/star-treks-interracial-kiss-deep-south-almost-2016-7. See the interview with Nichelle Nichols on the matter at https://www.youtube.com/watch?v=3hKKkGhEDoU.

14. The obituary of Roxie Roker, who played Helen Willis, the Jeffersons' neighbor, refers to her playing a role in television's first interracial couple. http://www.nytimes.com/1995/12/06/nyregion/roxie-roker-66-who-broke-barrier-in-her-marriage-on-tv-s-jeffersons.html.

15. Erik Hayden, "Poll: 46 Percent of Mississippi GOP Want to Ban Interracial Marriage," *Atlantic*, 7 April 2011, https://www.theatlantic.com/national/archive/2011/04/mississippi-republicans/349433/.

16. Nick Brown declared in 1992 that "no non-white man can have sanctioned sexual relations with a white woman" in film, though the previous year had seen the exploration of interracial sexual relationships in Spike Lee's *Jungle Fever* (1991). See Brown, "Race: The Political Unconscious in American Film," *East-West Film Journal* 6, no. 1 (January 1992): 8. It should be noted that the film *100 Rifles* (1969) featured sex scenes between James Brown and Raquel Welch, but because she was cast as Mexican, not white, little controversy arose over the interracial sex. Guerro, *Framing Blackness*, 79.

17. On the film received as "soft porn," see Sun, "Mandingo," where Sun recounts viewing the film in a theater "full of porn-addled racists"; Canby, "Film: Vapid 'Mandingo'"; and DeVos, "Expect the Truth," 9–11. For a more theoretical treatment of *Mandingo* as pornography, see Linda Williams, "Skin Flicks on the Racial Border: Pornography, Exploitation, and Interracial Lust," in *Porn Studies*, ed. Williams (Durham, NC: Duke University Press, 2004), 271–308.

18. DeVos, "Expect the Truth," 8, 10.

19. See, e.g., Kenneth Stampp, *The Peculiar Institution: Slavery in the Antebellum South* (1956; reprint, New York: Vintage, 1989), 350–61. Caution about deploying words that fail to convey the degradation of sexual acts between masters and slaves is found in Brenda Stevenson, *Life in Black and White: Family and Community in the Slave South* (New York: Oxford University Press, 1996), 240; and Angela Davis, *Women, Race, and Class* (New York: Vintage, 1983), 25.

20. Stampp, *Peculiar Institution*, 351, 354, 350.

21. Eugene D. Genovese, *Roll, Jordan, Roll: The World the Slaves Made* (New York: Vintage, 1974), 414–25. For a critique of Genovese's characterization and treatment of master-slave sexuality, see Diane Miller Sommerville, "Moonlight, Magnolias, and Brigadoon; or, 'Almost Like Being in Love': Mastery and Sexual Exploitation in Eugene D. Genovese's Plantation South," *Radical History Review* 88 (Winter 2004): 68–82.

22. Catherine Clinton, *The Plantation Mistress: Woman's World in the Old South* (New York: Random House, 1982), 199–222; Deborah Gray White, *Ar'n't I a Woman: Female Slaves in the Plantation South* (New York: Norton, 1985), 34, 61, 152, 164–65. John Blassingame, an African American historian, did not shy away from claiming that white men demanded sex from slave women "usually through force," but his treatment of the subject was fleeting. Blassingame, *The Slave Community: Plantation Life in the Antebellum South* (New York: Oxford University Press, 1972), 154–56.

23. The relationship between Hammond and Ellen was constructed, as Celine Parrañas Shimizu notes, not merely as a commentary on the sexual dynamics of slavery but also as a progressive, clear signal to moviegoers that a loving relationship across racial lines was not only possible but desirable. "Master-Slave Sex Acts," 49.

24. White, *Ar'n't I a Woman*, 27–40; Clinton, *Plantation Mistress*, 204.

25. Clinton, *Plantation Mistress*, 110–11, 137–38, 204; Anne Firor Scott, *The Southern Lady: From Pedestal to Politics, 1830–1930* (Chicago: University of Chicago Press, 1970), 3–21.

26. On the representation of black male sexuality in *The Birth of a Nation*, see Patricia Hill Collins, *Black Sexual Politics: African Americans, Gender, and the New Racism* (New York: Routledge, 2005), 65–66. On the historical construction of the black rapist, see Diane Miller Sommerville, *Rape and Race in the Nineteenth-Century South* (Chapel Hill: University of North Carolina Press, 2004), 1–18, 223–59.

27. On black feminism, see, e.g., Michelle Wallace, *Black Macho and Myth of the Superwoman* (New York: Dial, 1979).

28. Shimizu, "Master-Slave Sex Acts," 43–44.

29. A sampling of such works includes Martha Hodes, ed., *Sex, Love, Race: Crossing Boundaries in North American History* (New York: New York University Press, 1999); Hodes, *White Women, Black Men: Illicit Sex in the Nineteenth-Century South* (New Haven, CT: Yale University Press, 1997); Joshua D. Rothman, *Notorious in the Neighborhood: Sex and Families across the Color Line in Virginia, 1787–1861* (Chapel Hill: University of North Carolina Press, 2003); Annette Gordon-Reed, *Thomas Jefferson and Sally Hemings: An American Controversy* (Charlottesville: University Press of Virginia, 1997); Gordon-Reed, *The Hemingses of Monticello: An American Family* (New York: Norton, 2008); Catherine Clinton and Michele Gillespie, eds., *The Devil's Lane: Sex and Race in the Early South* (New York: Oxford University Press, 1997); Adele Logan Alexander, *Ambiguous Lives: Free Women of Color in Rural Georgia, 1789–1879* (Fayetteville: University of Arkansas Press, 1991); Thomas E. Buckley, "Unfixing Race: Class, Power, and Identity in an Interracial Family," *Virginia Magazine of History and Biography* 102 (July 1994): 349–80; and Sommerville, *Rape and Race in the Nineteenth-Century South*.

11

Mint Julep Melodrama
Jezebel

CATHERINE CLINTON

Jezebel, set in and around New Orleans in 1852 and 1853, introduces viewers to interwoven tropes of southern honor, sectionalism, class and gender divides, and racial stereotypes and concludes with the life-and-death dilemmas of a yellow fever epidemic. The historical figure named Jezebel—a queen of Israel who promoted sin and idolatry—first appears in the Old Testament and reappears in the Book of Revelations as an evil, manipulative emblem of her sex. *Jezebel's* lead character, Julie Marsden (Bette Davis), flaunts her reckless behavior in nearly 90 minutes of the 104-minute film. The Warner Brothers trailer of the 1938 film promised: "From the picturesque glamour of the old south a great actress draws the scarlet portrait of a gorgeous spitfire who lived by the wild desire of her untamed heart. . . . The story of a woman who was loved when she should have been whipped."[1]

In the antebellum South, *Jezebel* was a term linked to justification for rape and concubinage, since African American women were believed to be by nature lascivious and sexually insatiable and to initiate liaisons with white males. Feminist writers, most pointedly the African American activist Josephine St. Pierre Ruffin (1842–1924), have deconstructed this white supremacist "blame the victim" ideology, challenging the Jezebel stereotype since the late nineteenth century and discrediting this venomous misrepresentation (along with the stereotype of Mammy).[2] In the twenty-first century Jezebel has emerged as the brand name of an online magazine, self-described as "focused on celebrities, sex, feminism, and issues relating to women's empowerment." Thus, *Jezebel* requires context, and in the 1938 cinematic version Julie Marsden treads a fine line between rebeldom and retrograde, with the term a throwback to the biblical era. Her character sacrifices self for the higher purpose of moral redemption: not a happy ending but a true Hollywood one.[3]

The screenplay (co-written by John Huston and based on a 1933 stage play by Owen Davis) allowed a star turn for the lead actress under the direction of one of the industry's most esteemed directors, William Wyler. Yet *Jezebel* was considered a consolation prize, as the studio head, Jack Warner, had refused to buy the rights to *Gone with the Wind* for the studio's leading contract player: Bette Davis lost out to Vivien Leigh for the role of Scarlett O'Hara. In 1939 Davis won a second Oscar for her role in *Jezebel*, a few months before the screen version of Margaret Mitchell's bestseller premiered. Despite being overshadowed by the King Kong of plantation epics, *Jezebel* has remained a cult classic, highlighting several foundational themes of what the film scholar Edward Campbell Jr. has called "the Southern."[4]

The storylines for *Jezebel* and *Gone with the Wind* had dramatic parallels, which caused the latter's producer, David O. Selznick, to write to Jack Warner complaining of plagiarism. No lawsuit emerged, as both films drew on Lost Cause legends and themes. The French film scholar Taina Tuhkunen suggests that these two classics created a "crisis in representation" with a "modification of a feminine ideal."[5]

In *Jezebel*, the heroine, Julie Marsden, hopes to train her fiancé, banker Preston Dillard (played by Henry Fonda), much in the way she coaches her horses. Although critics have suggested her identification with the frisky colt she rides in on during her film entrance, it also demonstrates her fierce commitment to "breaking" those she loves.

In the opening scenes, Julie insists that Pres keep his promise to accompany her to Mme Poulard's to select a gown for an upcoming ball. She barges into the bank where he works just as he is negotiating to bring New Orleans into the nineteenth century—pitching investment in a $10 million railway scheme.

While a naysayer refers to a railroad engine as a "snorting teakettle," Pres Dillard warns his colleagues that they should not be "missing the parade." Dillard's ally on the board, Dr. Livingston (Donald Crisp), chimes in that New Orleans must alleviate unsanitary conditions so the community will not face an epidemic like the one that devastated the city in earlier decades.[6] This scene deftly limns the capitalism-versus-agrarianism concerns promoted in late-twentieth-century Genovesian theory.[7] But it also highlights the role played by Dillard, as reflected in work by James Oakes, Sven Beckert, and Edward

Julie Marsden (Bette Davis), accompanied by her beau, Preston Dillard (Henry Fonda), appears at the Olympus Ball in her infamous red dress in *Jezebel*.

Baptist, among others, who emphasize the business aspects of the antebellum South's "peculiar institution."[8]

The film outlines the North-South divide by portraying the South as turning its back on capitalism and modernity, a portrayal over which modern scholars wrangle. Preston Dillard, with a foot in each camp, struggles to reconcile the two. His fiancée's interruption is also a sign of changing times. Her invasion of the all-male preserve signals deeper danger, as Leslie Fishbein suggests: "Julie's rebelliousness threatens not only her relationship with Preston Dillard, but all of polite society and the business structure on which it rests."[9]

Pres's refusal to drop his work to go to the dressmaker triggers a dramatic turn of events, beginning with Julie's selecting a *red* dress to wear to the ball, a flagrant violation of local custom. Over loud objections from her guardian, Aunt Belle (Fay Bainter), Julie proclaims: "This is 1852, dumplin'. Not the Dark Ages. Girls don't have to simp around in white just because they're not married." She shocks her female listeners by making joking references to prostitutes and taking a swipe at their social hypocrisy.

Later that day, Julie and Pres, who brings along a walking stick to reinforce *his* mastery, have a memorable scene in her boudoir. As the two verbally spar, Julie pretends to defer, and he departs with a kiss. Next Julie asks Zette (a young enslaved woman who is dressed in an attractive costume to designate her status as a ladies' maid) to take a note to her former flame, Buck Cantrell (George Brent). The next night Cantrell discovers that Julie, swathed in red, wants *him* to escort her to the dance. He declines, refusing to be lured into her web. Preston appears and demands that she change gowns. Julie taunts him about his manhood, and when the game continues, Preston decides to call her bluff. When they walk into the Olympus Ball, the full force of public disapproval at the sight of her show-stopping red gown causes Julie to lose her nerve.

The scenes at the ball are remarkably effective in etching the stylized hauteur of southern conventions with a Kabuki-like precision. Many viewers forget that the dress's red color is *in our imagination* rather than on the screen, as director William Wyler shot his classic in black and white. The power of this scene is that it literally makes us "see red." "This colorization represents a trauma," suggests Tuhkunen, who further explains, "Bearing in mind the attachment of the classic southern movies to the image of the angel of the house, as well as to the white-red dichotomy, it is unsurprising that the synchronized emergence of the Jezebel and 'scarlet woman' in *Jezebel* and *Gone with the Wind* created such a shock effect."[10]

Among the gentlemen at the ball, small talk about the weather nearly escalates into a duel. As work on southern honor by Kenneth Greenberg, Bertram Wyatt-Brown, and others demonstrates, trivialities could accelerate into life-and-death matters.[11] In the film's most memorable sequence, Julie begs to be taken home, at which point Pres becomes the defiant one and tugs her onto the dance floor. As they begin to waltz, other couples retreat—and the music stops as only the two of them remain in motion. Pres confronts the orchestra and, despite Julie's humiliation, demands that the band play on, pulling his partner back onto the floor.

At the end of the evening, Preston deposits Julie on her doorstep and curtly bids her farewell. When she slaps him, he stiffly repeats, "Bye, Julie," before fading into the night. As Julie disconsolately stares out a window, her aunt urges her to go after him. She vows instead to feign cool indifference, insisting that he'll be back.

The film abruptly jumps forward a year—with "our heroine" still pining for her lost love, who did not return to her. Rather, Pres broke off their engagement and headed North. Meanwhile, Julie has been a shut-in chatelaine. Dr. Livingston suggests that Julie and her aunt retreat to the country because the threat from yellow fever is on the rise. He also tells the two women that Pres is on his way back to New Orleans, and so they plan a joyful homecoming at Halcyon, the family plantation.

Fonda and Davis are magnetic in their Halcyon scenes, particularly in their first encounter upon his return, when a contrite Julie plunges to her knees in a diaphanous white gown to express her apologies and beg Pres's forgiveness. This submissive gauzy posturing conforms to images of white southern womanhood.[12] Pres is visibly shaken, as Julie's rehearsed speech is interrupted by the entrance of a stranger from the North, Amy Bradford (Margaret Lindsay), who is introduced as Pres's new wife. From this moment, the plot spirals out of control, as Julie's calculations—much like those of her beloved South—are altered by Yankee realpolitik.

The final third of the film unfolds with interlocking dramas: Julie schemes to reclaim Pres's heart, both by baiting his new wife, with her northern ways, and by cornering Pres, hoping to rekindle passions. He's quick to dash her hopes and reject her advances, and he soon returns to New Orleans to tend to bank business, leaving Amy behind at Halcyon. Julie plots to create a rivalry between Pres and her longtime admirer Buck Cantrell, prodding the latter to defend her honor. But her plans go awry as it becomes Pres's younger brother, Ted, who takes up the challenge to a duel, in which he shoots and kills Buck. He's quick to blame the tragedy on Julie.

By then a yellow fever epidemic has engulfed New Orleans, and word reaches Halcyon that Preston is among those stricken by it. Distraught, Julie, with a slave as a guide, sneaks through the swamps to cross a tightly enforced quarantine line to get to the city. There she finds Pres half-dead and stations herself by his bedside to nurse him. Later a party from Halcyon that includes Pres's wife, Amy, arrives. When the authorities, as prescribed by law, come to transport Pres to the dreaded Lazarette Island for quarantine, Julie volunteers to accompany him and persuades Amy to let her go. This morality tale ends with a stalwart Julie and a pair of nuns atop a cart loaded with the infected and doomed. This "Jezebel" risks her own life to save her former sweetheart, hoping she can "wash away" her sins and redeem her good name.

The accuracy of this film is not in question, given that the story is fictional.

But since this is historical fiction, the question is how much authenticity is ladled out to engage viewers and carry the story forward. The lead character may be a nineteenth-century belle, but the universality of her struggle—to chafe against bonds that restrict women, to weather romantic storms—still resonates in contemporary times.

As a portrait of a particular time, place, and society, *Jezebel* draws heavily on claims from the Lost Cause. One critic dismissed it as "just too much hanging moss, too many darkies singing spirituals, and as always, too much Max Steiner."[13] This description mixes aesthetic and ideological jabs, which clouds appreciation of the film's layered meanings and wider appeal. Yes, the visually lush sets are exaggerated for effect, which had been a problem for plantation epics from D. W. Griffith's films onward.[14] And yes, the Max Steiner musical score lures the listener into "crescendo conditioning," as the music lulls and swells to cue filmgoers how to respond. (Steiner scored more than three hundred films, including, most famously, *Gone with the Wind,* and became known as "the father of film music.")

As in most "southerns" of the era, slavery is an offscreen affair or pushed to the sidelines. Onscreen black characters are deferential or comic, or both—but never autonomous, or equal. The enslaved characters featured in *Jezebel* are stock figures from the accommodationist playbook, designed to justify white mastery. Owen Davis's play five years earlier had emphasized "Julie's devotion to her servants," and romantic racialism continued as an undercurrent in the screenplay. The film offers familiar stereotypes that require forced joviality and deferential fawning; black characters must enhance or illuminate white lives only.

The audience is introduced to a number of black coachmen, with "comedic" bits inserted to make paternalism more palatable. Within these scenarios, slavery's ills are repudiated. Julie's relationship with her maid Zette is neither intimate nor hostile: Julie feels she can co-opt Zette by promising her one of her fanciest dresses, while Zette remains an enigma.

When Julie first gallops onto the screen, trying to tame a headstrong colt, she barks at the young black attendant—just a boy—trying to handle in her mare. The youngster, Ti Bat, is barely old enough to hold the reins, much less control a horse. Julie orders, "Don't stand there with your eyes bulging out." This caricatured image becomes emblazoned in viewers' minds, as Jezebel loudly commands and blacks struggle to meet her exacting demands. When Pres's bride suggests that *she* accompany her husband into exile, Julie remonstrates: "Do you know the Creole word for fever powder, for food and water? How to talk to an overworked black boy and make him feel he will help you?" From her opening dialogue until her final onscreen exchange, Julie's identity is refracted through scenes of authority and submission, heavily invested in the racial hierarchy and her role in it.

There are moments of genuine kindness and camaraderie on display as well, though curiously, they involve men more than women. At one point when he is offered a mint julep from Julie's African American butler, Uncle Cato, Pres Dillard suggests that they sidestep formalities and have a drink together. This would be in direct violation of slaveholders' rules of decorum, thus Uncle Cato begs off, saying he will take his drink into the kitchen to enjoy later. The ultimate lesson here was, and still is, to reassure that the best servants knew their place and stayed in it.

In the latter scenes at Halcyon, the camera pans black children gathering along the road hollering. "Carriages comin'." Whether in the yard or the parlor, in the kitchen or the boudoir, African Americans were not just plantation decor. Enslaved African Americans were required to "perform" their blackness, heightening southern distinctiveness, as an exotic alternative to the outside world. These moments—set pieces staged for effect—are in some ways authentic: nineteenth-century travelers' accounts reflect this kind of extravagant welcome. Yet saying that something is authentic does not make it "true," as we know that such moments were often staged, but it is part of the white South's sense of self-serving memory, part of its pride of place.

Equally key to the planter South's world-view, Pres's marriage to an outsider triggers anti-Yankee behavior at Julie's dinner table. This hazing does not necessarily win over an audience but might have been subversive, according to one critic who observed that "as it invokes the mythology of the Lost Cause, *Jezebel* criticizes rather than celebrates the South for its devout commitment to the war and its inability to recognize the reality of future defeat at the hands of the better-equipped industrial North."[15] At Halcyon, abolitionists are openly derided. While Preston and Buck spar verbally, Julie enjoys the show, purring like a feline, egging on the men through thinly veiled barbs. At one point Buck Cantrell confides: "I like my convictions undiluted, same as I do my bourbon." Although some of this dialogue may verge on the knife-edge of parody, bombast may have been the rule for white slaveholders creating their own set of facts.

As frustrations multiply during the homecoming gone haywire, Julie decides to join the plantation slaves gathered outside on the porch and works the crowd up into a frenzy of song—which strikes several false notes. The sing-along is intended to symbolize the intimacy of master/mistress and slave, and many a southern uses a black chorus to suggest a harmonious atmosphere. Yet Julie's manner in this scene belies any such harmony. Such interludes allow characters to "perform" whiteness, with blackness served up as a side dish to onlookers. Ironically, Julie leads a chorus of "Raise a Ruckus Tonight," which, unfortunately, hails from the postbellum era.[16] The music consultant erred more than once, as Bette Davis hums "Beautiful Dreamer," a tune that was not penned by Stephen Foster until 1864. While these may be small quibbles, they demonstrate Hollywood producers' indifference to approximating historical accuracy.

Yet every so often these clichéd moments strike a chord. Certainly, the film portrays the influence of the Code Duello within the Old South, with two official challenges featured, one resulting in a wounding, the other in a death. Women's objections to duels and men's indifference to women's objections were commonplace. Gossip recorded over these ritualized encounters was common and could have been lifted out of many an antebellum diary.

The film showcases New Orleans as a cultural *sui generis*, embodying the best and worst of the South simultaneously. One scholar claims that *Jezebel* depicts New Orleans as "the site of a dying culture whose gentility and charm depend upon the preservation of a civilized veneer, now threatened both by the rise of the entrepreneurial North and by its own internal decay."[17] The vivid and wrenching images of this city, particularly under siege from a deadly fever, resonate into the twenty-first century. "The post-Katrina discourse of a perpetually doomed southern city," according to another scholar, "evokes a myth that suggests a pattern in which New Orleans will succumb to tragedy over and over again. . . . And we cannot help but see Katrina as something out of *Jezebel*."[18]

The parallels between *Jezebel*'s urban backdrop and the community wards ravaged by Hurricane Katrina more than a century later create intellectual fodder. As Michael Bibler suggests, "If *Jezebel* eerily prefigures Katrina, it is not because Katrina is an example of history repeating itself. Rather, the film shows us that Katrina's aftermath might be better understood as a tragic realization of the long-standing fiction that has been told about New Orleans."[19] The South and particularly this Mardi Gras capital continue as cultural signifiers, as literary and cinematic touchstones.

Scholars in women's history and film studies appreciate the ways in which these competing narratives underscore issues of gender. Although Yankee women might be highlighted in this drama as progressive, the southern belle elicits begrudging admiration through her embodiment in this particular protagonist: "Julie's shrewdness and cunning, her ability to pry secrets from her slaves, her determination to struggle to survive."[20] And indeed, at film's end the triptych of Bette Davis/Julie/Jezebel glides toward her unknown fate—defying the consuming flames, booming cannons, and pestilence all around her. Davis, like many great actresses, rises above the material and gives her viewers much to discuss while passing the popcorn.

NOTES

1. Ida Jeter, "*Jezebel* and the Emergence of the Hollywood Tradition of a Decadent South," in *The South and Film*, ed. Warren French (Jackson: University Press of Mississippi, 1981), 31.

2. See Deborah Gray White, *Ar'n't I a Woman: Female Slaves in the Plantation South* (New York: Norton, 1985).

3. It was an ending that followed the stifling strictures imposed on filmmakers by the Motion Picture Production Code (known as the Hays Code, introduced in 1930 to create guidelines that censored many writers and directors for decades). The rule was that any deviation from morality, however alluring on screen, must result in disgrace, downfall, ruin, and often death to satisfy gatekeepers.

4. Edward Campbell Jr., *The Celluloid South: Hollywood and the Southern Myth* (Knoxville: University of Tennessee Press, 1981).

5. See Taina Tuhkunen, "Jezebel and Scarlett: When Hollywood Gets Its Hand on Dixieland Icons," [in French], in *Demain sera un autre jour: Le Sud et ses heroines a l'ecran* [Tomorrow is another day: The South and its heroines on screen] (Pertuis, France: Rouge Profond, 2013), 103.

6. See Jo Ann Carrigan, *The Saffron Scourge: A History of Yellow Fever in Louisiana, 1796–1905* (Lafayette: University of Louisiana at Lafayette Press, 2015); and Benjamin Trask, *Fearful Ravages: Yellow Fever in New Orleans, 1796–1905* (Lafayette: University of Louisiana at Lafayette Press, 2005).

7. See Eugene Genovese, *The World the Slaveholders Made: Two Essays in Interpretation* (New York: Pantheon, 1969).

8. See James Oakes, *The Ruling Race: A History of American Slaveholders* (New York: Norton, 1982); Sven Beckert, *Empire of Cotton: A Global History* (New York: Knopf, 2014); and Edward E. Baptist, *The Half Has Never Been Told: Slavery and the Making of American Capitalism* (New York: Basic Books, 2014).

9. Leslie Fishbein, "Women on the Fringe: A Film Series," *Film & History: An Interdisciplinary Journal of Film and Television Studies* 8, no. 3 (September 1978): 34.

10. Tuhkunen, *Demain sera un autre jour*, 127.

11. See Kenneth Greenberg, *Honor and Slavery: Lies, Duels, Noses, Masks, Dressing as a Woman, Gifts, Strangers, Humanitarianism, Death, Slave Rebellions, the Proslavery Argument, Baseball, Hunting, and Gambling in the Old South* (Princeton, NJ: Princeton University Press, 1998); and Bertram Wyatt-Brown, *Southern Honor: Ethics and Behavior in the Old South* (New

York: Oxford University Press, 1982). See also Joanne Freeman, *Affairs of Honor: National Politics in the New Republic* (New Haven, CT: Yale University Press, 2002).

12. See Catherine Clinton, *The Plantation Mistress: Woman's World in the Old South* (New York: Pantheon, 1982); and Clinton, *Tara Revisited: Women, War, and the Plantation Legend* (New York: Abbeville, 1995). See also Laura F. Edwards, *Scarlett Doesn't Live Here Anymore: Southern Women in the Civil War Era* (Urbana: University of Illinois Press, 2000); Sally McMillen, *Southern Women: Black and White in the Old South* (New York: Oxford University Press, 1991); Anya Jabour, *Scarlett's Sisters: Young Women in the Old South* (Chapel Hill: University of North Carolina Press, 2007); and Elizabeth Fox-Genovese, *Within the Plantation Household: Black and White Women in the Old South* (Chapel Hill: University of North Carolina Press, 1988).

13. Gary Carey, "The Lady & The Director: Bette Davis & William Wyler," *Film Comment* 6, no. 3 (Fall 1970): 21.

14. I suggest in *The Plantation Mistress* that ironically, *Mandingo* was one of the first southerns to visually demonstrate the gulf between the lavish town homes planters enjoyed and the more rough-hewn country estates, which were working plantations. Most southerns, taking their cue from *Gone with the Wind,* paint the country estates of the antebellum planters with lavish grandeur. Although parts of Quentin Tarantino's *Django Unchained* reflect some semblance of reality rather than a stylized hype, his film is more "un"-scientific fiction than authentic, and perhaps his plantation architecture is a nod to his faithful rerendering of scenes from *Mandingo,* to which he pays lavish homage. More accurate images of a working plantation rarely make it onto the large screen, although Steve McQueen's *12 Years a Slave* presented important alternatives with the slapdash squalor of Edwin Epps's home and with the images from an adjacent plantation, where Patsy takes tea with Harriet Shaw, its chatelaine.

15. Michael P. Bibler, "Always the Tragic Jezebel: New Orleans, Katrina, and the Layered Discourse of a Doomed Southern City," *Southern Cultures* 14, no. 2 (Summer 2008): 12.

16. One songbook—*The Liberated Woman's Songbook,* by Larry Silverman (New York: Collier Macmillan, 1972), 122–23—credits the following lyrics:

My old master promised me, That when he died he'd set me free, He lived so long his head got bald, He got out the notion of dyin' at all, (CHORUS:) Come along, little children, come along, Come while the moon is shining bright. Get on board, little children, get on board, We're gonna raise a ruckus tonight.

A second verse suggests that the mistress has promised to set "Sarah" free, but then the last verse takes a dark turn:

Yes, they both done promised me, But their promise didn't set me free, A dose of pizin helped them along, May the Devil preach their funeral song,

Selecting this particular "Negro folk song," with a verse implying that the enslaved might poison their owners to gain freedom, seems a fairly avoidable mistake.

17. Fishbein, "Women on the Fringe," 34.

18. Bibler, "Always the Tragic Jezebel," 7.

19. Bibler, "Always the Tragic Jezebel," 8.

20. Fishbein, "Women on the Fringe," 34.

SECTIONAL CRISIS
AND CIVIL WAR

12

From "Bleeding Kansas" to Harpers Ferry
via *Santa Fe Trail*

NICOLE ETCHESON

Santa Fe Trail is part western, part Civil War epic, and part love story, with occasional appearances by the railroad also bearing the name Santa Fe. This 1940 hodgepodge resulted from Warner Brothers' desire to exploit their star Errol Flynn's recent success in westerns, the box-office triumph of *Gone with the Wind*, and the Santa Fe Railroad's willingness to fund some of the movie's costs in return for the publicity.[1]

Upon graduating from West Point in 1854, J. E. B. Stuart (Flynn) and George Custer (Ronald Reagan) are assigned to the "suicide station" Fort Leavenworth, Kansas. The posting is dangerous because of the fighting in Kansas between abolitionists and proslavers. The newly fledged officers travel by railroad to the "blood-soaked ground" of Kansas Territory. A confrontation ensues when Oliver Brown (Alan Baxter), son of John Brown (Raymond Massey), "leader of the Abolitionists, whose bloody raids are terrorizing Kansas," tries to smuggle a family of slaves to free soil. Caught on the train, Oliver jumps off and rejoins his father's band. John Brown, spouting the "law of God," reprimands Oliver for abandoning the slaves. Posing as a minister, the elder Brown leads his band to collect crates of Bibles from freighters for whom Stuart and Custer are providing a protective escort. A crate breaks open and the contents are shown to be rifles, not Bibles, setting off a gun battle. Another of Brown's sons, Jason (Gene Reynolds), depicted here as half his actual age in 1854, is captured, although the real Jason Brown was never involved in his father's guerrilla activity. Wounded and agonizing over his father's use of violence, young Jason reveals that his father is at the house of Shubel Morgan in Palmyra. En route to the town, Stuart finds that Brown has burned out the settlers at Delaware Crossing in retaliation for Jason's death.

Stuart is captured scouting Palmyra, but Custer and the cavalry rescue him. A large group of African Americans have gathered at Morgan's farm. With the cavalry coming, Brown announces he will leave them. If the viewer didn't get the point that abolitionists are fickle allies, as evinced by Oliver's desertion, it is driven home by his father's willingness to abandon the people he addresses as "my children." At least John Brown has the grace to say good-bye before he sends them away to "fend for themselves as other free men do."

Oliver Brown is killed in the big battle scene that ensues when the cavalry arrives, although the real Oliver Brown died at Harpers Ferry. After the fight, Stuart predicts that Brown's force is broken forever, but Custer prophetically disagrees. Indeed, Brown is shown asking what he has done to displease the Almighty and vowing to continue wreaking God's vengeance. But a title card appears informing the viewer that Bleeding Kansas is over, as men lay railroad track. Stuart and Custer return to Fort Leavenworth, where both have been pursuing Kit Carson Holliday (Olivia de Havilland), the sister of a West Point classmate whom they met at graduation.[2]

Brown resurfaces, presenting his plan to capture the federal arsenal at Harpers Ferry to eastern supporters, led by Dr. J. Boyce Russell, a fictionalized Henry Ward Beecher. With the weapons from the arsenal, Brown will lead an army through the South, sparking a mass slave insurrection. Although the men protest that this will lead to civil war, they agree to fund the plan. At Brown's headquarters, depicted as a tent camp rather than the actual Maryland farmhouse, Brown's military expert, a fictional character named Carl Rader (Van Heflin), is unhappy about not being paid. Rader, who had attended West Point with Stuart and Custer, finds Stuart at a Washington, DC, ball and tells him of Brown's plan. Rader agrees to return to Brown and accompany the raid while Stuart, Custer, Robert E. Lee, and Jefferson Davis plan the response.

Brown and his men take hostages and occupy the arsenal's engine house, but the townspeople surround it. Brown sends out a hostage with a white flag but shoots him in the back when he tries to escape. When the cavalry arrives, Lee orders Stuart to offer Brown a chance to surrender. Brown refuses, whereupon Stuart waves his hat as a signal to open the attack. During the climactic battle scene, Brown shoots Rader for betraying him. After several assaults, the soldiers finally break into the engine house, and Stuart captures Brown.

All of *Santa Fe Trail*'s main characters, including John Brown (Raymond Massey), arrayed beneath a tagline promising action and death

In the penultimate sequence, Brown is hanged with all the major characters improbably present. John Brown makes a moving gallows speech, but Robert E. Lee gets the last word after Brown swings: "So perish all such enemies of the Union, all such foes of the human race." The finale abruptly shifts from Brown's execution to a resolution of the love triangle: Kit and Stuart are married on board a train car heading into the sunset. If the scene's music, "John Brown's Body," compromises the wedding's happy ending, it at least allows for a closing shot of the railroad.

So pervasive and egregious are the film's historical errors that before filming even started, the West Point historian protested "gross historical inaccuracies" in the script.[3] Custer graduated from West Point several years after Stuart, but in the film, as actor Raymond Massey wrote, "almost every general in the Confederate and Union armies seems to have graduated from West Point in the same class."[4] Kansas Territory was two years away from bleeding, and in any case, Stuart wasn't assigned to Kansas until 1855, and he would spend most of his time there fighting Indians. Stuart was a bystander when the army disbanded Brown's guerrillas and freed their prisoners after the Battle of Black Jack. That encounter did allow Stuart to identify Brown at Harpers Ferry three years later.[5]

The movie's Palmyra seems to be a combination of the New England settlement of Lawrence and the site of the Black Jack battle. Palmyra, which was just a stop on the Santa Fe Trail in the 1850s, is portrayed as a bustling settlement and a destination for runaway slaves. Lawrence was home to the territory's abolitionist community, but Black Jack was fought in open terrain, near the real Palmyra or Baldwin City. Brown's son Frederick, only mentioned in *Santa Fe Trail*, helped capture proslavery guerrillas at Black Jack. The army showed up a couple of days later and freed those prisoners. Shubel Morgan was not an actual person but one of John Brown's many aliases.[6]

Stuart was at the War Department when news arrived of the seizure of the federal arsenal at Harpers Ferry. It is true that Brown's military aide, the English mercenary Hugh Forbes, wrote to Secretary of War John B. Floyd warning of the plot, but Floyd did not take the warning seriously, and unlike in the movie, federal officials were taken by surprise. But unlike Rader, Forbes had the good sense not to go to Harpers Ferry. The movie captures well the atmosphere of hysteria that surrounded news of the raid, although it wildly exaggerates Brown's numbers. No hostages died, and the movie completely ignores the local defenders' savage treatment of captured raiders, the desecration of their bodies, and the presence of African Americans among Brown's band.[7]

Stuart served as an aide to Robert E. Lee, who was in Virginia settling his father-in-law's estate when he was given command of a detachment of Marines there. In Harpers Ferry, Stuart took Lee's offer of surrender to Brown at the engine house and signaled the Marines to attack. While the real Brown tried to negotiate, Raymond Massey's Brown flatly refuses, saying, "We prefer to die here." Ronald Reagan as Custer leads a cavalry charge, complete with troopers on horseback vaulting rail fences. There are even cannon blasting the engine house, which is portrayed as a large fort, built to be defended by riflemen and surrounded by stone walls. The real terrain at Harpers Ferry is far less open, the engine house smaller, and the Marines charged on foot without artillery support and with bayonets in order to avoid accidentally shooting Brown's white and black hostages. The movie's original battle scenario had Flynn as Stuart on the sidelines, but the director, Michael Curtiz, having decided it was a waste not to use the hero, incorporated shots of Flynn shouting orders and seeming to lead the final assault. Lieutenant Israel Green of the Marines not only led the attack but captured Brown.[8]

Stuart did enter the engine house after Green had subdued Brown. He took the still unconscious Brown's bowie knife as a souvenir and identified him. Stuart was not present at Brown's hanging, as he had returned to duty in Kansas. During the secession winter of 1860–61, Stuart positioned himself for either promotion in the United States Army or a place in the new Confederate army. He received both and chose the latter.[9]

Not only is the movie "preposterous as history," to quote the critic Ten Sennett, but it also has nothing to do with the Santa Fe Trail—the freighting route from Independence, Missouri, to Santa Fe, New Mexico—or the railroad. The critic Bosley Crowther's 1940 review was aptly titled "'Santa Fe Trail,' Which Is Chiefly a Picture about Something Else." Migrants to Kansas Territory traversed Missouri not by rail but by river steamboat; indeed, it was not until 1868 that construction began on the Atchison, Topeka, and Santa Fe Railroad.[10] The Underground Railroad was, of course, a figure of speech, not a literal means of transportation. Most of Kansas's northern settlers were not abolitionists but midwestern farmers who only resented proslavery interference in the territory more than they disliked African Americans. The Free Staters did import weapons in crates marked "Bibles," but there were no shoot-outs with the army. In fact, the Free Staters scrupulously avoided armed conflict with the military, knowing that it was the surest way to bring the full force of the federal government down on their movement.

Then there is the casting. Raymond Massey captured well the image of John Brown as the "fanatic, religious zealot." Wearing the beard Brown did not grow until after he left Kansas, Massey may have been made up with reference to the John Steuart Curry mural, in which Brown's outstretched arms encompass the coming Civil War. Although some suggest that Brown had a diagnosable personality disorder, historians today are quick to point out that what seemed like madness in the nineteenth century may have been Brown's lack of racism and passionate desire to end slavery. J. E. B. Stuart's image as the dashing cavalier fits well with the casting of Errol Flynn, but Stuart's West Point nickname, "Beauty," was actually a joke about his lack of physical attractiveness. Stuart, in fact, was a teetotaler who carried a prayer book, while the handsome Flynn was debauched even by Hollywood standards. A couple of years later, in *They Died with Their Boots On*, Flynn would be considered a good fit for George Armstrong Custer because Custer actually was a dashing figure—a gambler and a womanizer—who was constantly in trouble at West Point. But in *Santa Fe Trail* the genial Reagan plays Custer as faithful sidekick to Flynn's Stuart. Although Reagan portrays him as sympathetic to the antislavery movement, Custer was a doughface, a northern man who defended southern slavery, and he was also far too young to have participated in any of these events. As she did in many films, Olivia de Havilland as Kit Carson Holliday plays Flynn's love interest. Cyrus Holliday was indeed the founder of the Atchison, Topeka, and Santa Fe Railroad, and he did have a daughter, but there's no evidence Holliday or his daughter ever met Stuart, let alone Custer. Even the locations are obviously wrong. The Kansas and Harpers Ferry sequences were shot near Los Angeles, where the desert scrub resembles western Virginia even less than it does Kansas.[11]

Even worse than the consistent factual errors is the historical distortion. The kindest thing that can be said of *Santa Fe Trail* is that it doesn't assert states' rights as the cause of the Civil War, but Hollywood's prosouthern bias is on full display, along with a nationalism motivated by the looming war in Europe. The result is a film that condemns abolitionism and emphasizes sectional harmony. When Reagan's Custer asserts, "There's a purpose behind [Brown's] madness. One that can't easily be dismissed," Stuart does dismiss it, saying that it's not their job to decide the morality of slavery. Later Stuart tells Kit that "the South can settle her own problems without loss of pride of being forced into it by a bunch of fanatics." In a confrontation with Brown, Stuart insists that Virginians know slavery is a "moral wrong" and only need time before they, along with the rest of the South, abolish it. Kit tells the wounded Jason Brown that his father's cause may be just—even "great and good"—but his methods are "wrong—terribly wrong." Slavery is the cause, but the abolitionists, not the slaveowners, are at fault for starting the war. It is jarring to see Jefferson Davis and Robert E. Lee presented as stalwarts of the Union. In his commencement address at West Point Davis lectures the graduating cadets on their responsibility to their government and the need for "unity of spirit."[12]

Repeatedly, it is Massey's Brown who embraces destroying the Union. The film commentator Marc Eliot even says that Brown was portrayed so as to call to mind "Hitler's evil, murderous charisma." Rader and Brown's propaganda and conspiracy further heighten the comparison to the Nazis. Robert E. Morsberger notes that Rader hates not so much slavery as the slaveowning aristocracy and that, in the era of the House Un-American Activities Committee his lines about wiping wealthy southerners off the earth may have resonated as left-wing class warfare.[13] Massey's Brown is given some fine lines referring to slavery as "a dark and evil curse laying all over this land" and "a carnal sin against God that can only be wiped out in blood," lines that not only sound like the real John Brown but capture the abolitionist sense of slavery as the United States' original sin. But the actual slaves play a small role, continuing a Hollywood tradition that has persisted to the era of *Lincoln* and *Free State of Jones,* in which a white savior is needed to free the slaves.[14]

Santa Fe Trail might be dismissed as simple Lost Cause propaganda if not for the ambivalent portrayal of John Brown. Not even Flynn's Jeb Stuart disputes the justice of Brown's cause; he merely insists that Brown's agitation is unnecessary to achieve abolition. Director Curtiz echoes Henry David Thoreau's depiction of Brown as a Christ figure in the execution scene, which the film historian Robert Matzen described as "reminiscent of every crucifixion-of-Christ picture ever made."[15] After exchanging a few remarks with the sheriff, whom Brown asked not to keep him waiting, John Brown said nothing more at his hanging. But the scriptwriter Robert Buckner gives Brown a speech from the gallows. The first, and invented, portion is replete with Calvinist sentiments: "I am only walking as God foreordained I should walk. All my actions, even the follies leading to this disaster, were decreed to happen long ages before this world began." Then Massey intones the words that Brown handed his jailer on a slip of paper as he was taken away for his execution: "I John Brown, am now quite certain that the crimes of this *guilty land* can never be purged away but with Blood." Instead, of completing Brown's text, however, Massey says, "Aye, let them hang me. I forgive them and may God forgive them for they know not what they do," evoking Christ's words from the Cross.[16]

Like the abolitionists, slaves are treated ambivalently. A settler identifies the black family on the train as "the trouble: Negro Slaves." This is a view that Frederick Douglass once deplored when he complained that Abraham Lincoln "strangely" told blacks they were the cause of the Civil War.[17] Rader is given powerful lines about slavery's cruelty, stating that southerners know how to handle horses as they do their slaves—"with a strap across their back." This admission of slavery's violence is compromised because it is the northerner, Rader, who equates human beings with beasts and whose violence to animals is contrasted with Stuart's gentleness.

In addition to the black family on the train and a butler at the military ball, there are numerous African Americans on Shubel Morgan's farm. Film critics have seen them as "childish dupes" of Brown, but they hauntingly sing "No More Auction Block for Me" and ask questions about freedom's meaning that echo Civil War–era debates about freedmen's rights. After the fight, a black woman binds up Stuart's wounded arm. He calls her "mammy," and she fits the stereotype, stout and speaking in dialect. She left home because "Old John Brown said he's going to give us freedom but shuck'ins, if this here Kansas is freedom than I ain't got no use for it, no sir." Her husband agrees that he'd just as soon go back to Texas. (Most self-liberated slaves in the territory came from Missouri, not from faraway Texas.) They are Hollywood's "happy darkies," or they would be if only they hadn't fallen into the abolitionists' clutches.[18] In case the viewer has failed to understand who truly cares for African Americans, one of the liberated slaves says of the Virginian Stuart, "That white man talk like he's a friend."

It is not just the African American characters who are caricatures. The movie leaves most of the emotional "work" of the Civil War to Olivia de Havilland's Kit. Although Kit is a tomboy, she dons petticoats when she's needed to nurse Jason Brown or bemoan the bloodshed.[19] Back in Kansas, she laments that Americans are trying to decide slavery "by words in the east and by guns in the west." She foretells the Civil War by translating the prophecies of an Indian woman, who predicts that the army friends will one day be not only "great in battle" but "bitter enemies" and that the war has already started in the East, foreshadowing the film's next segment at Harpers Ferry. (To resolve the love triangle, the Indian woman helpfully predicts that Custer will fall in love with a blonde, rather than the brunette Kit, whereupon Kit promptly introduces

Custer to a pretty blonde who happens to be Jefferson Davis's daughter!) At Brown's execution, Kit denies that she's crying for the condemned man: "I see something else up there; something much more terrible than just one man."[20]

As Marc Eliot wrote, the grafting of the John Brown saga onto what was originally intended as a western resulted in a film that "made no historical sense."[21] This did not stop *Santa Fe Trail* from being a box-office success, "a celluloid epic" according to *Variety*. Critics and historians carped about the historical inaccuracies, but the audience no doubt enjoyed the dashing cavalry battles as well as the romantic sparring between Flynn and Reagan over de Havilland. The portrayal of slavery and African Americans fit longstanding literary, historical, and cinematic stereotypes, while Massey's blood-and-thunder portrayal of Brown cemented the image of the abolitionist as puritan fanatic. In a powerful critique, Oswald Garrison Villard called the movie a "travesty of history" with a "distinctly pro-slavery" slant.[22] He was right.

NOTES

1. Peggy A. Russo, "John Brown Goes to Hollywood: *Santa Fe Trail* and *Seven Angry Men*," in *Terrible Swift Sword: The Legacy of John Brown*, ed. Russo and Paul Finkelman (Athens: Ohio University Press, 2005), 190–212, esp. 198; Robert Matzen, *Errol & Olivia: Ego & Obsession in Golden Era Hollywood* (Pittsburgh: GoodKnight, 2010), 136–37.

2. A number of film historians have identified De Havilland's character as named Halliday, but the name in the credits is Holliday.

3. Matzen, *Errol & Olivia*, 137.

4. T. J. Stiles, *Custer's Trials: A Life on the Frontier of a New America* (New York: Knopf, 2015), 4; Raymond Massey, *A Hundred Different Lives* (Boston: Little, Brown, 1979), 262. In the movie, Stuart and Custer graduate with James Longstreet, George Pickett, John Bell Hood, and Phillip Sheridan. Matzen, *Errol & Olivia*, 137.

5. Emory M. Thomas, *Bold Dragoon: The Life of J. E. B. Stuart* (New York: Vintage, 1986), 46–47. For a history of the Civil War in Kansas, see Nicole Etcheson, *Bleeding Kansas: Contested Liberty in the Civil War Era* (Lawrence: University Press of Kansas, 2004).

6. Etcheson, *Bleeding Kansas*, 40, 64–65; Terry Beckenbaugh, "Battle of Black Jack," Civil War on the Western Border, accessed January 2017, http://www.civilwaronthewesternborder.org/encyclopedia/battle-black-jack.

7. See Stephen B. Oates, *To Purge This Land with Blood: A Biography of John Brown* (New York: Harper & Row, 1970), 200–201; and Robert E. Morsberger, "Slavery and *The Santa Fe Trail*, or John Brown on Hollywood's Sour Apple Tree," *American Studies* 18 (Fall 1977): 87–98, esp. 95.

8. Thomas, *Bold Dragoon*, 54–57; Morsberger, "Slavery and *The Santa Fe Trail*," 95; Matzen, *Errol & Olivia*, 141; Robert E. McGlone, *John Brown's War against Slavery* (Cambridge: Cambridge University Press, 2009), 282, 289, 298–99.

9. Thomas, *Bold Dragoon*, 58–59, 65–67.

10. Ted Sennett, *Warner Brothers Presents: The Most Exciting Years—from "The Jazz Singer" to "White Heat"* (New Rochelle, NY: Arlington House, 1971), 168; Keith L. Bryant Jr., *History of the Atchison, Topeka and Santa Fe Railway* (New York: Macmillan, 1974), 3–4, 7–8, 15; Bosley Crowther, "'Santa Fe Trail,' Which Is Chiefly a Picture about Something Else, Opens at the Strand," *New York Times*, 21 December 1940, http://www.nytimes.com/movie/review?res=9B04E2DD173BE03ABC4951DFB467838B659EDE&pagewanted=print; Matzen, *Errol & Olivia*, 136, 147.

11. "Santa Fe Trail," *Variety*, 18 December 1940; Thomas, *Bold Dragoon*, 3, 18, 41–42, 53; Thomas McNulty, *Errol Flynn: The Life and Career* (Jefferson, NC: McFarland, 2004), 109, 122; Stiles, *Custer's Trials*, xvi, 20–22; Craig Miner, *Kansas: The History of the Sunflower State, 1854–2000* (Lawrence: University Press of Kansas, 2002), 97–99; Matzen, *Errol & Olivia*, 141. See also Merrill D. Peterson, *John Brown: The Legend Revisited* (Charlottesville: University of Virginia Press, 2002), 113–14; Sennett, *Warner Brothers Presents*, 168, 171; Russo, "John Brown Goes to Hollywood," 193. For Brown's religion, see Louis A. DeCaro, *Fire from the Midst of You: A Religious Life of John Brown* (New York: New York University Press, 2002). On Brown's psyche, see Kenneth R. Carroll, "A Psychological Examination of John Brown," in Russo and Finkelman, *Terrible Swift Sword*, 118–37; and Oates, *To Purge This Land with Blood*, 329–34. For a discussion of differing interpretations of Brown, see David S. Reynolds, *John Brown, Abolitionist: The Man Who Killed Slavery, Sparked the Civil War, and Seeded Civil Rights* (New York: Knopf, 2005), 7–8. John Wayne turned down the part of Custer because he didn't like Flynn. Marc Eliot, *Reagan: The Hollywood Years* (New York: Harmony Books, 2008), 118. For an excellent description of how badly Harpers Ferry was depicted, see Oswald Garrison Villard, "History and the Movies," *Saturday Review of Literature*, 1 March 1941, 9.

12. See Edward D. C. Campbell Jr., *The Celluloid South: Hollywood and the Southern Myth* (Knoxville: University of Tennessee Press, 1981); Stephen Vaughn, *Ronald Reagan in Hollywood: Movies and Politics* (New York: Cambridge University Press, 1994), 57, 81, 87–91; and Larry J. Easley, "The Santa Fe Trail, John Brown, and the Coming of the Civil War," *Film and History* 13, no. 2 (1983): 25–33, esp. 28.

13. Eliot, *Reagan*, 118. See also Vaughn, *Ronald Reagan*, 87–91; Russo, "John Brown Goes to Hollywood," 192; and Morsberger, "Slavery and *The Santa Fe Trail*," 90.

14. *Lincoln*, dir. Steven Spielberg (2012); *Free State of Jones*, dir. Gary Ross (2016); Charles M. Blow, "White Savior, Rape or Romance?," *New York Times*, 27 June 2016, https://www.nytimes.com/2016/06/27/opinion/white-savior-rape-and-romance.html?_r=0.

15. Matzen, *Errol & Olivia*, 141–42. See Henry David Thoreau, "A Plea for Captain John Brown," in *Meteor of War: The John Brown Story*, ed. Zoe Trodd and John Stauffer (Maplecrest, NY: Brandywine, 2004), 225–32.

16. Oates, *To Purge This Land with Blood*, 351–52. Brown had to wait several minutes while the troops present took their places. Luke 23:34.

17. Frederick Douglass, "Oration Delivered on the Occasion of the Unveiling of the Freedmen's Monument in Memory of Abraham Lincoln," accessed February 2017, https://memory.loc.gov/cgi-bin/query/r?ammem/murray:@field(DOCID+@lit(lcrbmrptoc12divo)).

18. Vaughn, *Ronald Reagan*, 87–91; Pauline Kael, quoted in *The Blue and the Gray on the Silver Screen: More Than Eighty Years of Civil War Movies*, by Roy Kinnard (Secaucus, NJ: Carol, 1996), 81; Campbell, *Celluloid South*, 13; Easley, "*Santa Fe Trail*," 80.

19. Martha Tomhave Blauvelt, *The Work of the Heart: Young Women and Emotion, 1780–1830* (Charlottesville: University of Virginia Press, 2007), 3–9; Judith M. Kass, *Olivia de Havilland* (New York: Pyramid, 1976), 36–37.

20. Matzen, *Errol & Olivia*, 141–42. Matzen amusingly comments that the assembled cast— Flynn, De Havilland, and Reagan—were "struggling for the motivations about what they are witnessing" in this scene. The actors "stand there like uncomfortable waxwork figures, relying on a Hungarian [director Curtiz] to figure it all out for them." Flynn, in particular, hated having so small a part in so important a scene.

21. Eliot, *Reagan*, 121.

22. Campbell, *Celluloid South*; Villard, "History and the Movies."

13

Abraham Lincoln on Film

MICHAEL BURLINGAME

Among several screen depictions of Abraham Lincoln, three stand out: John Ford's *Young Mr. Lincoln* (1939), Robert E. Sherwood's *Abe Lincoln in Illinois* (1940), and Steven Spielberg's *Lincoln* (2012).

Young Mr. Lincoln, starring Henry Fonda and based on a script by Lamar Trotti, "has come to be regarded by many as one of the greatest Lincoln portrayals of all time," according to one authority on cinematic representations of the sixteenth president.[1] Trotti was nominated for an Oscar, and Fonda won second place for best actor in the New York Film Critics Circle awards. In 1945 the eminent Russian director Sergei Eisenstein said of it: "Of all American films made up to now, this is the film that I would wish, most of all, to have made," for it had "an astonishing harmony of all its component parts, a really amazing harmony as a whole."[2]

The movie focuses on an imaginary courtroom drama loosely based on the legendary 1858 "Almanac Trial" in Springfield, in which Lincoln defended an accused murderer, Duff Armstrong, son of good friends from his New Salem days. (The film transposes this episode to make it one of the earliest of his legal career and sets it in New Salem.) Lincoln saved the lad by successfully impeaching the testimony of the prosecution's star witness, who claimed that bright moonlight had enabled him to observe the nighttime murder. Using an almanac, Lincoln showed that the moon had been so low in the sky at the time of the murder that the witness could not have seen what transpired.

In the movie's opening scene at New Salem, the twenty-two-year-old Lincoln campaigns for the legislature with an "aw, shucks" speech, based on a plausible, documented account of his remarks that suggests he ran a simple campaign. In fact, he launched his candidacy with a careful, detailed appeal

Henry Fonda as Lincoln in *Young Mr. Lincoln*

that ran in a local newspaper. A family named Clay purchases goods at the store where Lincoln works by offering to pay with a copy of Blackstone's *Commentaries on the Laws of England*, which Lincoln accepts in lieu of cash. (He actually bought the book at an auction.) As he eagerly peruses that dry tome, an attractive young woman, Ann Rutledge, encounters him. She flirts, praising his intelligence and ambition; he modestly demurs, protesting (accurately) that he had less than twelve months' formal schooling. After she points out that he has educated himself (which he did), he indirectly declares that he loves her. In fact, Lincoln did fall in love with Ann Rutledge and evidently became engaged to her, but she died before they could wed. Historians long dismissed the story of Ann Rutledge as a myth, but recent scholars have concluded that it actually took place.[3]

In the following scene, Lincoln places flowers on Ann's grave and says that he may become a lawyer, though he has his doubts. From the grave she seems to urge him on. In fact, by then he had been studying law for some time. Lincoln was far more distraught by the death of Ann than the film indicates, so much so that his friends feared he might kill himself.

While the opening sequence in New Salem depicts that village romantically, deemphasizing its crudeness, the next scene, set in Springfield, shows the rough side of frontier life when Lincoln deals with his first law case, *Hawthorn v. Woolridge*. When the two belligerent parties to the suit, who had fought bloodily, engage in fierce mutual recriminations, Lincoln calms them down and gets them to resolve their differences with a compromise. In reality, this was his first case, and he may well have sought such an outcome, having often urged fellow attorneys to "discourage litigation" and "persuade your neighbors to compromise whenever you can."[4]

In the next scene—a July Fourth celebration—Mary Todd (Marjorie Weaver) makes her first appearance, accurately portrayed as a flirt. She tells Lincoln that she has heard good things about him, especially as a member of the state legislature. He says (inaccurately) that he no longer serves in that body. Lincoln participates in a rail-splitting competition, which realistically depicts how wedges and a maul were used. (He had split many rails, honestly earning his later political sobriquet, "the Railsplitter.")

That night, while Springfielders celebrate, outside town a deputy sheriff is killed while fighting two sons of the Clay family. Darkness makes it difficult to see the struggle clearly. Well-liquored townsmen, impulsively concluding that the Clay lads are guilty, charge the jail where they are held in order to lynch them. Lincoln intervenes and condemns mob violence, which was widespread in the 1830s. (His first major speech in Springfield was on that subject.) He persuades the mob to disperse by quoting a biblical verse extolling mercy. (He knew the Bible quite well and often quoted from it. Moreover, he was famously merciful.) While this confrontation is fictional, during the 1832 Black Hawk War Lincoln did prevent a lynching when an Indian entered his regiment's camp with a safe-conduct pass.

Mary Todd again takes the initiative, inviting Lincoln to a party. There he modestly calls himself a "jack-leg lawyer" (in fact he said he was a "mast-fed lawyer"), tells amusing stories to men while the music plays (which he often did at such events), and accepts her invitation to dance, which he does badly (as in real life). He is unresponsive to her advances. (She was the aggressor in their courtship, for he was quite passive around women.)

Lincoln visits the Clay family and is especially kind to the matriarch (Alice Brady), who reminds him of his own mother. (She in fact resembles Mrs. Armstrong, who had been a surrogate mother to Lincoln in New Salem.) He agrees to defend her sons even though he is relatively inexperienced. (When Lincoln took on Duff Armstrong as a client, he had been practicing law for more than twenty years.) During his visit he is helpful, chopping wood, reading and writing letters, just the sort of things he did for many others in New Salem.

The film then becomes a courtroom drama. During jury selection, Lincoln tells a few jokes (accurate) and delivers an impassioned defense of frontier women. (Lincoln was something of a protofeminist; during the Civil War he paid handsome tribute to the women of the North.) At the film's climax he uses an almanac (as he had done in the Duff Armstrong trial) to prove that the key prosecution witness could not have seen the murder.

Since the film's plot is largely fictional and narrowly focused, it reveals little about Lincoln's political career or his personal life but much about his character, accurately portraying Lincoln's positive qualities. He appears to be a folksy, self-deprecating, likeable, humorous, good-natured, courageous young man and an able lawyer. But as Mark Reinhart contends, the portrait is excessively idealized: "*Young Mr. Lincoln* presents Lincoln as a mythical hero, not so much a man as he is a larger-than-life symbol of the American spirit. . . . While this makes for fine, stirring drama, it paints a misleading portrait of what Abraham Lincoln was really like in life."[5] In his twenties and thirties, Lincoln cruelly employed sarcasm, ridicule, and demagoguery to attack opponents.[6] This uglier side of the young Lincoln is missing from the film.

The director John Ford loved Americana, and in *Young Mr. Lincoln* he not only served up only a heaping dish of patriotism (with a Norman Rockwell–like Fourth of July celebration) but also explored a darker side of life in frontier America (with a lynch mob storming a jail). The 1939 movie seems dated and remote from the concerns of modern audiences.

That is not true of a movie released the following year, *Abe Lincoln in Illinois*, starring Raymond Massey, directed by John Cromwell, and based on Robert E. Sherwood's 1938 play of the same name. At that time, Europe trembled on the brink of a war pitting Hitler against the democracies. Massey, who had played the role on stage, told an interviewer:

> There really isn't such a great difference between Lincoln's fight and ours. In Lincoln's time the specific issue was slavery. Today it has taken a different form. But if you substitute the word dictatorship for the word slavery throughout Sherwood's script, it becomes electric with meaning for our own time. Try it on his answer to Douglas in which he scores the policy of "indifference to evil" and the fellows who hold that "there is no right principle for action but self-interest."

That was old Abe talking and he was saying it just as much to our own time as he was to the world of the Eighteen Sixties.[7]

According to Sherwood, his play was "the story of a man of peace who had to face the issue of appeasement or war."[8] The playwright wrote to a relative that Lincoln represented "all the contrasted qualities of the human race—the hopes and fears, the doubts and convictions, the moral frailty and superhuman endurance, the prescience and neuroses, the desire to escape from reality, and the fundamental, unshakeable nobility. . . . He was a living American and in his living words are the answers . . . to all the questions that distract the world today."[9] As the historian Bruce Chadwick has noted, "The subliminal message of the film was that Lincoln, and the horrific Civil War, *did* end the evil of slavery. Now . . . another war was needed to stop a second evil, Nazism."[10] In the early twenty-first century, when democracies are under attack from antidemocratic Islamic jihadists, the movie's underlying message seems more relevant than ever.

In the introduction to the published version of his play, Sherwood wrote: "The playwright's chief stock in trade is feelings, not facts. . . . He has been granted . . . considerable poetic license to distort and embellish the truth; and he generally takes advantage of far more license than he has been granted."[11] The film does indeed take liberties with the truth, portraying Lincoln as a fundamentally passive man who needed his wife, Mary Todd (Ruth Gordon), to instill ambition, and needed his law partner, William H. Herndon, to goad him into opposing slavery. In fact, Lincoln's own ambition resembled a powerful rocket propelling him upward; his wife merely provided an afterburner. While Herndon was, to be sure, more of an abolitionist than his partner, from his youth Lincoln had hated, loathed, and despised slavery, and he had denounced it publicly at the age of twenty-eight.[12]

The film opens in a log cabin with twenty-one-year-old Abe reading Shakespeare. His rough father, Thomas, expresses contempt for Abe's enthusiasm for books, and his benevolent, pious stepmother offers the young man encouragement. This brief treatment of young Lincoln's parents accurately depicts the family dynamic, their poverty, and Lincoln's love of books in general and Shakespeare in particular. He accepts an offer to help take a flatboat to New Orleans and only reluctantly leaves the family. In reality, he was eager to escape from his illiterate, unambitious, ignorant father and the crude, backward, superstitious frontier world he represented. Lincoln and his sire got along poorly,

Raymond Massey as Lincoln facing Republican political advisers who urge him to run for the presidency in *Abe Lincoln in Illinois*

in part because Thomas regularly yanked his son out of school and hired him to neighbors in order to supplement his meager income.

As actually happened, the flatboat hangs up on a milldam at New Salem, where Abe settles. Returning from New Orleans, he arrives in that village on election day and sees a veteran of the Revolutionary War (fictional) haranguing skeptical villagers. Apropos of this scene, Brian Snee observes: "More than any other Lincoln film, *Abe Lincoln in Illinois* presents its hero as the direct descendent of the framers of the Constitution and the realization of their vision for the United States."[13] At New Salem, Lincoln successfully wrestles Jack Armstrong, leader of the village toughs. In fact, Lincoln did not win that epic match, but his courage, strength, and good-natured willingness to accept Armstrong's violation of the rules impressed the local residents.

Though the film shows Mentor Graham teaching Lincoln grammar, Graham could not fairly claim much credit for Lincoln's mastery of that subject, for Lincoln wrote that he had "studied with nobody."[14] And while the movie garbles some details about his romance with Ann Rutledge, it does accurately show that she was first engaged to another man, who seemingly abandoned her; that Lincoln loved her; and how her death affected him. The script, however, does not indicate that she loved him in return, though in life she did.

When Lincoln first arrives in New Salem, he implausibly says, "I don't want to be no politician." In fact, he thirsted for political distinction. His decision to run in 1832 was not made, pace the film, in response to an appeal by leading Springfield Whigs. Lincoln's service in the Black Hawk War of 1832 is cursorily sketched, starting with his election as a captain. In the film, he accepts that post reluctantly, but in fact he was delighted to win it.

Lincoln served four terms in the Illinois state legislature, where he played an important role in moving the capital to Springfield and in passing legislation designed to create a statewide infrastructure network. He also dared to condemn slavery as "based on injustice and bad policy."[15] The film ignores those accomplishments and misleadingly suggests that he ducked the slavery issue. Lincoln is shown to be reluctant to run for Congress, though in fact he eagerly did so. In the film, he tells his friends who urge him to enter the race: "I'm opposed to slavery but I'm even more opposed to getting myself into trouble." In reality, as a congressman he boldly framed a bill to abolish slavery in the District of Columbia.

Lincoln's troubled courtship of Mary Todd is misrepresented. He is shown to be a rival of Stephen A. Douglas, who in fact never seriously pursued her, and the notion that Lincoln left Mary at the altar has been thoroughly discredited. He did, however, break the engagement in person rather than in a letter, at the insistence of his closest friend, Joshua Speed, as the film shows. The film also accurately suggests that Mary was the aggressor, that Lincoln demonstrated little real affection for her, and that her sister and brother-in-law opposed the match. His later reconciliation with Mary is unmotivated, though in all likelihood she seduced him and thus trapped him into matrimony.

The Lincolns' woe-filled marriage is portrayed accurately. Sherwood called Mary Todd "a very strange and pathetic person," "tremendously ambitious," and "snobbish."[16] Her hard, shrewish nature is vividly illustrated twice in the film: when she berates Lincoln after he belatedly tells her that eastern politicos are about to call on them, and again on election night 1860, when she joins her husband to follow the returns. As she begins to show signs of hysteria that evening, he suggests that she go back home. She replies heatedly: "I won't go home! You only want to be rid of me. That's what you've wanted ever since the day we were married—and before that. Anything to get me out of your sight, because you hate me!" After urging some friends who are present to depart, he curses her: "Damn you! Damn you for taking every opportunity you can to make a public fool of me—and yourself! It's bad enough, God knows, when you act like that in the privacy of our own home. But here—in front of people! You're not to do that again. Do you hear me? You're never to do that again!" In fact, she often embarrassed him in public, and he usually bore her tirades with equanimity. Occasionally, however, he did react angrily. Overwhelming evidence shows that she made his home life miserable, rendering him truly "a man of sorrows."

In the film's most important sequence, depicting the Lincoln-Douglas debates of 1858, the speeches of both candidates are patchworks of their various statements. Lincoln's is a brilliant pastiche of some of his finest utterances. Known as the "credo speech," it was the hit of the 1938 play, sounding like a thinly veiled attack on the looming totalitarianism of the time, as it did in the film as well. Throughout the film Stephen A. Douglas is treated rather gently. Sherwood described him as "honorable, able, and a fine patriot,"[17] when in fact he was during the 1858 senatorial campaign a drunken, race-baiting demagogue.

The film concludes with the presidential election of 1860. Implausibly, on the eve of his victory Lincoln is made to say: "Yes—we've fought the good fight—in the dirtiest campaign in the history of corrupt politics. And if I win, I must fill all the dishonest pledges made in my name." To be sure, his managers at the Republican national convention in Chicago did strike unauthorized bargains with the Indiana and Pennsylvania delegations, and Lincoln's two weakest cabinet choices were from those states, and yet no evidence suggests that he thought the election was anything like the dirtiest in history. Equally implausible is Herndon's description of Lincoln as "a man who has never wanted anything in his life but to be let alone, in peace!" The ambitious Lincoln wanted much more out of life than that. In the final scene, Sherwood makes an unsatisfactory pastiche of Lincoln's eloquent farewell to Springfield, one of his oratorical masterpieces.

Far broader in scope than *Young Mr. Lincoln*, *Abe Lincoln in Illinois* tells a good deal about Lincoln's public and private life, though not without important distortions, especially regarding Lincoln's ambition and his hatred of slavery. A major advantage of the film, as Mark Reinhart noted in 2009, is that Raymond Massey "captures the unique characteristic that Lincoln was said to have possessed in life of being grotesque while at the same time instantly likable. In fact, there are moments in *Abe Lincoln in Illinois* when Massey recreates Lincoln better than any other film impersonation in history."[18]

Today, Reinhart might well be inclined to bestow that accolade on Daniel Day-Lewis, the Oscar-winning star of Steven Spielberg's 2012 film, *Lincoln.* Like *Young Mr. Lincoln,* the movie has a narrow focus: the president's role in securing congressional passage of the Thirteenth Amendment in 1865 (abolishing slavery throughout the land, not just in the Confederate states). The movie accurately shows that Lincoln thought it essential to have Congress pass the amendment before the war's end, lest courts overturn his 1863 Emancipation Proclamation after the cessation of hostilities, thus paving the way for reenslavement of the freedmen. Lincoln emerges as a profoundly committed champion of black freedom, as in fact he was.

One of the more striking features of Spielberg's film is its generally accurate portrayal of the Lincoln marriage.[19] Mary Lincoln (Sally Field) is made to say to her husband: "All anyone will remember of me is I was crazy and I ruined your happiness." Although it is highly unlikely that she would have been so self-critical, she was indeed mentally unbalanced and made Lincoln's married life "a domestic hell on Earth," as William Herndon put it.[20]

In a scene in which the First Couple argue about their eldest son's desire to join the army, Mary fiercely accuses Lincoln of resenting the young man: "You've always blamed Robert for being born, for trapping you in a marriage that's only ever given you grief and caused you regret." Much evidence suggests that Mary trapped Lincoln by seducing him and then insisting that they marry immediately to protect her honor. She delivered Robert slightly less than nine months after the wedding. She could not have known right away if she were pregnant, but she might have been, and this knowledge could have impelled a man with an exceptionally tender conscience and a highly developed sense of honor (like Lincoln) to marry her despite strong misgivings. Earlier those misgivings had led him to break the engagement. He had done so because, as he confided to a friend, "he thought he did not love [her] as he should and that he would do her a great wrong if he married her."[21] To a woman friend Lincoln declared: "It would just kill me to marry Mary Todd."[22]

Mary had taken the initiative throughout the courtship. Orville H. Browning, a close friend and political ally of Lincoln, told an interviewer, "Miss Todd was thoroughly in earnest [in] her endeavors to get Mr. Lincoln," and he stated

Sally Field as Mary Todd Lincoln with Daniel Day-Lewis as her husband in
Ford's Theater on the night of his assassination in *Lincoln*

flatly that there "is no doubt of her exceeding anxiety to marry him."[23] The
sister-in-law of Lincoln's host in Springfield, William Butler, thought that Mary
"certainly made most of the plans and did the courting" and "would have him
[Lincoln], whether or no." She alleged that "it was the talk of Springfield that
Mary Todd would marry him in spite of himself."[24] According to her cousin
Martinette Hardin, Mary wanted Lincoln back after he broke their engagement
and had "made up her mind that he should marry her at the cost of her pride
to show us all that she was not defeated."[25]

Other considerations make it seem likely that Mary Todd seduced Lincoln.
It would not have been out of character, for her ethical sense was imperfect.
As First Lady, she accepted bribes, padded expense accounts and payrolls, appropriated wages from White House servants, tried to raid the stationery fund,
disguised personal expenses in government bills, helped peddle cotton-trading
permits, and engaged in other illegal activities.[26] Moreover, when she wed she
was nearly twenty-four, rapidly approaching the status of old maid. (At that
time, women in Sangamon County on average married at nineteen.)

The circumstances surrounding the wedding, which took place on one day's notice, are curious. Its abruptness startled Mary's sister Elizabeth Edwards. Aristocrats like the Edwardses and the Todds customarily threw elaborate weddings. On the day he got married, Lincoln appeared and acted "as if he were going to the slaughter." While dressing for the ceremony, he was asked where he was going. "I guess I am going to hell," came the reply. He said to his groomsman, James Matheny: "I shall have to marry that girl." Matheny reported that Lincoln "often" confided "directly & indirectly" that "he was driven into the marriage." According to Matheny, Mary Todd "told L. that he was in honor bound to marry her."[27]

Though Spielberg's film won high praise and received two Oscars (for best actor and best production design), important errors mar it.[28] Most seriously, it suggests that Lincoln was torn between a desire to end the war and a desire to free the slaves. But there was no such tension. The Confederates had been trying to persuade northerners that peace could be had and the union restored only if Lincoln dropped emancipation as a prerequisite for Confederate surrender. But in fact, Jefferson Davis would accept nothing short of Confederate independence. Lincoln had said as much in his December 1864 annual message to Congress (what today would be called the State of the Union address).

Equally egregious is the scene in which Lincoln imperiously rises from his seat and shouts at some political allies: "I am the president of the United States of America, clothed in immense power. You will procure me these votes." The source of that quote is a Massachusetts congressman who was recalling what someone told him about events that had transpired more than twenty years earlier. It is highly uncharacteristic of Lincoln, and most scholars do not credit it. Doris Kearns Goodwin, however, cited it in her book *Team of Rivals*, upon which the screenplay is partly based.

In the film, Mrs. Lincoln warns her husband that he must win passage of the amendment or else: "If you fail to acquire the necessary votes, woe unto you, sir. You will answer to me." In fact, the First Lady was no abolitionist. In 1856, a year when her husband campaigned widely for John C. Fremont, the presidential nominee of the antislavery Republican Party, she wrote to her half-sister that she favored Millard Fillmore, candidate of the anti-Catholic, anti-immigrant American Party: "If some of you Kentuckians, had to deal with the 'wild Irish,' as we housekeepers are sometimes called upon to do, the south would certainly elect Mr Fillmore next time."[29] That letter casts serious doubt on the belief, held by some, that Mary Lincoln was an enthusiastic opponent of slavery. Moreover, she reportedly objected to her husband's plan to issue the Emancipation Proclamation. As the president made a fair copy of that historic document, she, according to her eldest son, "was very much opposed to the signing of the Emancipation Proclamation" and interrupted him, "inquiring in her sharp way, 'Well, what do you intend doing?'" He replied: "I am a man under orders, I cannot do otherwise."[30]

Other misleading features of Spielberg's film include its portrayal of the House of Representatives as a lively deliberative body; having Connecticut representatives vote against the amendment; depicting Radical Republicans (represented by Pennsylvania congressman Thaddeus Stevens) as vindictive supporters of a harsh peace; having Lincoln slap his son Robert; having Lincoln meet with the shady lobbyists deployed by Secretary of State William Henry Seward to win support for the amendment; showing relatively few blacks as slaves, as residents of Washington, or as agents in their own emancipation; suggesting that the Peace Democrats rather than War Democrats dominated their party in 1865; indicating that the Republican Party was badly split over emancipation at that time; having Lincoln argue that the amendment was necessary to shorten the war; and portraying influential members of the Blair family of Missouri as opponents of the amendment.[31]

As Michael Vorenberg, author of the unacknowledged book upon which most of the movie is evidently based,[32] concluded:

> At its best, *Lincoln* demonstrates that good history can enrich a film. To be sure, there are minor inventions, distortions, and omissions that help keep the film coherent and entertaining and do not rewrite history in any significant way. Other choices represent more serious transgressions—not simply because they get history wrong but because they get it wrong unnecessarily. Doing justice to history does not have to come at the price of boring or confusing audiences. *Lincoln* makes that point like few other films have. Yet, in leaving unchallenged some of the more damaging myths of the era of the Civil War and Reconstruction, *Lincoln* misses the opportunity not simply to be a better history but to be a better film.[33]

In sum, the three movies under consideration have high entertainment value, pleasing general audiences, but for students of history they resemble foods that tickle the palette but provide little nutrition. The films also call to mind an Italian expression: *se non è vero, è ben trovato* (even if it's not true, it's a good story).

NOTES

1. Mark Reinhart, *Abraham Lincoln on Screen: Fictional and Documentary Portrayals on Film and Television*, 2nd ed. (Jefferson, NC: McFarland, 2009), 222.

2. Jay Leyda, ed., *Film Essays and a Lecture by Sergei Eisenstein* (New York: Praeger, 1970), 140.

3. John Evangelist Walsh, *The Shadows Rise: Abraham Lincoln and the Ann Rutledge Legend* (Urbana: University of Illinois Press, 1993).

4. Notes for a Law Lecture, in *Collected Works of Abraham Lincoln*, ed. Roy P. Basler et al., 9 vols. (New Brunswick, NJ: Rutgers University Press, 1953–55), 2:81.

5. Reinhart, *Abraham Lincoln on Screen*, 221.

6. Michael Burlingame, *The Inner World of Abraham Lincoln* (Urbana: University of Illinois Press, 1994), 147–60.

7. *New York Times*, 30 October 1938.

8. Harriet Hyman Alonso, *Robert E. Sherwood: The Playwright in Peace and War* (Amherst: University of Massachusetts Press, 2007), 192.

9. Alonso, *Robert E. Sherwood*, 193.

10. Bruce Chadwick, *The Reel Civil War: Mythmaking in American Film* (New York: Knopf, 2001).

11. Robert E. Sherwood, *Abe Lincoln in Illinois: A Play in Twelve Scenes* (New York: Charles Scribner's Sons, 1940), 188.

12. Burlingame, *Inner World of Abraham Lincoln*, 236–67, 20–56.

13. Brian J. Snee, *Lincoln before Lincoln: Early Cinematic Adaptations of the Life of America's Greatest President* (Lexington: University Press of Kentucky, 2016), 95.

14. Autobiography Written for John L. Scripps, in *Collected Works of Lincoln*, 4:65.

15. Protest in Illinois Legislature on Slavery, 3 March 1837, in *Collected Works of Lincoln*, 1:75.

16. Sherwood, *Abe Lincoln in Illinois*, 197.

17. Sherwood, *Abe Lincoln in Illinois*, 233.

18. Reinhart, *Abraham Lincoln on Screen*, 27.

19. The following account of the Lincolns' domestic life is taken from Michael Burlingame, *Abraham Lincoln: A Life*, 2 vols. (Baltimore: Johns Hopkins University Press, 2008), chaps. 6, 7, and 25.

20. William H. Herndon, *Herndon on Lincoln: Letters*, ed. Douglas L. Wilson and Rodney O. Davis (Urbana: University of Illinois Press, 2016), 185.

21. Interview with Mrs. Alexander R. McKee (née Martinette Hardin), "A Romance of Lincoln," clipping identified as "Indianapolis, January 1896," Lincoln Financial Foundation Research Collection, Allen County Public Library, Fort Wayne, Indiana.

22. Sarah Rickard, interview by Nellie Crandall Sanford, *Kansas City Star*, 10 February 1907.

23. Orville H. Browning, interview by John G. Nicolay, Springfield, 17 June 1875, in *An Oral History of Abraham Lincoln: John G. Nicolay's Interviews and Essays*, ed. Michael Burlingame (Carbondale: Southern Illinois University Press, 1996), 2.

24. Rickard interview.

25. McKee interview.

26. Michael Burlingame, "Mary Todd Lincoln's Unethical Conduct as First Lady," in *At Lincoln's Side: John Hay's Civil War Correspondence and Selected Writings*, ed. Burlingame (Carbondale: Southern Illinois University Press, 2000), 185–203.

27. James Matheny, interview by William Herndon, 3 May 1866, in *Herndon's Informants: Letters, Interviews, and Statements about Abraham Lincoln*, ed. Douglas L. Wilson and Rodney O. Davis (Urbana: University of Illinois Press, 1998), 475.

28. Michael Vorenberg, "Spielberg's *Lincoln:* The Great Emancipator Returns," *Journal of the Civil War Era* 3 (2013): 549–72.

29. Justin G. Turner and Linda Levitt Turner, eds., *Mary Todd Lincoln: Her Life and Letters* (New York: Knopf, 1972), 46.

30. *Christian Science Monitor*, 12 February 1935.

31. Vorenberg, "Spielberg's *Lincoln.*"

32. Michael Vorenberg, *Final Freedom: The Civil War, the Abolition of Slavery, and the Thirteenth Amendment* (Cambridge: Cambridge University Press, 2001).

33. Vorenberg, "Spielberg's *Lincoln*," 570.

14

Glory
"Heroism Writ Large, From People Whom History Had Made Small"

JOHN DAVID SMITH

Edward Zwick's award-winning 1989 film *Glory,* from Kevin Jarré's script, is a moving tribute to the generally undervalued role that black soldiers played in the Union army during the Civil War—a story never before told in movies. The film chronicles the early history of the Fifty-fourth Massachusetts (Colored) Infantry, which, thanks to *Glory,* became one of the most famous US Army regiments in American history. One critic wrote, "It's the most overdue war movie ever made, filled with terrible beauty, richness and grandeur."[1] In an important sense *Glory* is revisionist history, informing viewers that blacks, not just whites, fought in the Civil War and contributed to overthrowing slavery and reuniting the nation and "that white soldiers had no monopoly on valor."[2]

Glory introduced the history of black troops in the Civil War and reached far more people than any monograph ever could have. It also added to "the public's knowledge of critical contributions to the development of the United States by individuals of African ancestry."[3] Unlike the caricatures of blacks in *The Birth of a Nation* (1915) and *Gone with the Wind* (1939), *Glory* offered "a greater variety of black characters," picturing them "as heroic combatants and . . . realistic figures who grow and develop rather than remaining static stereotypes, docile or comic servants."[4] "It is certainly rare for the power of a social revolution to come through in a Hollywood movie," wrote the reviewer in the Marxist *Workers Vanguard.* "But that is what you see in *Glory,* the moving story of the first Northern regiment of black troops in the Civil War."[5] "Arms in the hands of slaves had been the nightmare of Southern whites for generations," the historian James M. McPherson observed. "In 1863 the nightmare came true."[6]

Following President Abraham Lincoln's January 1, 1863, Emancipation Proclamation (which authorized the recruitment of African Americans), Massachusetts abolitionists, led by Governor John A. Andrew, conceived of recruiting a black regiment, to be officered by whites, to fight the Confederates. It would become "a regiment fit to showcase the cause of freedom."[7] Most whites, however, doubted that blacks possessed the "manhood" to fight the Confederates.

Andrew disagreed. In early 1863 he dispatched black and white abolitionists, including Frederick Douglass, throughout the North to recruit men for his new regiment. "We can get at the throat of treason and slavery through the State of Massachusetts," Douglass proclaimed.[8] Quickly recruits assembled at the Readville, Massachusetts, training site. To command the Fifty-fourth, Andrew appointed Robert Gould Shaw, the twenty-five-year-old scion of Boston abolitionists and a captain in the Second Massachusetts Infantry, colonel of the black unit. Andrew considered the new regiment "perhaps the most important corps to be organized during the whole war," "a model for all future colored regiments." He informed Shaw: "I know not . . . when, in all human history, to any given thousand men in arms there has been committed a work at once so proud, so precious, so full of hope and glory as the work at once committed to you."[9]

Glory portrays the training and mobilization of the men of the Fifty-fourth, their first observations of slavery as the regiment enters the South, and the presence of racism in the Union ranks. The unit first participated in the sacking of Darien, Georgia, on June 11, 1863, and then engaged Confederates at the Battle of Grimball's Landing on James Island, South Carolina, on July 16. The film focuses largely on the regiment's bold and climactic assault on Fort Wagner, the Rebels' bastion on Morris Island, South Carolina, on July 18. With this futile attack the Fifty-fourth etched its place in history and historical memory.

At dusk, with Shaw in the lead, six hundred men of the Fifty-fourth crossed sand dunes in disciplined rows, then traversed muddy terrain and stormed Fort Wagner, charging unflinchingly into the deadly fire of the Rebels' guns. "Fort Wagner is the Sebastopol of the rebels," a corporal in the Fifty-fourth reported.[10] Although the Union troops penetrated the fort's walls, the Rebels eventually threw them back. Their valiant charge cost the regiment dearly—272 men killed, wounded, and missing, 42 percent of its effectives. Shaw took a shot in the chest while leading his men over Fort Wagner's parapet. The Confederates, contemptuous of a white officer commanding black troops, stripped Shaw's body and dumped it in a ditch along with the bodies of dead enlisted

Jimhi Kennedy, Denzel Washington, and Morgan Freeman as early recruits
in the Fifty-fourth Massachusetts Infantry in *Glory*

men. When, following the battle, federal officers appealed to Confederates to
reclaim Shaw's body, a Rebel officer replied disdainfully, "We have buried him
with his niggers."[11] The black Civil War veteran and pioneer historian George
Washington Williams interpreted Shaw's interment as an apotheosis. "Colonel
Shaw was saluted by death and kissed by immortality."[12]

Although the regiment's attack had no military significance, it immediately
assumed symbolic meaning in the northern press and among African Americans. Two days after the ill-fated attack, Douglass's eldest son, Sergeant Major
Lewis Douglass, informed his fiancée: "We charged that terrible battery on
Morris Island . . . and were repulsed. . . . This regiment has established its
reputation as a fighting regiment, not a man flinched, though it was a trying
time. Men fell all around me. A shell would explode and clear a space of twenty
feet. . . . How I got out of that fight alive I cannot tell, but I am here."[13] The
black troops and their white officers became martyrs who sacrificed themselves
in the cause of black freedom. According to the historian Willie Lee Rose, "It
was at Battery Wagner that the tide of public opinion was fully turned on the
question of arming the Negro."[14] McPherson maintains that had the Fifty-

fourth "done nothing else in the war," its service on Morris Island "elevated it to the deserved status of most famous of the 166 black regiments in the Union Army."[15]

No one came to appreciate their contributions more so than Lincoln. Following the Fifty-fourth's attack on Fort Wagner, he threatened to retaliate against Confederate prisoners if the Rebels failed to treat captured black soldiers as prisoners of war. Soon after Lincoln celebrated those blacks who, "with silent tongue, and clenched teeth, and steady eye, and well-poised bayonet," had fought the insurgents.[16] Others too commemorated Shaw and his command. In 1897 Augustus Saint-Gaudens honored them in a bronze bas-relief sculpture, the *Shaw Memorial*, on Boston Common. In 1960 Robert Lowell memorialized Shaw and his men in his poem "For the Union Dead." The men of the Fifty-fourth remain the most celebrated of the 179,000 black soldiers who fought in the war.

Inspired to create *Glory* by Saint-Gaudens's *Shaw Memorial*, Zwick and Jarré based their film on Shaw's letters at Harvard University and on two histories of the Fifty-fourth, Peter Burchard's *One Gallant Rush* (1965) and Richard Benson and Lincoln Kirstein's *Lay This Laurel* (1973). The cinematographer Freddie Francis filmed *Glory* in Savannah and Jekyll Island, Georgia, as well as in Olustee, Florida, the site of an important Union defeat in February 1864 in which the Fifty-fourth participated.[17] To assure authenticity to the smallest detail, especially in scenes depicting camp life, combat, and militaria, the filmmakers employed 125 Civil War reenactors.[18] As a result *Glory*'s battle scenes are unsurpassed in their realism and accuracy. James McPherson judged *Glory* "not only the first feature film to treat the role of black soldiers in the American Civil War; it is also the most powerful and historically accurate movie about that war ever made." He considered the portrayal of the Fifty-fourth's attack on Fort Wagner "through bursting shells and murderous musketry, losing men every step of the way but continuing right up the ramparts and breaching the parapet . . . the most realistic combat footage in any Civil War movie I have seen."[19]

Glory begins largely through the eyes and words of Shaw (Matthew Broderick). The supporting cast comprises four invented characters, all enlisted men: the ex-slaves Silas Trip (Denzel Washington), John Rawlins (Morgan Freeman), and Jupiter Sharts (Jihmi Kennedy) and the free black Thomas Searles (Andre Braugher). Upon assuming his command, Shaw appears uncertain about the fighting qualities of his men. But as *Glory* unfolds, the black soldiers convince

Shaw of their worth as soldiers and men. After living and fighting with the Fifty-fourth, Shaw no longer views blacks as inferiors to be uplifted, but rather as men with feelings and talents and as creditable soldiers. As the film critic Roger Ebert noted, thrown into the crucible of war, Shaw and his men developed a reciprocal relationship. "It is up to the troops themselves to convince him they can fight—and along the way they also rightly provide him with some insights into race and into human nature, a century before the flowering of the civil rights movement."[20]

Critics nonetheless found much to fault in Glory's character development, especially its framing the powerful story of the black troops' baptism in fire from Shaw's perspective rather than from that of his men. "Why did we see the black troops through his eyes—instead of seeing him through theirs?" asked Ebert.[21] Others complained that in Glory Shaw becomes "the great white savior who dares to take command of the first black regiment, built them into a strong fighting force, and gave this life on their behalf. . . . There are no autonomous blacks in the film, only blacks led by whites."[22] At best, the historian Marilyn Richardson quipped, Glory's black characters were "prototypes from central casting."[23]

The film critic David Nicholson judged Glory "a little like . . . a photograph of a group of blacks and whites where the whites are front and center and in focus, while the blacks remain at the edges, in shadow and slightly blurry." Missing are "the interior lives of the men who fought in the Fifty-fourth." Nicholson further chided Glory for fictionalizing its black characters. "The real story of the men who joined the 54th Massachusetts is even more powerful and more moving than that told in 'Glory.' They left their own record in letters to family and friends . . . and many were literate."[24] The historian Gerald Horne argues that Glory might in fact have proven "more dramatic" had the film included real characters such as Sergeant William H. Carney, whose heroic act in saving the Fifty-fourth's flag after its route at Fort Wagner earned him the Medal of Honor. He was the first African American to receive this honor.[25]

In addition to historical inaccuracies, Glory also contains questionable uses of artistic license. First, Massachusetts and other northern states received credit toward their draft quotas by recruiting blacks for their regiments, thereby freeing whites from military service. To a degree, then, race exploitation, not sheer abolitionist ideology, motivated Andrew to establish the Fifty-fourth. Glory also gives viewers the false impression that most of the Fifty-fourth's recruits were fugitive slaves. They were largely freemen. In a similar vein, the film suggests wrongly that the Fifty-fourth was the vanguard regiment of black soldiers recruited in the Civil War and that its attack on Fort Wagner was the first military action by African American troops in the war. Black troops had organized as early as the summer of 1862 in South Carolina, Louisiana, and Kansas; by the time of Lincoln's proclamation five blacks regiments had organized. Significantly, prior to the Fifty-fourth's assault on Fort Wagner, black troops had distinguished themselves in combat at Milliken's Bend and Port Hudson, Louisiana. By ignoring those black troops already in the field, Zwick and Jarré exaggerated the Fifty-fourth's importance while overlooking how the regiment differed in various ways from other black units.[26] They also misled viewers in portraying Shaw as volunteering to lead the charge on Fort Wagner. Actually, General George C. Strong asked Shaw if he wished to lead the attack, and he jumped at the chance to prove his men's valor.[27]

Additional lapses include *Glory*'s simplification of Shaw's racial attitudes. Shaw was a paternalist, never an abolitionist. Before February 1863 he "had never associated with black people," and he "still had prejudices against them." Like many whites, Shaw harbored doubts about how well blacks would fight. After months commanding black troops, he informed his wife: "They are perfectly childlike . . . and are no more responsible for their actions than so many puppies."[28] Similarly, the film simplifies the motivations of the men who served in the Fifty-fourth. While many no doubt volunteered to fight to free the slaves, the soldiers most certainly had various reasons for volunteering, including a commitment to preserving the Union.

Glory also contains fabrications that weaken its historical authenticity. In the film the Fifty-fourth attacks Fort Wagner from the north; the regiment's assault actually came from the south. The film also includes a fictitious scene in which Shaw orders Trip to be flogged for leaving camp without permission. (The audience later learns that he did so to search for shoes.) The War Department, however, had banned whipping in 1861. As the historian Joseph T. Glatthaar explains, the gratuitous whipping scene "gives the public a sense that black soldiers would endure such abuse when in fact they would not."[29] That scene also suggests erroneously that the Fifty-fourth was ill-equipped. In Readville the men resided in wooden barracks, not in tents, and received uniforms, including shoes.

Glory includes other errors of historical detail as well. While for eighteen months the regiment did refuse to accept any pay rather than accept unequal pay (white soldiers received thirteen dollars per month, while black troops received seven), it did so at Shaw's suggestion, not by a spontaneous eruption by the enlisted men. This discriminatory practice continued until June 1864, when Congress equalized the pay of black and white troops. And the Fifty-fourth was not the only black unit to protest the pay inequality.[30] Still other historical slips mar *Glory*. The Fifty-fourth organized in February 1863, not three months earlier. The film portrays Douglass as an elderly man (in 1863 he was a vigorous forty-five-year-old), and it gives his recruiting efforts short shrift.[31] Shaw did not accept the command of the Fifty-fourth at a Boston soiree; he received Andrew's offer at winter quarters in Virginia. Shaw initially spurned the appointment, accepting the colonelcy a day later after wrestling with his conscience.[32]

These errors notwithstanding, *Glory* successfully introduced viewers to the black troops' commitment to the Union cause. As Horne notes, "It may be difficult for a two-hour film to grapple with the subtle complexities of the past; . . . perhaps all we can ask is if the basic thrust of the film has been true to history. *Glory* easily passes this test."[33] In assessing *Glory*'s accuracy, the historian Thomas Cripps differentiates between "an evocative credibility" and "an authenticated dissertation." In *Glory*'s case, he writes, "a tolerable credibility requires only that the details *ring* true rather than claim truth: the trigger housings and the flash pans of the muskets, the badges on the kepis, the mundane details of Boston teatime as well as Carolina campfires allow us to believe that the accompanying story seems true enough to carry the freight of its meaning."[34]

Not only is *Glory* generally accurate but it underscores "war with a clear ethical goal that goes beyond questions of national self-interest." The film also succeeds in placing blacks more in the forefront of popular culture than previous Civil War films had done, correcting Lost Cause stereotypes of blacks as docile and passive, and addressing such questions as the meaning of freedom and the centrality of human rights. The men of the Fifty-fourth made a moral choice to fight for what they believed in, freedom for the slaves and black equality.[35] Their story resounded far and wide, confirming "the wisdom of black recruitment" and inspiring others to join Lincoln's army.[36] "In a very real sense," writes the historian Donald M. Jacobs, "*Glory* is a modern monument to the many examples of black bravery in the Civil War," fully akin to Saint-Gaudens's sculpture.[37]

Glory, like all movies, reflects the cultural imperatives and values of its day. Zwick considered the film a "good story," one "redressing historical misperception, providing positive role models and doing whatever it can to contribute to healing the commonality of purpose between people."[38] Manifesting the liberal racial mores of the late 1980s, *Glory* sought "to raise public awareness of historical racism and the role of Africans and African Americans."[39] White racism runs through the film like a leitmotif—from the fictional Irish drill instructor, who insults the recruits with racial slurs; to Shaw, who orders that Trip be whipped like a slave; to white Union troops who hurl racist slurs at the black soldiers.

In true Hollywood war-movie fashion, the recruits ultimately bond, finding community on the eve of their big battle. They "testify" at a regimental camp gospel meeting, signifying their commitment to African American brotherhood and emancipation.[40] In that scene Trip proclaims: "Y'all's the onliest family I got. And—I loves the 54th. Ain't much of matter what happens tomorrow—we men, ain't we?"[41] And just as Trip overcomes his skepticism of Shaw and of whites generally, Shaw overcomes his doubts about blacks. Ultimately he and his men find "unity in glory and sacrifice."[42]

Viewers found meaning in *Glory*'s themes of reconciliation and unity. For example, following Boston's Charles Stuart murder case in October 1990, Monica Fairbairn, director of the city's Museum of Afro American History, hoped that *Glory* would promote "the process of healing" within her black community. It touched upon persons, places, and subjects of "real historical significance for black people," she said.[43] In Washington, DC, David Miller, a drug-prevention teacher, took his inner-city students at Shaw Junior High School (named for Colonel Shaw) to see *Glory*. "These kids need to be fed the image of these courageous black soldiers," Miller explained. "If we could teach a generation of students to see how they need to stand together and help each other, we could eliminate the drug problem." *Glory* taught twelve-year-old Chris Landon that blacks had fought in the Civil War. "We owe them our life. They died for our country." Ninth-grader Frank Sykes explained that had he had the chance, he would have joined the Fifty-fourth. "They were fighting for a cause, for their freedom."[44] *Glory* inspired James Hayes, a black accountant in Atlanta, to become a Civil War reenactor. "I realized that it [the Civil War] was not only a very painful period. It also was a heroic period."[45]

While *Glory* mythologized the Fifty-fourth, the film nevertheless holds meaning in contemporary debates over racial justice.[46] According to the critic Marc Bernadin, "The magic of 'Glory' comes from the film itself. It speaks of heroism writ large, from people whom history had made small."[47]

1. Jay Carr, "'Glory': War Film Filled with A Terrible Beauty," *Boston Globe*, 12 January 1990, 36.

2. Geoffrey C. Ward, "Some Fought for Freedom, Some for Glory," *New York Times Book Review*, 17 November 1991, 36.

3. Joseph T. Glatthaar, review of *The Massachusetts 54th Colored Infantry*, in *Journal of American History* 78 (December 1991): 1166–67.

4. Hernán Vera and Andrew M. Gordon, *Screen Saviors: Hollywood Fictions of Whiteness* (Lanham, MD: Rowman & Littlefield, 2003), 27.

5. Francis Daly, "Black Soldiers Fight for Freedom: A Review," *Workers Vanguard*, 26 January 1990, 16.

6. James M. McPherson, "The 'Glory' Story," *New Republic*, 8 and 15 January 1990, 27.

7. Michael C. C. Adams, "Seeking Glory: Our Continuing Involvement with the 54th Massachusetts," *Studies in Popular Culture* 14, no. 2 (1992): 12.

8. Frederick Douglass, "Men of Color, to Arms!," [21 March 1863], in *The Life and Writings of Frederick Douglass*, ed. Philip S. Foner, 4 vols. (New York: International, 1952), 3:318.

9. John A. Andrew to Francis G. Shaw, 30 January 1863, and Andrew speech at Readville Camp, 18 May 1863, quoted in *A Brave Black Regiment: The History of the 54th Massachusetts Volunteer Infantry, 1863–1865*, by Luis F. Emilio (1894; reprint, New York: Da Capo, 1995), 3, 27.

10. J.H.G. [James Henry Gooding] to *New Bedford Mercury*, 20 July 1863, in *On the Altar of Freedom: A Black Soldier's Civil War Letters from the Front*, ed. Virginia M. Adams (Amherst: University of Massachusetts Press, 1991), 38.

11. Quoted in McPherson, "'Glory' Story," 26.

12. George Washington Williams, *A History of the Negro Troops in the War of the Rebellion* (1887; reprint, New York: Fordham University Press, 2012), 138.

13. Lewis Douglass to Amelia Loguen, 20 July 1863, in *Letters from Black America*, ed. Pamela Newkirk (New York: Farrar, Straus & Giroux, 2009), 230.

14. Willie Lee Rose, *Rehearsal for Reconstruction: The Port Royal Experiment* (1964; reprint, Athens: University of Georgia Press, 1999), 258.

15. McPherson, "'Glory' Story," 26.

16. Order by the President, 30 July 1863, and Abraham Lincoln to James C. Conkling, 26 August 1863, in *The Collected Works of Abraham Lincoln*, 8 vols., ed. Roy P. Basler (New Brunswick, NJ: Rutgers University Press, 1953), 6:357, 410.

17. C. Peter Jorgensen, "The Making of 'Glory,'" *Civil War Times Illustrated* 28 (November/December 1989): 53–56.

18. Gary W. Gallagher, *Causes Won, Lost, and Forgotten: How Hollywood and Popular Art Shape What We Know about the Civil War* (Chapel Hill: University of North Carolina Press, 2008), 95; Jorgensen, "Making of 'Glory,'" 55–58.

19. McPherson, "'Glory' Story," 22, 26.

20. Roger Ebert, review of *Glory* in *Chicago Sun-Times*, 12 January 1990, Weekend Plus section, 46.

21. Ebert review.

22. Vera and Gordon, *Screen Saviors*, 28.

23. Marilyn Richardson, "Taken from Life: Edward M. Bannister, Edmonia Lewis, and the Memorialization of the Fifty-fourth Massachusetts Regiment," in *Hope and Glory: Essays on the Legacy of the 54th Massachusetts Regiment*, ed. Martin H. Blatt, Thomas J. Brown, and Donald Yacovone (Amherst: University of Massachusetts Press, 2001), 295n31.

24. David Nicholson, "What Price 'Glory'? The Movie May Be Stunning, But It's Surpassed by the Past," *Washington Post*, 21 January 1990, G1.

25. Gerald Horne, review of *Glory* in *American Historical Review* 95 (October 1990): 1142.

26. Glatthaar review, 1166.

27. Peter Burchard, *One Gallant Rush: Robert Gould Shaw and His Brave Black Regiment* (New York: St. Martin's, 1965), 133.

28. Robert Gould Shaw to Annie Shaw, 26 June 1863, in *Blue-Eyed Child of Fortune: The Civil War Letters of Robert Gould Shaw,* ed. Russell Duncan (Athens: University of Georgia Press, 1992), 291n5, 360.

29. Joseph T. Glatthaar, quoted in Nicholson, "What Price 'Glory'?"

30. Burchard, *One Gallant Rush*, 115–16.

31. David W. Blight, "The Meaning of the Fight: Frederick Douglass and the Memory of the Fifty Fourth Massachusetts," *Massachusetts Review* 36 (spring 1995): 141–53.

32. McPherson, "'Glory' Story," 27.

33. Horne review, 1143.

34. Thomas Cripps, "*Glory* as a Meditation on the Saint-Gaudens Monument," in Blatt, Brown, and Yacovone, *Hope & Glory*, 239, emphasis in the original.

35. Paul Haspel, "The War in Film: The Depiction of Combat in *Glory*," in *The Civil War in Popular Culture*, ed. Lawrence A. Kreiser Jr. and Randal Allred (Lexington: University Press of Kentucky, 2014), 153, 154, 168.

36. Martin Blatt, "Hope and Glory," *CRM*, no. 11 (1998): 25.

37. Donald M. Jacobs, review of *Glory* in *Public Historian* 12 (Summer 1990): 161.

38. Armond White, "Zwick on His Feet: Fighting Back," *Film Comment* 26 (January 1990): 24.

39. Jeremy D. Stoddard and Alan S. Marcus, "The Burden of Historical Representation: Race, Freedom, and 'Educational' Hollywood Film," *Film & History: An Interdisciplinary Journal of Film and Television Studies* 36 (Fall 2006): 31.

40. Thomas Cripps, "Frederick Douglass: The Absent Presence in *Glory*," *Massachusetts Review* 36 (Spring 1995): 154, 155, 162; Robert Burgoyne, "Race and Nation in *Glory*," *Quarterly Review of Film & Video* 16, no. 2 (1997): 147–51.

41. Haspel, "War in Film," 163–64.

42. Heike Bungert, "*Glory* and the Experience of African-American Soldiers in the Civil War: An Attempt at Historical Film Analysis," *Amerikastudien* 40, no. 2 (1995): 280.

43. Carol Flake, "In Troubled Times, 'Glory' Pulls People Together," *Boston Globe*, 13 January 1990, Living Arts section, 9, 13.

44. Thomas Bell, "D.C. Teachers Praise 'Glory''s Message," *Washington Post*, 18 January 1990, 1.

45. Lee May, "Lessons of Glory," *Atlanta Journal/Atlanta Constitution*, 24 October 1993, M4.

46. Morris Dickstein, "Going to the Movies: War!," *Partisan Review* 57, no. 4 (1990): 612; Tom O'Brien, "At War with Ourselves," *Commonweal* 117 (9 February 1990): 84–85.

47. Marc Bernardin, "What to Watch: Video," *Entertainment Weekly*, 16 February 2001, 76.

15

"And Does it Matter, After All, Who Wins?"
The Movie *Gettysburg* and Popular Perceptions of the Civil War

LESLEY J. GORDON

Michael Shaara's 1974 Pulitzer Prize–winning novel *The Killer Angels,* written in the shadow of Vietnam, conveys a message on the wastefulness of warfare. Characters bemoan that honorable men would go to battle with such effectiveness to murder one another. College professor turned officer Joshua Chamberlain, the novel's ostensible hero, reflects on a speech he authored years earlier inspired by Shakespeare: "What piece of work is man . . . in action how like an angel." His father had responded, "Well, boy if he's an angel, he's sure a muderin angel."[1]

Twenty years later, when the director Ron Maxwell brought Shaara's novel to the big screen, the message of war's senselessness remained, although convoluted. It was 1993. The Clinton era was just beginning, and the country was nearly a decade away from its "war on terror." *Gettysburg* appeared two years after Ken Burns's widely popular PBS series *The Civil War,* marking renewed popular interest in the conflict and its times. Indeed, Maxwell seemed to consciously echo some of Burns's techniques by his use of contemporary photographs, maps, and a sweeping musical score. Several scenes were filmed on the actual battle site, and thousands of reenactors participated as extras. Maxwell apparently mortgaged his home to retain rights to the novel, spending ten years trying to raise money to make the film. It was clearly a labor of love for both him and his main financier, Ted Turner, who made a cameo appearance in the film.[2]

Still, when the movie premiered in October 1993, it was largely a box-office flop.[3] Other movies vied for audiences' attention that fall, including *The Remains of the Day, Rudy,* and *The Piano.* Nonetheless, critics praised the movie for its realism and for what was perceived to be minute attention to historical detail. Stephen Holden, writing for the *New York Times,* applauded the film's "stately tone and meticulous attention to detail," which Holden believed made it feel "more like a documentary than a dramatic film." The movie, Holden stated, successfully conveyed a "visceral sense of what fighting a war used to be like."[4] Desson Howe, reviewing the film for the *Washington Post,* agreed, telling his readers: "You'll get an evocative feel for the might of pre–Desert Storm—not to mention pre–World War I—cannon fire."[5] A travel writer for the *Chicago Tribune,* noting the uptick in visits to the National Military Park in the weeks following the film's release, described the movie as "painstakingly authentic" and a "magnificent wide-screen reenactment."[6] Yet, most film critics complained of the film's "bloated screenplay," uninspired acting, and "redundant and dull" battle scenes.[7] The film is excessively long, more than four hours, and after limited showings it reappeared as a miniseries, the project's original intent, on TNT, attracting many more viewers.

Since its release in 1993, *Gettysburg* continues to inspire reviews and reflection. In 2004 Bruce Chadwick listed the film as the fourth best Civil War film "ever" for the popular magazine *American Heritage.*[8] Chadwick, who also has written a complete book on Civil War movies, calls *Gettysburg* "well balanced," praising its use of reenactors and on-location shots. "The movie," Chadwick declared, "is justifiably a favorite of Civil War enthusiasts."[9] In 2008 the *Time* writer Richard Schickel noted "minor" flaws in the film "compared with the acuity of the film's best characterizations, the vaulting scale of its design and, above all, its old-fashioned belief that history, besides being instructive in itself, can—and should—be a great movie subject."[10] One reenactor looked back fondly at his experience in the film: "I have never had a more intimate experience with history as I did the day we filmed that scene on the actual battlefield."[11]

Indeed, the movie's fans enthusiastically praise *Gettysburg's* aura of historical authenticity. An unattributed blog post on the University of Mary Washington's website maintains: "Nothing can ever be 100% accurate once creative license is taken into account, but the film *Gettysburg* gets as close to accurate as they come." The blogger adds: "Military strategy and tactics for both the Union and Confederate armies are accurately depicted as are the command orders. The motivation of both sides and individual leadership are also well portrayed."[12] Maxwell, who also wrote the screenplay, insists that historical accuracy was always his goal. He explains:

The Civil War was a brutal episode in our history. More than a half million were killed or wounded. Tens of thousands were made refugees. The suffering was beyond our reckoning. Individual heroism and courage, duty and honor, only make sense in the context of these trials and tribulations. I have not shied away from either in this screenplay. The last thing the world needs is a mindless, glossy entertainment on the Civil War. None of us wants that, so it is important to accept the seriousness of this challenge: to keep our eyes wide open, to be relentlessly honest, to refrain from perpetuating myth and folklore—to get to the truth of the matter. Nothing will be more dramatic and nothing will be more worthwhile.[13]

Despite Maxwell's assertions, the film's accuracy has been a point of contention for many historians since its release. In 1994, in a special issue of the *Journal of American History*, Gary Gallagher pronounced the movie a faithful rendition of Shaara's book, with interpretations of the battle and the war "by turns revisionist and conventional." The movie, Gallagher argued, was conventional in the way it focused on famous generals and a single climactic battle, yet revisionist in its downplaying of slavery and soldiers' complex motivations.[14]

The showcasing of the Confederate general James Longstreet and the Union colonel Joshua Chamberlain as leading protagonists challenges not only the traditional narrative but also historical facts. Missing is the controversy surrounding Longstreet's uneven performance on July 2, and there is even some questioning about the direct role played by Chamberlain and his Twentieth Maine Regiment in the pivotal moment on Little Round Top.[15] In addition, as Gary Gallagher insists, Lee's men, and even Lee himself, appear to lack any strong attachment to their new nation.[16] Two captured southern soldiers talk vaguely of defending their "rats," and Confederate officers abstractly compare the Union to a gentlemen's club. In one scene, Longstreet suggests that the South should have first freed its slaves and *then* attacked Fort Sumter, as if slavery could be easily shed like an old, unwieldy set of clothes weighing down the new nation. Lee is oddly passive and grim throughout, although a scene in which his soldiers surround him shouting adoring cheers rings true.[17] The portrayal of Union soldiers as inspired abolitionists is equally misleading: Chamberlain addresses a demoralized regiment of Maine soldiers, idealistically praising the Federal army as "something new": "We are an army out to set other men free."[18] The fictional Irish sergeant Buster Kilrain reasons that all men, including African Americans, should be judged "one at a time," giving no hint of the ugly anti-Irish sentiment prevalent in the Union army or the virulent racism.[19]

The movie succeeds in conveying central tenets of the Lost Cause, including its emphasis on the battle's alleged decisiveness, the uniform bravery of Confederate troops, the downplaying of slavery, and the admiration of Lee by his men.[20] The portrayal of George Pickett as a foppish, perfumed dandy is also more Lost Cause mythology than historical reality.[21] In addition, the film perpetuates the deceptive image of a heroic "brothers' war," making memory of the battle, in William Blair's words, "as familiar and comfortable as today's rural landscape covers the scars beneath."[22] Soldiers' close attachment to their individual regiments is certainly noteworthy and accurate, although the film misleadingly implies that only proud Virginians took part in Pickett's Charge. In a particularly melodramatic moment, General Lewis Armistead, doomed to death during Pickett's Charge, rattles off celebrated Virginia bloodlines to the British observer Colonel Arthur Fremantle.

The film seeks to entertain and reassure its perceived audience and not to offend or distress.[23] The theme of testing one's courage, defined as an essential quality of white manhood, is central. Individuals die and suffer, but the expansive level of brutality or destruction that the battle wrought on its participants and the town itself are largely absent.[24] Through the sensory power of film, *Gettysburg* instead evokes an emotional desire for a time long past and, as Jim Weeks describes, "a golden age of valor."[25]

This affirmation of celebrated manly warfare has no real place for noncombatants. Women and African Americans play no active role in the movie's plotlines. Chamberlain refers dismissively to prior armies fighting for women "and some other loot," and Armistead remembers fondly General Winfield S. Hancock's wife, Myra, as the "most perfect beautiful woman I'd ever seen."[26] Two nameless white women appear briefly to witness marching federal troops, one asking if their shirts need mending. The lone African American man in the film, a fugitive slave, injured and cowering when found by Union troops, is mute. Chamberlain orders food for him, but the slave, as well as the implications of his presence, quickly disappears from the film's main action. When Lee at one point inquires whether there has been "any trouble with the local population," an aide responds that there has been "no trouble," although he adds that "there are some local women who claim we have taken all their food." Lee urges his army to behave properly and "with respect to all civilian populations at all times."[27] And as Armistead rallies his troops for that final,

Martin Sheen as Robert E. Lee and Tom Berenger as James Longstreet
on the set of *Gettysburg*

fateful charge, he urges them to fight not just for their beloved homeland but for their wives and sweethearts.

An outpouring of scholarship has shown decisively that women and slaves were not by any means mere bystanders in this battle or in the war in general. Lee's men kidnapped untold numbers of free blacks during his invasion of Pennsylvania under the false pretense that they were fugitive slaves.[28] Local civilians, including black and white women and children, endured the fear and terror of war at their doorsteps, many acting as nurses and cooks in the battle's immediate aftermath and as cleanup crews in the weeks and months that followed.[29] Gettysburg was not staged and not bloodless, and it certainly was not the end. As we know, the war raged on for two more long years.

Missing too is any sense of the deeper division that became more stark by 1863, not just the divide between Union and Confederate armies but the "war within," as historians have called it, which tore communities apart. Eighteen sixty-three was marked by bread riots in the South and draft riots in the North and by a war weariness that descended heavily on soldiers and civilians alike. The movie really is traditional military history, albeit not the most accurate version of it.

Yet for all its emphasis on "drums and trumpets," *Gettysburg* offers mixed messages concerning the control leaders actually exhibit in battle. The focus on famed individual officers implies that these men are all-powerful, their failings and strengths determinant of their armies' success. However, Lee repeatedly suggests that "all is in God's hands," and John Buford on the eve of the fighting ruefully predicts wasted lives lost and "men in tall hats and gold fobs" thumping their chests, "saying what a brave charge it was."[30] In an extended exchange between Lee and Longstreet after the shocking failure of Pickett's Charge, Lee grimly predicts that the war will continue. "Does it matter after all, who wins?" he asks. "Is that ever really the question?"[31] This, as Gallagher has noted, is a startling response from Lee, who in actuality "cared passionately about Confederate independence."[32]

In 1993, the year of the film's release, Charles Royster published *The Destructive War*.[33] In many ways, this was the start of what some today call the "antiwar turn" or the "dark turn" in the field of Civil War history.[34] Royster's searing portrayal of major figures, including Stonewall Jackson and William Sherman, emphasized the war's brutality and suffering. In the more than twenty years since, there has been renewed attention to the trauma of war. *Gettysburg* tries to show that destruction, but with mixed results. The battle and the war are reduced to the frayed friendship of officers. One of the final scenes of the movie depicts the Chamberlain brothers embracing, exhausted and filled with emotion at having each other after all they have witnessed. This moving shot seems to convey, literally, the ideal of a "brothers' war."

Gettysburg as a film (like Shaara's novel) is both repelled by and attracted to war's violence. Battle is wasteful but glorious, admirable but useless. Gettysburg's chaos and shock are largely missing; in its place are men determined to prove their courage and honor, something audiences and the larger American public still seem to believe the Civil War can offer them.

NOTES

1. Michael Shaara, *Killer Angels* (New York: David McKay, 1974), 126.

2. Richard Corless, "Gettysburg: The Great Battle That the Movies Ignored," *Time*, 3 July 2013, http://entertainment.time.com/2013/07/03/gettysburg-the-great-battle-that-the-movies-ignored/.

3. The budget was $25 million, and box-office sales came to only $10,731,997. See http://www.the-numbers.com/movies/year/1993 and also http://gettysburg.umwblogs.org/.

4. Stephen Holden, "When War Was All Glory and Bands and Death," *New York Times*, 8 October 1993.

5. Desson Howe, "Battle Lines Sharply Drawn," *Washington Post*, 8 October 1993.

6. Michael Kilian, "Gettysburg: Movie Gives the Civil War Battlefield a New Birth," *Chicago Tribune*, 28 November 1993. Indeed, it appears that there was nearly a 20 percent increase in visits to the battlefield in 1994 from the previous year, which seems to have been tied directly to the film's premiere. See Jennifer Murray, *On a Great Battlefield: The Making, Management, and Memory of Gettysburg* (Knoxville: University of Tennessee Press, 2014), 143.

7. Quotations are from, respectively, Holden, "When War Was All Glory," and Hal Hinson, "Gettysburg: Battle Fatigued," *Washington Post*, 8 October 1993.

8. See Bruce Chadwick, "Actor against Actor: What Are the 10 Greatest Movies Ever about the Civil War?," *American Heritage*, August/September 2004, 64–66. http://www.americanheritage.com/content/actor-against-actor. The other three films were, in order of ranking, *Glory, Gone with the Wind,* and *Roots.*

9. Chadwick, "Actor against Actor."

10. Richard Schickel, "Who Will Go with Me!," *Time*, 21 July 2008, http://content.time.com/time/subscriber/article/0,33009,1825127,00.html.

11. Brian James Egan, "Part I: My Experience on set of movie 'Gettysburg,'" *O Say Can You See?: Stories from the National Museum of American History* (blog), http://americanhistory.si.edu/blog/2012/10/my-experience-on-set-of-the-movie-gettysburg-1.html.

12. "Historical Accuracy," *Gettysburg* (blog). http://gettysburg.umwblogs.org/historical-accuracy-3/.

13. Ron Maxwell, "Poetic License," http://www.ronmaxwell.com/commentary/essays#poetic license.

14. Gary W. Gallagher, review of *Gettysburg*, in "The Practice of History: A Special Issue," *Journal of American History* 81, no. 3 (December 1994): 1399.

15. In a fascinating essay probing the varying and incomplete descriptions of the action on Little Round Top, Burton Crompton concludes that "there is no true history or account that one can rely upon to represent what actually happened." See Compton, "History Thrice Removed: Joshua Chamberlain and Gettysburg," in *Memory and Myth: The Civil War in Fiction and Film from "Uncle Tom's Cabin" to "Cold Mountain,"* ed. David Sachsman, S. Kittrell Rushing, and Roy Morris Jr. (West Lafayette, IN: Purdue University Press, 2007), 257.

16. Gary W. Gallagher, "Hollywood Has It Both Ways: The Rise, Fall, and Reappearance of the Lost Cause in American Film," in *Wars within Wars: Controversy and Conflict over the American Civil War*, ed. Joan Waugh and Gary W. Gallagher (Chapel Hill: University of North Carolina Press, 2009), 166.

17. Most critics and historians complain of Martin Sheen's performance as problematic, but Brian Wills observes "hints of complexities" in Sheen's Lee, stating, "No one took the loss of Gettysburg harder than Marse Robert, and Sheen captures the pathos on screen." See Brian Steele Wills, *Gone with the Glory: The Civil War in Cinema* (Lanham, MD: Rowman & Littlefield, 2007), 157.

18. *Gettysburg* script, http://www.script-o-rama.com/movie_scripts/g/gettysburg-script-transcript-civil-war.html.

19. *Gettysburg* script.

20. Gallagher, "Hollywood Has It Both Ways," 164–65.

21. Lesley J. Gordon, *George E. Pickett in Life and Legend* (Chapel Hill: University of North Carolina Press, 1998), 106–20.

22. William A. Blair, "The Brothers' War: Gettysburg the Movie and American Memory," in *Making and Remaking Pennsylvania's Civil War*, ed. Blair and William Pencak (University Park: Pennsylvania State University Press, 2001), 246. See also Wills, *Gone with the Glory*, 155. For more on the movie's (and the novel's) success in spreading mythology about Gettysburg, see Craig A. Warren, *Scars to Prove It: The Civil War Soldier and American Fiction* (Kent, OH: Kent State University Press, 2009), 119–59.

23. At least one author has complained of Maxwell's "desire to avoid offending any segment of the audience by refusing to 'take sides.'" See Roy Kinnard, *The Blue and the Gray on the Silver Screen: More Than Eight Years of Civil War Movies* (Secaucus, NJ: Carol, 1996), 274.

24. The book that best explores the lasting legacy of the battle's aftermath is Margaret S. Creighton's *Colors of Courage: Gettysburg's Forgotten History* (New York: Basic Books, 2005).

25. Jim Weeks, *Gettysburg: Memory, Market, and an American Shrine* (Princeton, NJ: Princeton University Press, 2003), 176. See also Jenny Barrett, *Shooting the Civil War: Cinema, History, and American National Identity* (New York: Tauris, 2009), 120–21.

26. *Gettysburg* (1993) Movie Script, http://www.springfieldspringfield.co.uk/movie_script.php?movie=gettysburg.

27. *Gettysburg* (1993) Movie Script.

28. The kidnapping of free blacks is a controversial and, until recently, largely overlooked consequence of Lee's campaign. There is no evidence that Lee directly ordered such practice,

but it appears that other high-ranking officers, including Longstreet and Pickett, openly approved of it. See Frank Reeves, "Confederates' 'Slave Hunt' in the North a Military Disgrace," *Pittsburgh Post Gazette*, 30 June 2013, http://www.post-gazette.com/news/state/2013/06/30/Confederates-slave-hunt-in-North-a-military-disgrace/stories/201306300221; David G. Smith, "The Capture of African Americans during the Gettysburg Campaign," in *Virginia's Civil War*, ed. Peter Wallenstein and Bertram Wyatt-Brown (Charlottesville: University of Virginia Press, 2005), 137–51.

29. Creigton's *Colors of Courage* explores the many ways local white and black women, in particular, were part of the battle and its aftermath.

30. *Gettysburg* script.

31. *Gettysburg* script.

32. Gallagher, "Hollywood Has It Both Ways," 166.

33. Charles Royster, *The Destructive War: William Tecumseh Sherman, Stonewall Jackson, and the Americans* (New York: Vintage, 1993).

34. The best overview of this historiographical trend is by Yael Sternhell, although notably she does not use the term *dark turn*. See Yael Sternhell, "Revisionism Reinvented? The Antiwar Turn in Civil War Scholarship," *Journal of the Civil War Era* 3, no. 2 (June 2013): 239–56. On the overall "dark turn" and the need for more traditional military history, see Gary Gallagher and Katherine Shively Meier, "Coming to Terms with Civil War Military History," *Journal of the Civil War Era* 4, no. 4 (December 2014): 492.

16

Martin Scorsese's *Gangs of New York*
Racial Ambiguity in New York City's Five Points

GRAHAM RUSSELL GAO HODGES

Martin Scorsese's 2002 epic *Gangs of New York*, once puckishly called "*Gone with the Wind* as narrated by Travis Bickle" by *New York Magazine*, stands as one of the most vivid cinematic re-creations of nineteenth-century New York City. Scorsese yearned to transform Herbert Asbury's classic 1928 history of New York's Five Points gangs from the time he first saw it on a friend's bookshelf in 1970.[1] Equally influential was Raoul Walsh's 1933 film *The Bowery*. Adapting Asbury's book proved to be a deeply personal project for Scorsese, given that he had grown up close to the Five Points neighborhood of Lower Manhattan. Over the decades, Scorsese worked with the screenwriter Jay Cocks to create a film script. But ups and downs in Scorsese's career kept the project in limbo until the late 1990s, when the agent Michael Ovitz approached the director with a proposal to use Leonardo DiCaprio as the star. Harvey Weinstein took over as producer, and after lengthy negotiations DiCaprio signed on to costar with Daniel Day-Lewis.[2]

In this essay I examine *Gangs of New York* through the prism of race. Race has often been a troublesome quality in Scorsese's films, with notably egregious examples in the negative critical response to the interracial relationships in *Mean Streets* (1973) and the nasty, sexually vengeful cuckold of *Taxi Driver* (1976), played by the director himself. Yet most critics ignored the issue of race in *Gangs of New York*. Patrick McGee, who has written the most extensive commentary on the film, argues that race is a paramount characteristic of the "modern" and that Scorsese simply uses his artistry to uncover the unpleasant social mores of his film's characters and perceived notions of violent Irish prejudice against African Americans. The film makes significant use of Chinese

Americans to expand the plot. A close examination, however, indicates that much of the racism in *Gangs of New York* unnecessarily marginalizes blacks and Asians and is more revealing of the exacting director's personal vision than a useful portrait of nineteenth-century Irish New York City.[3]

I can accept that racism existed aplenty in the nineteenth century and that the Draft Riots of 1863, the major climax of the film, had strongly racist causes. I have argued earlier that there was a fair amount of interracial cooperation and love between Irish and black New Yorkers in antebellum Five Points.[4] While most commentary on *Gangs of New York* has examined it through an Irish lens, this essay switches that lens to see the film from African American and Chinese American perspectives, which have taken on a new relevance in light of the recent resurgence of white nationalism and racism.

Gangs of New York does not fit easily into any of Robert Brent Toplin's four types of historical drama. The film does not truly present a heroic figure. Nor does it use the past to reflect current controversies or make the past relevant to the present. Scorsese's recasting of history brings the film closer to Toplin's description of historical drama as artistic license.[5]

The production of the epic was beset by problems. It was filmed at the Cinecitta Studios in Rome, where a nearly mile-long set re-created the Five Points neighborhood as a rabbit's warren of breweries, bars, factories, churches, opium dens, underground saloons, and secret tunnels that reached in every direction. Critics acknowledge that whatever they saw as the film's other flaws, its set admirably captured the Five Points' seedy, rough-and-tumble ambience. Scorsese and Day-Lewis researched and practiced the working-class argot of the 1850s, striving to emulate the accent of the period.[6]

Scorsese scrupulously attended to every detail, down to the amount of dirt ground into each garment. The director traveled everywhere on the set in a golf cart among the hundreds of Italian extras. Weinstein was on the set many times. Weinstein and Scorsese battled over dozens of details and expenses. Cost overruns ballooned, exceeding the projected $83 million budget by $20 million.[7]

The film was a middling hit. Upon its release, *Gangs of New York* seemed poised to become a blockbuster, given the subject and presence of the highly popular actors Daniel Day-Lewis and Leonardo DiCaprio, who had just stared in the film *Titanic*, the highest-grossing film of the era. That was not to be for *Gangs*, which earned $194 million on domestic and foreign sales. While not in the same league as *Titanic*, *Gangs of New York* put Scorsese back on solid ground among Hollywood producers and remains one of his biggest successes to date. I cite these statistics to indicate that *Gangs of New York* remains a significant marker in Hollywood's often tentative embrace of the American past. My judgment, however, is that the film is not widely screened in classrooms across the country, probably because of its length, Scorsese's penchant for gore, and the production's factual errors.[8]

Scorsese, who fancies himself a history buff, hired the highly regarded scholar Tyler Anbinder as a historical consultant. How much Scorsese used Anbinder's knowledge is debatable. Despite the director's meticulous attention to detail, the film is troubled, as a number of scholars have written, with errors of historical fact and no real social-historical content.[9]

Scorsese's vision is in line with the perceived historical wisdom that New York City's gang warfare of the era stemmed from Irish immigrant tensions, culminating in the Draft Riots of July 13–16, 1863. In that uprising, Irish mobs roamed the streets of Manhattan burning buildings and murdering scores of black citizens. It was the worst act of domestic racial terrorism in nineteenth-century New York City. Historians have blandly described the riots as an expression of white working-class resentment against the liberal elites of the city, rather than emphasizing that African Americans were the victims of the murderous violence and later volunteered by the thousands to fight in the Union army. As Clifton Hood has recently argued, the rioters focused their violence not on the elite but on innocent blacks, who were tortured and murdered in the streets. Scorsese augmented this view by considering the riots as a key moment in the "birth of the modern," in a city, and, by extension, a nation, riven with ethnic tribalism and conflicts. The film ends by fast-forwarding to New York's skyline in the 1990s.[10]

Scorsese's film is bookended by riots. The first is fictional and takes place in 1846; and at the end, of course, are the infamous Draft Riots of 1863. In the mid-1840s, nativist Protestants were taking on Irish Catholic immigrants. In the heat of one such confrontation between the two, Bill the Butcher (Day-Lewis) strikes a blow that kills a leader of the Irish gang, "Priest" Vallon (Liam Neeson). His young son, Amsterdam, witnesses his father's death, thus setting up the showdown between the two antagonists seventeen years later, after the orphan has grown into a young man (DiCaprio) out for vengeance. Jenny (Cameron Diaz) serves as a love interest and a prize to be won in battle between the two men. Though the film has been criticized for its excessive violence, the street battles in the early part of the film are based somewhat on actual Catholic and Protestant gangs of that period, the Dead Rabbits and the Bowery B'hoys.[11]

Day-Lewis's character is an archetypical Bowery B'hoy—greedy, racist and nativist, a ward heeler and gang leader. Adorned with a stovepipe hat, period clothing, greasy, flapping hair, and a glass eye featuring the American eagle, Day-Lewis exudes the quotidian masculinity of the B'hoy, a precursor of gendered modernity. His violence is casual and instructive to his subject. Bill denounces Irish immigrants as "working for a nickel what a n——would work for a dime and a white man for a quarter." Often, he conflates Irish and blacks in curses. Bill hates Abraham Lincoln and throws a knife at the president's poster during an angry rant against conscription. Later, Bill shouts "Down with the Union" during a stage performance of Uncle Tom's Cabin, and his gang pelts the actor playing Lincoln with rotten fruit.[12]

Race in Gangs of New York is more complicated than Bill's nativist cries. Black and Chinese music make up a significant portion of the song tracks. During an early sequence, Priest Vallon leads his gang through an underground series of tunnels. On the sidelines are African Americans engaged in an African dance that, as McGee notes, is combined with an Irish jig, in a forerunner of twentieth-century tap dancing, made famous by Bill "Bojangles" Robinson. Blues songs alternate with white folk songs. African drums reveal Jenny's anger when she brushes off Amsterdam.

There are fleeting glimpses of black individuals or couples in crowds or on the streets. Chinese men mingle with black women. The most frequently seen black man is Amsterdam's companion Jimmy Spoils (Lawrence Gilliard II), the sole outsider in the otherwise Irish gang the Dead Rabbits. Spoils was too young to be in the original gang, but he is a constant member of Amsterdam's crew before and after reformation of the gang. Spoils is omnipresent at gang meetings. He walks through the streets close by Amsterdam. They joke together in a pawn shop, drink whiskey in the streets, and board a ship intending to loot it. Nominally Catholic, Spoils serves as a pallbearer helping Amsterdam Vallon shoulder the coffin of a murdered priest. Boyle, a member of Bill's gang, objects to Spoils's presence in a Catholic church and proclaims that "no n—— can ever be a member of the Dead Rabbits."[13]

Sexuality and race intersect in complicated ways in the film. During a missionary-sponsored dance, Jenny picks Amsterdam out of a line for her partner after refusing several other young men. Jimmy Spoils stands two places behind Amsterdam and conceivably could have been a choice had Jenny turned

Jimmy Spoils, played by Lawrence Gilliard II, is the most omnipresent black figure in *Gangs of New York* as Amsterdam Vallon's (Leonardo DiCaprio) sidekick in the Dead Rabbits gang. Spoils often has to bear the brunt of crude racism and is later killed in the Draft Riot.

down Amsterdam. However, during the ensuing dance, in which some fifteen couples take part, Jimmy is without a partner.

Unlike black men, white men are allowed to cross racial lines. Bill, despite his many racist proclamations, relaxes with a Chinese prostitute (Eliane Chappuis) in a brothel. While the bare-breasted woman strokes Bill's shoulder, he talks with Amsterdam across a table. Entertaining the latter is a bare-breasted black woman of the night (Roberta Quaresima). Later, Bill is found in a room with two naked women, one white, the other Asian. There is an easy familiarity between prostitute and client. When his consort tries to get Bill to go upstairs, he asks her if they have ever been together before. Amsterdam and his woman share an opium pipe. At one point, Boss Tweed (Jim Broadbent) arrives and consorts with another black prostitute (Marta Pilato). Clearly, black women are only sexual objects in the film, even for avowed racists like Bill.[14]

Chinese culture in the film represents danger and degradation. One of the film's lengthiest segments takes place in a Chinese opera house/opium den. According to several estimates and the 1855 New York State Census, forty Chinese were men living in Lower Manhattan in 1860; an accounting for 1859 came up with thirty-eight Chinese around the Five Points, though scholars accept that census takers may have skipped some buildings reputed for violence. Nearly all of these Chinese men were sailors, peddlers, clerks, and laborers. Only after the Civil War and the development of a real Chinatown did Chinese New Yorkers develop such industries as cigar making and laundry work. Most lived in the heavily Irish Fourth Ward.[15]

Unlike much of the film's coverage of African Americans, its presentation of Chinese characters has credible aspects. Earlier in the film, Amsterdam, Bill, and Jenny spend time in an opium den, though it serves as a mere backdrop. Opium was legal at the time. Chinese New Yorkers commonly used opium, as did other members of the city's proletariat. Moreover, there was historical precedent for the scene at the Chinese opera house/opium den. Featuring dancers in full regalia performing operatic gestures, the scene is very elegant. As virtually all Chinese male immigrants or visitors to New York City before 1965 were from southern China, one presumes that the actors were performing Cantonese opera, which was popular with the more populous California Chinese. Indeed, despite the paltry number of Chinese in New York City in the 1850s, the Tong Hook Tong Dramatic Company, together with American investors, including P. T. Barnum, were planning in 1852 to present Cantonese opera. The production would be fully staged, elaborately costumed, authentic Cantonese opera, direct from Guangzhou and San Francisco. The production was to be part of the Crystal Palace Exhibition in New York in 1853, the major event of the year. Sizable sums of money were promised to stage the operas. When the thirty-six performers arrived, the finances were in chaos, and one George A. Beach, the producer, declared insolvency. The opera company was stranded. Eventually Beach found sufficient funds to stage performances at Niblo's Garden, with tickets priced at a modest fifty cents, much downscale from the planned price of six dollars at the Palace. The performances received excellent reviews, but, unhappily, Beach absconded with all the receipts. After several weeks of despair, a group of merchants helped the performers return to San Francisco, ending legitimate Chinese theater in New York City for some time to come.[16]

Giving further credence to Scorsese's presentation in *Gangs of New York*, Niblo's was a favorite of Bowery B'hoys, and it was reasonable to think that they might have attended a performance. However, the key moment of the scene is an attempted assassination of Bill the Butcher, leading to another of the numerous melees in the film. The scene fits into the overall construction of the motion picture, which often has lead performers strutting around the streets making stylized proclamations and speeches that invariably led to violence. While the performers on stage are Chinese, the audience is made up entirely of working-class Irish. The opera is no more than a backdrop for

Chinese opera, or more likely Cantonese opera, was new and exotic in antebellum New York, long before the presence of a substantial Chinese community in the city. In *Gangs of New York*, the Chinese performances serve as milieu rather than dramatic presentation.

the attempted murder. At the end of the scene, Bill, who survives the attack, dismissively gestured toward several of the dancers and shouts, "Get these monkeys out of here," proclaiming that now it's time for "a night of America." As Bill eulogizes Vallon, Chinese observers are pushed out of the room. Later, during a contested election, Bill's gang forces Chinese to the polls.[17]

By dwelling on Bill's racism, Scorsese missed a real chance to say something meaningful. The Chinese population of New York City was a bachelor society, with far more men than women. For mates, Chinese men frequently turned to Irish women. Virtually all the Chinese men with families recorded in the New York State census of 1855 had Irish wives.[18] Had Scorsese not been so invested in his limited view of race relations in New York, he might have placed some of these couples in the audience at Niblo's rather than only presenting Chinese as marginalized stage props. My argument about the Chinese presence in this film is similar to the liminal quality of black representation.

The film's lack of diversity is evident in casting decisions. Generally, actors and the crew are union workers; experience and screen time are highly valued. *Gangs of New York*, as mentioned, was largely filmed in Rome, so the crew was largely Italian. It is striking, however, how very few actors were black or Asian. There were almost no nonwhite crew members. Lawrence Gilliard II is the highest-billed nonwhite actor. Gilliard was a relative newcomer when he was cast in the role of Jimmy Spoils; later he became a widely known television actor. Eliane Chappuis, the daughter of a Vietnamese mother and a Swiss father, had several credits before playing a Chinese whore in *Gangs of New York*. Kathy Shao-Lin Lee, whose dancing enlivens the nightclub scene, was able to get a few more parts in succeeding years. Sai-Kit Yung, who has a speaking role at the Chinese opera house, used that credit to gain a part in *Batman Begins* (2005) and ample television appearances. The remaining nonwhite actors in *Gangs of New York* list the film as their sole experience or had limited exposure before or after. Basil Chung, who played an elderly Chinese man at the opera house, appeared in an episode of *Dr. Who* in 2005 but has no other credits.[19] Jian Su and Man Cao played acrobats in *Gangs* but have no other credits. Of the crew members, whose selection was presumably bias-free, only Ivy Fong is credited.

The film's narrative culminates in the Draft Riots. In the most extensive commentary on the historical validity of the production, Patrick McGee agrees with Iver Bernstein and others that the Draft Riots were fused with class resentment. In the film, however, while actual blacks are rare, race is predominant. In one important example, Bill fulminates against President Abraham Lincoln's Emancipation Proclamation, using racial slurs and invective. In another scene, the audience mocks a performance of the popular play derived from the novel *Uncle Tom's Cabin*. In gratuitous language, Bill derides another Irishman as no better than a "n——." The character, named McGinn, then attacks the nearest group of blacks. Later, the nativist Bill refers to arriving Irish as no better than "niggers." While some may maintain the historical accuracy of such epithets, they are jarring to the ear and have little to do with the plot. Rather they marginalize.[20]

One of the most significant acts of vandalism by the draft rioters was the burning of the Colored Orphan Asylum on 23rd Street. In the film, an announcer, presumably from a telegraph office, reads from a teletype that the mob is headed toward the asylum. A billboard poster of Frederick Douglass is burned. Had Scorsese had a sufficient budget, he would have included the conflagration. Not being able to afford the scene rankled him as he considered the film incomplete without this episode. One has to wonder, given the director's penchant for racial invective, whether he would have included the mob's sparing of the children. At any rate, racial attacks in the film are somewhat subdued, given the degree of actual violence directed toward local blacks. The film briefly depicts the lynching of one black man and the murder of Jimmy Spoils and makes fleeting reference to the torching of the Colored Orphan Asylum.[21]

Others have noted the historical errors in the film. I point instead to the stereotypical use of racial groups. When blacks or Asians are present, they serve as little more than human scenery, making the film even less relevant for today's audiences. Even the character of Jimmy Spoils seems an anomaly. Scorsese could have done much more.

NOTES

1. Peter Rainer, "Old World Charm, a review of *Gangs of New York*," *New York Magazine*, 23 December 2002; Richard Schickel, *Conversations with Scorsese* (New York: Knopf, 2011); Herbert Asbury, *The Gangs of New York: An Informal History of the Underworld* (New York: Knopf, 1928).

2. Tom Shone, *Scorsese: A Retrospective* (London: Thames & Hudson, 2015), 198–99; Schickel, *Conversations with Scorsese*, 226. I have used the standard DVD version of the film (Los Angeles: Miramax Pictures, 2002).

3. Patrick McGee, *Bad History and the Logics of Blockbuster Cinema* (New York: Palgrave, 2012), 87. McGee's discussion of *Gangs of New York* is by far the most extensive, covering pages 69–144 in his book. See also Nathan Jérémie-Brink, "Black and Irish Conflicts in 'Gangs Of New York,'" *Eat This Scroll* (blog), 2 February 2013, https://eatthisscroll.wordpress.com/2013/02/13/black-and-irish-conflicts-in-gangs-of-new-york/.

4. Graham Russell Hodges, "'Desirable Companions and Lovers': Irish and African Americans in the Sixth Ward, 1830–1870," in *The New York Irish*, ed. Ronald H. Bayer and Timothy J. Meagher (Baltimore: Johns Hopkins University Press, 1996).

5. Robert Brent Toplin, *History by Hollywood*, 2nd ed. (Urbana: University of Illinois Press, 2010), 3–8.

6. A. O. Scott, "To Feel A City Seethe," review of *Gangs of New York*, *New York Times*, 20 December 2002; *Martin Scorsese Interviews*, ed. Robert Ribera, rev. ed. (Jackson: University Press of Mississippi, 2017), 181–82.

7. Shone, *Scorsese*, 200; Vincent LoBrutto, *Martin Scorsese: A Biography* (Westport, CT: Praeger, 2008), 370.

8. McGee, *Bad History*, 72.

9. Timothy Gilfoyle, "*Gangs of New York*: Why Myth Matters," *Journal of Urban History* 29, no. 5 (2003): 620–30; Daniel J. Walkowitz, "*The Gangs of New York*: The Mean Streets in History," *History Workshop Journal* 56 (2003): 204–9; Vincent Di Girolamo, "Such, Such, Were the Bhoys. . . . ," *Radical History Review* 90 (2004): 123–41; J. Matthew Gallman, "Gangs of New York," *Journal of American History* 90, no. 3 (2003): 1124–26; Shone, *Scorsese*, 201.

10. The key work here is Iver Bernstein, *The New York City Draft Riots: Their Significance for American Society in the Age of the Civil War* (New York: Oxford University Press, 1990). See also McGee, *Bad History*, 64, 128, for a summary of this argument. For a new argument, see Clifton Hood, *In Pursuit of Privilege: A History of New York City's Upper Class and the Making of a Metropolis* (New York: Columbia University Press, 2017), 159.

11. Walkowitz, "*The Gangs of New York*."

12. McGee, *Bad History*, 74–75, 80–82. Bill's rants are at disc 1, 00:17 and 1:15–16.

13. McGee, *Bad History,* 118; John Kuo Wei Tchen, *New York before Chinatown: Orientalism and the Shaping of American Culture, 1776–1882* (Baltimore: Johns Hopkins University Press), 73. For Spoils in the Dead Rabbits, see *Gangs of New York,* disc 1, 38:55 and 1:01; and disc 2, 00:39.

14. *Gangs of New York,* disc 1, 1:20–24.

15. Tyler Anbinder, *Five Points: The Nineteenth-Century New York City Neighborhood That Invented Tap Dance, Stole Elections, and Became the World's Most Notorious Slum* (New York: Free Press, 2001), 396–98; Tchen, *New York before Chinatown,* 76.

16. Tchen, *New York before Chinatown,* 86–89. See also McGee, *Bad History,* 120.

17. For 1850s references to Chinese as subhuman curiosities, see Tchen, *New York before Chinatown,* 97–131.

18. Tchen, *New York before Chinatown,* 77–79, 159–63; Anbinder, *Five Points,* 420. For incidents, see *Gangs of New York,* disc 2, 00:17.

19. For Gilliard, see http://www.imdb.com/name/nm0319142/?ref_=ttfc_fc_cl_t14. For Elaine Chappuis, see http://www.imdb.com/name/nm0152671/?ref_=ttfc_fc_cl_t65#actress. For Kathy Shao-Lin Lee, see http://www.imdb.com/name/nm1290111/bio?ref_=nm_ov_bio_sm. For Sai-Kit Yung, see http://www.imdb.com/name/nm0950954/?ref_=ttfc_fc_cl_t38. For Basil Chung, see http://www.imdb.com/name/nm1307302/?ref_=ttfc_fc_cl_t39.

20. McGee, *Bad History,* 84, 93–95, 115.

21. Schickel, *Conversations with Scorsese,* 227–28; Sarah Mulhall Adelman, "Permitted to Proceed Unmolested": Childhood and Race in the Burning of the Colored Orphan Asylum," *Commonplace* 17, no. 2 (March 2017).

17

The Assassin's Accomplices
Guilt, Innocence, and Redemption in *The Prisoner of Shark Island* and *The Conspirator*

JONATHAN D. SARRIS

Abraham Lincoln's life has provided endless source material for historians and filmmakers alike—and so has his death. Indeed, the events of late April 1865 seem almost tailor-made for storytellers, whether their preferred genre is fiction or nonfiction. Both *The Prisoner of Shark Island* (1936) and *The Conspirator* (2010) focus on the lives of accused members of the Lincoln assassination conspiracy. Each film dramatizes the plight of one of the accused, who is portrayed as a scapegoat wrongly prosecuted by vengeful Union officials meting out victors' justice to innocent white southerners. In seeking to exonerate two of the alleged conspirators, Samuel Mudd and Mary Surratt, these films echo the notes of the Lost Cause mythology that arose after the Civil War.

But this is not to say that the two films are identical. *Shark Island* was made while the mythology of the Lost Cause still held sway, and the film openly indulged in the romanticization of the plantation South. *The Conspirator* was made after the civil rights movement by an avowedly liberal actor-director, Robert Redford. But Redford had very different ideological reasons for depicting an innocent southern lady as a victim of the Union, reasons that had nothing to do with the original purposes of the Lost Cause but rather reflected the rancorous aftermath of the American wars in Iraq and Afghanistan in the early twenty-first century. Thus we have two films that proceed from the same assumption—that southerners were wrongfully prosecuted by federal officials after the Civil War—but have different purposes and reasons for telling their stories, both embedded in the times and events that surrounded the films' creation.

John Ford had a penchant for making films about the past, from the reign of Mary Stuart to the gunfight at the O.K. Corral. *The Prisoner of Shark Island* fits squarely within this oeuvre. Together, Ford and the Georgia-born screenwriter Nunnally Johnson crafted a portrayal of one of the most interesting characters involved in the Lincoln assassination, Dr. Samuel Mudd, whose decision to provide medical assistance to John Wilkes Booth in the hours following the assassination led to a prison sentence for aiding the president's murderer. The film was released on Abraham Lincoln's birthday in 1936.[1]

Ford's Samuel Mudd (Warner Baxter) is a kind "country doctor" who lives a simple life in the Maryland countryside southeast of Washington with his doting wife, Peggy (Gloria Stuart), at the end of the Civil War. Their lives are shattered on the stormy night when John Wilkes Booth and his coconspirator David Herold pound on the door asking for help. The good doctor, not knowing who Booth is or what he's done, treats his broken leg and sends him into the night. For this simple act of kindness Mudd is arrested the next day by vengeful Union soldiers. A drumhead military trial follows for Mudd and the other accused conspirators, at which the saintly physician eloquently protests his innocence before being shouted down by hard-hearted judges. As his helpless wife looks on, the other accused conspirators swing from the gallows, and Mudd himself is sentenced to life at hard labor.[2]

Mudd is condemned to a hellish military prison at Fort Jefferson in the Dry Tortugas, Florida, where he is starved, beaten, and tortured. After a failed, desperate escape attempt, Mudd is thrown into a dungeon along with his loyal former slave Buck. Salvation comes in the form of an outbreak of yellow fever that paralyzes the fort. The good doctor springs into action, assisting the post surgeon to treat the stricken prisoners. When the men recover, the commandant personally intervenes with President Andrew Johnson to secure a pardon for Mudd. The film closes with Mudd and Buck returning home to Maryland and their families, and "Dixie" plays cheerfully over the closing credits.[3]

To the extent that the film gets the history right, it is mostly the little touches of physical detail and staging that add authenticity to its depiction of the Civil War era. The rousing torchlight "illuminations" that filled the streets of Washington, DC, on the night of Robert E. Lee's surrender; the jerry-rigged splint the real doctor fashioned for Booth on the fateful night; the monogrammed boot the assassin left at the house—all these ring true. The harsh conditions of Mudd's incarceration at Fort Jefferson are generally realistic though exaggerated. As shown in the film—and the basis for its title—there really was a shark patrolling the watery moat surrounding the fort, although the poor creature was no superpredator: when the soldiers tried to feed it with live cats, the discombobulated shark was frightened off. Dr. Mudd did assist the medical personnel at the fort during the yellow fever epidemic, and his presidential pardon from Johnson recognized that "Samuel A. Mudd devoted himself to the care and cure of the sick, and interposed his courage and skill to protect the garrison."[4] But the film's interpretive framework is problematic. Not only does Ford misstate Mudd's role in the Lincoln conspiracy; he also echoes racist arguments about the nature of slavery and the causes of the Civil War itself that were at the very heart of the Lost Cause myth.

Despite the Mudd family's remarkable 150-year-long quest to rehabilitate Mudd's image and formally reverse his conviction, history tells a far more complicated story about the relationship between Samuel Mudd and Lincoln's assassins. In the film, Mudd has no political allegiance to the Confederacy and even praises the sixteenth president in an early scene, saying, "Old Abe's all right after all" and opining that Lincoln's merciful attitude is "the only salvation we Southerners can look for." But the real Samuel Mudd was a slaveholder, a secessionist, and an ardent opponent of the Union. He raged against "Pharisaical, covert, stealthy, and cowardly" northerners. He despised Republicans and abolitionists for "ram[ming] down our throats their religious convictions." The federal government was nothing but a bunch of "sheep-stealing dogs," Mudd ranted, and Lincoln himself was the engine of a dangerous "revolution" that intended to force his will upon the South and the US Constitution.[5]

The doctor did more than spout harsh words during the war. He was active in a pro-Confederate network of spies, saboteurs, informants, and guerrillas in southern Maryland. While the movie Mudd is a stranger to Booth, the real doctor was well acquainted with the killer before the assassination. Booth actually stayed at Mudd's home while reconnoitering potential escape routes through southern Maryland, and later Mudd conferred with Booth in Washington, DC, even introducing him to a key coconspirator, fellow Marylander John H. Surratt.[6] Mudd's prevarications to pursuing Union authorities hunting the fleeing Booth cast further doubt on the doctor's claims of innocence. At his trial, Mudd's muddled story faced more challenges as witness after witness testified about his previous meetings with Booth, his contacts with Confederate agents, and his apparent efforts to mislead federal officials. His words and actions did not seem to be those of a wholly innocent man, and it was doubtless this untrustworthy tone that led the military court to give him such a harsh sentence. Whether or not Mudd was an active coconspirator, John Ford's portrayal of a simple, innocent man caught up in a maelstrom of northern revenge bears little resemblance to historical fact.[7]

But Ford's distortion of history goes far beyond the guilt or innocence of one man. The larger problem with his movie is that it repeats racial myths about the Civil War and Reconstruction. Unlike in many movie depictions of the Civil War era, black characters appear frequently throughout the film. But they are all in service of the racial ideology of the Lost Cause, validating the paternalistic view of black people as subservient, childlike, or savage. To the extent that the film uses black characters to legitimize Samuel Mudd, it also legitimizes the propaganda of the Old South and Jim Crow eras, which stereotyped African Americans as incapable of responsibility and self-government, better off under the care of white caretakers, who knew what was best for them.

In the film, "Massa Sam" cares for his black dependents with a mix of fatherly affection, fair discipline, and amused tolerance. When Yankee carpetbaggers show up near the Mudd place to preach the virtues of emancipation to the credulous former slaves, Mudd orders Buck and the others to throw the Yankee off the place and get back to work. The hands cheerfully comply. (This scene may be attributable to screenwriter Nunnally Johnson's southern roots. He recalled that his Georgia-born parents refused to visit the northeastern states "because of the New England carpetbaggers during Reconstruction days.") Buck loyally serves the family throughout the trial and even poses as a Union soldier to gain access to Fort Jefferson so he can help engineer his former master's escape. Through it all, Buck personifies "the faithful devotion [of] . . . the slaves of the Southern people during our great four years' war for independence."[8]

When the action of the movie shifts to the doctor's imprisonment, the racial politics become even more explicit. The African American troops guarding the fort are depicted as slovenly and incompetent, speaking in broad dialect. When the epidemic strikes the garrison, the black soldiers cower and roll their eyes in fear, refusing to aid the sick or even leave their barracks. In one of the film's most revealing moments, Dr. Mudd assumes control of the hospital in the crisis and orders the black soldiers to assist him. When they refuse, Mudd takes on the persona of an angry master, cajoling and humiliating the black men, threatening them with hanging, warning, "They'll choke you, choke you till your eyeballs pop out and your tongue swells up"—a shocking evocation of the real-life lynchings that were all too common in the 1930s. Overawed by Mudd's threats, the black men quickly fall into line, saying, "That ain't' no

Yankee talking jus' to hear hisself talk, that's a Southern man, and he mean it." Ultimately the fort is saved because Samuel Mudd is the only man who knows how to treat black men as the subservient children they are.[9]

These scenes are actually quite compatible with the real Samuel Mudd's views on race. The doctor owned eleven slaves before the Civil War and believed that black servitude had been ordained by God. While he was imprisoned at Fort Jefferson, Mudd's racial sensibilities were affronted by the presence of black soldiers, and he raged at being forced to suffer "the humiliation of being guarded by an ignorant irresponsible & prejudiced Negro soldiery." Like many southern whites, Mudd foresaw a bleak future for the white race in a South ruled by black men. "Our white population is wonderfully diminishing by death and other causes," Mudd wrote despairingly. "The negroes will soon be in the majority." Indeed, Samuel Mudd's escape attempt was spurred by his desperation to escape black rule at Fort Jefferson. "Could we have had a white regiment . . . to guard the place," Mudd wrote after his recapture, "no thought of leaving should have been harbored," but being ordered about by black men had been "more than I could submit to."[10] So, while *The Prisoner of Shark Island* does not reflect the current state of historical scholarship on the Civil War, emancipation, or Reconstruction, the film accurately reflects the real Samuel Mudd's views on race and slavery. But while today these views are seen as detestable, in 1936 they were mainstream.

Advocates for racial justice condemned the film at the time of its release and objected to its portrayal of African Americans. The NAACP urged protest against the film, as it had for *The Birth of a Nation*, and the black-owned *Chicago Defender* branded *Shark Island* "an anti-Negro picture," lamenting "that the main impression created by the film is that Negroes are inferior individuals and cowards." Even Hollywood's censoring body, the Motion Picture Code, was uncomfortable with the film and cautioned Ford and Johnson to avoid any material that "tends to bring up racial differences or prejudice between the black and white races."[11] But this was not a majority view. When the *New York Times* panned the film in 1936, it critiqued the derivative plot but said nothing about racial stereotypes.[12] Ford and Johnson created a fictionalized work of history that was very much in the mainstream of 1930s film depictions of slavery, race, and the Old South, recasting the history of the Civil War and emancipation as a tragedy for the white South. In the process, the film elevates as innocent a man who well might have been guilty and celebrates a cause and culture that definitely were.

Seventy-three years later, a very different filmmaker took on the aftermath of the Lincoln assassination. Robert Redford's *The Conspirator* tells the story of Mary Surratt, the first woman ever executed by the US government. Like Samuel Mudd's, her case is a textbook example of a rush to judgment. Like Mudd's, Surratt's case has been a cause célèbre for legions of writers, artists, and scholars. And like Mudd's, her story found a skilled storyteller to bring her case to the screen with the intent of exonerating an innocent person of a terrible crime. As a director, Robert Redford seems to be everything that John Ford was not— quiet, deliberate, unprolific, self-conscious of film as an art. And unlike the conservative Ford's, Redford's filmmaking is shaped by his political liberalism.

The Conspirator begins on the night of the Lincoln assassination, in a city gripped with fear and chaos. As Booth's coconspirators are rounded up one by one, a military commission is organized to try the accused, including Mary Surratt (Robin Wright), owner of "the nest that hatched the plot" and the mother of one of Booth's closest associates. Mary is assigned an idealistic young army attorney named Frederick Aiken (James McAvoy), who is reluctant at first to defend a woman he considers guilty but relents because "she deserves a defense." As Aiken gradually becomes convinced of Mary's innocence, he battles heroically against a military justice system that is bent on vengeance and tramples civil liberties. After an unfair trial at the hands of prejudiced judges, Mary is found guilty. Aiken tries one last legal gambit to have the conviction appealed by a writ of habeas corpus from a civilian court. But Secretary of War Edwin Stanton (Kevin Kline) blocks the move, insisting that Mary "be given a swift, sure and harsh sentence." Mary Surratt thus marches with the other conspirators to the gallows, where she stoically faces her doom, leaving Aiken to ponder the fate of justice.[13]

Does Redford's film hew closer to history than John Ford's did? We are certainly primed to expect more recent films to be more "authentic" then the costume dramas of the distant past, since they often have bigger budgets and fewer content restrictions and are marketed to more savvy modern audiences. *The Conspirator* strives to be taken seriously as an interpretation of the past in a way John Ford's *Shark Island* probably did not. The effort shows. To an even more heightened degree than Ford, Redford works to re-create the physical world of 1865 in minute detail. Consider the scene depicting Lincoln's evacuation from the theater to the Petersen House after Booth's attack. It seems almost documentary in its realism—from the panicked throng outside Ford's Theater, to the way the stricken president is laid crosswise on the bed, to

Mary Surratt (Robin Wright) under military escort to her execution in *The Conspirator*

Mary Lincoln's emotional breakdown. The execution of Surratt and the other convicted conspirators on July 7, 1865, is also striking in its verisimilitude. The Fort Pulaski National Monument near Savannah is a convincing stand-in for the prison yard in at the Old Arsenal in Washington, and the procedures of the execution itself are searingly authentic, from the umbrella used to shield Mary from the July sun as she ascended the gallows to the way the prisoners were tied and hooded; these little touches are almost enough to make the viewer believe along with Theodore Roosevelt that history has "the power to embody ghosts, to put flesh and blood on dry bones, to make dead men living before our eyes."[14]

But like *The Prisoner of Shark Island*, Redford's film has a point of view and functions at a point in time. And Redford's interpretation, like Ford's, has as much to do with the then current social and cultural milieu as it does with the realities of 1865. Redford clearly wants to teach lessons with *The Conspirator*, not primarily those of history but rather those of certain dangerous trends in American politics of the early twenty-first century. In service of that goal, his film unwittingly echoes elements of the Lost Cause mythology that portray the South and southerners as victims of the overweening power of the federal government.[15]

The Prisoner of Shark Island and *The Conspirator* / 197

The film's interpretation of the Surratt trial is firmly fixed on two fundamental assumptions—that Mary Surratt was not guilty of a capital offense
and that the use of military tribunals to try civilians was unjust and illegal.
Redford's Surratt is a proud southern woman and a Confederate patriot in her
own way, but she is more or less a passive witness to her son John's involvement with Booth. She is condemned by the unscrupulous machinations of
witnesses who, Redford strongly suggests, lie on the stand to implicate Mary
and save their own skins. The truth is more complicated. All the conspirators
stayed in or visited Surratt's Washington, DC, boardinghouse frequently and
planned much of their operation there. Booth also used her home in southern
Maryland as a safehouse during his flight, and the aforementioned witnesses
claimed consistently that Surratt had helped transport weapons and supplies
at Booth's request. Surratt was also directly implicated by one of the four main
conspirators, George Atzerodt, who remembered Booth discussing Mary's
mission to southern Maryland. For the assassination historian Edward Steers,
these pieces of circumstantial evidence are compelling reasons to believe that
Mary Surratt aided and abetted the conspiracy. It certainly seemed so to the
judges on the tribunal, who had no trouble believing that a woman who had
had regular contact with Booth and the other known conspirators must have
been involved in some integral way.[16]

Redford's second argument, about the illegitimacy of military tribunals,
is even more pronounced. Repeatedly Redford shows the judges to be deeply
prejudiced against the defendants, shouting down defense counsel, quashing
exculpatory evidence, and coaching prosecution witnesses on the stand. As in
Shark Island, the civil courts are portrayed as the only hope for the innocent
accused, and much of the film's plotline revolves around lawyer Aiken's attempt
to remove Mary from the jurisdiction of military judgment. The choice to try
the conspirators in military tribunals was indeed controversial at the time of
the trial, and in reality Mary Surratt's other lawyer, Reverdy Johnson (played
in the film by Tom Wilkinson), argued strenuously that the proceedings were
unconstitutional, just as he does in the movie. But here again the historical
record is not crystal clear, and interpretations change. Several scholars have
pointed out that the decision was validated by both the attorney general of the
United States and President Andrew Johnson. There were good reasons for a
military trial, including the difficulty of finding impartial jurors and the fact
that the assassination of the commander-in-chief during wartime was an act
of enemy combatants, who should be subject to military justice.[17]

Redford takes a side in these arguments, which is his prerogative, just as it is for historians. But his argument is weakened by heavy-handed scenes that tend to the inflammatory. For example, when Anna Surratt (Evan Rachel Wood) testifies in her mother's defense, the court forbids her to see her mother, an act of deliberate cruelty that causes Anna to break down in sobs. The fact that the court took no such action might seem a minor quibble, but it substantiates the portrayal of a vengeful federal government inflicting misery on helpless southern women. Even less excusable is Redford's portrayal of Edwin Stanton as a scheming villain who subverts law and morality in order to punish the innocent. From the moment he appears at the Petersen House, Kevin Kline's Stanton is the hot-blooded heart of vengeance, heedless of the legal niceties. "They assassinated our President, and someone must be held accountable! The people want that," Kline growls. When the military tribunal recommends imprisonment rather than death for Surratt (as really did occur), Stanton simply orders the tribunal to change its recommendation and ignores the writ of habeas corpus Aiken has secured from a federal judge. All this is laughable. The real Stanton had no direct role in the trial once the military tribunal was established; that power went to Judge Joseph Holt, who ran the proceedings independently. And it was President Johnson, not Stanton, who refused to grant Mrs. Surratt clemency (although he later claimed that he had never been told of the tribunal's recommendation for leniency).[18]

What is missing from Redford's tale is at least as relevant as what he includes, and the film misses opportunities to deal with the Surratt trial in historical context, which would have revealed political flashpoints that are much more interesting than a dry courtroom drama. The real political battle of titans going on over the assassination trial wasn't between Stanton and Aiken. It was between President Johnson and the man who actually ran the trial—Judge Joseph Holt, whose role is minimized in the film. Holt, head of the Bureau of Military Justice, was the engine of the proceedings, and it was he who urged a robust prosecution of Mudd and Surratt. A friend of President Lincoln and a fellow Kentuckian, Holt had twin motivations for his vigorous prosecution. First, he was determined to prove a connection between the assassination plot and the Confederate president, Jefferson Davis.[19] As a result, Holt kept his foot on the pedal during the prosecution and favored executing Mary Surratt despite the tribunal's recommendation that she be sentenced to life in prison. Second, Holt became convinced that prosecuting Davis and other former Confederate officials was a vital component of a larger mission: enforcing a stringent Reconstruction on the South that would use federal power to protect the rights of former slaves. This put Holt at odds with President Andrew Johnson, who favored leniency for the South and cared little about the fate of the freed people. As Holt and Johnson became more antagonistic, the legacy of the trials became a political football, especially with regard to Samuel Mudd and Mary Surratt. In 1869 President Johnson pardoned Mudd and released Surratt's remains from the Old Arsenal yard to her family in an attempt to burnish his reputation as a friend to white southerners and a supporter of leniency toward the former Confederacy. Any of this material would have provided Redford's film with high-stakes political intrigue that arguably would have been much more exciting than what he invented, but it was not to be.[20]

Another missed opportunity for Redford is in the treatment of gender in the Surratt trial. It would seem that a film with a female protagonist would be fruitful ground for injecting some of the considerable recent scholarship on the issue into the mainstream. The defense strategy of Surratt's lawyers was tied innately to conceptions of womanhood in the Victorian era. In the real trial, Mary Surratt's status as a woman, with all that entailed in 1865, was central to her defense. In essence, Aiken argued that Mary's status as a proper lady made her incapable of such a violent crime and, furthermore, that that same status entitled her to the protection of men. His summation held Mary up as the epitome of her sex—"a woman born and bred in respectability . . . whose unfailing attention to the most sacred duties of life has won for her the name of 'a proper Christian matron.'" But Redford ignores this gender dynamic, and the version of Aiken's speech included in the film cuts the heart out of the historical reality of Surratt's defense.[21]

But if Redford's film contains errors, it may be because he had bigger fish to fry. Just as John Ford functioned within a culture and a society still dominated by the Lost Cause, Redford also paints on a canvas framed by contemporaneous events. It is impossible to view *The Conspirator* outside the context of America's wars in Iraq and Afghanistan in the early twenty-first century and the struggle to define rules of war and jurisprudence in an age of insurgency and terrorism. The key touchstone for the film was the system of military tribunals set up under the George W. Bush administration to handle terrorist cases outside the civil-court framework. Defenders of this approach argued that military tribunals were an acceptable compromise between the rule of law and national security, and to bolster their case they used historical examples such as the military trials of saboteurs during World War II and the Lincoln-assassination trials. Those on the left, including Redford, disagreed. In interviews given at the time of the film's release, he made clear that the trial of Mary Surratt offered a cautionary tale for the present day, arguing that "the fact that this woman who ran a boarding house was tried and put to death in a military tribunal" was a dangerous parallel to the present state of affairs. The director also warned that "messing with the Constitution has been going on since the time of Lincoln" and that events like the Surratt trials show "what prejudice and bias can do to justice." Kevin Kline also saw contemporary relevance in the film, comparing his ruthless, amoral Stanton to Vice President Dick Cheney.[22]

Doubtless the liberal Redford would be appalled by the suggestion that in defending Mary Surratt he was unwittingly embracing the line of the Lost Cause argument that portrayed white southerners as innocent victims of a rapacious federal government. And it would be a mistake to say that *The Conspirator* is cut from the same ideological cloth as *The Prisoner of Shark Island*. Each director had his own agenda for casting the Lincoln trials as he did. What is inarguable is that each film used the past to convey messages about the present, consciously or unconsciously. And ultimately, these films reveal much more about 1936 and 2010 than they do about 1865. "When the legend becomes fact, print the legend," advocates a character in John Ford's *The Man Who Shot Liberty Valance*.[23] Both these films follow that advice.

NOTES

I dedicate this essay to my father, Louis G. Sarris, who taught me to love John Ford movies.

1. Dan Ford, *Pappy: The Life and Times of John Ford* (Englewood Cliffs, NJ: Prentice Hall, 1979), 94–97; Tom Stempl, *Screenwriter: The Life and Times of Nunnally Johnson* (San Diego: A. S. Barns, 1980), 53–56.

2. *The Prisoner of Shark Island*, dir. John Ford (20th Century Fox, 1936), DVD.

3. *Prisoner of Shark Island*.

4. *Washington National Intelligencer*, 11 April 1865; *Washington Evening Star*, 12 April 1865; *Frank Leslie's Illustrated Newspaper*, 10 June 1865; Elizabeth Leonard, *Lincoln's Avengers: Justice, Revenge, and Reunion after the Civil War* (New York: Norton, 2004), 69; Thomas Reid, *America's Fortress: A History of Fort Jefferson, Dry Tortugas, Florida* (Gainesville: University Press of Florida, 2006); 84–89, 118; Nettie Mudd, *The Life of Dr. Samuel A. Mudd* (New York: Neale, 1906), 258–59; "Samuel A. Mudd's Pardon," 8 February 1869, quoted in Elden Weckesser, *His Name Was Mudd: The Life of Dr. Samuel A. Mudd, Who Treated the Fleeing John Wilkes Booth* (Jefferson, NC: McFarland, 1991), 221.

5. Edward Steers Jr., *His Name Is Still Mudd: The Case against Doctor Samuel Mudd* (Gettysburg, PA: Thomas, 1997); *Prisoner of Shark Island;* Samuel Mudd to Orestes Brownson, 13 January 1862, excerpted in Mudd, *Life of Dr. Samuel A. Mudd,* 341–46.

6. Ben Pittman, *The Assassination of President Lincoln and the Trial of the Conspirators* (Birmingham, AL: Notable Trials Library, Gryphon Editions, Inc., 1989), 170–71; Edward Steers Jr., *Blood on the Moon: The Assassination of Abraham Lincoln* (Lexington: University Press of Kentucky, 2001), 66–68; Terry Alford, *Fortune's Fool: The Life of John Wilkes Booth* (Oxford: Oxford University Press, 2015), 190–93; Thomas Conrad, *The Rebel Scout: A Thrilling History of Scouting in the Southern Army* (Washington, DC: National, 1904), 62–63.

7. Pittman, *Assassination of Abraham Lincoln,* 168–70; Louis J. Weichmann, *A True History of the Assassination of Abraham Lincoln and of the Conspiracy of 1865* (New York: Knopf, 1975), 68–69; Edward Steers Jr., *The Trial: The Assassination of President Lincoln and the Trial of the Conspirators* (Lexington: University Press of Kentucky, 2003), lxxx–lxxxvii; Leonard, *Lincoln's Avengers,* 125–28.

8. *Prisoner of Shark Island; Confederate Veteran* 2, no. 11 (November 1894): 336; Stempl, *Screenwriter,* 21; David W. Blight, *Race and Reunion: The Civil War in American Memory* (Cambridge, MA: Belknap Press of Harvard University Press, 2001), 259–60.

9. *Prisoner of Shark Island.*

10. Mudd, *Life of Samuel A. Mudd,* 345; Pittman, *Assassination of Abraham Lincoln,* 170–71; Mudd, *Life of Samuel A. Mudd,* 130–31, 144, 350–51.

11. *Chicago Defender,* 28 March 1936; Ellen Scott, *Cinema Civil Rights: Regulation, Repression, and Race in the Classical Hollywood Era* (New Brunswick, NJ: Rutgers University Press, 2014), 26.

12. *New York Times,* 13 February 1936.

13. *The Conspirator,* dir. Robert Redford (2010; Lionsgate, 2011), DVD.

14. James L. Swanson, *Manhunt: The 12-Day Chase for Lincoln's Killer* (New York: Harper Perennial, 2006), 90–94; Leonard, *Lincoln's Avengers,* 67–101; Theodore Roosevelt, *Annual address of the president of the American Historical Association, delivered at Boston, December 27, 1912,* in *American Historical Review* 18, no. 3 (1913): 473–89.

15. *The Conspirator;* Robert Redford, interview by Christianne Amanpour, *This Week,* 10 April 2011, http://abcnews.go.com/Politics/robert-redford-politics-today-pretty-grim-now/story?id=13337715.

16. Pittman, *Assassination of Abraham Lincoln,* 85–86, 116–17; Weichmann, *True History,* 133–34; Steers, *Blood on the Moon,* 137–43; Alford, *Fortune's Fool,* 260; Leonard, *Lincoln's Avengers,* 104–5.

17. *New York Herald,* 31 May 1865; Pittman, *Assassination of Abraham Lincoln,* 251–63; Davis Miller Dewitt, *The Judicial Murder of Mary R. Surratt* (Baltimore: John Murphy, 1895); Louis Fisher, *Military Tribunals: Historical Patterns and Lessons,* CRS Report No. RL42458 (Washington, DC: Congressional Research Service, 2004), https://fas.org/sgp/crs/natsec/RL32458.pdf.

18. *The Conspirator;* Leonard, *Lincoln's Avengers,* 8–11, 64–73.

19. Leonard, *Lincoln's Avengers,* 63–65; William Tidwell, *April '65: Confederate Covert Action in the American Civil War* (Kent, OH: Kent State University Press, 1995), 1–14.

20. Leonard, *Lincoln's Avengers,* 265–90.

21. Catherine Clinton and Nina Silber, eds., *Divided Houses: Gender and the Civil War* (Oxford: Oxford University Press, 1992); Pittman, *Assassination of Abraham Lincoln*, 298–99; Leonard, *Lincoln's Avengers*, 120–22; Robert Redford, director's commentary, *The Conspirator*.

22. Redford interview; Redford, director's commentary; Louis Fisher, *Military Tribunals and Presidential Power: American Revolution to the War on Terrorism* (Lawrence: University Press of Kansas, 2005).

23. *The Man Who Shot Liberty Valance*, dir. John Ford (Paramount, 1962).

IV

THE LOST CAUSE, RECONSTRUCTION, AND THE WEST

18

Historical to a Fault
Gary Ross, *Free State of Jones,* and the (Eventual) Destruction of the Lost Cause

JOSEPH M. BEILEIN JR.

In the middle of the 2016 film *Free State of Jones,* Gary Ross, the screenwriter and director, makes perhaps the clearest articulation of his central point. Following a brief but intense battle scene in March 1864, Newt Knight (Matthew McConaughey) and his interracial and intergender band of Unionist guerrillas drive Confederates soldiers out of Ellisville, Mississippi. Then, the victors remove the Confederate battle flag and in its place raise the Stars and Stripes. For these men and women, black and white, former slaves and poor farmers, the Confederate flag symbolized slavery, white supremacy, the exploitation of both white and black people by wealthy slaveholders, and, of course, treason. In hastily pulling down that symbol of so much hate, greed, and corruption and replacing it once again with a symbol of freedom, hope, democracy, and humanity, they seek to redeem their homeland. Not a few scenes later, Knight—a white yeoman farmer and a deserter from the Confederate army—stands under that flag and declares to his gathered followers that Jones County will now be its own sovereign state, in which all God's children will be considered free and all men will reap what they sow. As depicted in this film, the community not only reversed the backward-looking dream of the Confederacy but was so revolutionary that even today's mainstream American audience might struggle to recognize the interracial, egalitarian community that once lived under the Stars and Stripes.[1]

Free State of Jones is a film that sets out to overturn much of the traditional narrative of the Civil War. As Ross said, "It was very much on my mind to set that record straight." In particular, Ross aims to take down the Lost Cause, which is responsible for much of what Americans think about the war, themselves, others, and their places in this country. At its most basic, the Lost Cause is the idea that white southerners seceded and fought the Civil War to protect their rights—individual liberties and states' rights—and that the cause of the war was not slavery. The Lost Cause promotes the idea that slavery was a benevolent institution and that the slaves themselves preferred their shackles to freedom, were loyal to their owners, and would have remained savages if not for the civilizing efforts of their paternalist benefactors. With this in mind, the war is remembered as one of self-defense, or the "War of Northern Aggression," as it is still known in some parts of the country. Finally, a key fixture of the basic argument is that white southern men were outnumbered and had far fewer resources than their Yankee enemies. In this light, Confederate soldiers are always depicted as pious, chivalrous, and brave. Although academic historians have dismantled the Lost Cause, the perpetuation of this ultimately dangerous constellation of myths in popular culture has allowed the white South to seemingly win the fight for the memory of the Civil War.[2]

In making a film that seeks to discredit the Lost Cause, Ross's screenplay was guided by the excellent research and inspired writing of Victoria Bynum, one of the most innovative and respected social historians to work in the field of Civil War studies. According to Ross, "Victoria Bynum, a very good historian, wrote the first book on [Newt Knight] which was an academic investigation." Bynum's book, *The Free State of Jones: Mississippi's Longest Civil War* (2001) was the first to tell the full story of the Knight family, other related kinship networks, and the Jones County rebellion. Bynum's narrative begins in the colonial period and concludes in the mid-twentieth century. She traces the extended familial bonds that made up Knight's Company and ultimately the interracial community that grew out of the war. Ross's film draws mostly from part 2 of Bynum's book, in which she lays out the factors that led to the creation of the army of Confederate deserters and Unionists who coalesced in Jones County and the ways in which they directly challenged the Confederacy. Here Bynum displays the inclusive nature of the war: it was not just a war between men on the battlefield but an intergender war that destroyed any notion of a boundary between the home and the front. Furthermore, some of the most powerful analysis offered by Bynum reveals the intersection between gender identity, racial identity, and politics in the era of Reconstruction and beyond. Indeed, *The Free State of Jones* effectively changes the chronology of the war, demonstrating that it did not end in Mississippi in 1865 but continued on for a century afterwards.[3]

While Bynum's *Free State of Jones* offered Ross the best book from which to build his film, the challenge posed by the American film industry's perpetuation of the mythical Civil War is formidable. Beginning with *The Birth of a Nation* (1915), the Lost Cause has been a staple of movies about the Civil War. *The Birth of a Nation*, which was released during the Jim Crow era, remains the most overt, blunt depiction of the Lost Cause. In it, the conflict is a "war of northern aggression," in which wealthy, white southern slaveholders are victims, abolitionists are deformed opportunists, and African Americans are either loyal pets or ignorant, base, and violent animals. These alternative facts presented in the film were readily accepted and even celebrated, with President Woodrow Wilson equating the film to "writing history with lightning." Perhaps more shocking, the film inspired the second iteration of the Ku Klux Klan. The 1939 film *Gone with the Wind* told a Lost Cause story from a different perspective. With the white female protagonist, Scarlett O'Hara, struggling with a war that shattered her world, the audience sees the destruction of the southern homefront, the noble attempt by southerners of all stripes to fight back—even the loyal slaves, who believe the Yankees and carpetbaggers to be the real enemies—and ultimately some redemption in rebuilding the world in a way that resembled their antebellum paradise. More recently films, like *Gettysburg* (1993) and *Gods and Generals* (2003), as well as Ken Burns's documentary *The Civil War* (1990), continue to offer doses of the Lost Cause, trying to remove some of the taint of slavery, treason, and brutality in their depictions of the Confederate participants.[4]

There have been a few attempts before *Free State of Jones* to make films that reject the Lost Cause. *Glory* (1989) told the story of the Massachusetts Fifty-fourth Volunteer Infantry Regiment, a colored unit made up of black enlisted men led by white officers, which saw notable action in South Carolina as a part of campaign to penetrate the defenses of the city of Charleston in 1863. A critically important film, it shows the scars of slavery as well as the humanity and agency of black men, leaving little doubt as to the true cause of the war and the fallacy of the Lost Cause. The film's major drawback is that it is, at its core, a story told from the perspective of a white officer, Robert Gould Shaw, and thus an inevitable white-savior narrative. This trope is hammered home in the final scene, in which Shaw's body is tossed into a mass grave with the bodies of his men, arms splayed as if on the cross. *Lincoln* (2014) also works to chip away at the Lost Cause. Working through the complex story of congressional passage of the Thirteenth Amendment, it offers a window into the efforts of the radicals—true radicals—to abolish slavery, while Confederate agents and their northern Democratic allies attempted to negotiate a peace in which slavery would remain intact. Here Lincoln appears less as a white savior—although there is something inevitable about this part of the story—and more as the pragmatic politician who works to get the votes he needs to secure the change to the Constitution that the nation needs.[5]

While these films are both relatively accurate in their portrayals of the war, *Free State of Jones* works harder to emphasize *all* the themes established in the realms of social and cultural history than any film to date. Ross opens his narrative by rejecting any notion of the romance of war, replacing it with brutality. Like so many other films about war, *Free State of Jones* opens with an unnamed battle, an immediate, full immersion in combat that works to reorient the viewer's sense of time, place, and action. More like the opening scene of *Glory*, which depicts a moment in the battle of Antietam, than it is like the depiction of the D-Day landings in Steven Spielberg's *Saving Private Ryan*, the battle does not last very long. A force of Confederate infantry make an ill-fated assault on prepared Union infantry and artillery, who quite literally blow holes in the soldiers in gray. The viewer is shown a man's head blown apart and other bits and pieces of carnage. While the actual combat on screen remains relatively brief, the action then follows Newt Knight, the stretcher bearer, as he moves a wounded officer to a hospital tent. Just as they do in front of the enemy's cannons, here too men suffer and die. The point is as simple as it is powerful: war is hell.[6]

Immediately after this opening scene, Ross takes down the idea that slavery was not the cause of the war. Newt Knight sits beside a fire and reads from the pages of a newspaper an announcement of the "twenty Negro" law. Knight tells those around him that just as the Confederacy was conscripting men—obviously middling, yeoman, and poor men and boys—into the army, the Confederate government had passed a law allowing men with twenty or more slaves to leave the army and return home. In allowing the wealthiest men to avoid the gruesome realities of the conflict, it left the poorer white men to be saddled with the burden, doing more than their fair share. In other words, the war was to become a rich man's war but a poor man's fight, at least for white southerners. Following this realization and the death of a boy who was kin to him and dragged into the war unwillingly, Knight deserts the army.[7]

Upon his return to Jones County, Knight sees for the first time the plight of white women in the war. The Confederate home guard is depicted in the film as a parasitic institution, taking whatever it wants from the women and children who are left on the farms. One such household is occupied by a woman and her daughters. While the woman is obviously capable, it is evident that she has struggled to take care of her family in the absence of her menfolk. Adding insult to injury, not only did the Confederate army take her man but now they want all of her food, which would almost certainly result in starvation for her and her daughters. Knight arrives and inspires these women to resist. When the home guard do show up, they find themselves looking down the barrels of pistols, shotguns, and rifles wielded by a woman and little girls. This scene makes obvious the importance of women in Knight's war against the Confederacy.[8]

Ross then proceeds to expose the hideous nature of slavery. While Knight is acting as the local Robin Hood, his hideout is in a swamp—a fitting southern American stand-in for Sherwood Forest. Here he has been taken in by a small community of runaway slaves, who seem to accept him as a fellow outlaw. While the connections between these outcasts—slaves who voted with their feet and a white man who ostensibly did likewise—are clear, their differences must not be overlooked. Skin color is one difference, of course, but the real distinction between a free man and a slave lies in the iron contraption welded around the neck of Moses (Mahershala Ali), a persistent runaway, to keep him from trying to escape through the tangled swamp. While it did not work, the spikes of the so-called slave collar were intended to catch the vines, underbrush, and branches and either hold him so that the slave catcher could grab him or knock him to the ground, in which event his neck would likely snap. Knight removes this medieval device from Moses, and the two become close friends. Over time they are able to unite the most radical members of the white community with the black community of Jones County.[9]

The central focus of *Free State of Jones* is on the guerrilla war waged by Knight, Moses, their female kin, and other white and black men against the Confederate army in Jones County, Mississippi, which reached its peak in 1864. Ross's depiction of guerrilla warfare adheres to current scholarship of irregular conflict in the Civil War. *Free State of Jones* shows that the warfare was built on kinship relations and the yeoman household. From these vital networks, a gender, age, and racially inclusive guerrilla warfare emanates. While men continue to do most of the shooting, killing, and dying, women are no less invested. These women operate what scholars have come to call the domestic supply line, providing food, clothing, information, and ammunition. The household's division of labor is on full display as Knight's followers harvest their corn, with the men going out to the fields and plucking the ears of corn from the stalks and then delivering full baskets of ears to their women, who then shuck them for ready consumption. This is a community at war.[10]

This biracial, mixed-gender army achieves success against the Confederates. Two small but pitched battles show the complete victory over the local Confederate forces. In addition to the battle for Ellisville, we are shown an ambush staged during a churchyard burial service in which the Confederate troops are caught off guard by women pulling pistols from their skirts and men popping out of coffins. The women, using gendered expectations to shield their identities as gun-toting guerrillas, open fire, as do black men hiding behind gravestones and springing up to shoot down Confederates, thus taking on those who intended to return them to bondage. The scene ends with Newt Knight following the Confederate commander into the church and slowly strangling him to death. Overall, the ambush conveys to viewers that the guerrillas were united, clever, and ultimately willing to do what they had to in order to win.[11]

For Ross, Knight's greatest achievement was to effectively unify yeoman whites and slaves. Yet their joining forces was not without some friction, as one of the most telling scenes reveals. During a barbeque held in the swamps to celebrate their successful harvesting their crops before the Confederate home guard could take them, a racial confrontation breaks out among Knight's compatriots. As many of the revelers rest after glutting themselves on pork and corn, Moses makes his way to the roasted pig for his share of the meat. One of Knight's white followers approaches him, tells him to stop, and calls him a "nigger." Moses's response is to ask, "And you ain't?" The implication is clear to the audience but not to the man who has accosted Moses. Enter Knight, who explains to his white friend that what Moses means to say is that if he is a nigger, then aren't you as well? After all, these black men only worked for the planters, but you poor whites were willing to fight and die for them. Moses has flipped the commonly understood definition of the word *nigger* from one that signifies racial distinction to one that signifies class difference.

Free State of Jones makes an important contribution to the story of Reconstruction by showing that the conflict continued to rage on after the Confederacy surrendered in 1865. Ross shows how the alliance between the poor whites of Jones County and the black community (then free) mostly falls apart. While some radicals like Knight and a few others stick with their black allies, Jones

County—like so much of the South—quickly slides back into something akin to the antebellum status quo. Planters retain power over the black population, who lose what little power they had. One scene reveals that black men and women even lose power over the integrity of their families, as Moses's son is legally kidnapped and reenslaved under the apprenticeship law passed as a part of the Mississippi Black Codes. Although Knight resolves the issue by purchasing the boy's freedom, the exchange shows that the government, the courts, and white society worked in concert to achieve white supremacy.

Even sadder, the yeoman and poor whites again ally themselves with the wealthy whites and are happy to use violence against black men. In the most emotional, if predictable, scene of the film, Moses is chased down and lynched for his political activity. While the act itself takes place off screen, Moses's lifeless, bloodstained body tells the story: he was beaten, his genitalia were cut off, and then he was hanged. Although the film accurately demonstrates that the political activity of black men threatened white supremacy, the justification for most such lynchings was that the victim of the lynching had been accused, often erroneously, of sexually assaulting or otherwise defiling a white woman.[12]

Ross makes an admirable attempt to show the connections between more contemporary events and the Civil War. In what is the most unique part of the film, there are several jump cuts from the 1860s action to a mid-twentieth-century trial of Davis Knight, a descendant of Newt Knight, to determine his race on the basis of miscegenation from that earlier era. Unfortunately, its periodic insertion into the film just does not work as well as it should. While *Free State of Jones* is ostensibly a love story between Newt Knight and a black woman named Rachel (Gugu Mbatha-Raw)—a love story that is symbolic of the potential love between the white and black races—that romance plays second fiddle to the Robin Hood story and the larger class-based theme. Yet this message is no clearer than the attempts to fit the miscegenation trial into the story of the war, which Ross thought "was important just for the continuity and continuum." But it has the opposite effect. At the most basic level, a viewer understands what is going on, but it drains momentum from the Civil War–era narrative. Likewise, the audience never sees enough of the later miscegenation conflict to truly understand its deeper significance. When Davis Knight gives his final plea of not guilty, there is no building momentum, no overwhelming tension, and so viewers are not moved as much as they should be. Ross just tried to do too much.[13]

There is something to be said for films diverting from the historical script.

Newt Knight (Matthew McConaughey) and his soon-to-be second wife, Rachel (Gugu Mbatha-raw), together in the swamp in *Free State of Jones*

As Ross said in a number of interviews and in a blog dedicated to the film, he did the research and was dedicated to a film that was true to the history. He also said that "there are so many things that fall into a very pat Hollywood construct," meaning that the film industry requires filmmakers to stick to a sort of formula. In challenging this formula and allowing historical accuracy to drive his filmmaking, Ross may have shackled himself to a story that does not lend itself to the packaging required of a major motion picture. To cover as much historical content as Ross clearly wanted to include, it would have taken multiple films or an altogether different format, such as the now prolific cable miniseries with their multiple installments. Using one component of this complex history—the class conflict, the romance between Rachel and Newt Knight, or even just the miscegenation trial—as a frame through which to focus the fuller story might have generated the payoff the story should provide. This is not to criticize Ross for being too historical. And this is certainly not a critique of the inclusion of the Davis Knight trial in the film, which by itself is arguably the film's most illuminating segment. Rather, it is to say that while film has strengths, especially in contrast to written history, there are things that film just cannot achieve as well.[14]

Free State of Jones is far from a failure. Ross set out to tell a story that challenged Hollywood's simplistic and long-standing Lost Cause versions of the Civil War and its aftermath, and he succeeded. "I felt a certain satisfaction finally being able to set a lot of the history straight," Ross said after the film's release, "and that was very satisfying for me, because that post-war era since then hasn't really been examined and it needs to be." One hopes that more filmmakers will take up the work of academic historians. Scholars are actively researching and writing about elements of the Civil War that have something new to say about our country and our identity as Americans today. Even if these filmmakers have to sacrifice aspects of the history to make sure that their films are seen and audiences are moved, it is necessary to continue chip away at the Lost Cause in popular culture. And one hopes that films such as this will lead the intellectually curious to the great historical monographs that fill our libraries and present them with the *real* history. Reading the incredible stories that course through our past will bring the greatest satisfaction, because the truest stories cannot so easily fit onto the silver screen, unless, of course, that silver screen is in one's mind.[15]

NOTES

1. *Free State of Jones*, dir. Gary Ross (Burbank, CA: STX Entertainment, 2016).

2. The Ross quotation is from an interview Ross gave to Crave Online on 22 June 2016, "Gary Ross on 'Free State of Jones' and Setting the Record Straight," http://www.craveonline .com/entertainment/1002567-interview-gary-ross-free-state-jones-setting-record-straight #84×2Y18Ljjy65ixY.99. For a primer on the Lost Cause and its insidious postwar effects on American memory, see David W. Blight, *Race and Reunion: The Civil War in American Memory* (Cambridge, MA: Harvard University Press, 2001).

3. Victoria E. Bynum, *The Free State of Jones: Mississippi's Longest Civil War* (Chapel Hill: University of North Carolina Press, 2001). For the quotation about Bynum, see "Gary Ross Interview: The Real History of Free State of Jones," 23 June 2016, in http://www.denofgeek. com/us/movies/free-state-of-jones/256533/gary-ross-interview-the-real-history-of-free-state-of- jones. In making a commitment to historical accuracy, unlike other filmmakers, Ross created an innovative way to interface the film and history, basically by footnoting the film. For Ross's footnotes on the film, see http://freestateofjones.info/.

4. Gary W. Gallagher, *Causes Won, Lost, and Forgotten: How Hollywood and Popular Art Shape What We Know about the Civil War* (Chapel Hill: University of North Carolina Press, 2008), 41–90.

5. Gallagher, *Causes Won, Lost, and Forgotten*, 91–134.

6. The brutality and apparent randomness of death on the conventional battlefield of the Civil War is now commonplace in the literature. For a foundational work in this area, see Gerald Linderman, *Embattled Courage: The Experience of Combat in the American Civil War* (New

York: Free Press, 1987). The work that is most responsible for emphasizing the sheer brutality of guerrilla warfare is Michael Fellman, *Inside War: The Guerrilla Conflict in Missouri during the American Civil War* (New York: Oxford University Press, 1990).

7. The impact of the twenty-slave law has been debated by historians and writers for some time. For an example of a work that shows it to be divisive, see David Williams, *Bitterly Divided: The South's Inner Civil War* (New York: New Press, 2008), 58.

8. For more about the historical contributions of women to the Unionist cause in Jones County, see Bynum, *Free State of Jones*, 106–10. For an in-depth analysis of the plight of women, especially those marginalized by race, class, and wartime struggle, see Bynum, *Unruly Women: The Politics of Social and Sexual Control in the Old South* (Chapel Hill: University of North Carolina Press, 1992).

9. One of the best works on runaway slaves and the practice of running away is John Hope Franklin and Loren Schweninger, *Runaway Slaves: Rebels on the Plantation* (New York: Oxford University Press, 2000). For methods of keeping the slave community in line, see Sally E. Hadden, *Slave Patrols: Law and Violence in Virginia and the Carolinas* (Cambridge, MA: Harvard University Press, 2003).

10. Bynum, *Free State of Jones*, 93–129. For other examples of this new school of thought on the workings of guerrilla warfare, see Joseph M. Beilein Jr., *Bushwhackers: Guerrilla Warfare, Manhood, and the Household in Civil War Missouri* (Kent, OH: Kent State University Press, 2016); Matthew C. Hulbert, *The Ghosts of Guerrilla Memory: How Civil War Bushwhackers Became Gunslingers in the American West* (Athens: University of Georgia Press, 2016); Beilein and Hulbert, *The Civil War Guerrilla: Unfolding the Black Flag in History, Memory, and Myth* (Lexington: University Press of Kentucky, 2015); and LeeAnn Whites, "Forty Shirts and a Wagonload of Wheat: Women, the Domestic Supply Line, and the Civil War on the Western Border," *Journal of the Civil War Era* 1 (March 2011): 56–78.

11. There was no pitched battle of Ellisville, nor would there have been in a guerrilla war in which guerrillas were looking to hit soft targets. Also, Ross admits in his footnotes to the film that something like the ambush at the church took place, but it occurred near a creek bed. See http://freestateofjones.info/.

12. Bynum, *Free State of Jones*, 136, 150–52.

13. Bynum, *Free State of Jones*, 177–90; "Gary Ross Interview."

14. http://freestateofjones.info/. See also "Gary Ross on 'Free State of Jones' and Setting the Record Straight."

15. "Gary Ross Interview."

19

Sommersby
Identity, Imposture, and (Re)construction in the Post–Civil War South

TOM LEE

Set in the immediate post–Civil War South and based on a 1982 French film, *Le retour de Martin Guerre* (hereafter *The Return of Martin Guerre*), 1993's *Sommersby* has at its core a question of identity. At the beginning of the Civil War, John Robert "Jack" Sommersby (Richard Gere) leaves Vine Hill, Tennessee, to join the fighting. For six years, his wife, Laurel (Jodie Foster) awaits word of her husband. Then, unexpectedly, an unnamed Confederate (also played by Richard Gere) appears. He knows details about the people of the community and looks like the soldier who rode away. However, his appearance and manner differ sufficiently that there is reason to doubt that he is the same man who left. Laurel's acceptance of the Confederate veteran as her husband proves to be crucial to his acceptance by the community and to the unfolding of the movie's plot even as the actions and views of the returned Jack—his views on race and class—lead him toward the conundrum over identity and honor that seals his fate. Antebellum misdeeds, contemporary prejudices, and personal jealousies doom the returned Jack Sommersby's efforts to bring prosperity, harmony, and love to the little town decimated by war.[1]

The mystery of whether the Jack Sommersby who returns is the real Jack Sommersby may be less significant to the film than trailers for the movie asserted. More central is the way in which the new or returned Jack differs from the antebellum Jack who left. The figure who appears in Vine Hill seeks what he never had. Transformed by the war and its consequences, he draws Laurel and many of the people of Vine Hill into his crusade to build a world less reconstructed than wholly new, but there is always resistance. In the wake of

Sommersby's release, film critics and reviewers focused predominantly on the identity crisis and the romance at the heart of the film's story, but the story at the heart of *Sommersby* may well be about much more. In the early 1990s, at a time of momentous international change, issues of race, economics, and culture captured the attention of Americans. As they had at watershed moments throughout their history, Americans faced a moment of decision about what being an American would mean and how the future would unfold. In 1993, *Sommersby*'s filmmakers challenged viewers to consider contemporary issues through the lens of a historical moment of great fluidity at the end of the Civil War, when the course of Reconstruction and human relations in the United States had yet to harden again after tremendous upheaval. Through *Sommersby,* they offered up an allegory for Reconstruction, or more precisely what they understood Reconstruction to have been, what Eric Foner termed in 1988 "America's unfinished revolution."[2]

Throughout most of the film, the Australian director Jon Amiel maintains the tension surrounding the returned Sommersby's identity. For all of his successful displays of familiarity and his ability to name local residents, the man whom the town accepts as Jack Sommersby struggles at times to remember people and events from before the war. Virtually all his missteps can be explained away as lapses of memory following a long absence, but there are plenty of hints that he is not the man who left. One of the most concrete examples occurs when the local cobbler compares the returned Jack's foot with a pattern used for a previous pair of boots and discovers the returned Jack's foot size to be smaller. More important and persuasive, however, are patterns of behavior. As Jack is reintroduced to Vine Hill, viewers learn that the man who left embodied many of the most vulgar attributes of the honor-bound, southern cavaliers' system of patriarchy. He was a wastrel and a hellion who drank, played at cards, womanized, and relied on the threat of violence even in his own home. The returned Jack behaves in ways utterly at odds with his prewar character.[3]

Only Laurel's embrace ensures Sommersby's acceptance by the community, but hints of doubt linger in Jack and Laurel's relationship as the two engage in a figurative dance around the question of his identity. In a highly symbolic scene crucial to the film, viewers are drawn to ask whether Laurel's early coldness toward Sommersby results from her doubts about his identity, memories of mistreatment, or apprehension about relinquishing the independence she experienced in his absence. After appearing at Laurel's bedroom door asking her to shave off his beard, Sommersby sits with Laurel standing behind him. As she begins to shave him with a straight razor, Sommersby fishes for insight about their life together, asking eventually if love had drawn her to him. She pauses, the razor firmly against Sommersby's throat, which he holds extended as if signaling to her that his fate rests in her hands. Then, the razor still poised, she offers a response broken by halting pauses. "Could 'a been [love]," she says, "if you had been the least . . . little . . . bit . . . kind." After a further pause, Laurel continues shaving, and when she finishes, she holds a mirror up for Sommersby. "What do you think?" he asks. "I'm thinkin' who is this man sitting in my kitchen?" she replies. Laurel's response offers little more to resolve the mystery of Sommersby's identity than it does to reveal Laurel's own inner thoughts, yet it is significant. The man sitting before her, whether noticeably physically different in body or different in spirit and personality, is not the Jack Sommersby who left Vine Hill. Sommersby's true identity matters less than what his presence represents: not restoration but hope for a future different from the past. Over time, Laurel grows ever closer to the man who now inhabits her home until finally she and Jack consummate their relationship in a night of sexual passion, a far cry from the passionless, violent, and sexless marriage that viewers learn existed before Jack went off to war.[4]

Sommersby's activities as an agent of change begin in earnest when he announces a scheme to save the town and his own family's fortunes. At a town meeting that includes African American families, Sommersby argues that burley tobacco could be grown in Vine Hill and would be the community's salvation. To all willing to join him, he promises the use of a piece of his land, tools, and fertilizer in return for half of the crop. He promises that once he has made enough money from the system to pay his mortgage, he will allow growers to buy their piece of land at a fair price, and he extends the offer to local freedmen. When asked how, without cash or collateral for credit, he will provide the tools and livestock and buy seed, he asks the townspeople to contribute what little of value they have. Already resistant to combining with blacks in the endeavor and questioning Sommersby's willingness to part with land hard won by his father, most townspeople react with scorn, emphasizing their poverty. When it appears that they are about to balk at Jack's scheme, however, Laurel rises and offers a treasured ruby brooch that she had protected during the war. Over the following days, townspeople bring forward their goods to contribute. Sommersby takes sole responsibility for selling the goods and securing the seed, and the town becomes twisted by anxiety as the days pass without his return. Again, the importance of Sommersby's identity seems diminished, for the identity of the man who rode off with the hopes and possessions of Vine Hill's residents matters less than whether he returns and the community survives.

Sommersby does return, and the tobacco crop is planted and flourishes, but as the crop matures, events occur that shatter the promise of renewal. Even as Laurel embraces the possibility of a new life, including a pregnancy, Orin (Bill Pullman), a local man and apparent veteran who is missing a leg and who had been courting Laurel in Jack's absence, harbors ambitions to marry her. As Laurel becomes more distant, the jilted Orin becomes the chief doubter of Sommersby's identity and the chief instigator of doubt in others. In the tobacco field, Orin tricks Sommersby into confirming his suspicions that the returned veteran is an imposter. On the same day, three drifters who seem familiar with Sommersby arrive, and Sommersby drives them off with a tobacco knife. Later, Orin confronts Laurel, calling her acceptance of the imposter sinful, and fights with Sommersby in a barn, threatening to destroy all that is being built in order to save Laurel. When he fails, Orin uses Sommersby's new-found, inclusive attitudes toward freedmen to bring local night riders to visit the Sommersby house. Finally, as the harvest is under way, marshals arrive with a warrant to arrest John Robert "Jack" Sommersby for murder.

Led to Nashville to stand trial for the murder, the man who has assumed the role of Jack Sommersby faces the choice that will decide his fate. In the courtroom, overseen by an African American (James Earl Jones), eyewitnesses draw a figurative noose around Sommersby's neck. Faced with forfeiture of the man she loves, Laurel agrees to participate in a plan hatched by Orin to save the defendant from the gallows by undermining his claim to being John Robert Sommersby. On the stand, willing to face the opprobrium of accepting a man who is not her husband, Laurel testifies that the defendant is not her husband. Another witness, who was among the night riders, identifies the defendant as Horace Townsend, an unscrupulous con man who taught briefly in a small town, absconded with a large sum of money meant for school construction, impregnated a young woman before abandoning her, and deserted during the war before being captured. Were he to abandon his claim to the name Sommersby, Townsend could avoid the penalty of a crime that he did not commit, but his admission would nullify his contracts with the people of Vine Hill, confirm Laurel's dishonor, and make his new baby illegitimate under the law. He determines to reaffirm his claim, appeals to the people of Vine Hill, and

In a pivotal courtroom scene from *Sommersby*, Horace Townsend (Richard Gere) challenges Laurel (Jodie Foster) to affirm his claim to be Jack Sommersby.

calls Laurel back to the stand. While still refusing to acknowledge him to be Jack Sommersby, she acknowledges that he is her husband.

As in *The Return of Martin Guerre*, a court's verdict leaves only the gallows for the imposter. While the two films share a significant number of plot points and character types, they also differ in significant ways. In both, an imposter takes the place of a missing soldier, and his successful imposture depends upon the acquiescence of the soldier's wife. Indeed, the romantic attachment between the wife and the imposter, a feeling that had not existed to the same degree between wife and husband, becomes an explanation as to why a wife who likely recognizes the imposture nonetheless accepts the imposter. Similarly, in both films the imposter's challenging of cultural, familial, and social norms triggers his ultimate demise.

For all that the two films share, however, two significant differences shed light on the significance of *Sommersby* and the message bound up with its story. In 1976 the historian Natalie Zemon Davis, a specialist on early modern European peasant society, encountered the story of Martin Guerre and realized its cinematic potential. In 1980 she traveled to France to locate filmmakers willing to produce a movie based on the incident and was introduced to two filmmakers who had already begun work on developing the Martin Guerre story for the screen. The resulting film reflected the influence of Davis's knowledge of relevant fashion and customs. Thus, while *The Return of Martin Guerre* was based on a documented, sixteenth-century incident that occurred in a French peasant village, *Sommersby* is a purely fictional story owing no allegiance to any specific historical incident. The filmmakers' decision to set their film during Reconstruction was a conscious one fraught with cultural meaning. A change in plot marks another telling difference. At the end of *The Return of Martin Guerre*, the cuckolded husband reappears to confront the imposter, condemn his faithless wife, and claim his lost property and position, but Jack Sommersby, as viewers learn, lies buried and cannot return.[5]

The reasons for these choices seem clear enough. The end of the Civil War marked a moment in American and southern history in which the old order had been toppled, or at least temporarily deposed, and a new order, which had yet to form, could still be shaped. Like most historical films, *Sommersby* makes its share of questionable historical claims. For instance, the lore surrounding the development of white burley tobacco holds that the first crop was grown in 1864 along the Ohio River. While Tennesseans grew both dark fire-cured tobacco and bright or yellow flue-cured tobacco commercially before and after the Civil War, the odds seem slim that Tennesseans in a small, mountain-encircled village in the years immediately after the war would have had the technical skill set to grow burley or that they could have grown a sufficient burley crop to make marketing in Lexington, Louisville, or even Nashville profitable. Indeed, not until the 1920s did burley gain widespread acceptance by mountain farmers.

Two other incidents reflect the more subtle ways that filmmakers shaped their presentation of the past in order to convey their message. While Townsend's plan for growing tobacco relied on sharecropping, a system found throughout southern commercial agriculture, the cooperative nature of his scheme, his promise to sell his land to tenants, and his invitation to freedmen to join the scheme bespeaks of a racial and class egalitarianism that could have existed only on the most radical edges of Reconstruction. The trial offers another example. Because it involved a white murder victim and white defendant, and because of the prejudices that still existed in Tennessee in 1866, the oversight of a case like Sommersby's by an African American judge stretches credibility. While African Americans did hold some legislative positions in Tennessee and did serve as magistrates, these opportunities came well after the Civil War, and not until 1868 was Tennessee's ban on African American officeholding and jury service lifted.[6]

In a 1993 interview, the screenwriter, Nicholas Meyer, explained that making Judge Isaacs black was a conscious choice. A telling exchange from the film reveals why. While cross-examining the nightriding, white witness who identified him as Horace Townsend, Townsend asserts that the witness's real motivation for making his revelations is to stop him "from selling land to a colored man who'd then be a landowner on a level with yourself." Later, after being chastised by Judge Isaacs for using profanity, the witness assumes the mantle of whiteness and commands the judge to hold his tongue in his presence. "You sit up there in judgment of nobody!" fumes the witness. "In two years, when the Yankees are gone, you will be back in the field where you belong." In the exchange, the filmmakers rightly expose the racism that so shaped Reconstruction, reminding viewers that hard-won victories, symbolized by the presence of Judge Isaacs, could be reversed. Judge Isaacs's status and Townsend's anachronistic attitudes on race and class suggest what might have been. By stretching historical possibility, the filmmakers reveal their understanding of the immediate postwar period as one of potential transformation. Yet, conservative forces remain potent. Townsend's individual, fictionalized story becomes allegory. There was to be no dramatic return of the real Sommersby in a last-minute courtroom appearance, but Sommersby's crimes, misdeeds, and abuses claw at Townsend throughout the film. As Townsend's untimely death suggests, the New South that might have been would not escape the powerful hold of the Old South.[7]

The fluidity of the fictionalized historical moment both allows and demands that individuals make choices about identity. One of *Sommersby*'s subtleties is an undercurrent of Homeric epic throughout. As the opening credits for *Sommersby* roll, viewers follow Gere's then unidentified character on the journey that will bring him from an unmarked grave to Vine Hill. He passes through scenes of destruction and death, racial violence and rebuilding. Witness to the waste of war and hate, the unnamed Confederate, like all archetypal heroes, has been transformed by the experience of his journey. He is a changed man, and all that was familiar is new and strange. Later, while assuming the identity of Jack Sommersby, Horace Townsend surprises Laurel by reading Homer to her and to Robert, Laurel's son. The classics scholar Robert J. Rabel has argued that all retellings of the Martin Guerre story prior to *Sommersby* took for granted a classical understanding of the individual as possessing a stable, unchanging ego. The self could be disguised, but it could not be fundamentally altered in character. In *Sommersby,* he argues, elements from *The Return of Martin Guerre* and classics like the *Odyssey* are blended to create a story about identity with existential choice at its core. When Horace Townsend buries Sommersby's body at the beginning of the film, he might as well be burying himself. His journey through war has remade him. Not only is he a new man literally when he shows up in Vine Hill seeking to assume Jack Sommersby's identity but, as his devotion to Laurel, to his new child, and to the people of Vine Hill reflects, he is not the Horace Townsend who used and abandoned people before the war. "Horace Townsend is dead," he says to Laurel on one occasion when she seeks to discover his true identity. However, who he is matters less than who he is understood to be. The self was never more than a created thing, as Townsend's actions attest when he chooses death over loss of the Sommersby name. Especially in moments of extreme historical flux, identities can be remade. Change is possible, the filmmakers appear to argue.[8]

Sommersby appeared at a moment of change and possibility. In 1989, a decade's worth of resistance by the Solidarity labor union led to elections in Poland, and Eastern Europeans breached the Hungarian border and the Berlin Wall. In 1991, US forces achieved a sweeping military victory against Iraqi forces in Operation Desert Storm, the United States' first major international military intervention since Vietnam. The same year, tensions in the Soviet Union, unleashed in part by Mikhail Gorbachev's reforms, led to the political disintegration of the United States' Cold War enemy, the Soviet Union. Domestically, in the 1992 presidential election voters chose Bill Clinton, the first president of the United States to be born after World War II and a chameleonlike politician with youthful and multiracial appeal who campaigned as an agent of change. Crucial to Clinton's victory were promises to correct economic inequities that since the late 1970s had ripped away the security of the American middle class and blue-collar workers. Also crucial was a unique appeal to African Americans. In the 1980s, the rap lyrics of N.W.A. and other hip-hop artists reminded Americans of the racial anger that had bubbled in inner-city neighborhoods like South Central Los Angeles. In 1992, in the wake of the acquittal of LAPD officers charged with the videotaped 1991 beating of Rodney King, riots broke out in Los Angeles, and smaller riots occurred in other US cities. Not only had the first Reconstruction failed to correct America's racial divide but the rioting appeared to affirm that the twentieth century's civil rights movement, the so-called Second Reconstruction, also had failed to achieve its promise. With the Cold War seemingly over, with the United States seemingly on the verge of unparalleled hyperpower status, and with technology seemingly having begun to revolutionize how Americans lived and worked, the time seemed ripe for a new generation of leaders to address long-standing issues.[9]

By the early twenty-first century, the promise for change that had seemed so potent in the early 1990s had resolved itself in impotence, the victim of events and trends already present but perhaps still veiled in the earlier decade. While *Sommersby* performed moderately well against competing films in 1993 and remains available in digital video, it never became a blockbuster or significantly impacted the nation culturally.[10]

The release of *Sommersby* marked yet another return of Martin Guerre and the story of an imposter's failed effort to reach for a prize, a new life that proved to be just beyond reach. Despite the ambitions of the filmmakers and producer Richard Gere, *Sommersby* falls short. Too much seems contrived for moral effect, too much feels wooden and unnatural, and too much feels anachronistic. A trailer for the film sums up the troubling dissonance. "She knew his face, his touch, his voice," says a narrator. "She knew everything about him but the truth." Really? The character Horace Townsend is made to give voice to very late-twentieth-century views that even in 1993 were more attuned to Hollywood than to most small towns in Tennessee. As an allegorical figure, Townsend becomes a man or character out of time and thus truly an imposter. By focusing on his reconstruction and failing to deal more honestly and fully with the limitations and complexities of the years following the Civil War, the filmmakers neglect the influence and persistence of systemic historical factors that affect human behaviors and limit human choices. As most scholars of the South duly recognize, the past does not simply let slip its hold over the present. That much we see in *Sommersby*, but its filmmakers ignore the equally important point that while reconstructing the past to serve the present may convey a message, it hardly encourages understanding.[11]

NOTES

1. *Sommersby*, dir. Jon Amiel (1993; Burbank, CA: Warner Home Video, 1999), DVD; *Le retour de Martin Guerre*, dir. Daniel Vigne (1982; Los Angeles: Orion Home Video, 1996), VHS.

2. Roger Ebert, review of *Sommersby*, 5 February 1993, RogerEbert.com, "Reviews," http://www.rogerebert.com/reviews/sommersby-1993; Eric Foner, *Reconstruction: America's Unfinished*

Revolution, 1863–1877, Francis Parkman Prize Edition (New York: History Book Club, 2005), title page.

3. *"Sommersby* (1993): Full Cast & Crew," IMDb, accessed 12 November 2016, http://www.imdb.com/title/tt0108185/fullcredits?ref_=tt_ov_st_sm.

4. "Sommersby Script—Dialogue Transcript," Script-O-Rama, accessed 10 February 2017, http://www.script-o-rama.com/movie_scripts/s/sommersby-script-transcript-gere-foster.html.

5. Todd Purdum, "Martin Guerre and the Princeton Scholar," *New York Times,* 13 November 1983, http://www.nytimes.com/1983/11/13/nyregion/martin-guerre-and-the-princeton-scholar.html; Robert Finlay, "The Refashioning of Martin Guerre," *America Historical Review* 93, no. 3 (June 1988): 555.

6. *Nashville Union and Dispatch,* 22 March 1868, 2; *Nashville Union and American,* 26 October 1870, 1; *Nashville Union and American,* 3 November 1870, 1; "This Honorable Body: African American Legislators in 19th Century Tennessee," entry for Sampson Keeble, Tennessee State Library and Archives, accessed 7 January 2017, http://sharetngov.tnsosfiles.com/tsla/exhibits/blackhistory/keeble.htm; Bobby L. Lovett, *The Civil Rights Movement in Tennessee: A Narrative History* (Knoxville: University of Tennessee Press, 2005), 232; Paul Bergeron, Stephen Ash, and Jeanette Keith, *Tennesseans and Their History* (Knoxville: University of Tennessee Press, 1999), 171; Department of the Interior, Census Office, "Report on the Culture and Curing of Tobacco in the United States," by J. B. Killebrew, in *Report on the Productions of Agriculture as Returned at the Tenth Census,* vol. 3 (Washington, DC: Government Printing Office, 1883), 177, http://usda.mannlib.cornell.edu/usda/ AgCensusImages/1880/1880a_v3–01.pdf.

7. James Earl Hardy, "'Sommersby''s Historical Accuracy," *Entertainment Weekly,* 6 August 1993, http://ew.com/article/1993/08/06/sommersbys-historical-accuracy/; "Sommersby Script—Dialogue Transcript."

8. Justine McConnell, *Black Odysseys: The Homeric Odyssey in the African Diaspora since 1939* (Oxford: Oxford University Press, 2013), 155–79; Robert J. Rabel, "Impersonation and Identity: 'Sommersby,' 'The Return of Martin Guerre,' and the 'Odyssey,'" *International Journal of the Classical Tradition* 9, no. 3 (Winter 2003): 391–406.

9. Daryl A. Carter, *Brother Bill: President Clinton and the Politics of Race and Class* (Fayetteville: University of Arkansas Press, 2016), 4–5; Steven M. Gillon, *The American Paradox: A History of the United States since 1945,* 3rd ed. (Boston: Cengage Learning, 2012), 330–54.

10. The movie opened on 7 February 1993 on 1,432 screens and grossed more than $8 million in its first weekend in the United States, eventually grossing $50 million in the United States and $140 million worldwide. That year, it competed against *Jurassic Park, The Fugitive, Mrs. Doubtfire, Schindler's List,* two films based on John Grisham novels, and *Philadelphia* among other films, and its gross receipts ranked twenty-sixth among all competitors. Reviews were mixed. "Top-US-Grossing Feature Films Released 1993–01–01 to 1993–12–31," IMDb, http://www.imdb.com/search/title?title_type=feature&year=1993,1993&sort=boxoffice_gross_us,-desc; Jason Drake, review of *Sommersby, Sight and Sound* 5 (2012): 56–57; Clifford Terry, "Sommersby Has Nowhere to Go after the War," *Chicago Tribune,* 5 February 1993, http://articles.chicagotribune.com/1993–02–05/entertainment/9303175721_1_laurel-sommersby-jack-sommersby-martin-guerre.

11. *Sommersby* trailer, IMDb, accessed 7 January 2017, http://www.imdb.com/videoplayer/vi3079209241?ref_=tt_pv_vi_aiv_1; Foner, *Reconstruction,* xxvii.

20

Knights of the Twenty Years' War
Race and American Exceptionalism in *The Hateful Eight*

MATTHEW E. STANLEY

For the filmmaker Quentin Tarantino, the Big American Question—the substratum of our national identity, our progress and agony, our unity and division, and even how and why different Americans hope, aspire, and dream the way they do—seems to reside in the Civil War era. And its particulars are written in cold blood.

Perhaps it is only appropriate for an artist who trades in irony and violence that the principal questions of American history unfold in the Old South and the West. Detractors have charged Tarantino, with his so-called postmodern sensibilities, with promoting gratuitous profanity and oversaturated bloodletting. But he reveals one of his most telling interpretations—his metahistory, perhaps—in one character's incapacity to suffer a particular category of violence in his 2012 film, *Django Unchained*. The revenge fantasy's primary character bond is between two dashing and honor-bound horsemen: the film's namesake, Django "Freeman," a former slave seeking to liberate his subjugated wife; and Dr. King Schulz, a German immigrant and racial liberal whose surname and cosmopolitanism summon the radical politics of his (likely) Forty-Eighter background and whose title and first name invoke a certain legendary civil rights icon.[1] For the viewer, it soon becomes evident that Django's only white ally—and the film's only redeeming white character—is not an American. Tarantino barbarously illustrates this point. Midway through the film, the protagonists witness a savage, fatal dog attack against a defenseless field hand. Rather than bearing witness to a national sin in microcosm, Schulz looks away. A proficient killer in his own right, the German is nevertheless physically unable to watch this most extreme culmination of plantation violence. When the sadistic master, clearly amused by the incident, asks what could possibly be wrong with the nauseated Schulz, Django explains that his compatriot from Düsseldorf just isn't "used to Americans."

What, then, does it mean to Quentin Tarantino to be "used to" Americans? What is the national default? What lies at the core of the American experience? It is not only significant that, in a genre that has consistently lionized former Confederates, from Ethan Edwards to Josie Wales, the protagonist in this western is an exemplar of slave agency who, in his final confrontation, squares off not against a literal white oppressor but against a loyal (and ingeniously preservation-oriented) house slave who represents the very internalization of white oppression and the antithesis of black self-liberation.[2] In a fictive moment that would make the real-life slave rebel Charles Deslondes or Nat Turner blush, Django explodes the prevailing racial hierarchy by, quite literally, reducing the Big House—that pecuniary and emotional marrow of the Old South slaveocracy—to smoldering ruins. Tarantino's opus, which is part spaghetti western, part southern gothic, and part chamber drama, is historical fantasy, to be sure. But the film's power structures—African Americans and immigrants as branded outsiders—and its racial hierarchies—economic power and legal statecraft centered on the systematic exploitation of minorities authored by a white ruling class and enforced by their aspirational *Herrenvölker*—speak to something quite genuine about the very nucleus of American origins and national exceptionalism.

That exceptionalism is white supremacy, and if Tarantino's filmic philosophy of history is any guide, its social and cultural methodization during the Civil War era continues to shape our national myths, our collective values, our identities, and our material lives. In flipping the Lost Cause genre, *Django Unchained* depicts what one reviewer called "a two-hour-plus lecture on racism in American film . . . an extended fuck you to D. W. Griffith and John Ford, John Wayne, and Clint Eastwood."[3] It is also notable that the director locates not simply white supremacy but the white ruination of black bodies at the center of American history and identity. Tarantino's coupling of *Django* with *Inglourious Basterds* (2009) posits "slavery and racism as a proto-fascist function of capitalism" and an analogy between enduring American white supremacy and Nazism.[4] American fascism, then—with its ties to exclusive property rights and corporate capitalism, from slavery and sharecropping to convict leasing and the carceral state—is an extension of white supremacy rooted in the Middle Period.

Tarantino expands upon these themes of national character, in both subject matter and intellectual sophistication, in *The Hateful Eight* (2015). Here a series of character studies and vignettes set in the Reconstruction-era West become a metaphor for the black experience in American history. If *Django* represents history as it should have been—clear-eyed and replete with self-liberation and justice—then *The Hateful Eight* represents history as it was—mysterious, unnecessarily catastrophic, ironically violent, and morally inconclusive.

Accentuated by the cinematographer Robert Richardson's hazy blue-white palette and Ennio Morricone's ominous score, the mountainous setting invokes isolation and dread. An impending snowstorm in the Wyoming Rockies mirrors the mounting racial and sectional tension inside Minnie's Haberdashery, a one-room cabin in which most of the film is set. Wartime Unionists grow more and more skeptical of wartime rebels, and vice versa. All of them are mistrustful of the lone black man (though *black* is not the word they typically use to describe him), who is the first character to realize that all is not what it seems.

The film's motley characters, like the axiomatic "knights" (or perhaps "samurai") of *Reservoir Dogs* (1992), are dangerous men (and one woman) with shadowy and somewhat interconnected backgrounds, centering primarily on their Civil War experiences, enduring sectional loyalties, and racial identities. The principal players include an African American veteran cavalry officer, Major Marquis Warren (Samuel L. Jackson), who moves west following the war; Warren's acquaintance and fellow bounty hunter John Ruth (Kurt Russell, parodying John Wayne); Ruth's prisoner, Daisy Domergue (Jennifer Jason Leigh); Chris Mannix (Walton Goggins), an ex-Confederate paramilitary; an unrepentantly racist Confederate general, Sanford "Sandy" Smithers (Bruce Dern); and a cadre of other thieves and imposters.

The Civil War is not over for these men. While Ruth is an avowed, sentimental Unionist, Mannix, the "Scourge of South Carolina" and the son of the notorious Confederate Erskine Mannix, fought in a unit, "Mannix's Marauders," notorious for killing emancipated black people. "I don't drink with rebel renegades and I sure as hell don't break bread with 'em," Ruth snaps. Mannix, conversely, defends "The Cause": "When niggers are scared, that's when white folks are safe." Smithers, still donning his Rebel gray, jests about "Yankee sons of bitches" and northern "blue bellies," and he and Mannix seethe at the witness of a free black man. A verbal brawl erupts over the infamous (and fictitious) "Battle of Baton Rouge," in which Smithers, who "doesn't acknowledge niggers in uniforms," sanctioned the massacre of an entire United

States Colored Troops (USCT) unit. Mannix sides with Smithers; Ruth sides with Warren; and they divide the haberdashery into "northern" and "southern" sides, the fireplace representing "Georgia," and the bar, "Philadelphia."

Most consequentially, Major Warren, a proficient killer of Confederates who burned down the fictional Wellenbeck Prison, possesses a letter from Abraham Lincoln, with whom he claims to have shared correspondence during the late war. The letter has a seductive effect on white people, and Warren uses this to his advantage throughout the film. Ruth, who weeps while reading it, becomes furious when Warren admits that the Lincoln note is in fact a fake. Warren counters: "You got no idea what it's like being a Black man facing down America. The only time Black folks is safe is when white folks is disarmed." The Lincoln letter, and the entire fiction of Warren's correspondence with Lincoln, has just such a disarming effect. The "lie," Warren explains, is a necessary survival technique. It affords him protection.

Cabin fever quickly sets in, and layers of the enigma unfold. "Bloody shirt" becomes outright bloodletting as Warren reveals that he killed Smithers's son. In a sadistic (and likely fictive) act of revenge, Warren claims that he made his prisoner, the son of "the bloody nigger killer of Baton Rouge," perform fellatio on him in exchange for the promise of a blanket. The ever-constricting quarter become a gore-soaked purging ground for racial and sectional grudges, and most of the key players are violently dispatched. In a model of unsubtle suggestion, Warren's genitals are mutilated by a white man. The film's final chapter, "Black Man, White Hell," sees Warren and Mannix unceremoniously coexecute the "lyin' bitch" Domergue via brutal hanging, thus concluding nearly three hours of gradating, bisecting threads of racial, gender, and regional hate and prejudice: white men who hate black men; Yankees who hate Rebels; men who hate women; and even a black woman who hates Mexicans. Badly wounded, Mannix has a change of heart and now requests the Lincoln letter. Awestruck, Mannix and Warren read it together as they both fatally bleed out.

For Tarantino, particularly given his brand of camp, satire, and pulp fiction, where does mere entertainment end and the director's social philosophy begin? Warren demonstrates few of the self-liberating or liberal democratic impulses that US historians associate with African American soldiers and freedpeople. There is no broader discussion of structures, statecraft, or, most notably, black political and economic rights—all themes scholars have deemed central to the understanding of the postwar era. Unlike with Django "Freeman" in Mississippi and Tennessee, emancipationism is not explored with Marquis Warren in this far corner of the West.

Yet allusions to other racial, imperial, and ideological facets of "Greater Reconstruction" are obvious.[5] Like a character plucked from the imagination of William Faulkner, Smithers represents the deposed agrarian chieftain, perhaps driven from place and power by the new and more urban regional bourgeoisie described by Charles Beard and C. Vann Woodward as a part of the "Age of Capital," to use Eric Hobsbawm's term.[6] His defeated but defiant attitude is a metaphor for the Old South plantocracy. Similarly, like the concept of "race riot" or the wartime "battles" of Fort Pillow, Olustee, and Poison Spring, the "Battle of Baton Rouge" serves as a euphemism for what were, in fact, white massacres of black soldiers during and after the war.[7] Intentionally or not, Minnie's fate—the murder of a black female landowner—is a symbol for both the violent "redemption" of Reconstruction and the white theft of black lives and property, one of the defining themes of American history. The beneficiaries of this kleptocracy are men like Mannix, a member of the white elite who ends up (as sheriff) on top of the postwar power structure. And whereas the figurative emasculation of a white man by a black man plays on the most acute and intimate of white fears, the literal emasculation of Warren by a white man speaks to something true in the American record.

Tarantino's handling of violence, gender, and especially race has been met with vocal resistance, both popular and academic. Like a Marquis de Sade sporting 70 mm Panavision, Tarantino has long established himself as a master satirist for the MTV age, employing hyperviolence, hyperracism, and hypersexism as burlesque to mock or jolt or anger, perhaps for the sake of improving. Perhaps not. Indeed, cultural critics have long debated Tarantino's pervasive use of the "n word" and Blaxploitation tropes, not in the service of political commentary but (according to his detractors) for shock value or superficial pop or aesthetic effect.[8] The director's personal comments on race and blackness have also stirred controversy, drawing charges of insensitivity, unacknowledged privilege, and racial appropriation.[9] Yet, whatever the gravity of Tarantino's sins—sins that should not be dismissed or go unscrutinized—the filmmaker's imagery and messaging have consistently cut against stock racial and gender types. Raised by a single mother, he has a well-earned reputation, for instance, for challenging traditional gender roles, patriarchal expectations, and male hegemony through smart, strong (even dangerous) leading women in *Pulp Fiction*

(1994), *Jackie Brown* (1997), *Kill Bill: Vol. 1* (2003), *Kill Bill: Vol. 2* (2004), *Death Proof* (2007), and *Inglourious Basterds* (2009).

Tarantino's views on racial politics outside the confines of his artistic medium are particularly well known. In recent years he has been active in the Rise Up October movement, which drew attention to police violence against African Americans, and has proven a vehement critic of the Confederate flag, calling it the "American swastika."[10] His works have been banned and boycotted by "family values" groups, police unions, and various elements of the Alt-Right. As Adilifu Nama maintains, "Tarantino's films are not merely movies that entertain; they symbolize racial anxieties circulating throughout American society."[11] In the case of *Django* and *The Hateful Eight*, that circulation has come to include all American history, and the Civil War era in particular, which the director appears to view as *the* critical period in the historical development of American race relations.

Biracialism appears central to this social philosophy both in real life and on film. Interracial alliance has served as a frequent plot stratagem for Tarantino: Vincent Vega and Jules Winnfield in *Pulp Fiction*, Jackie Brown and Max Cherry in *Jackie Brown*, the multiethnic women of *Death Proof*, Shoshanna Dreyfus/Emmanuelle Mimieux and Marcel in *Basterds*, and both Django "Freeman" and King Schulz and Calvin Candie and Stephen in *Django*. As old acquaintances and veterans of the War of the Rebellion, Major Marquis Warren ("The Bounty Hunter") and John Ruth ("The Hangman") appear to fit into this schema. Except they do not. Rather than mirroring Django and Schulz as relatively equal partners—antiracist allies whose relationship is one of shared responsibility and sacrifice—Warren and Ruth exhibit a less equitable power dynamic.

Their imbalanced relationship is revealed through *The Hateful Eight*'s most effective plot device and Tarantino's metonymy for the history of American race relations: the Lincoln letter. Warren, a black man traveling alone in a violent corner of a hostile continent, possesses a fake letter from Abraham Lincoln on his personage because it has a "disarming effect" (a double entendre in light of contemporary white-on-black police violence) on white folks that shields him from bigotry on all sides. Born out of self-preservation, and an example of what W. E. B. Du Bois designated the "double consciousness" of being both black and American, the letter carries a certain social capital for which Warren's melanin content disqualifies him (and in this case saves his life during a blizzard).[12] The fiction that a black soldier shared a private relationship with the "Great Emancipator" and "Savior of the Union" not only elevates Warren but also liberalizes Lincoln, and by extension white Unionists.

Mannix inverts Warren's assertion that black people are only safe when white people are "disarmed," both literally and figuratively, by insisting that white people are only secure when black people are scared. A psychological manipulation of the oppressor that was honed on the plantation, this is the quintessence of their time and of all time: white advantage relies on unremitting coercion underwritten by capital and, when that advantage is seriously challenged, explicit terror.

The Lincoln letter is a self-protective ruse that reads like a metaphor for our times. The note underscores the long history, especially among African Americans, of American minorities' creative, deliberate, and shrewd self-defense. This self-sanctuary has existed historically as a response not only to the white-on-black violence of Reconstruction or the coercion, displacement, and extermination of people of color by white people in the American West but also, more immediately, to the sheer vulnerability of black lives in Ferguson, Missouri; Baltimore; Chicago; Minneapolis–St. Paul; Charleston, South Carolina; and everywhere else in the United States. When Warren explains that "the only time Black folks are safe is when white folks are disarmed," he might as well be speaking for Trayvon Martin, Mike Brown, Freddie Gray, or Sandra Bland. It is noteworthy that the intended audience of Warren's Lincoln letter is not seething white supremacists, impossible allies whose racial world-views are firmly entrenched. Rather, the audience is white Unionists, racial liberals. John Ruth is, after all, a "well-meaning" racist who deems himself a situational ally of the black veteran. He becomes palpably disappointed—heartbroken even—when he realizes that the letter is counterfeit, in part because it serves to expose the hypocrisy of his own "good" cause.

This trope squares with Robert Penn Warren's "Treasury of Virtue." The Southern-born novelist, who declared the Civil War "the biggest lie the nation ever told itself," explained that the aftermath of the Civil War engendered two socially corrosive, deeply cherished historical misconceptions. Countering the South's "Great Alibi," the idea of southern victimhood that downplays slavery as the sectional conflict's root cause, the "Treasury of Virtue" was, according to Warren, the North's "psychological heritage" wrought by the war. That "treasury," in all its sanctimoniousness, shifts the locus of troubled race relations southward, indicting the former slave states and exonerating the more liberal

North through a moral geography, thus speaking to the heart of northern—and therefore American—pathos, myth, and identity. If the white southerner feels trapped by history, the white northerner feels redeemed. Part of "the lie" of American history—what Warren termed a "mechanism for evading reality"—is the same self-delusion displayed by John Ruth's naïve internalization of the Union cause.[13]

The Lincoln letter also serves as an allegory for liberalism in Obama's America. It is a premeditated, comforting narrative of congenial, paternalistic race relations intended for white liberal audiences who entertain ideas about postracialism; or who suggest that racial disparities are born out of black culture or pathology rather than hundreds of years of white kleptocracy; or who focus on property rights or various forms of victim-blaming in the event of black political protest rather than acknowledging persistent white-imposed black disadvantage and validating black pain. These are the melanin-deficient publics who "believe" the Lincoln letter, who believe the captivating lie that is designed specifically to make white people feel good.

What does it mean that the black veteran and the South Carolina terrorist "teamed up" and (presumably) died together while the latter admiringly read the fake Lincoln letter? Is the coexecution of Domergue, her face now beaten to a gory pulp, suggestive of a continued, transracial patriarchy? Is this shared manhood and misogyny, specifically the hatred of a double-crossing "bitch," meant to transcend even vast racial divides? Or is the apotheotic bloodbath, so evocative of earlier Tarantino films, intended to have a purging effect, implicating all in a national sin of white supremacy? Perhaps. Viewers less familiar with Tarantino's routine are left to interpret the film's gratuitous male-on-female violence as indefensible, as either absurdism or failed humor. Meanwhile, the age of #MeToo—a topic on which Tarantino has provided his own mea culpa—gives such questions newfound resonance.[14]

In fact, the audience is left to wonder about the dialectics of race and class within American racial capitalism. Does the filmmaker view racism from a Marxian perspective, as an incipiently top-down social and legal construct that creates a "false consciousness" among alienated "white" workers, who, their environments shaped by dominant classes and established institutions, then contribute to capital's capacity to exploit them by eschewing any attempt at biracial cross-class alliance? Is the "white privilege" of Tarantino's world a materially negligible difference that white elites give to nonelite whites in order to sustain a social system that brutalizes black people and exploits white labor?

W. E. B. Du Bois referred to this mostly nonmaterial white advantage—one that impedes the capacity of white workers to organize across racial lines for the collective benefit of *all* nonelites—as the "psychological wage" of white social privilege over African Americans "in exchange" for blacks' being exploited by the ruling class.[15] Martin Luther King Jr. also decried such racialized capitalism as giving the white working class the "satisfaction of . . . thinking you are somebody big because you are white."[16]

Or does Tarantino conceive of American racism more as herrenvolkism, wherein the benefits of whiteness are more than felt and in which roughly united white people, who, according to the historian David Roediger, "define and accept their class position by fashioning identities as 'not slaves' and 'not blacks,'" also create racism independent of the ruling class?[17] The "relational" role of race, the hegemonic role of elite whites, and the compliant and essential role of working-class white men—slave drivers, plantation hands, slave patrolmen, coachmen, trackers, mining-company grunts, and cow punchers—in upholding the racial power structure in both *Django* and *The Hateful Eight* suggest some vague combination of materialism *and* critical whiteness theory, perhaps Tarantino's latent rejection of what is often, in fact, a false binary.[18] Perhaps Mannix embodies the falseness of white consciousness, still applauding the Lincoln letter (the lie) even as the last survivors tortuously bleed to death. The blood-soaked finale, unlike the fictive catharses of *Basterds* and *Django*, brings discomfort and unease. Whether directed from above, by those with the resources to create and ascribe, or reshaped and sustained from below, by those with less social power, the consequences of whiteness are, for everyone, unredeemed, or less than fully redeemed, pain and disquietude and tragedy.

Tarantino has been adamant about his desire to make a movie about the life of the militant abolitionist John Brown. This is unsurprising, as Brown's life and ideas would no doubt reaffirm the director's technical and ideological bent: race and racism, black-white alliance, revenge killing, and a violent reckoning—in the case of the Civil War, the ultimate violent reckoning. But a John Brown film would also constitute a first for Tarantino: a turn away from fantasy and toward a more authentic history. Perhaps the manipulating tonic of the Lincoln letter, the theme of biracial misogyny, and the seductive power of nationalist myths have already brought Tarantino halfway there. Indeed, within the context of American racial history, *Django Unchained* functions as the Lincoln letter (the lie), and *The Hateful Eight*, the reality. Just as the Lincoln letter absolves John Ruth, Django's triumph offers white audiences "redemption from the sins of the past." If the revisionist *Inglourious Basterds* and *Django* are "states of exception" about how the past *should have* played out, *The Hateful Eight* is about how it *did* play out.[19]

From John Winthrop to John L. O'Sullivan, and from Ronald Reagan to Dick Cheney, the myth of American exceptionalism—embraced across both major political parties—has always revealed far less about any categorical American innateness than it has about the mentalities, aspirations, interests, and self-understandings of affluent white men.[20] Far from benign, American exceptionalism has served as justification for territorial expansion, human enslavement and genocide, religious mission, immense material inequality, political and economic encroachment, and military intervention.[21] In *The Hateful Eight*, Tarantino befittingly joins white supremacy to American exceptionalism in the West, the most appreciable site (or perhaps "crime scene") of manifest destiny. Although his illustration is less cerebral and less purposeful than that of the writer James Baldwin or Toni Morrison or the filmmaker Steve McQueen, whose prose and images have not merely displayed the primacy of European-ized ideas and white power over black lives to the American ethos but in fact gone beyond the exceptionalist paradigm in an attempt to recontextualize the entirety of the American past, Tarantino's chief trope is nevertheless a potent one.[22] The Lincoln letter, as a window into segregated black and white worlds, an example of the subtle manipulation that minorities require in order to self-preserve, and a source of the national exceptionalism white people internalize in order to rationalize this disequalizing arrangement, is a fitting "Big Idea" concerning four hundred years of uniquely asymmetrical race relations. It is the director's American metaphor and the answer to an ongoing American Question. Maybe the workings of imperial ideology best enable us to see how race, the production of which subverts class consciousness and upholds class structures, rather than class solidarity, which challenges racist configurations, has so often become the overriding distinction in American social life.

The Hateful Eight is not about Reconstruction; it uses Reconstruction as a parable for "racecraft" in the age of Obama, Ferguson, Black Lives Matter, and the white nationalism of Donald Trump and for American history more broadly. "Black Man, White Hell" indeed. Yet the two-decades-long national struggle—the "twenty years' war"—over questions of political union, slavery, and black civil rights simultaneously stemmed from, challenged, and reframed ideas and systems of white supremacy, ideas and systems that proved both the origin source of America's unique social violence and a critical component of its ruling-class hegemony. By the measure of Tarantino's Civil War–era duplet, slavery, and the racialized configurations of violence and power it continues to engender, is the most exceptional aspect of American exceptionalism.[23]

NOTES

1. On the human-rights politics of Forty-Eighters, see Bruce Levine, *The Spirit of 1848: German Immigrants, Labor Conflict, and the Coming of the Civil War* (Urbana: University of Illinois Press, 1992); and Mischa Honeck, *We Are the Revolutionists: German-Speaking Immigrants and American Abolitionists after 1848* (Athens: University of Georgia Press, 2011).

2. Rodney M. D. Fierce, "The Exceptional N*gger: Redefining African American Identity in *Django Unchained*," in *Movies in the Age of Obama: The Era of Post-Racial and Neo-Racist Cinema*, ed. David Garrett Izzo (Lanham, MD: Rowman & Littlefield, 2015), 54.

3. Oliver Speck, ed., *Quentin Tarantino's "Django Unchained": The Continuation of Metacinema* (New York: Bloomsbury, 2014), 2; Adam Serwer, "In Defense of Django," *Mother Jones*, 7 January 2013, motherjones.com/mixed-media/2013/01/tarantino-django-unchained-western-racism-violence.

4. Adilifu Nama, *Race on the QT: Blackness and the Films of Quentin Tarantino* (Austin: University of Texas Press, 2015), 11.

5. Richard White, *The Republic for Which It Stands: The United States during Reconstruction and the Gilded Age, 1865–1896* (New York: Oxford University Press, 2017), 105.

6. See Charles A. Beard and Mary R. Beard, *The Rise of American Civilization*, vol. 2 (New York: Macmillan, 1927); and C. Vann Woodward, *Origins of the New South, 1877–1913* (Baton Rouge: Louisiana State University Press, 1951), 150–58; Harold D. Woodman "Sequel to Slavery: The New History Views the Postbellum South," *Journal of Southern History* 44 (November 1977): 523–54, referring to the New South as an "emergent bourgeois society"; and Eric Hobsbawm, *The Age of Capital, 1848–1875* (New York: Vintage Books, 1975).

7. On wartime Confederate-on-black soldier massacres and collective memory, see John Cimprich, *Fort Pillow: A Civil War Massacre and Public Memory* (Baton Rouge: Louisiana State University Press, 2005); and Kevin M. Levin, *Remembering the Battle of the Crater: War as Murder* (Lexington: University Press of Kentucky, 2012).

8. For a definition and history of *Blaxploitation*, see Ed Guerrero, "The Rise and Fall of Blaxploitation," in *The Wiley-Blackwell History of American Film*, ed. Cynthia Lucia, Roy Grundmann, and Art Simon (New York: Wiley-Blackwell, 2012), 435–69.

9. For one of the best treatments of Tarantino and race, see Sean Tierney, "Quentin Tarantino in Black and White," in *Critical Rhetorics of Race*, ed. Michael G. Lacy and Kent A. Ono (New York: New York University Press, 2011), 81–97.

10. Qin Xie, "Confederate Flag is the 'American Swastika,'" *Daily Mail*, 2 January 2016, http://www.dailymail.co.uk/news/article-3382113/Confederate-flag-American-Swastika-s-damn-time-people-questioned-says-Quentin-Tarantino.html.

11. Nama, *Race on the QT*, 12.

12. W. E. B. Du Bois, *The Souls of Black Folk* (Chicago: A. C. McClurg, 1903), 3, 202.

13. Robert Penn Warren, *The Legacy of the Civil War* (New York: Random House, 1961), 58–59.

14. Jodi Kantor, "Tarantino on Weinstein: 'I Knew Enough to Do More Than I Did,'" *New York Times*, 19 October 2017.

15. W. E. B. Du Bois, *Black Reconstruction in America, 1860–1880* (New York: Harcourt, 1935), 700.

16. Martin Luther King Jr., "The Drum Major Instinct" (sermon, Ebenezer Baptist Church, Atlanta, 4 February 1968).

17. David R. Roediger, *The Wage of Whiteness: Race and the Making of the American Working Class* (New York: Verso, 1991), 13.

18. Jonathan A. Glickstein, *American Exceptionalism, American Anxiety: Wages, Competition, and Degraded Labor in the Antebellum United States* (Charlottesville: University of Virginia Press, 2002), 93.

19. Speck, *Quentin Tarantino's "Django Unchained,"* 2–11.

20. Louis Hartz, *The Liberal Tradition in America: An Interpretation of American Political Thought since the Revolution* (New York: Harcourt, 1955). Writing in the midst of the Cold War consensus, Hartz argues that the source of American exceptionalism lies in a lack of class consciousness owing to the absence of a feudal tradition, resulting in a Lockean liberal unanimity (often unchallenged and unthinking) around free-market capitalism, property rights, and the connection of individual merit with one's ability to succeed in the marketplace.

21. Donald E. Pease refers to American exceptionalism as "state fantasy," internalized by citizens and used by policymakers as spiritual and intellectual justification of the state will. Pease, *The New American Exceptionalism* (Minneapolis: University of Minnesota Press, 2009).

22. Deborah L. Madsen, *American Exceptionalism* (Jackson: University of Mississippi Press, 1998), 150–52.

23. There is a substantial literature on the links between racism and American exceptionalism and between whiteness and empire and manifest destiny. See esp. Reginald Horseman, *Race and Manifest Destiny: The Origins of American Racial Anglo-Saxonism* (Cambridge, MA: Harvard University Press, 1981); Rick Halpern and Jonathan Morris, eds., *American Exceptionalism? U.S. Working-Class Formation in an International Context* (New York: St. Martin's, 1997); and Fabian Hilfrich, *Debating American Exceptionalism: Empire and Democracy in the Wake of the Spanish-American War* (New York: Palgrave Macmillan, 2012).

21

The Silver Lining of "Bad History" at the Movies
Reconstruction, Confederate Exiles, and *The Undefeated*

MATTHEW CHRISTOPHER HULBERT

Hunkered beneath a tattered St. Andrew's cross, equally haggard Confederate soldiers look out over a battlefield. The time and place are not identified, but the report of heavy guns soon signals the start of another engagement. Up and down the Rebel line, explosions send men and shrapnel flying—the former to their death by way of the latter. The barrage precedes a Union cavalry charge; after mounted troopers overrun the Confederate defenses, a savage, hand-to-hand struggle ensues, and the few survivors in gray are forced to hobble off in retreat.

Just as the battle ends, a messenger arrives with news from the War Department. The entire battle had been for nothing: Lee had surrendered to Grant three days earlier at Appomattox. The Union colonel John Henry Thomas (John Wayne) thoughtfully takes stock of the Confederate dead. America's national bloodletting is finally over, but not quite soon enough for these men, their lives sacrificed for a cause already lost. Now regretting the headlong assault, Thomas parlays with a one-armed Confederate major and is more than a little disturbed to learn that unlike the Yankees, the Rebels had known of Lee's surrender *before* the battle. They had chosen to fight on, outgunned and outnumbered, despite the momentous news. "I don't think you understand Major, the war is over," Thomas states incredulously. The major, at peace with the decision to fight, politely retorts that his men will remain under arms because "this is our land [and you are trespassing on it]."

On this defiant timbre, the battlefield scene in *The Undefeated* (1969) gives way to a sequence of roads swollen with newly emancipated slaves, free but unsure where to go or what to do. We also see weary ex-Confederates journeying home, with minds still sharp enough to fight but bodies unwilling to answer the bugler's call. And then there are the lone chimneys that dot the southern landscape, the calling cards of the Union's pivot to hard war on the Confederate homefront after the election of 1864. Rather abruptly, essentially in the time it takes the opening credits to roll, the war is over, and most former Confederates, now burdened with the sting of defeat, have started rebuilding homes and piecing shattered lives back together.

Colonel James Langdon (Rock Hudson) is not like most former Confederates. Once the scion of an affluent slaveholding family, the colonel outfitted his own Confederate regiment during the war and bankrupted himself in the process. Now, as spring turns to summer 1865, Langdon is unable to pay the taxes due on his land and faces foreclosure. The bank will seize his estate and sell it at auction. One scene in which Langdon throws would-be buyers off his land—an interracial pair of smooth-talking carpetbaggers hoping to buy the plantation for pennies on the dollar—makes it abundantly clear that this space (not to be confused with cultural concepts of "place") can no longer be his home. So Langdon is leading the remnants of his unit to Mexico, where they will continue to live as Confederates, under the auspices and protection of His Imperial Majesty Maximilian I. Before beginning the long trek, though, Langdon burns the family's marble-columned "big house" to the ground, a gesture that symbolized the end of one life and plans for another to rise from the ashes.

The character of James Langdon is undoubtedly modeled after Major General Joseph Orville Shelby, a well-known and formerly affluent Confederate cavalry commander from western Missouri. In June 1865, Shelby, his once-vaunted "Iron Brigade," and a small caravan of other high-ranking ex-Confederate officers and politicians trudged through the South Texas heat. Gone were the days of great cavalry raids in the borderlands, and with them the hope that Missouri might be pulled out of the Union's clutches and delivered to the Confederacy. Though still legally unconquered—Shelby's men never technically surrendered to Union forces—they did not travel in the direction of any meaningful military objective. History and legend generally agree that Shelby's men tapped their last reserve of pomp and circumstance at Eagle Pass, ceremoniously sinking their pennant in the Rio Grande before crossing the border into French-controlled Mexico. No longer on Union soil, and far from the waning authority of Confederate leaders, Shelby and his fellow exiles would not comply with Robert E. Lee's wishes to make the process of political reunion as swift and painless as possible. Instead, this unlikely coterie of rene-gade generals, deposed governors, wanderlust soldiers, and outlawed guerrillas had something more quixotic in mind.[1]

Once settled in Mexico, Shelby and company were utterly determined not to relinquish their southern status. With generous subsidies from Maximilian I—brother of the Austrian emperor Franz Joseph I and in many ways the unfor-tunate dupe of France's Napoleon III—these "Confederados" established a col-ony midway between present-day Mexico City and Veracruz. Maximilian had reigned over the Second French Empire since spring 1864; he was popular with a small group of Mexican monarchists and now the Confederates but reviled by the lower classes as an invading dictator. In honor of their Habsburg patron's wife, Empress Charlotte of Belgium (sister of the notorious King Leopold), the Confederates christened the new settlement Carlota. The support of an autocrat as well connected as Maximilian to the high thrones of Europe by blood and marriage made it seem possible for the Confederados to re-create their antebel-lum life cycles on Mexican soil. That being the case, they built new homes and plotted out haciendas; they worked closely with recruitment agencies back in the United States to help lure other disillusioned southerners to join them; and they theorized about how best to ensnare Mexican peasants with de facto wage slavery in a nation where bondage de jure had long since been abolished. In short, even after the fall of Richmond and Lee's surrender in Wilmer McLean's living room—and even after the passage of the Thirteenth Amendment—these men were attempting to have their Confederate cake and eat it too.[2]

In *The Undefeated*, however, Langdon and the Confederates are not the only Civil War veterans with business south of the Rio Grande. Viewers next reunite with John Henry Thomas and his men, not in their blue coats and striped cavalry pants, but in the garb of western cowboys. By miraculous coincidence, Thomas has resigned from the Union army and, with the help of his former officers, is driving a herd of three thousand horses to Mexico. Maximilian's re-gime is locked in a bitter power struggle with an insurgency headed by Benito Juarez, the democratically elected president of Mexico whom Maximilian deposed upon seizing power. The emperor is thus willing to pay top dollar for new cavalry mounts. Along the way, the parties of Thomas and Langdon come into repeated contact, even celebrating the Fourth of July together. A friendship is quickly established between the two colonels, and an interracial romance blossoms between Langdon's teenage daughter, Charlotte (Melissa Newman), and Thomas's adopted Cherokee son, Blue Boy (Roman Gabriel).

In the film's final plot twist, Langdon's regiment is tricked by a band of Juaristas commanded by General Rojas (Tony Aguilar). Posing as supporters of Maximilian, the Mexican revolutionaries use a welcome party to lure the Confederates into a fortress courtyard and then take them hostage. Much like Maximilian's military forces, the Juaristas are in dire need of horseflesh, so Rojas refuses to release Langdon's people unless the colonel can persuade his new friend Thomas to hand over his entire herd. Rojas gives Langdon a deadline for delivery of the horses, after which he will begin executing Confederate officers. Not surprisingly given Thomas's amicable nature throughout the film, he and the other Union vets agree to bail out the would-be Confederados. But before they can ride to the rescue, they must first fight their way through a regiment of French soldiers not keen to lose their new mounts to the Juaristas. "We got ourselves mixed up in somebody else's war," Thomas observes wryly, before he and his men blast their way to safety and escape with the herd.

Meanwhile at Durango, where Langdon's exiles are imprisoned, Rojas observes the passing of the deadline and begins lining up the first group of Confederate officers to be shot. At the last possible moment, the pounding of equine feet announces the arrival of Thomas and Langdon with the ransom. Viewers expecting a fight between the Union-Confederate forces and the Juaristas are quickly disappointed. Rojas and his men honor their promise and free the Confederate prisoners, which is apparently good enough for Thomas. Following an awkward scene in which Rojas, Langdon, and Thomas all drink toasts to both Benito Juarez and the United States, a quick change of setting has the two former groups traveling together, bound for the States—not as Unionists and Confederates but intermingled as *Americans*. To drive home this new spirit of reconciliation, Blue Boy and Charlotte will be married; Thomas hints that he will marry Langdon's sister-in-law (whose first husband his regiment killed at Chickamauga) and move west to start a ranch; and Langdon, the man once so convinced of his inability to live on American soil that he torched his ancestral home before departing, proudly announces that he will run for Congress. Better still, the only character left out of the reconciliatory spirit and whom *all* the ex-pats despise equally is a southerner who traveled to Mexico with the Confederates but had not fought for *either* army during the war. Because he hadn't been manly enough to choose a side when North and South split, he cannot reap the benefits of reunion.

If any aspect of *The Undefeated* stands on solid historical footing, it's the motivations and intentions of Confederate exiles traveling to Mexico in 1865. Just like James Langdon early in the film, the first Confederados were not planning to sit out the worst of Reconstruction and then return to the United States when tensions eased. Langdon does not burn his house simply to spite the carpetbaggers he assumes would buy it at auction; in that moment, he intends never to return and regain it. Nor did Shelby and company plan to make their new homes in Maximilian's empire anything but permanent; they established newspapers, they brought their families, they worked with recruiting agents, and they tried to persuade other friends and relatives to join them in the warm, sunny, farmer-friendly climate of Mexico. Like the fictional Langdon, Shelby and his comrades believed that they could transplant the cultural place of the Old South ("home") to a new geographical space in Mexico. They simply needed a government friendly to their cause, land to develop, and financial backing—all of which an absolute ruler like Maximilian could, and did, supply for as long as he was in power.[3]

According to the historian David Blight, in the aftermath of the Civil War a group mainly interested in preserving southern white supremacy aligned with the "Reconciliationists," a bloc mainly interested in letting bygones be bygones for the sake of reuniting the nation. The war's legacy of emancipation—and the "Emancipationists," who championed it—constituted the collateral damage of this unholy political alliance. The importance of slavery as the root cause of the Civil War and its destruction as the conflict's signature achievement would not be touted, but rather squelched, to facilitate the process of sectional healing. While subsequent scholars, most notably Caroline Janney, have attempted to refine Blight's narrative, it remains standard among scholars and in the classroom. Thus, in getting the motive elements of the Confederados' story correct, it looks initially as though *The Undefeated* will force viewers to confront a crucial idea about Reconstruction: that when we zoom in a little closer than meta, not all ex-Confederates fit neatly within these three ideological categories.[4]

Unfortunately, once Langdon's regiment leaves American soil, the film's historical moorings come hopelessly loose. Following their brief captivity, the Confederates happily head back to their old homes after less than a week in Mexico. But Shelby and many of the southerners who ventured with him to Carlota in 1865 remained in voluntary exile for nearly two years. In 1867, nationalist forces led by Juarez infiltrated Maximilian's military collegium and toppled the imperial government from within. As Napoleon III refused to intervene with French troops, the monarchs of Europe ignored the hysterical pleading of Empress Charlotte and stood by while Maximilian was captured and executed by a firing squad. Without imperial subsidies and military protection, the positions of virtually all Confederate exiles living in Mexico suddenly became untenable; men who had planned to coerce Mexican peasants to cultivate their land in a wage system that eerily resembled slavery were no longer welcome after their benefactor's violent demise. Thus it was only when the Second Mexican Empire collapsed beneath them that the clear majority of exiles came slinking home to begin the process of reintegrating themselves into southern society after years abroad.[5]

In the film, it's just the opposite. Not only do Langdon's fictional Confederates prove to be inept as exiles but they lose their colonial aspirations after far less prodding than Shelby's group received—long before a colony has even been established to abandon! They come home in good spirits, having never laid eyes on Maximilian, Charlotte, or their subsidized land, ready to roll up their sleeves and restart their lives as Americans. All at once, the conclusion of *The Undefeated* misrepresents what the Confederados did in Mexico and why they returned to the United States. More critically, in doing so, the film reimagines their counternarrative as a fable of the Reconciliationist orthodoxy, complete with reunion-minded moral and multiple happy and patriotic endings.

The groundwork for this commemorative bait-and-switch was laid long before in one of Langdon's earliest scenes. Before departing for Mexico, the colonel gives his grandfather's pocket watch to an elderly freedman, presumably after he'd been a slave to multiple generations of Langdons. The receiver of the watch, though unnamed, is clearly touched by the gesture, and his facial expressions hint that he would rather remain in Langdon's service than face the uncertainties of life as a free man. From this exchange we are meant to understand that Langdon had been a slaveholder but a paternalistic, or "good," master, the kind of master who might be quickly absolved of his past sins and welcomed back into the American fold. And sure enough, by the end of *The Undefeated* virtually all memory of Langdon as a white supremacist slaveowner who squandered his own money waging a war for slavery against the US government is forgotten. Rather than representing the exception to mainstream historical renditions of Reconstruction, Langdon has become the perfect embodiment of the White Supremacist-Reconciliationist alliance that scaffolds such interpretations.

As a Reconciliationist-themed picture, *The Undefeated* would appear to fit within the organizational model for Civil War films outlined by the historian Gary Gallagher, the other three categories being Union Victory, Lost Cause, and Emancipationist. However, per Gallagher—who labels *The Undefeated* "spectacularly wretched"—it is merely one of a slew of films that "superficially fit the genre but are really westerns dressed up in ill-fitting Civil War garb." The historian Brian Wills concurs, describing the film as "less a Civil War piece than a western" and "more entertaining than educational." "Often," Wills concludes, "films like *The Undefeated* were excuses to offer the standard western fare without the baggage of historical veracity."[6]

As I've argued elsewhere, it isn't worth debating whether these films look like westerns, because they do. Given the subject matter, it would be stranger if *The Undefeated* did *not* look western. The more important message to be conveyed is that it's quite possible for a film to take place in the West (to be a western in the literal, geographical sense) and still tell a legitimate story about the Civil War and its place in memory and pop culture. And in fairness to *The Undefeated*, while Gallagher is correct in observing that Rock Hudson's southern drawl is "so bad it must be heard to be believed," the movie actually avoids many of the signature components we'd expect of a western produced in the 1960s. The script is without a marquee gunfight or showdown; it features a Native American character, but not as a savage enemy or a war chief on the prowl; and while Thomas's men swap their uniforms for cow-punching gear, Langdon's men wear theirs throughout the film. Perhaps most surprising of all, the director, Andrew McLaglen, and his screenwriters exercised an admirable (and frankly, unexpected) degree of restraint in not forcing a final battle scene between the combined Union-Confederate force and the Juaristas. That is, *The Undefeated* doesn't feature a penultimate battle scene in which white Americans triumph over Mexican or Native American foes, which was so common to pictures of the period.[7]

None of this is to contend, though, that the film is particularly well made; its flaws have more to do with acting and dialogue than with a crisis of genre identity. Made in the phase of John Wayne's career most generously described as "slightly past prime," *The Undefeated* utilized a combination of the Duke's "elder statesman" status and his comedic talents. This gave Colonel John Henry Thomas more in common with G. W. McLintock (*McLintock*, 1963) and Rooster Cogburn (*True Grit*, 1969) than with the lead characters of his earlier, more serious films, such as Ethan Edwards (*The Searchers*, 1956), Colonel John Marlowe (*The Horse Soldiers*, 1959), or Tom Doniphon (*The Man Who Shot Liberty Valance*, 1962). For co-lead Rock Hudson, the best years of his career were long in rear view by 1969. (His last hurrah, the 1968 film *Ice Station Zebra*, has

The clothing of Colonel James Langdon (Rock Hudson) and Colonel John Henry Thomas (John Wayne) illustrates how popular imaginings of the Civil War and the "Wild West" come together throughout *The Undefeated*.

become a cult classic but did little to reignite Hudson's fading star.) Following *The Undefeated*, he appeared in a few forgettable films and then moved on to equally forgettable roles on television. Later generations remember Hudson less for his roles in highly regarded films like *Magnificent Obsession* (1954), *Written on the Wind* (1956), and *Giant* (1956) than for being one of the first high-profile American celebrities to succumb to AIDS-related complications, at a time when the Reagan administration sought to minimize attention paid to the disease.[8]

Civil War historians have a stake in how their specialties are portrayed on-screen and regularly attempt to serve as gatekeepers, determining which pictures "count" or belong within the genre of true Civil War and Reconstruction films. Frequently, we criticize films—far better films than *The Undefeated*, it's worth mentioning—for not perfectly representing a historical event or character: a military unit ascribed undue credit during a battle; an attack launched from the incorrect cardinal direction; a plausible but unevidenced event taking place in the slave quarters to enrich a plot; even something so trivial as an officer's uniform having the wrong buttons or epaulets. And often these are the films historians actually enjoy or at least find tolerable. Other pictures, like *The Undefeated* or *Mandingo* (1969) or *Santa Fe Trail* (1940), are repeatedly dismissed outright or categorized as not being "real" films about the Civil War era because while they are based on actual historical events, people, institutions, and ideas, they take great liberty with "interpretation" or butcher well-established chronologies or don't look the way most would expect. (In the case of *The Undefeated*, as we know, it looks too western.)

In truth, *The Undefeated* does not fail to tell the story of Shelby and other Confederate exiles in Mexico well because it is a western masquerading as a Civil War film or even because it's laden with second-rate performances; it ultimately fails because it's a film about the Civil War and Reconstruction full of mostly "bad" or warped history. On one hand, the film's plot trajectory unquestionably squanders an opportunity to familiarize Americans with a counternarrative Reconstruction experience, and one that was international to boot. On the other hand, though, it would be foolish to expect otherwise from a major Hollywood studio. Production houses are in business to make money, not to win the praise and admiration of a tiny segment of the population trained to know better. This tension between potential and expectation brings us to the silver lining of *The Undefeated*'s lost opportunity: it underscores once and for all the importance of historians' directly engaging with "bad" historical movies.

This is categorically not to say that scholars should be concerned with the accuracy of every film based loosely on real historical events. Nor is it to say that it is the job of professional historians to defend the sanctity of "real history," if such a thing even exists, by not allowing Hollywood to have the last word with the public. (In all honesty, that battle is unwinnable, and we know it.) Rather, it is to say that if *The Undefeated* is ignored because of its bad history, the moment is lost and wasted in which we might blueprint the political and social forces—the Civil War centennial, the civil rights movement, growing opposition to the war in Vietnam—that deemed Colonel James Langdon circa 1865 more useful, more marketable, and more patriotic in America circa 1969 as a sanitized icon of reconciliation than as a truer reflection of Joseph Shelby and his band of Confederate exiles.

The writers behind *The Undefeated* clearly had access to the historical version of the Confederados' story, but the ahistorical final product is the result of a cause-and-effect relationship. In other words, bad history on screen is not necessarily a coincidence; historical inaccuracy in one form was directly influenced and molded by other historical forces—by broader patterns in Civil War remembrance and legacy building. In this light, there is something to be learned yet from James Langdon's short trip south of the border and his triumphal return alongside John Henry Thomas: clearly not what actually happened in the waning days of the Second French Empire but why Hollywood called them home to America *together*.

NOTES

1. On Shelby and company's trek into Mexico, see John Newman Edwards, *Shelby's Expedition to Mexico* (Kansas City, MO: Kansas City Times Steam Book and Job Printing House, 1872); Edwards, *Shelby and His Men* (Cincinnati, OH: Miami Printing and Publishing, 1867), 547; Anthony Arthur, *General Jo Shelby's March* (New York: Random House, 2010); and Edwin A. Davis, *Fallen Guidon: The Forgotten Saga of General Jo Shelby's Confederate Command* (Santa Fe, NM: Stagecoach, 1962). Other Confederate exiles included Jubal Early, Sterling Price, John B. Magruder, H. W. Allen, Alexander Terrell, and Pendleton Murrah.

2. For other accounts of general conditions in imperial Mexico, see Fitzhugh Lee to Colonel Kimmell, 12 August 1866 and 1 October 1867, Fitzhugh Lee Papers (1866–1887), Special Collections, Earl Greg Swem Library, College of William & Mary, Williamsburg, Virginia. On the origins of Carlota, see Carl Coke Rister, "Carlota, a Confederate Colony in Mexico," *Journal of Southern History* 11, no. 1 (1945).

3. John Newman Edwards to Fanny and Edmonia Edwards, 6 April 1866, Special Collections, State Historical Society of Missouri, Columbia (hereafter SHSMC); John Newman Edwards to Fanny Edwards, 18 September 1866, SHSMC; John Newman Edwards to Thomas Edwards, 18 September 1886, SHSMC; John Newman Edwards to Fanny and Edmonia Edwards, September 1865, SHSMC. Colonists paid one dollar per acre for land at 6 percent interest, and they were expected to repay the loan within five years if they did not buy the land outright. As Edwards notes in the letter of 6 April to his sisters, the land was probably worth twenty to thirty times more than a dollar per acre, and many colonists took on several hundred acres at a time.

The *Mexican Times* included articles on local news in the colony itself, as well as news from the United States. Front-page material included the prices of goods, recent arrivals to the colony, the fallout from defeat and Reconstruction, and the activities of Confederates who remained in America. (Regarding the activities of Confederates who remained in America, the paper provided both news and gossip, in which the romantic, gossipy, and dramatic Edwards excelled.) The most complete run of the *Mexican Times* is available in the Special Collections Library at Louisiana State University.

For information on official recruitment agencies and on waves of ex-Confederate colonists who did seek temporary respite or profit, see Todd Wahlstrom, *The Southern Exodus to Mexico: Migration across the Borderland after the Civil War* (Lincoln: University of Nebraska Press, 2015), xvi–xviii, xxii, 3–5, 13–24.

4. See David W. Blight, *Race and Reunion: The Civil War in American Memory* (Cambridge, MA: Harvard University Press, 2003). Caroline Janney contends that historians must take greater care to distinguish between the true meanings of *reunion* and *reconciliation* when con-

sidering the "Blight Thesis." Janney, *Remembering the Civil War: Reunion and the Limits of Reconciliation* (Chapel Hill: University of North Carolina Press, 2013).

5. Edwards, *Shelby's Expedition to Mexico*, 128–38; "Dispersion of the Confederate Colony at Cordova," *New York Tribune*, 22 June 1866; "The Confederate Colony in Mexico," *Richmond Examiner*, 16 January 1866; "The French at Vera Cruz: Description of the Retiring Army," *New Orleans Daily Picayune*, 3 March 1867. Empress Charlotte was not physically present at the execution of Maximilian. She was sent back to Belgium under the supervision of her brother King Leopold to lobby for European support against Juarez. After Maximilian's death, Leopold had Charlotte committed to an insane asylum under "dubious" medical circumstances. Edwards penned an obituary for Charlotte in 1870 entitled "Poor Carlota," which appeared in the *Kansas City Times* on 29 May of that year.

6. Gary Gallagher, *Causes Won, Lost, and Forgotten: How Hollywood and Popular Art Shape What We Know about the Civil War* (Chapel Hill: University of North Carolina Press, 2008), 54; Brian Wills, *Gone with the Glory: The Civil War in Cinema* (Lanham, MD: Rowman & Littlefield, 2007), 94–96.

7. Matthew C. Hulbert, *The Ghosts of Guerrilla Memory: How Civil War Bushwhackers Became Gunslingers in the American West* (Athens: University of Georgia Press, 2016), 240–46; Hulbert, "Texas Bound and Down: An Untold Narrative of Missouri's Guerrilla War on Film," *Journal of the West* 50, no. 4 (Fall 2011): 27–33; Gallagher, *Causes Won, Lost, and Forgotten*, 54–55.

8. On the Reagan administration's response to the AIDS crisis in the 1980s, see "The Age of AIDS," *PBS Frontline*, https://www.pbs.org/wgbh/pages/frontline/aids/; and "Ronald Reagan and AIDS: Correcting the Record," Real Clear Politics, http://www.realclearpolitics.com/articles/2014/06/01/ronald_reagan_and_aids_correcting_the_record_122806.html.

22

Custer's Last Stands
Remaking a Frontier Legend in Hollywood Film

KEVIN WAITE

George Armstrong Custer fell at the hands of a mixed force of Sioux, Cheyenne, and Arapaho warriors on June 25, 1876. Since then, writers and directors have killed him hundreds of times over again, turning his death at the Battle of the Little Bighorn into a touchstone of American popular culture. For a so-called last stand, Custer's final moments have had very little finality. The dust had barely settled along the banks of the Little Bighorn before historians, poets, and partisans began constructing a literary monument to the fallen thirty-six-year-old cavalry commander. These early eulogists—including American literary icons like Walt Whitman and Henry Wadsworth Longfellow—cast Custer in the role of the archetypal frontier hero: daring and dashing in the advance guard of white civilization. But Custer also attracted his fair share of detractors, who claimed that his hubris and tactical blunders had cost the lives of some two hundred men under his command. While the mythologizers and apologists outnumbered the critics in the first decades after his death, the anti-Custer camp had begun to grow quickly by the mid-twentieth century.[1]

This battle over Custer's legacy has reached across an astounding range of mediums and genres: poems, histories, memoirs, comic books, stage productions, pageants, paintings, lithographs, trading cards, and even whiskey advertisements. But it is through film that both Custer the heroic frontiersman and Custer the mad blunderer have achieved their fullest expression.[2] Custer himself was practically tailor-made for the silver screen. As a Union cavalry commander during the Civil War, he led from the front in a wide-brimmed hat, crimson scarf, and black velvet coat trimmed with gold braid; as colonel of the Seventh Cavalry during the subsequent Indian Wars, he swapped his velvet jacket for a fringed buckskin suit, though he kept his signature scarf and hat. Some of the very first films of the silent era featured Custer in all his battlefield finery and flair, and he proved an equally popular Hollywood hero in subsequent decades. Then, by midcentury, two major American wars—one against German Nazism, the other against Vietnamese Communism—threw the conflicting representations of Custer into stark relief. *They Died with Their Boots On* (1941) was released just before the United States entered World War II, and *Little Big Man* (1970) hit theaters at the height of the Vietnam conflict. Taken together, they represent not only the opposing poles of Custerology but also a sea change in the American attitude toward its military establishment.

They Died with Their Boots On (1941)

Raoul Walsh's 1941 film is a stirring piece of military propaganda and a dismal piece of history. It pits Custer (Errol Flynn), the peerless cavalry commander and moral crusader, against a cabal of corporate swindlers from the East and a horde of undifferentiated Indians from the West. Virtually single-handedly, Custer exposes the crony capitalism of the Gilded Age and preserves America's western frontier for white settlement. Short of elevating Custer to the US presidency, Walsh does everything that directorial license will allow to exaggerate the influence of his hero. Custer saves the Union at Gettysburg; he reinvigorates America's frontier defenses after the war; he thwarts the machinations of railroad tycoons; and he saves the US military from almost certain annihilation in the northwestern territories—all with effortless charm and good looks.

Errol Flynn is broad shouldered and quick witted in the role of Custer. He bursts onto the scene as a new cadet at West Point before the outbreak of the Civil War, attired in a flamboyant, homemade military uniform and toting a portrait of Napoleon's cavalry commander, Joachim Murat. Flynn's Custer soon displays a penchant for coldcocking haughty superiors, while simultaneously winning the esteem of certain influential individuals, such as the academy's commander, Philip Sheridan, and later General Winfield Scott. In this regard, the film is not entirely wide of the historical mark. Custer did indeed rile some superiors during his West Point years, amassing a full scorecard of demerits and ultimately graduating thirty-fourth in a class of thirty-four. But he also

Errol Flynn as a young George Armstrong Custer during his
West Point years in *They Died with Their Boots On*

possessed a rare ability to ingratiate himself with those in command, and he used their patronage to rise rapidly through the army's ranks during the Civil War, winning the single star of a brigadier general by age twenty-three.[3]

To fully catalog the film's inaccuracies would require an entire dedicated volume. Many of the falsehoods, however, serve an explicit purpose: to celebrate America's martial past. Two weeks after *They Died with Their Boots On* reached theaters, Japan bombed Pearl Harbor and the United States began mobilizing for war. American viewers were therefore primed for stirring stories about military triumph and selfless sacrifice. And if the historical Custer didn't exactly fit that role, the mythologized Custer certainly did. Dozens of films and books had already presented Custer as a heroic martyr, so when viewers streamed into theaters in 1941 they knew exactly what to expect. His name had become shorthand for martial valor—at a time when Americans craved precisely that.

For a nation marching off to a global conflict, Walsh's Civil War scenes were reassuringly bloodless. True, Custer sustains a wound at the battle of First Bull Run, but he does so while leading a heroic counterattack against the Confederate advance, and he's rewarded with a medal and the tender ministrations of four female nurses as he convalesces. (The film conveniently neglects to mention that Bull Run ended in an embarrassing rout of the Union army.) In short, a conflict that claimed the lives of some 750,000 men is transformed into high adventure, complete with flashing cavalry sabers, speedy promotion, a long string of Union victories, and even the courtship of a beautiful young woman, Libbie Bacon (Olivia de Havilland), who would become Custer's wife.

The film also carefully sidesteps any direct mention of slavery or sectional conflict—a notable feat, considering that it spans the secession crisis, the Civil War, and Reconstruction. In an early scene, after the slave South breaks from the Union and West Point's southern-born cadets march out of the academy, their commander, Philip Sheridan, offers no resistance or even criticism. Instead, he orders the band to strike up "Dixie" for his rebellious cadets. Northerners and southerners may shoot at one another in a few battlefield scenes, but there is no real enmity between American soldiers in *They Died with Their Boots On*. After the war, the North and the South reconcile seamlessly—ignoring the fact that Custer himself was an outspoken critic of military reconstruction and the various protections that Republicans attempted to extend to African Americans.[4]

True to the common cinematic tropes of the period, the film trades liberally in racial caricatures. Hattie McDaniel plays Callie, the superstitious African American maid and confidante of Custer's future wife. She reads her mistress's romantic fortunes in a teacup and clutches at a rabbit's foot as she orchestrates the courtship of Custer and Libbie. In some ways, this is a reprise of McDaniel's Oscar-winning portrayal of Mammy in Gone with the Wind (1939). In both roles, she mixes homespun wisdom and unquestioning loyalty to her white employers/owners. Viewers could be forgiven if they assumed that McDaniel was once again playing the role of a slave—although we can intuit that Callie is indeed free, given that she resides in Ohio. That the film restricts African Americans to the role of grinning servants is not surprising, however. Hollywood films of the period were not in the habit of challenging racial conventions (see Gone with the Wind from two years earlier), and They Died with Their Boots On reduces virtually every character to its crudest stereotype—dashing cavalier, greedy industrialist, whooping Indian, loyal black servant.

This is not to say, however, that the film is unworthy of scholarly attention. From a historian's perspective, They Died with Their Boots On displays rare insight through its narrative framing. By presenting the full sweep of Custer's career, from his youthful days at West Point during the secession crisis to his death on the Northern Plains (in present-day Montana) in 1876, the film traces the continuities between the Civil War and the Indian Wars that followed. A number of characters from the film's Civil War scenes reappear in the postwar West as soldiers, traders, and politicians, with all their vices and virtues intact. This transfer of personnel reflects an important historical fact. Many of the Union's commanders, such as William Tecumseh Sherman, Philip Sheridan, O. O. Howard, and John Pope, used lessons learned from Civil War battlefields in new campaigns against the Indians of the Great Plains. Historians such as Steven Hahn and Elliot West have recently suggested ways to reinterpret the wars of the mid-nineteenth century as a continuous process of state-making rather than a series of discrete military actions.[5] They Died with Their Boots On certainly doesn't deserve credit for any degree of conceptual sophistication, but in bridging the Civil War and subsequent Indian Wars, it at least acknowledges the parallels between events that are all too often seen in isolation.

At the heart of the film is a Manichean struggle—not a struggle between slavery and freedom, North and South, or even savagery and civilization but one between the forces of greed and the representatives of martial virtue. This struggle comes to the fore in the second half of the film, after the close of the

Civil War and Custer's brief return to civilian life. A pair of executives approach Custer in his drawing room, offering him the presidency of a railroad corporation, with an annual salary of ten thousand dollars. All they ask in exchange is the use of his good name in their business ventures. Custer immediately refuses, claiming defiantly, "My name stands for something." In truth, Custer was a chronic gambler and speculator who hobnobbed with New York's financial elite and proved all too ready to exploit his fame for a quick profit.[6] But Flynn's Custer is entirely devoid of such mercenary instincts. True, he turns to drink to lubricate his transition from military to civilian life. But this is meant primarily as a critique of the stultifying effects of inaction, and not of Custer himself. The message here is clear: war is ennobling; peace is emasculating; and politicians and industrialists are not to be trusted.

Fortunately for Custer, a new post as commander of the Seventh Cavalry at Fort Lincoln saves him from himself. It does not, however, save him from the intrigues of corporate profiteers. The struggle that began in his drawing room moves west to the Dakota Territory, where military contractors and railroad tycoons attempt to poison Custer's frontier peacekeeping. Short of twisting their waxed moustaches, these businessmen fulfill nearly every stereotype of devious villainy. "Here's to money and long may she jingle," toasts one of the leaders of this lot. To which Custer answers in rebuttal, "You can take glory with you when it's time to go." By this account, it's bow-tied plutocrats, and not uniformed soldiers, who stand guilty of destroying the Indians' way of life. Whereas Custer personally grants Crazy Horse political sovereignty in the Black Hills, these eastern magnates conspire to drive a railroad across Sioux ancestral lands, thus making inevitable the fatal clash between the Seventh Cavalry and Crazy Horse's braves.

Custer—who built much of his postwar fame on the killing of Indians, including noncombatants—is thus absolved of any guilt in this fanciful rescripting of his military career. He rides into the film's climactic battle sequence, not because he wishes to destroy Indian resistance, but because without his aid the entire US frontier army would likely face annihilation. It is an act of sacrifice, not conquest. At the Little Bighorn, his relatively small detachment of cavalrymen attempts to hold off an inexhaustible mass of Sioux warriors in order to provide cover for the rest of the army. Wielding two revolvers and a saber, Custer stands tall in his buckskin finest against wave after wave of Indian attackers as his men drop beside him.[7] Low-angle shots amplify Custer's heroic stature, and a stirring rendition of "Garyowen" provides the accompaniment for his last stand.[8] When Custer finally falls, he does so as a blameless martyr, and not as a tactical blunderer.

Walsh saves his most egregious contortions of historical fact for the film's final scene. In it, several of the main characters, including Philip Sheridan and two of the corporate racketeers, gather shortly after receiving word of Custer's death. Sheridan openly acknowledges that the Seventh Cavalry's actions at Little Bighorn saved the entire territory from the Sioux. He then ushers Libbie into the room, and she delivers word of Custer's final letter, penned on the eve of his death. To the dismay of the plutocrats, it exposes the fraud of their railroad corporation, orders its dissolution, and then demands that all Indians under Crazy Horse be protected against further American encroachments. Sheridan's assessment of the letter serves as both the final words of the film and as Custer's eulogy: "Your soldier won his last fight after all." Through this imaginative retelling of a great American military debacle, Custer's last stand becomes a triumph, simultaneously, for the US Army, for western settlement, for business ethics, and most implausible of all, for Native American rights. The film thus insists that neither Custer nor his many men died in vain.

Little Big Man (1970)

In contrast, Custer's death in Little Big Man is all vanity. Richard Mulligan plays a ranting, raving, and utterly incompetent Custer in this 1970 antiestablishment classic, a complete departure from the cool-headed heroism of Errol Flynn. The divergence in these biographical portrayals mirrored a broader shift in the popular attitude toward the US military. Fewer than thirty years separated the release dates of Little Big Man and They Died with Their Boots On, but in that time a large swath of the American public had become disenchanted with, if not aggressively opposed to, the policy of armed intervention. Whatever romance war possessed in the early 1940s had been sufficiently drained by 1970, after a decade of military quagmire in Vietnam by 1970. Put simply, the political and military failings of the Vietnam era dealt a death blow to the heroic myth of George Armstrong Custer. And Arthur Penn's unapologetically ideological Little Big Man put the nail in that coffin.

Based on Thomas Berger's novel of the same name, Little Big Man tells the story of Jack Crabb (Dustin Hoffman), who claims to be the lone white survivor of the Battle of the Little Bighorn. Like Berger's novel, Penn's film is narrated by a 121-year-old Crabb from his rest home. The story begins with the murder of Crabb's family and his adoption by a band of Northern Cheyenne under the leadership of Old Lodge Skins, played brilliantly by the Native actor Chief Dan George. For the next several decades of his life, Crabb drifts between warring white and Indian societies, unable to fully assimilate into either yet equally unable to escape. He acquires and then loses both a white and an Indian wife, as well as a host of allies and enemies. Crabb survives a nearly endless series of scrapes, shoot-outs, and massacres, even as virtually every other character around him falls victim to this frontier violence.

For such a blood-soaked epic, Crabb's narrative—in both the novel and the film—is consistently hilarious. However, the two comedies derive their humor from distinct techniques. Whereas Berger's novel is ironic and often subtle, Penn's humor relies largely on caricature and outlandishness, especially in its depiction of white society. The film's white characters range from unsavory and hypocritical to downright evil. Crabb crosses paths with an irritable pastor and his sexually voracious wife (Faye Dunaway), who preaches the virtues of abstinence as she sensually bathes him; a shyster who gradually loses body parts to the perils of his trade; and finally Custer himself. Custer is pettiness wrapped in buckskin; when he is not otherwise hunting Indians, he's grooming his golden moustache, flashing a toothy smile, and examining himself in any mirror within reach.

The heroes of *Little Big Man* wear war paint. Native Americans had been popular figures in Hollywood film since the beginning of the silent era at the turn of the century, but they generally played one of only two roles—the noble savage or the marauding villain—and usually the latter. By the 1960s, however, directors, screenwriters, and actors had become far more sympathetic (and occasionally even nuanced) in their depictions of native life.[9] This was partly in response to the fashionable counterculture of the era, which celebrated the perceived mysticism, spiritualism, and egalitarianism of American Indian societies, in stark contradistinction to the decadence and corruption of Western capitalism. Across 1960s America, communes sprang up, modeled on what were believed to be native customs and political culture. (Predictably, this fetishization of the Native American lifestyle reproduced plenty of old stereotypes.)

But Native Americans themselves also shaped their image in the public mind by assuming a prominent role in the civil rights movements of the era. In 1968 the American Indian Movement (AIM) was founded in Minneapolis in an attempt to protect Native Americans from police harassment. One year later, Native American leaders staged a dramatic occupation of Alcatraz, the former island prison, placing the national media spotlight on their long list of grievances against the federal government. And that same year, the Indian intellectual Vine Deloria published his bestselling manifesto, *Custer Died for Your Sins*.[10] Albeit often indirectly, the Red Power movement would make its mark on the silver screen.

Little Big Man is a product of both this growing interest in Indian political rights and the growing outrage over the Vietnam War. By 1970 it didn't take a particularly lively imagination to see the parallels between nineteenth-century US attacks on Indian populations and the ongoing campaign in Vietnam, which all too often targeted civilians. Penn made that analogy in one of the film's most haunting scenes, depicting the Seventh Cavalry's surprise attack on a Cheyenne encampment along the Washita River. The image of US soldiers cutting down every brown-skinned man, woman, and child in their path likely would have evoked associations with the My Lai Massacre, which had recently come to public attention. In fact, precisely a century separated the American attacks on the Washita (1868) and My Lai (1968). The casting of an Asian actress, Amy Eccles, in the role of Crabb's Cheyenne wife—who is mercilessly gunned down by Custer's troops as she attempts to flee the village with her infant child—was almost certainly intended to reinforce that parallel. Director Arthur Penn did little to disguise these ideological commitments. "Although I am focusing on history," he said in a press release, "I believe that the film is contemporary because . . . history does repeat itself."[11] Tellingly, the film does not depict the Cheyenne counterattack, which succeeded in eliminating a detachment of Custer's troops just outside the village. Penn's political message required a massacre, after all, and not a battle.

Something snaps in Custer between this Washita scene and the film's final battle sequence at the Little Bighorn. The cool-headed Indian killer becomes nothing short of a raving lunatic. While complaining of poison from the "goo-nads" and his feud with President Grant, Custer delivers a manically theatrical monologue to justify his advance to the Little Bighorn despite the warning signs. When the Seventh Cavalry encounters a mass of mounted Indian warriors, Custer's sanity devolves further. He seeks the low ground of the battlefield, fails to establish a defensive position, and proceeds to upbraid his own troops as they drop like flies around him. He then confuses Crabb with Ulysses S. Grant and reenacts his old grievances against the president at the

Richard Mulligan, as Custer in *Little Big Man*, takes two arrows in the back at the Battle of the Little Bighorn while the film's protagonist, Jack Crabb, played by Dustin Hoffman, looks on.

height of the battle. Just as he is about to execute Crabb—who had joined the Seventh Cavalry in an attempt to sabotage Custer after the Washita—Custer is struck by several arrows in the back. Custer's life ends as farce.

In this depiction of the battle, *Little Big Man* veers almost as far from the historical record as *They Died with Their Boots On*, albeit in the opposite direction. It also veers from Thomas Berger's fictionalized Custer, who, while driven half mad by ambition, nevertheless puts up a spirited defense at the Little Bighorn. And for this he earns the grudging respect of the novel's narrator, Crabb, who lives to tell the tale. For all his many failings, the historical Custer was a highly effective, often brilliant, battlefield commander. True, he fatally misjudged the strength of Crazy Horse's forces around the Little Bighorn. But past experience on the frontier suggested that such concentrations of Indian warriors were extremely rare. His tactical movements leading to Little Bighorn reflected overconfidence, not utter incompetence, and certainly not madness.[12]

Taking stock of Custer's capabilities as a battlefield commander requires taking stock of Native American military abilities as well.[13] Custer didn't defeat himself; he was defeated by a superior foe. His Lakota, Northern Cheyenne, and Arapaho adversaries outmatched and overwhelmed Custer's detachment of the Seventh Cavalry in a tactical masterstroke. But in Penn's retelling their military triumph at the Little Bighorn—or what they would call the Battle of the Greasy Grass—is little more than a fluke. Such a characterization is necessary in order to reinforce the film's implicit critique of the US military establishment and the ongoing debacle in Vietnam. Thus, the Indians of *Little Big Man* are victims, not victors. And Custer is their easy prey.

Conclusion

Few, if any, American figures have been killed so many times on the silver screen.[14] But these two films stand out above the rest of Custer's cinematic last stands. They remain monuments not only to Custer himself but to the historical moment in which they were produced. In 1941 Americans filed into movie theaters and marched off to war amid an upsurge of nationalist sentiment. *They Died with Their Boots On* capitalized on this spirit by presenting the unalloyed image of American military heroism. Conversely, by the time *Little Big Man* reached theaters in 1970, that midcentury moment of national pride and martial zeal had long since passed. To a war-weary nation, this ridiculous version of Custer mirrored the familiar failings of the US military in Vietnam—with all its arrogance, incompetence, and even atrocity. Whereas Custer had once been a vehicle for the celebration of America's military establishment, he now served as the embodiment of its ineptitude.

To be sure, Custer and his actions at the Battle of the Little Bighorn had come under scrutiny well before the Vietnam era. Shortly after his death, the Republican press blamed the deaths of Custer's men on the ignorance and arrogance of their commander.[15] And during the Great Depression, two highly critical appraisals of Custer, Frederic Van De Water's biography, *Glory-Hunter*, and Harry Sinclair Drago's novel, *Montana Road*, gained mass audiences. Then, in 1948 John Ford's *Fort Apache* landed another blow by casting Henry Fonda in the role of the egocentric and incompetent Colonel Owen Thursday, a thinly veiled stand-in for Colonel George Armstrong Custer.[16] The Seventh Cavalry and its commander would never again ride in untarnished glory in a major motion picture. We might therefore consider *They Died with Their Boots On* to be Custer's last stand in the role of Hollywood hero.

But it took a major military fiasco and the general jadedness of the Vietnam era to give that special edge to the Custer critique. Whereas earlier detractors had characterized him as capricious and cruel, Richard Mulligan's portrayal in *Little Big Man* added an element of farce. At some points authoritarian, at others incomprehensible, Mulligan's Custer brought the old frontier legend to new lows. And we may wonder if, in the American popular imagination, he will ever recover.

NOTES

1. For the long-lived debate over Custer's place in history, see Michael Elliott, *Custerology: The Enduring Legacy of the Indian Wars and George Armstrong Custer* (Chicago: University of Chicago Press, 2008); Brian W. Dippie, *Custer's Last Stand: The Anatomy of an American Myth* (Lincoln: University of Nebraska Press, 1976); Robert M. Utley, *Custer and the Great Controversy: The Origin and Development of a Legend* (Pasadena, CA: Westernlore, 1962); and Edward Caudill and Paul Ashdown, *Inventing Custer: The Making of an American Legend* (Lanham, MD: Rowman & Littlefield, 2015). For more general but related work on myth and the American frontier, see Richard Slotkin, *The Fatal Environment: The Myth of the Frontier in the Age of Industrialization, 1800–1890* (Norman: University of Oklahoma Press, 1985); and Henry Nash Smith, *Virgin Land: The American West as Symbol and Myth* (Cambridge, MA: Harvard University Press, 1950).

2. For the evolving myth of Custer in film, Paul Hutton's work is particularly useful. See Paul A. Hutton, "'Correct in Every Detail': General Custer in Hollywood," *Montana: The Magazine of Western History* 41, no. 1 (Winter 1991); and Hutton, "From Little Bighorn to Little Big Man: The Changing Image of a Western Hero in Popular Culture," *Western Historical Quarterly* 7, no. 1 (January 1976). See also Paul Stekler, "Custer and Crazy Horse Ride Again . . . and Again, and Again: Filmmaking and History at Little Bighorn," *Montana: The Magazine of Western History* 42, no. 4 (Fall 1992).

3. There is an extensive literature on the life of George Armstrong Custer, including, notably, Robert M. Utley, *Cavalier in Buckskin: George Armstrong Custer and the Western Military Frontier,* rev. ed. (Norman: University of Oklahoma Press, 2001); and T. J. Stiles, *Custer's Trials: A Life on the Frontier of a New America* (New York: Vintage, 2015).

4. Stiles, *Custer's Trials,* 211–54.

5. Steven Hahn, *A Nation without Borders: The United States and Its World, 1830–1910* (New York: Penguin, 2016), chap. 10; Hahn, "Slave Emancipation, Indian Peoples and the Projects of a New American Nation-State," *Journal of the Civil War Era* 3 (September 2013); Elliot West, *The Last Indian War: The Nez Perce Story* (Oxford: Oxford University Press, 2009), xvii–xxiii. What's sure to be the seminal work on this subject is in progress: Ari Kelman, *For Liberty and Empire: How the Civil War Bled into the Indian Wars* (New York: Basic Books, forthcoming). See also, Andrew E. Masich, *Civil War in the Southwest Borderlands, 1861–1867* (Norman: University of Oklahoma Press, 2017); Megan Kate Nelson, *Path of the Dead Man: How the West Was*

Won—and Lost—during the American Civil War (in progress); and Matthew C. Hulbert, *Ghosts of Guerrilla Memory: How Civil War Bushwhackers Became Gunslingers in the American West* (Athens: University of Georgia Press, 2016).

6. Stiles, *Custer's Trials*, 329–53, 420–28.

7. In popular depictions of his last stand, Custer is generally portrayed in a buckskin suit, saber in hand, with long, flowing golden hair. In truth, Custer's men carried no sabers into their fatal clash, and Custer himself had recently cropped his hair short.

8. Three men died while shooting the film's cavalry scenes. Hutton, "Correct in Every Detail," 40.

9. For the portrayal of Indians in film, see Jacqueylyn Kilpatrick, *Celluloid Indians: Native Americans and Film* (Lincoln: University of Nebraska Press, 1999); and Michelle H. Raheja, *Reservation Reelism: Redfacing, Visual Sovereignty, and Representations of Native Americans in Film* (Lincoln: University of Nebraska Press, 2010). For more on Native American representations more generally, see Philip Deloria, *Playing Indian* (New Haven, CT: Yale University Press, 1999); Shari M. Huhndorf, *Going Native: Indians in the American Cultural Imagination* (Ithaca, NY: Cornell University Press, 2001); and Robert F. Berkhofer, *The White Man's Indian: Images of the American Indian from Columbus to the Present* (New York: Vintage, 1979).

10. On the subject of George Armstrong Custer, Deloria had some choice words: "All tribes, even those thousands of miles from Montana, feel a sense of accomplishment when thinking of Custer. Custer binds together implacable foes because he represented the Ugly American of the last century and he got what was coming to him." Vine Deloria Jr., *Custer Died for Your Sins* (1969; reprint, New York: Macmillan, 1988), 148. For more on the Red Power movement, see Robert Chaat Smith and Robert Allen Warrior, *Like a Hurricane: The Indian Movement from Alcatraz to Wounded Knee* (New York: New Press, 1997); Joane Nagel, *American Indian Ethnic Renewal: Red Power and the Resurgence of Identity and Culture* (New York: Oxford University Press, 1996); and Alvin M. Josephy Jr., Troy R. Johnson, and Joane Nagel, eds., *Red Power: The American Indians' Fight for Freedom,* 2nd ed. (Lincoln: University of Nebraska Press, 1999).

11. Quoted in Hutton, "Correct in Every Detail," 53.

12. For lengthier assessments of Custer's performance at Little Bighorn that nevertheless come to similar conclusions, see Utley, *Cavalier in Buckskin,* 194–212; and Stiles, *Custer's Trials,* 454–55.

13. As Robert Utley wrote, "To ascribe [the Seventh Cavalry's] defeat entirely to military failings is to devalue Indian strength and leadership." Utley, *Cavalier in Buckskin,* 194.

14. If we expanded the category to include television shows and adopted a more capacious definition of *American figure,* the distinction would probably belong to either the Roadrunner or South Park's Kenny.

15. Custer was an outspoken Democrat. For a detailed account of the press response to the Little Bighorn, see James E. Mueller, *Shooting Arrows and Slinging Mud: Custer, the Press, and the Little Bighorn* (Norman: University of Oklahoma Press, 2013).

16. For the relationship between western film and western history, see Jon Tuska, *The American West in Film: Critical Approaches to the Western* (Westport, CT: Greenwood, 1985); and Wayne Michael Sarf, *God Bless You, Buffalo Bill: A Layman's Guide to History and the Western Film* (Rutherford, NJ: Fairleigh Dickinson University Press, 1983).

V

LATE-CENTURY ECONOMICS AND IMMIGRATION

23

Far and Away
The Stereotype of the Irish Immigrant Story

RYAN W. KEATING

The film *Far and Away* (1992) tells the story of Joseph (Tom Cruise), a poor Irishman who dreams of someday working his own land. His father's death sets Joseph on a course that ultimately leads him to America's shores. After a failed attempt to assassinate his landlord, Joseph meets Shannon (Nicole Kidman), and the two flee to America, where the promise of free land in Oklahoma awaits. Arriving in Boston, the two find the dream of land more distant than they originally thought, and they are cast into the city's immigrant community, where they struggle to save for their trip west and, ultimately, fall in love. Forced apart after Shannon is injured, the two reconnect in Oklahoma, where, in a climactic ending, together they claim their land, fulfilling the promise of America that drew so many immigrants to her shores. *Far and Away* provides viewers a detailed account of Irish immigration, from the push-pull factors that motivated men and women to travel more than three thousand miles from the land of their birth to their struggles in their adopted homeland and the quest for land ownership, a quest as deeply seeded in the Irish mind-set as it was in the American psyche and one that continues to drive Americans forward to this day. While the intertwined stories of Joseph and Shannon provide one of the most insightful treatments of nineteenth-century immigration that has come from Hollywood, ultimately the film, as one historian has noted "epitomizes a tendency in some Irish-American film-makers to distort not only historical events in Ireland, but simultaneously produce a myopic representation of the Irish in the construction of the US past."[1] The resulting narrative is a series of stereotypes loosely wrapped in historical fact that only really become useful as

Joseph (Tom Cruise) is confronted by Shannon (Nicole Kidman) before he attempts to assassinate her affluent (landlord) father in *Far and Away*.

teaching tools after they've been contextualized and firmly rooted in historical discussion.

Far and Away opens in Ireland in 1892, during a period of social and political strife when, the viewer is told, "the Tenant Farmers, after generations of oppression and poverty, have begun to rebel against the unfair rents and cruel evictions imposed upon them by their wealthy landlords." Historically, the landlord-tenant relationship was the crux of the social, political, and economic issues that plagued the relations between Irish and English and between Catholics and Protestants on that island. These relations also played a crucial role in Irish immigration, both as reasons for leaving for men and women who migrated to North America and as part of the collective diasporic memory of immigrants and their children.[2] To the film's credit, the opening scenes provide a fairly accurate snapshot of the issues that plagued Irish tenants throughout the century and led to the rise of the Irish Land League and to the Land War, which broke out during the last decade of the nineteenth century.

The broader social, political, and economic plight of the Irish tenant can be traced to the sixteenth century and the establishment of the Ulster Plantation, where, as part of a policy of surrender and regrants, Irish lords exchanged their Irish titles for English ones, surrendering their autonomy and that of the Irish monarchy (as nominal as it was) to England.[3] For the Irish Catholic tenant, the struggle first began with the arrival of Scottish Presbyterian settlers who served as the advance guard of the Protestant Reformation, slowly pushing Catholics off their land and securing English control over a vast majority of the island nation. This, combined with the passage of a series of anti-Catholic laws known as the Penal Codes, resulted in the subsequent decline of Catholic land ownership, so that by 1750 Catholics owned less than 5 percent of all Irish land.[4]

While many tenants struggled with rising rents and received no compensation for improvements they made on their holdings (as seen in the film when Stephen Chase arrives at the funeral to reclaim Joseph's family's land and improvements), laws requiring the subdivision of property equally among all living sons meant that by the time of the Famine, which began in 1847, most Irish were eking out a living on extremely small plots, and many farmers relied almost exclusively on the potato for their primary sustenance.[5] Irish nationalists, meanwhile, saw this suffering as the consequence of English domination over the island, which was solidified politically in 1801 with the Act of Union, which incorporated the Irish parliament into the English parliament and effectively eliminated Irish autonomy. Rebelling against England in 1798, 1803, 1848, and 1867, Irish nationalists struggled to make headway in the face of powerful English military responses and a generally unsympathetic population at home.

As Joseph tills his family's land, a confluence of events places him snugly within the larger history of Irish national agitation in the late nineteenth century. The important subplot revolving around the land question not only lays the groundwork for Joseph's immigration to America but also gives the viewer a taste of Ireland's struggle. Irish nationalism reemerged with force in the 1880s, led by Charles Stewart Parnell and William O'Brien, men who, as one historian noted, "forfeited the accolades of the revolutionary and post revolutionary generations by a principled commitment to constitutional agitation."[6] Over the course of the 1880s nationalists won an increasing number of seats in Parliament, culminating in the Home Rule Bill of 1886. This effort to bring Irish rule back to Ireland was ultimately defeated in large part owing to the "Orange Revolt" of Ulster Protestants, who vowed to remain a part of Great Britain, by military force if necessary.[7] After the failure of Home Rule, Irish politicians focused on the land question.[8] While agrarian violence was commonplace throughout the nineteenth century, it tapered off after the Famine (1847–55) only to be revived after 1887, when Irish politicians urged peasants to resist rising rents and unfair treatment by their landlords.[9] In the face of an economy in crisis, along with rising rents and tenancy at will, protesters sought stable rents and a degree of security. Ultimately, though, there was no cohesive organization, with participation "confined to tenants whose homes were under attack."[10]

This situation is reflected early in the film, and the class tensions exposed in the first scenes carry throughout the entirety of the movie. The issue of class is an important one and defined nearly years of conflict surrounding the Irish national question. The film opens with an impromptu protest by peasants over the arrival of a local landlord. Hardly unique within the history, this scene is important because of the lack of violence. As students of Irish nationalism know, the tragedy of the Irish question, at least during the long nineteenth century, was the inability of nationalists to motivate the masses to rise up against England. Suffering bred contempt: how would an Irish nation justify the potential sacrifice required to create it? Indeed, only after the executions of the leaders of the Easter Rising in 1916 did a militant national consciousness emerge among the masses.[11] Similarly, Joseph only becomes "radicalized" after the death of his father. The mocking response of the townsfolk to his decision to take up arms, however, speaks to broader apathy among peasants and to the tremendous task Irish nationalists faced during this period.

But Joseph's decision to murder Daniel Christie is driven as much by a deeper set of ideologies than simply revenge, for our man has an insatiable desire to better himself, and Daniel Christie stands in the way of that dream. Land. As his father notes in an eloquent deathbed soliloquy, "Without land a man is nothing. Land is a man's very own soul." And this motive drives Joseph to cultivate the poor soil of his father's lease, to seek out the man who confiscated that land, and, finally, to set his sights abroad. "America," murmurs his father, "that's what you're looking for and by god, if you manage it, your old da will be smiling down on you from heaven." In thse opening scenes the viewer finds the motivations behind Irish immigration on both sides of the Atlantic. The nuances of the tenant-landlord relationship, described by the 1880s as "distant, formal, and utilitarian," and the struggles of tenant farmers are clearly on display.[12] These struggles, combined with Joseph's desire for land ownership, is important. As one Irishman noted during the 1890s, "You can't rise in Ireland. . . . In order to succeed you must begin by leaving the country."[13] As Joseph carts seaweed to fertilize his land, he is all the while mocked by his brothers, who see little need to contribute to a household that only puts them further in debt. Their mocking, as well as his father's dying words, lays the groundwork for Joseph's immigration to the United States.

Joseph's attack on Daniel Christie and his run-in with Christie's daughter, Shannon, sets the stage for his "escape" from Ireland. In their interactions, *land* and *oppression* again emerge as the underlying forces behind immigration. For Shannon, as well as for Joseph, land ownership represents a form of independence and opportunity, freedom from the oversight of the landlord and the parents alike. Their goal of reaching Oklahoma also ties them to the broader American narrative, linking immigration to their adopted nation's westward growth. For the immigrants in this film, the lure of America is the lure of the West, propelling the characters forward and, in a sense, making them the embodiment of the American experience during this period.

Westward expansion is one of the defining themes of nineteenth-century America and of the historical memory of this period. In the late 1880s the federal government began to open the Oklahoma territory to settlement, which led to a series of land runs "in which," recalled one Sooner, "the settlers, starting on a signal, raced to find land to their liking and staked claims to it. . . . Each opening of a territory in Oklahoma." These events "brought from all over the country a new influx of people eager to claim land and establish homes and farms."[14] Although the land runs in the 1880s and 1890s were wild affairs (as illustrated at the conclusion of *Far and Away*), they did succeed in establishing a strong farming economy in the state. Furthermore, the opportunity for free land was enticing for reasons beyond simply land ownership. The economists Cecil Bohanon and Philip Coelho argue that "by entering on of the Oklahoma land contests an unskilled laborer [Joseph, in this case] could obtain an asset worth (at least) between $276 and $388 or between 74% and 103% of a year's income," and thus the risk was well worth the potential reward.[15]

However, while Irish immigrants may well have known of the opportunity to lay claim to free land, the realities of the trip west may have been daunting for poor men and women who had only recently arrived in America's eastern cities. In fact, census data provide an interesting tale of Irish migration to the Oklahoma Territory. Woods County, Oklahoma, was part of the Cherokee Strip, which was opened to settlement in 1893; ostensibly, it is a run for this land that is portrayed in *Far and Away*. In 1900, out of a total population of 33,693 living there, there were only 55 men and women of Irish birth and 119 of English birth. Thus, while immigrants like Joseph and Shannon may well have made the journey west, their experiences would have been the great exception rather than the norm. This does not mean that Irish immigrants were not part of the westward push during this period, for they settled throughout the West in cities such as Chicago, Milwaukee, Butte, Dubuque, and San Francisco. The historian David Emmons argues that the Irish, like many Americans, traveled west because "they knew the stories, had heard of the fabled promised lands." But, he claims, they did not go to tame the land; they chose to settle with other Irish, especially in urban areas, where they could monopolize certain industries.[16]

That Shannon knew of the opportunities in Oklahoma is not surprising. Numerous books on immigration and the American experience published at midcentury were available for readers in Ireland, and newspapers reported widely on the subject.[17] In April 1889, for example, The Irish Times noted that "ten thousand settlers crossed the Cherokee country . . . on their way to the Oklahoma preserved lands which are to be thrown open. . . . Great excitement still prevails in the neighbourhood of the Oklahoma district."[18] A year later the London Times reported on the opening of the Cherokee Strip and the "rush of 'boomers' to occupy the land."[19] As Joseph and Shannon escape the foggy dueling grounds of her father's estate, then, they become part of two complementary historical narratives. The first is the story of later-nineteenth-century Irish immigrants, men and women who left Ireland by choice, part of the group of "repressed Irish youth whose economic ambitions were inseparable from the desires for personal liberty."[20] But Joseph and Shannon are searching for more than just the promises of America. In the quest for land in Oklahoma they are responding to Horace Greely's famous exhortation, "Go West, young man!"; thus the story of Irish immigration becomes intertwined with that of manifest destiny and the American dream.[21]

Upon landing in Boston, Shannon loses the collection of silver spoons meant to fund the trip west. This plot twist allows the director to transition the film's narrative from immigration to arrival, as the duo are suddenly forced by circumstance into Boston's bourgeoning immigrant community. The film's success in displaying the struggles of the tenant farmer in Ireland is repeated in the scenes that take place in Boston, where viewers see a largely generalized but rather accurate account of the Irish American urban experience. Upon leaving their ship, Joseph and Shannon are immediately hounded by a young boy asking whether they are Irish. "I can take you to the ward boss," he says, "you can't get nothing without the ward boss." "Need work? Need lodging?" another young man calls out. "There are people [here] who hate the Irish."[22] Here, succinctly, are the political machine and the nativist movement, which served as two opposing pillars of the Irish American experience. The first offered recent immigrants the means of navigating the often hostile and stunningly new urban environments. The second worked diligently to combat the growing influence of Irish Catholics in the United States.[23] Furthermore, Joseph's skill with his fists and his alliance with the local ward boss provide a quick source of income and a sense of stability. Boston newspapers from the 1890s contain innumerable references to boxing, and the sport offered, in the historian Ralph Wilcox's words, a "ladder for socio-economic advancement." "Throughout history," Wilcox notes, "boxing has witnessed its greatest appeal among oppressed minorities, promising them a rapid escape from poverty and discrimination."[24] The 1880s and 1890s were a golden age for Irish boxing, led by John L. Sullivan, who reigned as heavyweight champion of the world from 1882 to 1892. Joseph personifies this part of the Irish immigrant experience and the ways in which immigrants were able to gain a leg up in the United States.

While in Boston, Shannon becomes the "typical" Irish immigrant woman. Her aristocratic background has little bearing on her place in her newly adopted homeland—perhaps a subtle commentary on class consciousness (or the lack thereof) in the United States at the time. Although her upbringing provided her with a certain set of skills (horseback riding and playing the piano, for example), Shannon lacks familiarity with the urban workplace and, thus, like thousands of other immigrant women, finds employment where she can. The struggles and harassment that Shannon faces during this part of the film provides important insight into the conditions of urban laborers during this period, in particular the lack of security for the unskilled. Irish immigrant women, the historian Hasia R. Diner contends, often "worked for paltry wages in mills, factories, and in thousands of private homes of the United States. They labored long hours and endured all of the dangers and discomforts associated with the lowest rank of the work force."[25] Shannon's experiences illustrate that plight. Her contempt for the hostility and harassment she faces reflects her own underlying disdain for the lower class that we see early in the film, but her background doesn't matter on the mean streets of Boston.

Shannon's wounding leaves the couple separated. While Joseph works his way west on the railroad (yet another nod to the Irish immigrant experience), Shannon reluctantly goes back to her family, who "escaped" from Ireland after tenants burned their estate. But the two reunite in splendid fashion during the Oklahoma Land Rush, laying claim to land and fulfilling their dreams. So the film ends well, perfectly summarizing the immigrant experience, from Ireland to the urban slums of the East Coast and then west, where land ownership fulfills both Irish and American ambitions. The struggles that Joseph and Shannon overcome mirror the larger immigrant experience in America, providing significantly more context than most films with Irish or Irish American characters. Over the course of two and a half hours *Far and Away* tells a complete story—from start to finish—of the experiences of the Irish immigrant at home and abroad, and does so in a way that gives the viewer significant, if broad, insight into both the determinants driving late-nineteenth-century immigration and the struggles of Irish men and women in America in the Gilded Age.

Despite these successes, the film struggles to tell the serious side of the Irish immigrant experience. The storyline ultimately becomes a parody of Ireland and the Irish that reinforces negative ethnic stereotypes and continues the long tradition of lampooning this immigrant group. The rise of nativism in the United States during the 1850s was a direct result of the massive influx of nearly three million immigrants between 1845 and 1854.[26] The arrival of poverty-stricken Irish Catholics fleeing the potato famine was cause for serious concern and led to an outpouring of animosity that continued well into the twentieth century. Nativist concern over the religion, poverty, fondness for alcohol, and unwavering loyalty to the Democratic political machines of this immigrant group caused considerable tension throughout this period. Important to this chapter, though, is the tendency to mock the Irish for their peculiarities. Such attitudes confronted the Irish in both Ireland and the United States and downplayed, I think, the very real struggles these men and women faced at home and abroad. *Far and Away*, in many regards, panders to these ethnic stereotypes, ultimately undermining the historical importance of the film's events by undercutting many scenes with mockery that echoes the anti-Irish attitudes of years past.

As England extended its control over Ireland, English Protestants increasingly portrayed the Irish in negative ways that highlighted attitudes of racial superiority and justified the paternalistic and outwardly colonialist attitudes espoused by the Protestant ascendancy. During this time, "British reporting on Ireland was crucially informed by the enduring stereotypes that constituted Irish identity. 'Paddy,' the objectified Irishman, was discursively constructed in leading articles, editorial cartoons, and letters to the editor using a number of different elements. The most important components in this manufacture were stereotypes of race, religion, and class."[27] For the English, such attitudes helped to explain away Ireland's many crises by "projecting the blame for Irish suffering onto the Irish themselves." Among these stereotypes were "Irish ig-norance, slavish devotion to priests and demagogues, indifference to squalor, and laziness."[28] Furthermore, "the ease of raising potatoes and their high yield gratified the Irish 'love of idleness and independence,' giving the peasant two-thirds of the year to do 'nothing but sleep, drink, or beg.'"[29]

Such stereotypes played well in the United States, where many looked with disdain upon the arriving Irish Catholic immigrants. The popular portrayal of "Paddy" "bore the stigma of the violent, drunken, rabble-rouser whose apelike physiognomy was witness to his degraded social and cultural development."[30] The "Paddy" was "a figure whose pathetic, comic, or malevolent qualities made him the supposed antithesis of the middle-class Englishmen or North Ameri-can."[31]

Editors throughout the United States quickly recognized the usefulness of these stereotypes in creating humorous quips for their readers. "An Irish-man," recounted the editors of the *Boston Evening Transcript*, "thus describes a wheelbarrow: 'It is a little carriage with one wheel, and the *horse* is a *man*.'"[32] New York readers learned that "A Paddy, writing from the West, says 'pork is so plenty that every third man you meet is a hog.'"[33] In North Carolina, some years later, "an Irishman was once brought before the magistrate charged with marrying six wives. The magistrate asked him how he could be so hard hearted a villian [sic]. 'Please, your worship,' said Paddy, 'I was trying to get a good one.'"[34] This type of commentary appeared hand in hand with darker portray-als of Irish immigrants produced by nativist newspapermen such as Thomas Nast, illustrating both the potential danger of these poor immigrants and their "ignorance," strange ways, and customs.

Unfortunately, the historical value of *Far and Away* is undermined by the fact that Ron Howard's epic is rife with ethnic stereotypes that diminish Ire-land's struggles and portray her people in rather negative ways. The opening scene panders to long-held portrayals of Irish idleness and drunkenness as viewers meet Joseph's father and his friend Danty in the local pub. Joseph Senior's liquor-laced assault on the local landlord is matched only by those of his elder sons Colm and Paddy, who emerge on the scene in a drunken stupor to berate their younger brother for "breaking your back on land that isn't your own." Their fighting, interrupted only by the arrival of their injured father, reinforces long-held negative perceptions of Irish men—perceptions that the English often used in the nineteenth century to justify the abuses they leveled at the subjugated Catholic masses. Indeed, the Irish nationalist John Mitchel's claim in the 1850s that "God sent the blight but the English created the Famine" reflected the popularly held belief that England and English landlords, motivated in part by negative perceptions of the Irish, used the tragedy of the famine to further strengthen their control over Ireland.[35] One English observer noted that the Irish "with a few exceptions are, as usual, idle, reckless, lazy, and improvident."[36] While Joseph appears to be the opposite, it is prudent to note that his attitudes are the *exception* among the attitudes of the Irish characters in the film, meaning that Howard's work actually reinforces prejudiced views of the very group whose story he is trying to commemorate.

Joseph's decision to take up arms against Daniel Christie is a serious one, reflecting the desperation that many poor Irish faced during the whole of the eighteenth and nineteenth centuries as they lost control over their land and, thus, political and economic power. The land question was of paramount importance to the Irish during this period, and Joseph's actions are tied to the long Irish tradition of using secret societies, agrarian agitation, and violence to curb the power of the landlord.[37] Handing over his musket, Danty passes the Irish revolutionary code to Joseph, urging him to give Christie "a proper taste of death" as the anonymous "Captain Moonlight." Yet the weapon, rusted with age and from lack of use, is a metaphor for Irish nationalism, which becomes clearer as his friends and neighbors openly mock Joseph and comes to fruition in his bungled attempt to enact revenge. Most Irish were not radicalized in the 1890s, and though the Gaelic Revival and offshoot organizations such as the Gaelic Athletic Association played important roles in reviving the national consciousness, historical evidence seems to suggest that participation in radical republicanism was rather limited. Yet the underlying message here is that Joseph's "cause" is actually a humorous misstep rather than a serious endeavor. In my opinion, this message undermines the Irish nationalist question broadly by suggesting that the motives driving men and women to resist English rule lacked seriousness or justification.

The inclusion of Nicole Kidman's character, apart from providing a the generic subplot of romance seen in nearly every major Hollywood film, is interesting, especially given the role that landed Anglo-Irish Protestant women played in the growth of Irish nationalism during this period. Women such as Maud Gonne and Constance Markievicz, upper-class members of the Protestant landed elite, made significant contributions to the nationalist cause through their involvement both in the Gaelic League, which fostered a cultural revival of Irish identity, and in more radical political groups such as the Daughters of Ireland and, later, Sinn Fein.[38] Howard could have modeled Shannon after Gonne and Markievicz, who, though born into privilege, recognized the plight of the Irish poor and threw themselves headfirst into the nationalist movements emerging at century's end.[39] Instead, the director chose to model his female lead after period stereotypes. She is portrayed as a silly and out-of-touch girl desperately seeking to rebel from her overbearing and "traditional" parents, and she does so by, among other things, refusing to ride her horse sidesaddle, playing a jazz ditty during family dinner, and ultimately stealing the family's silver spoons to fund her trip to America.

Certainly, Daniel Christie's aloofness suggests the conflict between English absentee landlords and their tenants. His reflection to Joseph on the morning of the duel—"I knew nothing of your family or their eviction. I'm sorry for their pain"—is a symbolic nod to the consequences of this relationship and to "the structure of social and political power in nineteenth-century Ireland," which revolved around the fortunes of the landed class. In other words, decisions that led to the eviction of Joseph's family were, for the landowner, a consequence of the economic realities, in which "income was stressed above investment."[40] Christie's later statement, as his home burns, that "this is no longer the Ireland of my birth," sums up this detachment, for that Ireland only existed in his disconnected reality. There exists, herein, an opportunity for Shannon's character to reflect some of the more radical changes taking place in Ireland during this period. Yet, although her storyline underscores a rebellious nature, ultimately her defiance is rather petty and influenced by the same naïve world-view as her father's. Her character too becomes a sad commentary on the ways modern Americans tend to view the English aristocracy of the late nineteenth century.

The Irish immigrant experience is, of course, incredibly complex and thus poses inherent difficulties for any filmmaker. At the most basic level, *Far and Away* accomplishes more than most films on this subject. The fact is that the land rush portrayed in the film, while a real historical event, could also be a metaphor for the Irish American experience more broadly; the hopes and dreams of America were, in reality, difficult to achieve. The struggles of Joseph and Shannon do, in fact, ultimately manifest in the achievement of their initial goal, land, which represents, of course, something much deeper: a sense of self-worth, individualism, and freedom. In one respect, their story is that of many Irish immigrants who arrived, struggled, and over generations pulled themselves up from the urban ghettos to become solidly middle-class Americans.

Viewers should be wary, though, of the ways the characters, their actions, their behaviors, and the situations they find themselves in minimize the immigrant experience by reinforcing negative ethnic stereotypes that have surrounded Irish men and women for more than two hundred years.

NOTES

1. Lance Pettitt, *Screening Ireland: Film and Television Representation* (Manchester, UK: Manchester University Press, 2000), 130.

2. See, e.g., Christine Kinealy, *This Great Calamity: The Irish Famine, 1845–52* (Dublin: Gill & Macmillan, 1994); Mary Daly, *The Famine in Ireland* (Dublin: Dundalgan, 1986); Nancy Curtin, *The United Irishmen: Popular Politics in Ulster and Dublin, 1791–1798* (New York: Oxford University Press, 1998); and James S. Donnelly, *The Great Irish Potato Famine* (Gloucestershire, UK: Sutton, 2001).

3. See, e.g., Brendan Kane, *The Politics of Culture and Honor in Britain and Ireland, 1541–1641* (Cambridge: Cambridge University Press, 2009); and Jane Ohlmeyer, *Making Ireland English: The Irish Aristocracy in the Seventeenth Century* (New Haven, CT: Yale University Press, 2012).

4. Kerby Miller, *Emigrants and Exiles: Ireland and the Irish Exodus to North America* (New York: Oxford University Press, 1985), 21–22.

5. Cormac O'Grada, *Black '47 and Beyond: The Great Irish Famine in History, Economy, and Memory* (Princeton, NJ: Princeton University Press, 1999), 17. On the importance of the potato, see O'Grada, *Black '47 and Beyond*; Kinealy, *This Great Calamity*; Daly, *Famine in Ireland*; and Donnelly, *Great Irish Potato Famine*.

6. Joseph O'Brien, *William O'Brien and the Course of Irish Politics, 1881–1918* (Berkeley: University of California Press, 1976).

7. O'Brien, *William O'Brien*, 33. On Ulster unionism, see Paul Bew, *Churchill and Ireland* (New York: Oxford University Press, 2016); Chris Dooley, *Redmond—A Life Undone: The Definitive Biography of John Redmond, the Forgotten Hero of Irish Politics* (Dublin: Gill & Macmillan, 2015); and Patrick Mitchell, *Evangelicalism and National Identity in Ulster, 1921–1998* (New York: Oxford University Press, 2003).

8. O'Brien, *William O'Brien*, 34.

9. R. F. Foster, *Modern Ireland: 1600–1972* (London: Penguin, 1988), 406–10.

10. O'Brien, *William O'Brien*, 36–37.

11. Peter Somerville Large, *Irish Voices: An Informal History, 1916–1966* (London: Pimlico, 2000).

12. Miller, *Emigrants and Exiles*, 386–89.

13. L. Paul-Dubois, quoted in Miller, *Emigrants and Exiles*, 414.

14. Louis A. Mossler, "Opening of the Cherokee Outlet," *Indiana Magazine of History* 50, no. 2 (June 1954): 167.

15. Cecil E. Bohanon and Philip P. Coelho, "The Costs of Free Land: The Oklahoma Land Rushes," *Journal of Real Estate Finance and Economics* 16, no. 2 (1998): 207.

16. Database of the 1900 census for Woods County, Oklahoma, constructed specifically for this project; David M. Emmons, *Beyond the Pale: The Irish in the West, 1845–1910* (Norman:

University of Oklahoma Press, 2010), 226–28. On Irish settlement patterns in the nineteenth and early twentieth centuries, see Ryan W. Keating, *Shades of Green: Irish Regiments, American Soldiers, and Local Communities in the Civil War Era* (New York: Fordham University Press, 2017); David M. Emmons, *The Butte Irish: Class and Ethnicity in an American Mining Town, 1875–1925* (Urbana: University of Illinois Press, 1990); Russell Johnson, *Warriors into Workers: The Civil War and the Formation of the Urban-Industrial Society in a Northern City* (New York: Fordham University Press, 2003); Emmons, *Beyond the Pale*; and Miller, *Emigrants and Exiles*.

17. Emmons, *Beyond the Pale*, 229.

18. "The Oklahoma Settlement," *Irish Times*, 20 April 1889.

19. "The United States," *London Times*, 17 March 1890.

20. Miller, *Emigrants and Exiles*, 415.

21. Horace Greely to R. L. Sanderson, 15 November 1871, Gilder Lehrman Collection, New York.

22. *Far and Away*, dir. Ron Howard (Universal City, CA: Universal Pictures, 1992), digital copy. All quotations below are from this version.

23. See, e.g., John Higham, *Strangers in the Land: Patterns of American Nativism, 1860–1925* (New Brunswick, NJ: Rutgers University Press, 2002); and Noel Ignatiev, *How the Irish Became White* (New York: Routledge, 1995).

24. Ralph Wilcox, "Irish American in Sports: The Nineteenth Century," in *Making the Irish American: History and Heritage of the Irish in the United States*, ed. J. J. Lee and Marion R. Casey (New York: New York University Press, 2006).

25. Hasia R. Diner, *Erin's Daughters in America: Irish Immigrant Women in the Nineteenth Century* (Baltimore: Johns Hopkins University Press, 1983), 72.

26. Tyler Anbinder, *Nativism and Slavery: The Northern Know Nothings and the Politics of the 1850s* (New York: Oxford University Press, 1992), 3.

27. Michael de Nie, *The Eternal Paddy: Irish Identity and the British Press, 1798–1882* (Madison: University of Wisconsin Press, 2004), 4–5.

28. de Nie, *Eternal Paddy*, 91.

29. de Nie, *Eternal Paddy*, 129.

30. Diner, *Erin's Daughters*, 72.

31. Miller, *Emigrants and Exiles*, 107.

32. "Sparks and Spangles," *Boston Evening Transcript*, 16 January 1843.

33. "True in Some Places, Too," *Jamestown (NY) Journal*, 2 February 1855.

34. *New Bern (NC) Daily Journal*, 11 November 1890.

35. Brian Jenkins, *Irish Nationalism and the British State from Repeal to Revolutionary Nationalism* (Montreal: McGill-Queens Press, 2014), 221; Tim Pat Coogan, *The Famine Plot: England's Role in Ireland's Greatest Tragedy* (New York: Macmillan, 2002); Christine Kinealy, *The Great Irish Potato Famine: Impact, Ideology, and Rebellion* (New York: Palgrave Macmillan, 2002), 153.

36. Kinealy, *This Great Calamity*.

37. Sean J. Connely, *Religion, Law, and Power: The Making of Protestant Ireland, 1660–1760* (Oxford: Clarendon, 1992); Foster, *Modern Ireland*, 292–94.

38. Robert Key, *The Green Flag: A History of Irish Nationalism* (London: Penguin, 1972), 425, 456–58.

39. See Anne Marreco, *The Rebel Countess: The Life and Times of Constance Markievicz* (London: Weidenfeld & Nicolson, 1967); and Sinead McCoole, *No Ordinary Women: Irish Female Activists in the Revolutionary Years, 1900–1923* (Madison: University of Wisconsin Press, 2003).

40. Foster, *Modern Ireland,* 374–75.

24

Silver Screen, *Bright Leaf*
Hollywood's Cigarette Habit

DREW A. SWANSON

In an 1890s auction-day scene, as the *Bright Leaf* protagonist Brant Royle bids up the sales price of tobacco to previously unseen heights to intimidate his business rivals, one prospective buyer turns to another and mutters, "We're being ruined by cigarettes."[1] This lament might very well serve as the movie's tagline, for the scenes that surround this auction vignette highlight the all-consuming and often destructive power of America's historic cigarette habit.

The 1950 film *Bright Leaf,* directed by Michael Curtiz (best known for *Casablanca* [1942]), spans two decades beginning in 1890 and follows a well-trod narrative path; it is a tale of ambition, revenge, and, ultimately, the destructive effects of greed. Royle, played by Gary Cooper, yearns to make a name for himself in the sleepy turn-of-the-century market town of Kingsmont, North Carolina, and along the way to avenge his father's poor treatment at the hands of the local tobacco manufacturers who once put the family out of business. With the assistance of the inventor John Barton's novel cigarette-rolling machinery, Royle amasses wealth by mass-producing newly fashionable cigarettes. His success displaces the old businessmen, epitomized by the august Major Singleton (Donald Crisp), who had once foreclosed on the Royle family farm. Indeed, Royle eventually drives Singleton to suicide, marries his daughter Margaret (Patricia Neal), and, completing his triumph, moves into Singleton's big white house on a hill overlooking Kingsmont. The poor boy has become the tycoon.

This noir rags-to-riches story quickly sours for Royle, however. His business tactics prove even more merciless than those of the manufacturers he displaces: he drives his competitors under, not content until they all meet his

Poster for *Bright Leaf,* showing Lauren Bacall as Sonia Kovac, Gary Cooper as
Brant Royle, and Patricia Neal as Margaret Royle (*far right*)

terms or go bankrupt; he arbitrarily fires employees; and he pursues a regional
and then national monopoly of cigarettes. One by one he alienates the people
who helped him rise to the pinnacle of the business, including Barton, sus-
pecting each of being as grasping as himself. Royle also makes a shambles of
his marriage and gets entangled in a romantic interest in another character,
Sonia (Lauren Bacall), a prostitute turned madam who is also his business
partner, having put up part of the initial investment in cigarette-manufacturing
machines.

Ultimately Royle's greed and paranoia prove his undoing. His wife, Margaret, turns out to be at least as calculating as he is: she secretly undercuts
his business and then leaves him as part of a long-brewing plot to avenge her
father's death. Sonia refuses Royle's desperate, apologetic advances, completely
dissolving the love triangle. And federal antitrust actions weaken his tobacco
company, proving that even Brant's business success was built on sand. The
denouement comes when a candle knocked over during Royle and Margaret's
final marital fight kindles a conflagration that burns the grand white house to

the ground. A desperate, wild-eyed Brant bars the fire brigade from combatting the flames, screaming, "I want to see it burn!" The films ends with Royle riding out of town, destitute, despondent, and crushed by his unbridled ambition.

The film was based on a book by the same name, written by the North Caro-linian Foster Fitz-Simmons and published just two years earlier. Fitz-Simmons's novel attempted to blend a Faulknerian sense of southern place with the muck-raking style of Upton Sinclair or Jacob Riis, drawing on southern gothic forms to reveal the dirt of tobacco dealings. As literature, it falls a little short of both marks, coming closer to melodrama than to tragedy or exposé. Both the book and the film fictionalize one of the New South's most famous industrial sto-ries. Royle stands in for James Buchanan Duke, progenitor of the American Tobacco Company (ATC), which dominated the nation's tobacco manufac-turing for two decades spanning the turn of the twentieth century, and the fictional Kingsmont represents Durham, North Carolina, the epicenter of early cigarette production. Americans, and southerners in particular, had marveled at the way Duke, the ATC, and Durham all seemed to go from unknowns to global icons overnight, a story made for Hollywood if ever there was one.

Although they both revolve around the story of Duke's life, there are more than minor differences between the novel and the film. The book is a *longue durée* story spanning three generations of Kingsmont life—roughly from the 1880s to the 1920s—along the way providing more detail about the social fabric of life in tobacco towns. Southern history and the legacy of the Civil War thus cast a longer shadow in Fitz-Simmons's story than on the big screen; stereo-types abound. It is no accident that the cigarette-rolling machine's inventor—the Connecticut Yankee John Barton—first appears in the book toting a carpet-bag. And the novel also draws on old southern tropes about race: for example, the firebrand whom Royle recruits to burn Major Singleton's warehouse is an African American named Maryland, tapping longstanding white fears of the black arsonist. As much as the novel draws on old stereotypes, it also connected to optimism about the New South's economic future more thoroughly than did the film. Fitz-Simmons ended his work with hope, suggesting that Royle had seen the error of his ways, and that he, and by extension the tobacco industry, might lead a kinder, gentler future life. Fitz-Simmons in no way rejected the industrialization of southern life, just its excesses.

The titular subject of both works, tobacco, is even more prominent a char-acter in Fitz-Simmons's book than in the film, backgrounding and at times overshadowing the human figures, seeming to compel people's actions through a powerful botanical determinism. For example, the protagonist of the third generation, James Barton (son of John Barton and Margaret Singleton, who rejects Royle's marriage schemes in the novel), becomes obsessed with plant breeding, attends North Carolina State University, and conducts experiments with improved tobacco strains and cultivation techniques that he hopes will improve the condition of the state's farmers. He marries Royle's daughter, symbolically fusing the interests of industry and state research to the benefit of the people of North Carolina.[2] At the end of the novel, Fitz-Simmons implies that Royle and Sonia perhaps have a chance to make their long-frustrated relationship work and that, by implication, so might tobacco and society in the Old North State.

As history, the film version of *Bright Leaf* leaves something to be desired. In relating the story of James Duke and the ascendancy of the ATC, it muddles some important details, the most crucial of which is that Duke's empire was never as consolidated as the film portrays, nor did it ever really crumble. The ATC did march to the pinnacle of a cigarette and chewing-tobacco empire, and federal antitrust action did dissolve the company as a monopoly in 1911, but the daughter businesses that resulted remained the masters of the tobacco universe, while Duke lived out his life in opulent splendor. Duke continued to be an important tobacco manufacturer, and he diversified into a range of other businesses that would prove important elements of the state's economy. In the early twentieth century Duke companies manufactured textiles, furnished municipal water, and generated electricity. Even the state's most prestigious institution of higher education was a part of this legacy: in 1924 Duke endowed a substantial portion of a $40 million trust on Trinity College, which promptly changed its name to Duke University to acknowledge its benefactor.[3]

Where the details are not wrong, the movie often lacks nuance. The examples are numerous. Like many technological-origin stories, *Bright Leaf* attributes the mechanization of cigarette making to one brilliant inventor, but the cigarette-rolling machine of James Bonsack (represented by Barton in the film) hardly appeared out of the blue. Manufacturers had long tinkered with various labor-saving devices, and Richmond's Allen & Ginter Company had even experimented with Bonsack's machine during the 1880s, before Duke's mechanics ironed out its worst flaws. Besides, dominating the cigarette market did not mean much in the late nineteenth century, as it accounted for such a small fraction of American tobacco production, and so Duke's ATC turned at least as much attention to plug tobacco as to cigarettes.[4] Kingsmont's parochial industrialists, epitomized by Major Singleton, hardly reflected the real size and complexity of the existing manufacturing industry that Duke conquered. Tobacco barons such as William Sutherlin of Danville, Virginia, had long wielded regional political and economic power, tying their tobacco businesses to railroad, bank, and fertilizer interests (and even more influential manufacturers held sway in Richmond and New York).[5] The farmers themselves (in North Carolina as well as in other states), largely pawns in the film, in reality worked hard to shape the industry, forming cooperatives and employing political activism in their campaigns to better rural conditions and resist the manufacturers' control.[6] Environmental limits posed by eroding and exhausting soils, insect pests, and plant diseases proved as challenging for growers as the greed of manufacturers (although the environmental details of North Carolina's Piedmont would have been hard to convey had Curtiz been so inclined, as *Bright Leaf* appears to have been filmed in California).[7] And African Americans, crucial agents in tobacco's story as both farm and factory workers, are but shadowy figures on the screen.[8]

But *Bright Leaf* is a Hollywood production, after all, restricted by the limits of two hours and the whims of moviegoing audiences, so perhaps it is too much to expect historical nuance. For all the inaccuracies, Curtiz's melodrama in fact captures essential elements of the South's tobacco and cigarette history. For example, in one memorable scene Major Singleton walks in on his elderly cousin Tabby (Elizabeth Patterson) puffing away on a clandestine cigarette, almost giddy with the pleasure of it. When Singleton accuses her of impropriety and treason, enjoying Royle's products with no thought of feminine modesty or family loyalty, she defends the habit: how could something so satisfying be wrong?

Tabby's defense captures the meteoric rise of cigarettes in the years spanning 1900 as well as a general American comfort with public smoking at the time of filming; figures throughout the movie light up, punctuating dramatic moments or contemplative scenes with wisps and curls of smoke. These stage smokers stood in for a real, ongoing national addiction to Camels and Lucky Strikes. Cigarettes, which only became the dominant consumer form of tobacco after World War I, had fostered greater tobacco usage than ever before. Their addictive power owed something to advertising—tobacco companies were nothing if not creative marketers, selling their products with posters, catchy doggerel, and by giving away baseball cards and pictures of pretty women—but the weed inside the paper wrapper played a role as well. Tabby does something in her smoking scene that tobacco consumers had rarely done before the advent of mass-produced American cigarettes: she inhales, fully and easily.

For centuries, the smoke produced by burning dried tobacco had been a hard pill to swallow, so to speak. Cigar and pipe smoke was basic in chemical content, with a high pH, making it difficult for smokers to draw into their lungs. Smokers who tried to inhale deeply often ended up coughing and sputtering, their body's reaction to the alkaline smoke. However, new curing methods used to produce bright leaf, a form of tobacco pioneered in the North Carolina and Virginia Piedmont in the mid-nineteenth century that became a primary ingredient in cigarettes, unintentionally (but momentously) resulted in tobacco with a new quality. Burning bright-leaf cigarettes produced acidic smoke. Consumers could fully inhale this smoke, which seemed to taste mild and smooth, into their lungs, where the tremendous surface area of the body's branching and absorptive alveoli pulled nicotine from the wisps and tendrils, to be quickly absorbed into the bloodstream. Cigarette smoke entered the body gently and then hammered the sensory system with a powerful and eventually addictive buzz. It would be nearly a century after the first cigarette rolled off Bonsack's machines before tobacco companies fully understood the biochemistry at work, but from the first they were happy to take advantage of consumers who seemed unable to resist the pleasures of cigarettes.[9]

Dependency can be psychological and cultural as well as biological, of course, and addiction in the film is not limited to cigarettes; almost everyone is hooked on something. Brant Royle is lured by power, money, social status, and revenge, and the tobacco business promises to serve as his path to these goals. Sonia cannot stay away from Brant even though she knows he represents only heartache. Margaret is addicted to stirring up trouble, attempting to escape the constricting bonds of gender and social norms in the small-town South. Major Singleton craves the status his industrial position confers and is bound to older ideas of behavior and honor. Enveloping these personal and individual desires are societal habits that ring true for post–Civil War North Carolina. Kingsmont, like the real towns of Durham, Winston-Salem, Wilson, and Oxford, hinges its rise on tobacco manufacturing, becoming as dependent on the tobacco companies and warehouses as their customers did on the cigarettes that rolled off the lines. And farmers found their wire in the blood in the promise of the next season, which must surely prove better than the present. *Bright Leaf,* for all its cheesy melodrama, conveys the importance of habit in history; there is a good deal of realism in its capture of the multiple forms of addictive power wielded by the burgeoning cigarette industry.

Bright Leaf reveals some fundamental truths of the era of its filming as well. The movie's comfortable embrace of cigarettes, even as it plays on the industry's early turmoil, reflects broader mid-twentieth-century American habits. If any year could be considered the apex of the cigarette in the United States, 1950 surely is a contender. World War II had accelerated already brisk tobacco consumption; packs of cigarettes had been a part of soldiers' kits, and Americans had handed them out as an inexpensive goodwill gesture in France, Italy, and Germany, where they had secured beachheads in new markets for North Carolina's manufacturers. And smoking on the home front had kept pace, with cigarette consumption growing by almost 50 percent during the war. Postwar prosperity kept sales brisk, and as in *Bright Leaf,* Hollywood regularly featured both heroes and villains lighting up.[10]

This consumer love was as yet largely untainted by health worries. The biologist Rachel Carson's popular-science bestseller, *Silent Spring,* with its indictment of the carcinogenic nature of a chemical culture, was still more than a decade away. The compounds used on tobacco crops that made their way into consumers' bodies, like maleic hydrazide-30, and pesticides like parathion, which occasionally proved deadly to tobacco farmers, received little popular press.[11] And even the tobacco companies at the time had no knowledge of the radioactive polonium-210 accumulating in smokers' lungs as a consequence of North Carolina farmers' years of spreading radon- and lead-bearing phosphates on their fields.[12] A few medical studies arguing that there were links between smoking and illness appeared in the 1940s and 1950s, but the game-changing 1964 Surgeon General's report declaring that cigarettes did indeed cause a range of cancers was not yet on the horizon.[13] Indeed, *Bright Leaf* audiences likely would have agreed with a Liggett & Myers Company slogan from just a few years previous touting the cigarettes streaming from Durham's factories as the producers of "employment for thousands, more pleasure for millions."[14]

Today the Hollywood version of *Bright Leaf* is perhaps as well known as the subject of the documentary filmmaker Ross McElwee's *Bright Leaves* (2003) as it is on its own merits. McElwee's introspective movie explores his own family's connection to the older film, which he believes to be a retelling of his tobacco-manufacturing ancestor John Harvey McElwee's battle with the industry titan James Duke. Eventually John Harvey McElwee succumbed to Duke's efficient (and ruthless) business practices, much as Major Singleton lost out to Brant

Royle. The documentary also grapples with Ross McElwee's personal struggles with his family's tobacco-peddling legacy. He is deeply conflicted, at once both proud of his association with the state's most famous industry and shamed by its legacy of disease and death.

McElwee's reflection on *Bright Leaf* revealed a degree of continuity in the regional conception of the industry. For all the changes that took place following the Surgeon General's 1964 report (McElwee, for example, visits a Duke University Hospital smoking-cessation clinic, where tobacco money now works to combat cigarette addiction), he portrays a state still hooked on the memory of tobacco culture as much as its residents remained addicted to nicotine. In various interviews, McElwee chats about the weed and Curtiz's film with relatives, friends, blue-collar workers, ill smokers, and farmers, all of whom seem more than a little nostalgic for North Carolina's superficially untroubled tobacco past. He ultimately declares the state's long history with the plant to be "like a fever dream," with its people enchanted by tobacco's "mysterious, dangerous powers of seduction."[15] On this Fitz-Simmons, Curtiz, and McElwee all agree.

What McElwee understood is that *Bright Leaf*, like North Carolina's real experience with tobacco, speaks to broader southern conceptions of the region's past. The Hollywood movie is a two-pronged tragedy: Royle's fall, dragging loved ones and a company down with him, is the obvious collapse, but a broader, tragic southern history of place threads through all as well. North Carolina's history is rooted in the legacies of soil, labor, and crop—a *terroir* of both environment and imagination, if you will—which fused concrete physical spaces with a terrain of the mind. *Bright Leaf*'s claim to represent something fundamental about southern place was rooted as much in its identification with tobacco as an emblematic staple for North Carolina as in its plot, in much the same way that Robert Penn Warren's *Night Rider* and Ellen Glasgow's *The Deliverance* bound the plant to Kentucky's and Virginia's respective historical heritages.[16]

Ultimately *Bright Leaf* is tough to come to terms with as a historical film because it is so hard to see its representations of people and tobacco through the haze of three eras of smoking. The film is set in the time of the nascent cigarette industry, when men like Duke began supplanting older forms of tobacco use with a new product, casting aside existing mores in favor of new consumer habits. But the movie also deals in mid-twentieth-century conceptions of smoking, imprinted as it is with the ideas of the cigarette's heyday, when Lauren Bacall lighting up was more likely to provoke thoughts of sex than it was thoughts of sarcoma in audience members. And watching today, we can hardly follow the drama without being distracted by our current epidemiological or economic understandings. We cannot avoid responding to a starlet's carelessly held cigarette with thoughts of millions of cases of lung cancer, a bent if not broken health-care system, Hispanic migrant workers toiling in green fields of tobacco, and booming Chinese markets in new smokers.

In this way perhaps *Bright Leaf* is the ultimate midcentury southern romantic tragedy. What it lacks in character development or believable relationships it more than compensates for with its focus on cigarettes. That nostalgia and romance can cling to addiction and a dependency on a commodity crop is a classic southern tale, after all, one worthy of serious attention and more than a little sorrow.

NOTES

1. *Bright Leaf*, dir. Michael Curtiz (Hollywood: Warner Brothers, 1950). The following descriptive paragraphs are based on the film.

2. Foster Fitz-Simmons, *Bright Leaf* (New York: Rinehart, 1948).

3. For this period of North Carolina's tobacco-manufacturing industry and Duke, good starting places include Allan M. Brandt, *Cigarette Century: The Rise, Fall, and Deadly Persistence of the Product That Defined America* (New York: Basic Books, 2007), chap. 1; Robert F. Durden, *Bold Entrepreneur: A Life of James B. Duke* (Durham, NC: Carolina Academic Press, 2003); and Nannie May Tilley, *The Bright Tobacco Industry, 1860–1929* (Chapel Hill: University of North Carolina Press, 1948). For an example of one company that resisted full integration into the American Tobacco Company and emerged from its dissolution as powerful as ever, see Michele Gillespie, *Katherine and R. J. Reynolds: Partners of Fortune in the Making of the New South* (Athens: University of Georgia Press, 2012), 104–10 and chap. 5; and Nannie M. Tilley, *The R. J. Reynolds Tobacco Company* (Chapel Hill: University of North Carolina Press, 1985), pt. 2.

4. Barbara Hahn, *Making Tobacco Bright: Creating an American Commodity, 1617–1937* (Baltimore: Johns Hopkins University Press, 2011), 92–96; Brandt, *Cigarette Century*, 26–31.

5. Hahn, *Making Tobacco Bright*, 70–75; Scott Reynolds Nelson, *Iron Confederacies: Southern Railways, Klan Violence, and Reconstruction* (Chapel Hill: University of North Carolina Press, 1999), 150–51, 168–69.

6. Evan Bennett, *When Tobacco Was King: Families, Farm Labor, and Federal Policy in the Piedmont* (Gainesville: University Press of Florida, 2014); Adrienne Monteith Petty, *Standing Their Ground: Small Farmers in North Carolina since the Civil War* (New York: Oxford University Press, 2013); Eldred E. Prince Jr. with Robert Simpson, *Long Green: The Rise and Fall of Tobacco in South Carolina* (Athens: University of Georgia Press, 2000), esp. chap. 4.

7. Drew Swanson, *A Golden Weed: Tobacco and Environment in the Piedmont South* (New Haven, CT: Yale University Press, 2014), chaps. 6 and 7.

8. On enslaved workers in tobacco factories, see Suzanne G. Schnittman, "Slavery in Virginia's Urban Tobacco Industry, 1840–1860Ð (PhD diss., University of Rochester, 1987). On postwar black growers, see Jeffrey Kerr-Ritchie, *Freedpeople in the Tobacco South: Virginia, 1860–1900* (Chapel Hill: University of North Carolina Press, 1999); and Lynda Morgan, *Emancipation in Virginia's Tobacco Belt, 1850–1870* (Athens: University of Georgia Press, 1992). On the continuing importance of African American laborers in tobacco factories at the time when *Bright Leaf* was filmed, see Robert R. Korstad, *Civil Rights Unionism: Tobacco Workers and the Struggle for Democracy in the Mid-Twentieth-Century South* (Chapel Hill: University of North Carolina Press, 2003).

9. Tara Parker-Pope, *Cigarettes: Anatomy of an Industry from Seed to Smoke* (New York: New Press, 2001), 67–68; Richard Kluger, *Ashes to Ashes: America's Hundred-Year Cigarette War, the Public Health, and the Unabashed Triumph of Philip Morris* (New York: Knopf, 1996), 6–7.

10. Parker-Pope, *Cigarettes*, 16–17; Iain Gately, *Tobacco: The Story of How Tobacco Seduced the World* (New York: Grove, 2001), 237–52; Elizabeth M. Whelan, *A Smoking Gun: How the Tobacco Industry Gets Away with Murder* (Philadelphia: George F. Stickley, 1984), chap. 8.

11. Sarah Milov, "Little Tobacco: The Business and Bureaucracy of Tobacco Farming in North Carolina, 1920–1965Ð (PhD diss., Princeton University, 2013), 245–62; Pete Daniel, *Toxic Drift: Pesticides and Health in the Post–World War II South* (Baton Rouge: Louisiana State University Press, 2007), 121–24; Rachel Carson, *Silent Spring* (Boston: Houghton Mifflin, 1962).

12. Brianna Rego, "The Polonium Brief: A Hidden History of Cancer, Radiation, and the Tobacco Industry," *Isis* 100, no. 3 (September 2009): 453–84.

13. Allan M. Brandt, "Difference and Diffusion: Cross-Cultural Perspectives on the Rise of Anti-Tobacco Policies," in *Unfiltered: Conflicts over Tobacco Policy and Public Health*, ed. Eric A. Feldman and Ronald Bayer (Cambridge, MA: Harvard University Press, 2004), 257–59; Kluger, *Ashes to Ashes*, 259–60; Gideon Doron, *The Smoking Paradox: Public Regulation in the Cigarette Industry* (Cambridge, MA: Abt Books, 1979), 12–13.

14. Liggett & Myers Tobacco Company, *Tobaccoland, U.S.A.* (New York, 1940), 8.

15. *Bright Leaves*, dir. Ross McElwee (New York: First Run/Icarus Films, 2003). For an anthropological exploration of rural North Carolina's current "addiction" to tobacco culture, see Peter Benson, *Tobacco Capitalism: Growers, Migrant Workers, and the Changing Face of a Global Industry* (Princeton, NJ: Princeton University Press, 2012), and for a similar Kentucky study, see Ann K. Ferrell, *Burley: Kentucky Tobacco in a New Century* (Lexington: University Press of Kentucky, 2013).

16. Robert Penn Warren, *Night Rider* (Boston: Houghton Mifflin, 1939); Ellen Glasgow, *The Deliverance: A Romance of the Virginia Tobacco Fields* (New York: Doubleday, Page, 1904).

25

Adaptation and Autonomy on the Lower East Side
The Jews of *Hester Street*

STEPHEN J. WHITFIELD

"Once I thought to write a history of the immigrants in America," Harvard's Oscar Handlin famously wrote in 1951. "Then I discovered that the immigrants *were* American history."[1] That claim, though vulnerable to scholarly accusations of overstatement, opens his classic account of the mass migration of the nineteenth century, *The Uprooted*. The year of its publication also marked the death of the most influential Jewish journalist ever to work in the United States. Abraham Cahan had been a founder as well as the longtime editor of the *Forverts* (also known as the *Jewish Daily Forward*). Established in 1897, it was the most widely circulated foreign-language newspaper in the nation as well as the most widely circulated Yiddish-language newspaper in the world. Cahan arrived in New York City in 1881 and bore the impress, according to the historian John Higham, of three cultures: Russian, Jewish, and American.[2] In 1896 Cahan published a novella, *Yekl: A Tale of the New York Ghetto*, which was adapted eight decades later into an independent film entitled *Hester Street*.

That 1975 production was the first film of the director and scenarist Joan Micklin Silver. Shot in black and white to convey a sense of authenticity, *Hester Street* avoids the trap of romanticizing the past, of pretending that a vibrant and cohesive community once immunized itself against the forces of fragmentation. In 1896 modernization was already shredding the bonds of continuity and stability. Faithful to its literary original, *Hester Street* is therefore free of sentimentality. The sadness of marital struggle—the crude attempt to transform a baffled, hurt wife into something that she is not—prohibits this film from wrapping its ambience in a comforting glow of nostalgia.

The distance of eight decades also enabled Silver to record the tensions among the uprooted with a certain critical detachment. Shifting the title of Cahan's tale from his male protagonist, she endows her movie with a feminist sensibility. At the end of the nineteenth century, when *Yekl* was published and when the story of *Hester Street* takes place, the plight of women was especially pronounced, and the options for impoverished urban women were especially grim. Stephen Crane's *Maggie: A Girl of the Streets* (1893) ends in a suicide; and Theodore Dreiser's *Sister Carrie* (1900) traces the pursuit of loneliness. But *Hester Street* becomes the address where the high tide of Victorian patriarchy meets its match, as a divorcee manages to achieve a measure of autonomy and chooses the pursuit of happiness instead of honoring the expectations of submissiveness.

But the movie also shows how high a price was exacted in the transplantation to the New World. For Gitl (Carol Kane), the ache of adjustment is real. She is confused and baffled by the challenges of language, custom, and economic survival. An urban legend has it that a disillusioned Italian immigrant picked up three lessons upon his arrival: (1) the streets were not paved with gold; (2) the streets were not paved at all; and (3) *I* was expected to pave them. America projected promises, but they were often unfulfilled. Within the chronological confines of 1896, *Hester Street* highlights the sense of displacement and homelessness that the female protagonist feels. In exposing the internal dynamics of Jewish life, the film reveals the clashes between men and women, between the secular and the pious, between the sweatshop boss and his workers.

Connubial conflict drew the special attention of the Yiddish stage and of early Yiddish films. For example, in Sidney M. Goldin's silent film *The Heart of a Jewess*, which Universal released in 1913, a wife works in a sweatshop to earn enough money to pay for her husband's passage to New York. His name, incidentally, is the same as that of Gitl's own husband: Jake. In Goldin's film, Jake achieves success by becoming a doctor and discards his wife so that he can marry wealth. The new fiancée dumps Jake, however, and the heroine marries the sweatshop foreman, who has loved her from the beginning.[3] The similarity to *Hester Street* suggests the frequency of marital incompatibility among immigrants. Had a noun like *Jewess* still been acceptable in 1975, Silver might well have called her own film *The Heart of a Jewess*.

Jake's own heart is cold. The very ferocity of the demands that Jake (Steven Keats) makes upon his wife to adapt quickly and fully to the New World and his

The classic 1907 photograph *The Steerage*, by Alfred Steiglitz, although taken on a ship traveling from New York to Europe, captures the class divisions that characterized immigrant transport at the turn of the century.

own infatuation with his already Americanized mistress, Mamie Fein (Dorrie Kavanaugh), constitute the assimilationist project on steroids. Once known as Yankele (a term of endearment in Yiddish) as well as Yekl, but now giving himself an American nickname, Jake is dedicated to jettisoning the burden of the past. When Gitl (Carol Kane) arrives at Ellis Island after three years of geographical separation, she fails at first to recognize her husband. Clean-shaven and dapper, Jake looks like a "nobleman." But to her horror, he clips off with scissors their son Yossele's long locks, which pious Jews favored, and renames him Joey. With a fury that exceeds the bounds of reason, Jake insists that his wife abandon the wig that signifies female modesty. And of course the sooner Gitl and Joey learn English, the smoother the velocity of assimilation. Ashamed that his wife from the Old Country is a *grune* (greenhorn), he pushes beyond decency the desire to be considered a "Yankee" and nothing else. Her piety and superstition embarrass him in this "educated" country called America. Because Gitl personifies what retards his wish to forge a new identity, this callow conformist drives her to seek a divorce. Jake is an extreme product of centuries of life in the Diaspora, which ensured a consciousness of Jewish difference in Christendom. *Hester Street* thus links private pain with collective history and remorselessly depicts the penalties Jews face as they struggle to fit in in America.

Jake's only redeeming feature is the pride he takes in his son, whom he thinks might even grow up to become president of the United States until Bernstein, the pious boarder whom Gitl will marry at the end of the film, undermines that far-fetched political fantasy by mentioning the constitutional requirement that occupants of the White House must be native-born. (A portrait of the incumbent, Grover Cleveland, is shown on the wall of the reception hall at Ellis Island.) With his unbounded aspirations and limited self-awareness, this "American feller, a Yankee," as he proclaims himself in the novella,[4] turns out to be quite easy to deflate. Especially effective at this assignment is Gitl's friend Mrs. Kavarsky (Doris Roberts), whose wisecracks display the tang of folk wisdom. When Jake continues his affair with Mamie, Mrs. Kavarsky admonishes him for his infidelity by announcing, "With one *tuchus* [rear end] you can't dance at two weddings." She refuses to be taken in by his rationale for his extramarital affair: "You can't piss on my back and call it rain." Undeterred, this newly minted "Yankee" nevertheless wants it all and wants it now.

He finds it easier to bully the bearded, skullcap-wearing Bernstein (Mel Howard). For him Jake has nothing but contempt. He scoffs at Bernstein's willingness to give English lessons (at twenty-five cents a pop) in the neighborhood, for what fool would want to learn the language from so obvious a *grune*? Bernstein joins the family in an excursion to the countryside but shows no curiosity when Jake teaches his son baseball. Understanding the "national pastime" is further evidence of Jake's hunger for inclusion in America. Cahan himself catered to the urgency of such yearning, and not only because *Yekl* was written in English. In 1909 the *Forverts* published an article on the fundamentals of baseball so that the process of adjustment might be accelerated. The central mission of the *Forverts* was to ease that process and, according to the literary scholar Donald Weber, to reduce the "distresses and deformations" entailed in "the struggle to be 'American.'"[5] Had the tale and the film been set a year later (in 1897), when the newspaper was founded, Bernstein might have found a journalistic remedy for the difficulties of adaptation to America.

But he shows no interest in discarding the claims of tradition. He is learned enough to be writing a biblical commentary in the cramped tenement apartment he shares with Jake and Gitl and their son. When Bernstein is about to leave the household because he cannot afford to pay the rent owing to the slack season, he is shown packing his books. Although he may be indigent, and his social status is low, Bernstein's inner life is rich because of his devotion to the study of the Talmud. In front of his small sewing machine Bernstein earns only six dollars a week, whereas Jake exults in making twice as much, reinforcing his disdain for his colleague. To be sure, their gross boss is no bargain and ought to remind viewers of Cahan's own socialist convictions. The boss comes close to being a coarse, overbearing, smirking anti-Semitic caricature. His girth suggests that he has prospered. Having risen from peddler to employer, he feels that he has earned the right to gloat. In the shtetl, scholars were admired, and they were considered catches for the daughters of wealthy families. Those who lacked the aptitude for religious study (like this boss) enjoyed a far lower status. But in the United States, the last shall be first. No wonder, then, that Bernstein curses the New World (*a klug zu Columbus!*—a pox on the Great Navigator!).

So why come to so uncongenial a country? Gitl wants to know. The answer reveals how the primacy of religious study in the Pale of Settlement, from which most eastern European Jews came, stigmatized pleasure. Students were forbidden to dream of seeing even the little finger of a woman, Bernstein tells Gitl. Such imaginings would constitute the equivalent of seeing a naked woman. Harboring thoughts that were considered lustful led the guilt-ridden Bernstein to realize that he could no longer remain in Russia. But on the Lower

East Side, the bachelorhood that seems to be his fate becomes another source of mockery, as the boorish Jake predicts that Bernstein, with his slim earning power, will only find a wife who is deaf or even a hunchback. But his fundamental kindness and unobtrusive demeanor are precisely what make him attractive to Gitl.

She will work in the grocery store they plan to buy, thanks to the three hundred dollars Jake and Mamie fork over so that the "American feller" can secure the divorce he desperately wants. Bernstein expects to continue his studies in the back of the store, an arrangement that will perpetuate the gender roles of the shtetl. Yet the newly constituted family lives in America, so Gitl subscribes to the dream of upward mobility. Can they escape from the relentless pressures of poverty? The ethos of the era encouraged such hopes. The *fin de siècle* marked the heyday of that faith in rising from rags to, if not riches, then at least the respectability of the middle class. At the end of the nineteenth century, no novelist was more popular than Horatio Alger. At the dawn of the twentieth century, no black autobiography was more popular than Booker T. Washington's *Up from Slavery* (1901); and at the Tuskegee Institute, which he headed in rural Alabama, the motto of the class of 1886 optimistically proclaimed: "There Is Always Room at the Top!"[6] Nor can it be mere coincidence that the novelist and critic William Dean Howells, the author of *The Rise of Silas Lapham* (1885), immediately discerned the value of *Yekl*, whose author would go on to write *The Rise of David Levinsky* (1917). In the contest between an ancient religious heritage and the materialism of modern America, Cahan sensed how the conflict would be resolved, how customs and perhaps even memories would have to be forfeited so that the social circumstances might be bettered.

Thus the end of *Hester Street*, with its hint that mercantile investment might lift the ambitious Gitl, her son, and her new husband out of the working class, foretells the Jewish encounter with modernity in the twentieth century. Gitl and Bernstein might well remain mired in a desperate struggle for survival on the Lower East Side, but the odds might favor Joey; without the weight of tradition to encumber him, he might achieve *embourgeoisement*. For at least half a century after the publication of *Yekl*, a sizable Jewish working class would remain more or less intact. But over the horizon, past Hester Street, in the outer boroughs of New York City and then nestling in the suburbs that flourished after World War II, the bulk of American Jewry would come to reside. In 1900 one government report had estimated that the average Jewish immigrant from eastern Europe arrived with nine dollars (compared with fifteen dollars for all immigrants).[7] From so precarious a footing, however, no ethnic group would ascend more quickly or more spectacularly than the Jews. None would show a greater devotion to the belief that opportunity for advancement beckoned. *Hester Street* highlights the anguish of adaptation, the tensions permeating the lives of the newcomers. But because they would prove to be resilient, their future would be more glowing in the century to come.

Gitl lands in one of the most densely concentrated neighborhoods on the planet, with families packed into cramped tenements and more immigrants arriving all the time. The Lower East Side is a thick ethnic enclave as well, which leads her to wonder where the Gentiles are. Where do *they* live? Somewhere past Rivington Street, she conjectures. (Gitl raises this question while on a picnic outside the city, an hour's train ride away, so she must have seen Gentiles on the train; and Italians and others lived on the Lower East Side as well.) *Hester Street* gives a speaking role to only one non-Jew, the immigration officer who doubts whether Jake and Gitl are married. They respond by producing a wedding certificate, written in Hebrew; but of course the official cannot read the *ketubah*, so without any gestures of hospitality he resignedly waves the family through. Who else is missing from the movie? Absent are policemen, politicians, criminals—all of whom operated on the Lower East Side. Nor do social workers or settlement-house representatives show up in *Hester Street*. Nor do any labor organizers try to enlist the sweatshop toilers in a union like the International Ladies Garment Workers Union. Because Joey is so young, no school is shown in the film, even though education would launch many of the children of the uprooted out of poverty and into material security. Thus the Jews in the film are largely on their own.

After learning from Gitl's letter from Russia of his father's death, Jake puts on a prayer shawl and seems to be mumbling the *kaddish*, the Aramaic prayer for the dead. He soon stops, however, either because he is overcome by grief or remorse, or because he has forgotten the words, or because he realizes how insincere his prayers are. No one in *Hester Street* is shown attending a synagogue, though an elderly rabbi, evidently an anachronistic holdover from the Old World, arranges for the divorce at the end of the film. But otherwise the power of the clergy does not reach very far into the community. In 1893, when Rabbi Hayim Vidrowitz arrived from Moscow and put up a sign identifying him as "Chief Rabbi of America," he was asked which authority had bestowed such a title. Vidrowitz replied: "The sign painter."[8] The influence of rabbis did not vanish, of course, and among the most famous was Abba Hillel Silver of

In *Hester Street*, Russian immigrants Yankel Bogovnik (Steven Keats) and his wife Gitl (Carol Kane) seek counsel from a rabbi (Zvee Scool).

Cleveland, Joan Micklin Silver's father-in-law. He grew up on the Lower East Side, though his father had reached the New World earlier. When the rest of the family joined him, Abba Hillel Silver was taken on that first day in New York to a barber, who sheared off his earlocks.[9] The future Zionist tribune was thus expected to resemble other American boys. Rabbi Silver's son Raphael, a realtor, was the producer of *Hester Street*.

Other than the allure of a dancing school, where single men and women can meet, *Hester Street* shows no leisure activities. No one attends a concert or a play, even though visitors like the expatriate novelist Henry James and the German sociologist Max Weber, attending Yiddish plays early in the twentieth century, found themselves fascinated by the raw emotional force that poured out on stage. *Hester Street* makes no pretense of aiming at a comprehensive depiction of the Lower East Side and cannot be censured because Silver failed to make an epic. But the scenes she filmed are quite consistent with the consensus of historical scholarship, and much effort was expended to convey an atmosphere of authenticity. The photographs the Danish immigrant Jacob Riis took and then used to illustrate his book *How the Other Half Lives* (1890) may have aided the production design. By 1975, however, the Lower East Side had changed so much that *Hester Street* was shot in Greenwich Village instead.[10]

Perhaps because the historical actuality of the Lower East Side is too distant to revive, because it no longer bleeds into the present, the historian Hasia R.

Diner called the locale of *Hester Street* "the focal point of American Jewish re-membrance." This was "the neighborhood [that] was canonized into its mythic status," the entry to a nation but also a place that could be locked into remem-brance.[11] Indeed so many memoirs, autobiographies, and scarcely fictionalized accounts of growing up on the Lower East Side or elsewhere in New York have poured from the presses that Robert Byrne felt obliged to entitle his 1970 novel about a midwestern parochial-school upbringing *Memories of a Non-Jewish Childhood*. Near the end of Diner's own monograph on "the sacralization of the Lower East Side," she claims that it marked a moment in "the loss of coherence in modern Jewish culture."[12] Not that the meaning of the flow of immigration can be entirely erased, however. Take the family history of the current minority leader of the US Senate, Democrat Charles Ellis Schumer, who was born and raised in Brooklyn. Chuck Schumer's middle name refers to Ellis Island. His daughter's name is Emma, after Emma Lazarus, who wrote the poem that is embedded at the base of the Statue of Liberty. On January 27, 2017, when President Trump issued an executive order banning immigrants and refugees from seven predominantly Muslim nations, that iconic statue was shedding tears, Senator Schumer announced.[13]

The release date of *Hester Street* gives it a special niche in the evolution of American Jewry. By 1975 American Jews had decisively won the right to be equal, without having fully asserted the freedom to be different. In 1964 *Fiddler on the Roof* opened on Broadway; it evoked both the fragility and peril of Jewish life of the shtetl, as well as the radiant value of America as a refuge. In 1976 Irving Howe's magisterial *World of Our Fathers* examined the vibrant texture of Jewish life in New York City, but its discontinuities were too obvious to ignore, hence the search for roots that his book reinforced. Other signs of that quest can be cited. Henry Roth's novel about a Lower East Side boyhood, *Call It Sleep* (1934), was rediscovered. A paperback edition of Hutchins Hapgood's ethno-graphic essay *The Spirit of the Ghetto: Studies of the Jewish Quarter of New York* (1902), appeared in 1966, three years ahead of Milton Hindus's anthology *The Old East Side*. Such evidence of retrieval came in the wake of Moses Rischin's pioneering volume, *The Promised City: New York's Jews, 1870–1914* (1962), dedi-cated to the supervisor of his doctoral dissertation, Oscar Handlin. *Hester Street* is not an isolated instance of interest in the Lower East Side at the end of the nineteenth century.

On its own the movie now activates collective memory. The playwright Sharyn Rothstein has announced that she will adapt the film to the stage.

(Rothstein's own great-grandmother came to the United States alone, at the age of sixteen, and lived on the Lower East Side.)[14] Nor has the legacy of Abraham Cahan himself evaporated. The newspaper he edited for over half a century persists, though the *Forverts* became an English-language weekly, the *Forward*, in 1990, nearly a century after the publication of *Yekl*. The most famous of Yiddish newspapers had become a weekly in 1983 and then, after various permutations, a monthly in 2016. Rukhl Schaechter is the first American-born editor of the Yiddish edition. She is no anomaly: ninety-nine years after the publication of *The Rise of David Levinsky*, women filled all the chief editorial and publishing jobs at the *Forward*. (It now appears in a digital edition as well.) The editor in chief of the newspaper Cahan founded, Jane Eisner, conjectured that he "might have raised an eyebrow or two at the ascension of all these women—and then plunged right in to join us as we maintain his journalistic legacy."[15] Is it fair to guess that Gitl herself would have been pleased?

NOTES

1. Oscar Handlin, *The Uprooted: The Epic Story of the Great Migrations That Made the American People* (New York: Grosset & Dunlap, 1951), 3.

2. John Higham, *Send These to Me: Jews and Others Immigrants in Urban America* (New York: Atheneum, 1974), 96–99.

3. J. Hoberman, *Bridge of Light: Yiddish Film between Two Worlds* (New York: Schocken, 1991), 31–32.

4. Abraham Cahan, *Yekl and the Imported Bridegroom, and Other Stories of Yiddish New York* (New York: Dover, 1970), 70.

5. Donald Weber, *Haunted in the New World: Jewish American Culture from Cahan to the Goldbergs* (Bloomington: Indiana University Press, 2005), 18.

6. John P. Roche, *The Quest for the Dream: The Development of Civil Rights and Human Relations in Modern America* (New York: Macmillan, 1963), 9.

7. Marshall Sklare, *America's Jews* (New York: Random House, 1971), 60.

8. Irving Howe, *World of Our Fathers* (New York: Harcourt Brace Jovanovich, 1976), 195.

9. Marc Lee Raphael, *Abba Hillel Silver: A Profile in American Judaism* (New York: Holmes & Meier, 1989), 1–2.

10. Joyce Antler, "Hester Street," in *Past Imperfect: History according to the Movies*, ed. Mark C. Carnes (New York: Henry Holt, 1995), 178.

11. Hasia R. Diner, *Lower East Side Memories: A Jewish Place in America* (Princeton, NJ: Princeton University Press, 2000), 7.

12. Diner, *Lower East Side Memories*, 163.

13. Sam Frizell, "The Face of the Opposition," *Time*, 20 February 2017, 31.

14. Talya Zax, "'Hester Street' Gets Its Chance on Stage," *Forward*, 30 December 2016, 31; BWW News Desk, "Broadway Vet Sarna Lapine to Direct Sharyn Rothstein's HESTER STREET," 26 January 2018, Broadway World, www.broadwayworld.com/article/Sarna-Lapine-To-Direct-Sharyn-Rothsteins-HESTER-STREET-20180126.

15. Jane Eisner, "Women Lead the Forward into Ambitious Digital Era," *Forward*, 1 July 2016, 16–17.

26

"We've Taken Old Gods and Given Them New Names"
The Spirit of Sankofa in *Daughters of the Dust*

ALLISON DORSEY

The twenty-fifth anniversary of Julie Dash's lyrical meditation on the strength of black family, community, and history, *Daughters of the Dust,* was celebrated with a theatrical re-release and received a Special Award from the New York Film Critics Circle in December 2016. The power of the film is undiminished; the themes remain salient, and the hunger for narratives that magnify the black female voice is not sated. The film was groundbreaking in 1991, as Dash was the first black female filmmaker to produce a feature-length film that was distributed in wide release. In that historical moment of Operation Desert Storm and the release of the taped recording of the brutal police beating of the twenty-five-year-old black taxi driver Rodney King, Hollywood and the mainstream film industry passed on the opportunity to embrace Dash and the dozens of talented black male and female actors whose skill had brought her vision to life. Contemporarily, in the face of revived racial strife, continued police violence, and a new civil rights movement, black filmmakers and creative artists from Ava DuVernay to Beyoncé continue to pay homage to Dash's artistry and vision.

The film remains a work of singular beauty, director Dash having captured the backdrop of slavery with images of the dust from red clay soil, black hands working bold blue indigo, the gray-brown bark of live oak trees draped with pale green Spanish moss, dull-colored sweet grass, and the golden dunes that fall away to white sand beaches. The narrative is nonlinear, the story told in and out of time. Smartly dressed New Negroes are poised in 1902, leaning into the twentieth century, with all its promise of equality and opportunity. "It was an age of beginnings, a time of promises. The newspaper said it was time for everyone, the rich and the poor, the powerful and the powerless."[1] Born free in the forty-one years since the start of the Civil War, these descendants of captured Africans seek to escape the legacy of enslavement, to escape both the limited opportunities and the violence that are the hallmarks of white supremacy and Jim Crow. Set in the lush low country of the Sea Islands, stretched along the coast of South Carolina and Georgia, the film opens as members of the Peazant family prepare to leave their ancestral home and the cultural traditions of the Gullah/Geechee and move to the mainland.[2]

A second story runs parallel to this tale of mobility and uplift. *Daughters of the Dust* resonates with the spirit of *sankofa*. Taken from the Akan language of Ghana, *sankofa* means "to go back and get," to retrieve wisdom from the past. The term, often represented by the coordinating symbol of a bird looking backward to pluck an egg from its own back, is part of a Ghanaian proverb, *Se wo were fi na wosankofa a yenkyi*, "It is not wrong to go back for that which you have forgotten."[3] The proverb calls us to return to the past, to remember who we have been, and to seek guidance for the future. Dash invites the audience to look to the antebellum period, to slavery, to retrieve those things from the past that might otherwise be lost: the lessons of African spirituality, the restorative power of self-love, and the strength of family and community solidarity that sustained those who survived enslavement and those who hope to thrive in freedom. The family matriarch and griot, great-grandmother Nana Peazant is the embodiment of the wisdom of the past. The lessons she shares unfold through the narration of the Peazant women, including the Unborn Child, Eula, Viola, Yellow Mary, and Haagar.

The audience steps into a story infused with an African-based spirituality at the heart of Gullah/Geechee religious beliefs and practices known as conjure and hoodoo. The result of a melding of the traditions from the Akan, Yoruba, Igbo, and Mende, of Christianity and Islam, these faith traditions allowed enslaved people to endure psychic pain and sorrow, physical injury and loss. "We've taken old gods and given them new names," says Nana Peazant as she encourages her family members to pay homage to traditions both ancient and new, African and American. Orishas, the pantheon of Yoruba lesser gods who intercede with Olodumare, the supreme being or most high god, are summoned through characters in the film, as Dash reveals in her handwritten notes in the margins of the film script.[4] Nana Peazant represents Obatala, the oldest of the orishas, wise keeper of consciousness. Elegeba, the god of the crossroads and the messenger between the worlds of the living and the spirits,

Actress Cora Lee Day as Nana Peazant, the matriarch and griot of the
Peazant family, in *Daughters of the Dust*

is present in the Unborn Child. Ogun, the god of iron, patron saint of all those
who work with metal, craft weapons of war, and seek justice, is manifest on
screen as Eli Peazant, who vents his frustration and anger while working as a
blacksmith. Yellow Mary, though not garbed in the traditional blue-and-white
dress, embodies Yemonja, the goddess of the sea. An outsider rather than a
member of the Peazant clan, Trulia represents Oshun, goddess of the Oshun
River, known for her sensuality, vanity, and jealousy. Other markers of African
religious syncretism are carefully placed throughout the film, including the
kalunga line painted on the back of a turtle and a glass of water placed beneath
a bed on an envelope.

Early in the film, Eli Peazant names many of the symbols, translating for
viewers who may not be familiar with or understand the symbols themselves
or their power to evoke *ashe,* "the power that animates all of creation; it comes
from the source of creation and is available to everything within the universe."[5]
Eli also rails at Nana Peazant for her "failure" to protect the family: "When
we were children, we really believed you could work the good out of evil. We
believed in the newsprint on the walls . . . Your tree of glass jars and bottles . . .
The rice you carried in your pockets. We believed in the spirit tree, the frizzled-
haired chickens . . . the coins, the roots and the flowers. We believed they
would protect us and every little thing we owned or loved." Disheartened and
frustrated at the knowledge that neither freedom nor Nana Peazant's conjuring

protected his wife, Eula, and fearful that the child Eula carries is the product of her rape, Eli is determined to turn his back on the culture of the past. He wishes to flee the site of Eula's shame and his humiliation, to escape their shared sorrow by leaving the island.

As she will many times in the film, Nana Peazant acts to help Eli and others understand the power of Gullah/Geechee faith traditions. Conjure is neither make believe nor magic that endows practitioners with the superhuman ability to change the course of human events. The signs and symbols, rituals and traditions, are only avenues to the past, to the spirit of the ancestors on whose strength and wisdom we draw in difficult times. "Call on those old Africans Eli. They'll come to you when you least expect them. They'll hug you up quick and soft like the warm sweet wind. Let them old souls come into your heart, Eli. Let them touch you with the hands of time. Let them feed your head with wisdom that ain't from this day and time. Because when you leave this island, Eli Peazant, you ain't going to no land of milk and honey."

The disfranchised and marginalized employ conjure to find succor and inspiration from loved ones who have gone before, who watch over us and love us still. Through Nana Peazant, Dash speaks plainly and clearly to the audience about the power of faith traditions born in the travails of the past. "I'm trying to learn you how to touch your own spirit! I am trying to give you something to take north with you—along with all your great big dreams." For viewers long past the turn of the twentieth century but mindful of the black dreams so long deferred, there is undeniable truth in Nana Peazant's vision. Black residents of the Sea Islands had by 1902 weathered storms both physical and political. Hurricanes damaged homesteads on the islands in 1893, 1894, and 1898, driving residents to the mainland. Equally impactful was the 1898 political storm in South Carolina, which drove black men away from the polls with virulent rhetoric, threats of violence, and a change in the state constitution. A mere six years later, black men also experienced disfranchisement in Georgia, whether "on the mainland" or on the islands.[6] Access to hard-won political rights and economic opportunity was slipping away from the "free born" descendants of those who survived slavery. Equally significant then and now, the descendants needed an internal sense of self to sustain them in the face of systemic racism and white supremacy in all its forms.

Understanding the enslaved past as a source of strength and guidance is not without challenge. *Daughters of the Dust* recounts the sufferings of the enslaved but also wishes to highlight the promise and hope of the future. Nana Peazant, who is the bridge to the past, recalls life for those enslaved on the islands: "This was the worse place to have been born during slavery. Our hands scarred blue with the poisonous indigo dye that built up all these plantations from swamp land. Our spirits numb from the sting of fever from the rice fields. Our backs, bent down forever with the planting and hoeing of the Sea Island cotton."

The film not only addresses the experiences of slavery in America but also raises the specter of the slave trade. Viola shares the story of the *Wanderer,* a ship "still running and hiding salt water Africans, pure breed" in 1858, with a skeptical Mr. Sneed. The elderly Muslim Bilal, also speaking with Sneed, confirms the tale. "I came here on a ship called the *Wanderer.*" But it is the telling and retelling of the story of Ibo Landing, on St. Simon's Island that evokes the special sorrow of the Middle Passage. The damaged carving of an African figure floats in the river, a visual reminder of the chained men, women, and children who walked into the sea. A conversation between Yellow Mary and Eula raises the threat of drowning at Ibo Landing. When questioned by Sneed, Bilal discounts the seemingly supernatural belief shared by the island dwellers that the Ibo captives took flight as they stepped into the sea: "Some say the Ibo flew back home to Africa. Some say they all joined hands and walked on top of the water. But, Mister, I was there. Those Ibo, men, women and children, a hundred or more, shacked in iron . . . when they went down in the water, they never came up. Ain't nobody can walk on water." Slavery in the Georgia low country did indeed offer horrors and great sorrow. The 1803 mass suicide at Ibo Landing and the brutal rending of family and community in the 1859 "Weeping Time" sale of more than four hundred slaves in two days recall the violent and dehumanizing experience of bondage in the region.[7]

The slave past offers yet another horror. Assaulted and shamed, Eula Peazant is the symbol of generations of black women dishonored by violence and sexual assault during slavery and afterwards. What The Unborn Child names as "my ma and daddy's problem" is a problem not just for Eula and Yellow Mary; the threat of ruination at the hands of white men hovers over all black women. Eula, like thousands before her, is encouraged to keep silent about the identity of her rapist for fear that Eli will risk death by seeking vengeance: "You've got a good man Eula. Somebody you can depend on. He doesn't need to know what could get him killed. There's enough uncertainty in life without having to sit at home wondering which tree your husband's body is hanging from. Don't tell him anything." How, then, are the members of the Peazant family, male and female, young and old, to embrace and draw strength from a past that carries such pain and violation? Nana Peazant gives voice to the link between the present and the past as she tries to calm Eli's fears: "You won't ever have a baby that wasn't sent to you. The ancestors and the womb, they're one, they're the same. Those in this grave, like those who're across the sea, they're with us. They're all the same. The ancestors and the womb are one. Call on your ancestors, Eli. Let them guide you. You need their strength." Angry and unable to accept this powerful truth, that all children born to black mothers are blessed gifts to the community, Eli focuses, as do other members of the family, on the idea of flight to a space of imagined safety and a future away from the island.

The women of the Peazant family successfully "call on the ancestors" to provide guidance and strength to the community. The Unborn Child explains, "Nana prayed and the old souls guided me into the New World." This spirit of a new life called by the ancestors works to soften Eli's hardened heart. The dutiful Christian Viola begins mockingly to recite the names of the islanders. As she continues, she moves from the present to the past, from names of the enslaved to names of the sites of their labors, her voice fading as she begins to list the names of the orishas, unconsciously calling them forth. "My own, I Own Her, I Adore Her, You Adore Her. We even have a Pete and Re-Pete. Sometimes these Islanders name their babies the day of the week or the season in which they were born. Not to mention everybody has several nicknames Goober, Boy Rat, Hail, Harvest, Winter, Pigden, Hardtime, Fantee, Cudah, Ocra, Yono, Cish, Alemine, Jackiemine, Jaspermine, Cornhouse, Binah, *Shango, Obatala, Oya-yansa, Yemonja, Eshu Elegeba*." Ultimately it is Eula, standing at the edge of Ibo Landing and reciting the story of the Africans walking into the sea, calling back the power of those sacrificed ancestors that helps claim her child. The old souls who send the Unborn Child and the ancestors who possess Eli in the graveyard allow him to release the rage and paralyzing fear and accept Eula's child as his own.

Calling on the ancestors also gives Eula the will to free herself, to free Yellow Mary and all the Peazant women from the corrosive power of shame. Defiant and impassioned, Eula breaks the culturally imposed silence surrounding sexual assault. She urges the assembled Peazant women to set aside their disapproval of Yellow Mary as a "ruint" woman. Eula confronts the long history of violence against black women. She recognizes how the experience and fear of sexual assault have warped the hopes and dreams of generations of black women: "Deep, inside we believed that they ruined our mothers, and their mothers before them. And we live our lives always expecting the worse because we feel we don't deserve any better. Deep inside we believe that even our God can't heal the wounds of our past or protect us from the world that put shackles on our feet."

Eula cautions that there is no escaping the threat of sexual assault by flight to the mainland, for white supremacy also lurks there. Rather, the Peazant women must learn to conquer fear with self-acceptance, to overcome racist stereotypes and internalized self-loathing with self-love. Just as Nana Peazant is the link to the past, Eula is the conduit to the future. She understands the need to reconnect with the spirit of the ancestors in order to touch the lessons from those who survived slavery; more importantly, she recognizes the need to move beyond the pain of the past if black women are to survive in freedom.

> If you love yourselves, then love Yellow Mary, because she's part of you. *Just like we're a part of our ancestors.* A lot of us are going through things we feel we can't handle alone. There's going to be all kinds of roads to take in life. Let's not be afraid to take them. We deserve them, because we are all good woman. Do you . . . do you understand who we are and what we have become? We're the daughters of those old dusty things Nana carries in her tin can. We carry too many scars from the past. Our past owns us. We wear our scars like armor, for protection. Our mother's scars, our sister's scars, our daughters' scars . . . thick hard ugly scars that no one can pass through to ever hurt us again. Let's live our lives without living in the fold of old wounds.

Her directive is clear. Black women can look to the past to draw strength from the ancestors, but they must also shed the weight of fear, sorrow, and shame in order to embrace the future with determination and hope. With Eula's soliloquy Dash invites black women to lay down the burden of the past and step into their own power. It is worth nothing that Dash's *Daughters of the Dust* foreshadows, by two years, a similar theme celebrated in Maya Angelou's poem *On the Pulse of Morning*:

> You the Ashanti, the Yoruba, the Kru, bought,
> Sold, stolen, arriving on a nightmare
> Praying for a dream.
> Here, root yourselves beside me.
> I am that Tree planted by the River,
> Which will not be moved.

I, the Rock, I, the River, I, the Tree
I am yours—your passages have been paid.
Lift up your faces, you have a piercing need
For this bright morning dawning for you.
History, despite its wrenching pain,
Cannot be unlived, but if faced
With courage, need not be lived again.[8]

Dash's *Daughters of the Dust* offers a new generation insight into self-love and empowerment. Many Americans, millennials and their elders, at once buoyed by the election of the nation's first black president, were traumatized and disheartened by the specious racialist attacks on the character of that president and of the black first family. Attempts to disparage the nation's highest-profile black female, first lady Michelle Obama, were understood by many as emblematic of a disrespect and hostility toward black womanhood in general. This enmity is the background, the green screen on which the deaths of unarmed black women and girls, including Tanisha Anderson and Sandra Bland; of black men, including Eric Garner and Freddie Gray; and of black children such as seventeen-year-old Trayvon Martin and twelve-year-old Tamir Rice at the hands of law enforcement have been projected, captured on surveillance footage, recorded on cell phones, and taped by police body cameras.[9]

There are uncomfortable parallels between nineteenth-century racial violence and contemporary police shootings. Young people and scholars alike have taken to social media to remind the wider world of the dangers of #Breathingwhileblack and demand those employed "to protect and serve" to simply #Stopkillingus. Guided by academic analysis of popular culture provided by young scholars, such as Candice Benbow's "Lemonade Syllabus," and thoughtful investigative journalism like Ta-Nehisi Coates's "The Case for Reparations," a new generation has cast its gaze backward in search of a useful past.[10] They wish to understand the structures that produced contemporary racial and class hierarchies. They also seek to understand how the ancestors, recent and ancient, fought for their freedom and safeguarded their souls in battle. Young black women have rediscovered intersectionality and joined renewed debates about the nature and usefulness of black feminism. In this moment, Julie Dash's mystical film shines a bright light on the way forward. *Daughters of the Dust*, a reclamation and celebration of black culture, family, and love, serves as a tutorial, a spirit guide to help the generations face (again) an old threat manifest in new forms. In the spirit of Sankofa, *Daughters of the Dust* calls to us: reach back, take what you need, and then stride forward with purpose and power.

NOTES

I thank Taylor Morgan for her editorial assistance and insightful suggestions.

1. Quotations are taken from the film *Daughters of the Dust,* dir. Julie Dash (New York: Kino Video, 1991), DVD. See "The Script," in Julie Dash, *Daughters of the Dust: The Making of an African American Women's Film,* with Toni Cade Bambara and bell hooks (New York: New Press, 1992).

2. On the history and culture of the Gullah/Geechee, see Margaret Washington, *A Peculiar People: Slave Religion and Community-Culture among the Gullah* (New York: New York University Press, 1988); Michael Gomez, *Exchanging Our Country Marks: The Transformation of African Identities in the Colonial and Antebellum South* (Chapel Hill: University of North Carolina Press, 1998); Philip Morgan, ed., *African American Life in the Georgia Lowcountry: The Atlantic World and the Gullah Geechee* (Athens: University of Georgia Press, 2010); Cornelia Walker Bailey, *God, Dr. Buzzard, and the Bolito Man: A Saltwater Geechee Talks about Life on Sapelo Island* (New York: Doubleday, 2000); and Melissa L. Cooper, *Making Gullah: A History of Sapelo Islanders, Race, and the American Imagination* (Chapel Hill: Universtiy of North Carolina Press, 2017).

3. See Shelia Petty, *Contact Zones: Memory, Origins, and Discourses in Black Cinema* (Detroit: Wayne State University Press, 2008); and Angela K. Beale, "Daring to Create Change Agents in Physical Education: The Sankofa Philosophy," *Journal of Physical Education, Recreation & Dance* 84, no. 4 (2013): 7–9.

4. See Jacob K. Olupona and Terry Rey, eds., *Òrìdà Devotion as World Religion: The Global-ization of Yorùbá Religious Culture* (Madison: University of Wisconsin Press, 2008).

5. Will Coleman, "'Amen' and 'Ashe': African American Protestant Worship and Its West African Ancestor," *CrossCurrents* 52, no. 2 (Summer 2002): 158–64, http://www.jstor.org/stable/24460537.

6. On disfranchisement, see Michael Perlman, *Struggle for Mastery: Disfranchisement in the South, 1888–1908* (Chapel Hill: University of North Carolina Press, 2001). On the 1893, 1894, and 1898 hurricane seasons, see Walter Fraser Jr., *Lowcountry Hurricanes: Three Centuries of Storms at Sea and Ashore* (Athens: University of Georgia Press, 2009).

7. On Ibo Landing and flying Africans, see Timothy Powell, "Summoning the Ancestors: The Flying Africans Story and Its Enduring Legacy," in Morgan, *African American Life in the Georgia Lowcountry,* 253–80. On the "Weeping Time" auction, see Malcom Bell Jr., *Major Butler's Legacy: Five Generations of a Slaveholding Family* (Athens: University of Georgia Press, 2004), 311–41; and Kristopher Monroe, "The Weeping Time: A Forgotten History of the Largest Slave Auction Ever on American Soil," *Atlantic,* 10 July 2014, www.theatlantic.com/business/archive/2014/07/the-weeping-time/374159/.

8. Maya Angelou: "On the Pulse of Morning," *New York Times,* 21 January 1993. Following in the tradition of President John F. Kennedy, President William Jefferson Clinton invited Angelou to read an original poem at his first inauguration in January 1993.

9. See Kimberlé Williams Crenshaw, "#SayHerName: Resisting Police Brutality Against Black Women," African American Policy Forum, http://www.aapf.org/sayhernamereport/.

10. For the "Lemonade Syllabus," see http://www.candicebenbow.com/lemonadesyllabus/. Candice Benbow is a young scholar and writer. Currently a doctoral candidate in religion and society at Princeton Theological Seminary, she is also a lecturer in women's and gender studies at Rutgers University. See also Ta-Nehisi Coates, "The Case for Reparations," *Atlantic*, June 2014, www.theatlantic.com/magazine/archive/2014/06/the-case-for-reparations/361631/. The public intellectual and journalist Coates is the author of *Between the World and Me* (2015) and *We Were Eight Years in Power* (2017) and writes for *The Atlantic*. His work is rooted in the study of history and most often speaks to issues of race and class in America.

FILMOGRAPHY

Abe Lincoln in Illinois. 1940. RKO Radio. Director: John Cromwell. Cast: Raymond Massey, Gene Lockhart, Ruth Gordon, Mary Howard, Alan Baxter, Howard da Silva. 110 min.

The Alamo. 1960. United Artists. Director: John Wayne. Cast: John Wayne, Richard Widmark, Laurence Harvey, Patrick Wayne, Chill Wills, Linda Cristal. 167 min.

The Alamo. 2004. Touchstone Pictures. Director: John Lee Hancock. Cast: Dennis Quaid, Billy Bob Thornton, Jason Patric, Patrick Wilson, Emilio Echeovarria. 137 min.

Amistad. 1997. Dreamworks. Director: Steven Spielberg. Cast: Matthew McConaughey, Djimon Hounsou, Anthony Hopkins, Morgan Freeman, Jeremy Northam, Nigel Hawthorne, David Paymer, Chiwetel Ejiofor. 155 min.

The Birth of a Nation. 2016. Fox Searchlight. Director: Nate Parker. Cast: Nate Parker, Armie Hammer, Penelope Ann Miller, Jackie Earl Haley, Gabrielle Union. 120 min.

Bright Leaf. 1950. Warner Bros. Director: Michael Curtiz. Cast: Gary Cooper, Lauren Bacall, Patricia Neal, Jack Carson, Donald Crisp, Gladys George. 110 min.

The Conspirator. 2010. American Film Company. Director: Robert Redford. Cast: Robin Wright, James McAvoy, Tom Wilkinson, Kevin Kline, Evan Rachel Wood. 122 min.

Daughters of the Dust. 1991. American Playhouse. Director: Julie Dash. Cast: Cora Lee Day, Alva Rogers, Barbarao, Umar Abdurrahamn. 110 min.

Far and Away. 1992. Imagine Films. Director: Ron Howard. Cast: Tom Cruise, Nicole Kidman, Thomas Gibson, Robert Prosky, Barbara Babcock, Cyril Cusack. 140 min.

Free State of Jones. 2016. Bluegrass Films. Director: Gary Ross. Cast: Matthew McConaughey, Guga Mbatha-Raw, Mahershala Ali, Keri Russell. 139 min.

Gangs of New York. 2002. Miramax. Director: Martin Scorcese. Cast: Leonardo DiCaprio, Daniel Day-Lewis, Cameron Diaz, Jim Broadbent, Liam Neeson, John C. Reilly. 167 min.

Gettysburg. 1993. Tristar Television. Director: Ron Maxwell. Cast: Tom Berenger, Martin Sheen, Stephen Lang, Richard Jordan, Andrew Prine. 271 min.

Glory. 1989. Tristar. Director: Edward Zwick. Cast: Matthew Broderick, Denzel Washington, Morgan Freeman, Cary Elwes, Andre Braugher. 122 min.

The Gorgeous Hussy. 1936. MGM. Director: Clarence Brown. Cast: Joan Crawford, Robert Taylor, Franchot Tone, Lionel Barrymore, Melvin Douglas, James Stewart. 103 min.

The Hateful Eight. 2015. Weinstein Company. Director: Quentin Tarantino. Cast: Samuel L. Jackson, Kurt Russell, Jennifer Jason Leigh, Walter Goggins, Tim Roth, Michael Madsen, Bruce Dern. 187 min.

Hester Street. 1975. Midwest Films. Director: Joan Micklin Silver. Cast: Steven Keats, Carol Kane, Mel Howard, Dorrie Kavanaugh, Doris Roberts. 89 min.

In the Heart of the Sea. 2015. Warner Bros. Director: Ron Howard. Cast: Chris Hemsworth, Benjamin Walker, Cillian Murphy, Brendan Gleeson, Ben Whitshaw. 122 min.

Jeremiah Johnson. 1972. Director: Sydney Pollack. Cast: Robert Redford, Will Geer, Delle Bolton, Josh Albee. 108 min.

Jezebel. 1938. Warner Bros. Director: William Wyler. Cast: Bette Davis, Henry Fonda, George Brent, Margaret Lindsay, Fay Bainter, Donald Crisp. 108 min.

The Journey of August King. 1995. Miramax. Director: John Duigan. Cast: Jason Patric, Thandie Newton, Larry Drake, Sam Waterston. 91 min.

Lincoln. 2012. Dreamworks. Director: Steven Spielberg. Cast: Daniel Day-Lewis, Sally Field, Tommy Lee Jones, David Straithairn, Hal Holbrook, Joseph Gordon-Levitt, James Spader. 150 min.

Little Big Man. 1970. Cinema Center Films. Director: Arthur Penn. Cast: Dustin Hoffman, Faye Dunaway, Chief Dan George, Richard Mulligan, Martin Balsam, Jeff Corey. 127 min.

Mandingo. 1975. Paramount. Director: Richard Fleischer. Cast: James Mason, Perry King, Ken Norton, Susan George, Brenda Sykes. 127 min.

The President's Lady. 1953. 20th Century Fox. Director: Henry Levin. Cast: Charlton Heston, Susan Hayward, John McIntyre, Fay Bainter. 96 min.

The Prisoner of Shark Island. 1936. 20th Century Fox. Director: John Ford. Cast: Warner Baxter, Gloria Stuart, Francis Ford, Harry Carey, Francis McDonald. 136 min.

The Revenant. 2015. Regency Enterprises. Director: Alejandro G. Inarritu. Cast: Leonardo DiCaprio, Tom Hardy, Domhall Gleason, Will Poulter, Forrest Goodluck. 157 min.

Santa Fe Trail. 1940. Warner Bros. Director: Michael Curtiz. Cast: Errol Flynn, Olivia de Havilland, Raymond Massey, Ronald Reagan, Alan Hale, William Lundigan. 110 min.

Sommersby. 1993. Warner Bros. Director: Jon Amiel. Cast: Richard Gere, Jody Foster, James Earl Jones, Bill Pullman, William Windom, Frankie Faison, Clarice Taylor. 114 min.

They Died with Their Boots On. 1941. Warner Bros. Director: Raoul Walsh. Cast: Errol Flynn, Olivia de Havilland, Arthur Kennedy, Charley Grapewin, Anthony Quinn, Sydney Greenstreet. 140 min.

12 Years a Slave. 2013. Fox Searchlight. Director: Steve McQueen. Cast: Chiwetel Ejiofor, Michael Fassbender, Lupita Nyong'o, Paul Giamatti, Sarah Paulson, Benedict Cumberbatch, Paul Dano, Alfre Woodard. 134 min.

The Undefeated. 1969. 20th Century Fox. Director: Andrew V. McLaglen. Cast: John Wayne, Rock Hudson, Antonio Aguilar, Roman Gabriel, Lee Meriwether, Merle Olsen. 119 min.

Young Mr. Lincoln. 1939. 20th Century Fox. Director: John Ford. Cast: Henry Fonda, Alice Brady, Marjorie Weaver, Richard Cromwell, Donald Meek. 100 min.

SELECTED FURTHER READING
Nineteenth-Century America on Film

Aquila, Richard. *The Sagebrush Trail: Western Movies and Twentieth-Century America*. University of Arizona Press, 2015.

Bandy, Mary Lea, and Kevin Stoehr. *Ride, Boldly Ride: The Evolution of the American Western*. University of California Press, 2012.

Barrett, Jenny. *Shooting the Civil War: Cinema, History and American National Identity*. Tauris, 2009.

Bogle, Donald. *Toms, Coons, Mulattoes, Mammies, and Bucks: An Interpretive History of Blacks in American Films*. Bloomsbury Academic, 2016. See esp. chapter 2, "Black Beginnings: From *Uncle Tom's Cabin* to *The Birth of a Nation*."

Burgoyne, Robert. *Film Nation: Hollywood Looks at U.S. History*. University of Minnesota Press, 2010. See esp. chapter 1, "Race and Nation in *Glory*."

Campbell, Edward D. C. *The Celluloid South: Hollywood and Southern Myth*. University of Tennessee Press, 1981.

Carnes, Mark. *Past Imperfect: History According to the Movies*. Henry Holt, 1995.

Carter, Everett. "Cultural History Written with Lightning: The Significance of *The Birth of a Nation* (1915)." In *Hollywood as Historian: American Film in Cultural Context*, ed. Peter C. Rollins. University Press of Kentucky, 1983.

Chadwick, Bruce. *The Reel Civil War: Mythmaking in American Film*. Knopf, 2001.

Coyne, Michael. *The Crowded Prairie: American National Identity in the Hollywood Western*. Tauris, 1998.

Cripps, Thomas. "The Absent Presence in American Civil War Films." *Historical Journal of Film, Radio, and Television* 14, no. 4 (1994): 367–76.

———. *Making Movies Black: The Hollywood Message Movie from World War II to the Civil Rights Era*. Oxford University Press, 1993.

———. *Slow Fade to Black: Negro in American Cinema, 1900–1942*. Oxford University Press, 1977.

Davis, Natalie Zemon. *Slaves on Screen: Film and Historical Vision*. Harvard University Press, 2002. See esp. chapter 4, "Witnesses of Trauma: *Amistad* and *Beloved*."

Delmont, Matthew. *Making Roots: A Nation Captivated*. University of California Press, 2016.

Fenin, George N., and William K. Everson. *The Western: From Silents to Cinerama*. Orion, 1962.

Gallagher, Gary. *Causes Won, Lost, and Forgotten: How Hollywood and Popular Art Shape What We Know about the Civil War*. University of North Carolina Press, 2008.

Guerrero, Ed. *Framing Blackness: The African American Image in Film*. Temple University Press, 1993. See esp. chapter 1, "From *Birth* to Blaxploitation: Hollywood's Inscription of Slavery," and chapter 2, "Slaves, Monsters, and Others: Racial Fragment, Metaphor, and Allegory on the Commercial Screen."

Hoberman, J. *An Army of Phantoms: American Movies and the Making of the Cold War*. New Press, 2011.

Hulbert, Matthew Christopher. *The Ghosts of Guerrilla Memory: How Civil War Bushwhackers Became Gunslingers in the American West*. University of Georgia Press, 2016. See esp. chapter 8, "Black Flags and Silver Screens."

———. "Texas Bound and Down: An Untold Narrative of Missouri's Guerrilla War on Film." *Journal of the West* 50, no. 4 (Fall 2011): 27–33.

Jackson, Robert. *Fade In, Crossroads: A History of the Southern Cinema*. Oxford University Press, 2017.

Kammen, Michael. *Mystic Chords of Memory: The Transformation of Tradition in American Culture*. Vintage, 1993.

McMahon, Jennifer, and B. Steve Caski, eds. *The Philosophy of the Western*. University Press of Kentucky, 2010.

McVeigh, Stephen. *The American Western*. Edinburg University Press, 2007.

Morey, Kathryn Anne, ed. *Bringing History to Life through Film: The Art of Cinematic Storytelling*. Rowman & Littlefield, 2014.

Rollins, Peter C., and John O'Connor. *Hollywood's West: The American Frontier in Film, Television, and History*. University Press of Kentucky, 2005.

Sachsman, David B., S. Kittrell Rushing, and Roy Morris Jr., eds. *Memory and Myth: The Civil War in Fiction and Film from "Uncle Tom's Cabin" to "Cold Mountain."* Purdue University Press, 2007.

Simmon, Scott. *The Invention of the Western Film: A Cultural History of the Genre's First Half-Century*. Cambridge University Press, 2003.

Slotkin, Richard. *Gunfighter Nation: The Myth of the Frontier in Twentieth Century America*. University of Oklahoma Press, 1998. See esp. parts 3, 4, and 5.

Smith, Andrew B. *Shooting Cowboys and Indians: Silent Western Films, American Culture, and the Birth of Hollywood*. University Press of Colorado, 2003.

Smyth, J. E. *Reconstructing American Historical Cinema: From Cimarron to Citizen Kane*. University Press of Kentucky, 2006. See esp. section 2, "Resolving Westward Expansion," and section 3, "The Civil War and Reconstruction."

Snee, Brian J. *Lincoln before Lincoln: Early Cinematic Adaptations of the Life of America's Greatest President.* Lexington: University Press of Kentucky, 2016.

Tompkins, Jane. *West of Everything: The Inner Life of Westerns.* Oxford University Press, 1992.

Toplin, Robert, ed. *Ken Burns's "The Civil War": Historians Respond.* Oxford University Press, 1996.

———. *Reel History: In Defense of Hollywood.* University Press of Kansas, 2002.

Verheoff, Nancy. *The West in Early Cinema.* Amsterdam University Press, 2006.

Walker, Janet, ed. *Westerns: Films through History.* Routledge, 2001.

Wills, Brian S. *Gone with the Glory: The Civil War in American Cinema.* Rowman & Littlefield, 2001.

Wright, Will. *Six Guns and Society: A Structural Study of the Western.* University of California Press, 1975.

CONTRIBUTORS

William L. Andrews is the author of *The Literary Career of Charles W. Chesnutt* (Louisiana State University Press, 1980) and *To Tell a Free Story: The First Century of Afro-American Autobiography, 1760–1865* (University of Illinois Press, 1986). He is a coeditor of *The Oxford Companion to African American Literature* (Oxford University Press, 1997) and *The Norton Anthology of African American Literature* (Norton, 2003) and general editor of *The Literature of the American South: A Norton Anthology* (Norton, 1998) and "North American Slave Narratives," http://docsouth.unc.edu/neh/. He has edited more than forty books on a wide range of African American literature and culture. In 2017 he was awarded the Jay B. Hubbell Medal for Lifetime Achievement by the American Literature Society of the Modern Language Association.

Donna J. Barbie is associate dean of the College of Arts and Sciences at Embry-Riddle Aeronautical University in Daytona Beach, Florida. In addition to writing *The Making of Sacagawea: A Euro-American Legend* (University of Alabama Press, 1996), she also contributed to and edited *The Tiger Woods Phenomenon: Essays on Golf's Fallible Superman* (McFarland, 2012) and more recently published "Bird Woman, Donna Reed, and A Gold Coin," in *We Proceeded On: Lewis and Clark Trail Heritage Foundation Journal* (2013). A devotee of historical films, she is particularly intrigued by films of nineteenth-century city life, such as *Hester Street*, probably because she was born and raised in Bismarck, North Dakota.

Joseph M. Beilein Jr. is associate professor of history at Penn State Erie, The Behrend College. He is the author of several essays that examine guerrilla warfare in the Civil War. He is the author of *Bushwhackers: Guerrilla Warfare, Manhood, and the Household in Civil War Missouri* (Kent State, 2016) and a coeditor of *The Civil War Guerrilla: Unfolding the Black Flag in History, Memory, and Myth* (University Press of Kentucky, 2015).

Michael Burlingame holds the Chancellor Naomi B. Lynn Distinguished Chair in Lincoln Studies at the University of Illinois at Springfield. He has written and edited many books about the sixteenth president, including the two-volume *Abraham Lincoln: A Life* (Johns Hopkins University Press, 2008), chosen by the *Atlantic* as one of the five best books of the year and the recipient of several awards, including the Lincoln Prize. He served as a consultant on Steven Spielberg's film *Lincoln*. When that noted director asked how he could illustrate the horrors of war without staging an epic battle scene à la *Saving Private Ryan*, Burlingame suggested that a vivid image of the horrors of the Civil War was the description of houses at Gettysburg just after the fighting there ended. Each house became a hospital, and outside the windows of those houses were piles of amputated arms and legs. Such limbs appear in the film in a different setting.

Catherine Clinton is the Denman Endowed Professor in American History at the University of Texas at San Antonio and International Research Professor at Queen's University Belfast. She is the author or editor of twenty-five books, including *The Plantation Mistress: Woman's World in the Old South* (Pantheon, 1982); *The Other Civil War: American Women in the Nineteenth Century* (Hill & Wang, 1989); *Southern Families at War: Loyalty and Conflict in the Civil War South* (Oxford University Press, 2000); and *Harriet Tubman: The Road to Freedom* (Little, Brown, 2005). She also served as a consultant on Steven Spielberg's *Lincoln* (2012), which was nominated for the Oscar for Best Picture.

James E. Crisp taught from 1972 through 2016 at North Carolina State University, where he is now professor emeritus of history. He most recently published "Who Were the Texians? The Creation of a Texas Identity in the Era of the Republic," in *Single Star of the West: The Republic of Texas, 1836–1845* (University of North Texas Press, 2017). In 2002 he worked briefly for Ron Howard in planning for the film *The Alamo*, which would star Billy Bob Thornton as Davy Crockett.

Allison Dorsey is professor of history at Swarthmore College. She received her MA and PhD from the University of California, Irvine. She is the author of "'The Great Cry Of Our People Is Land'! Black Settlement and Community Development on Ossabaw Island, Georgia, 1865–1900," published in *The Atlantic World and African American Life and Culture in the Georgia Lowcountry* (University of Georgia Press, 2010); "Black History *is* American History: Teaching African American History in the 21st Century," *Journal of American History* (2007); and *To Build Our Lives Together: Community Formation in Black Atlanta, 1875–1906* (University of Georgia Press, 2004). She is researching the lives of black freedmen along the Georgia seacoast. Self-identified fan girl and mother of a young filmmaker, she enjoys teaching the courses "History vs. Hollywood" and "History vs. Hollywood: the Black Edition," which invite students to study American history as depicted on film and analyze narratives created by the filmmakers.

Nicole Etcheson is the Alexander M. Bracken Professor of History at Ball State University. She is the author of *A Generation at War: The Civil War Era in a Northern Community* (University Press of Kansas, 2011) and *Bleeding Kansas: Contested Liberty in the Civil War Era* (University Press of Kansas, 2004), as well as numerous publications on Civil War and midwestern history.

Lesley J. Gordon is the Charles G. Summersell Chair of Southern History at the University of Alabama. Her publications include *General George E. Pickett in Life and Legend* (University of North Carolina Press, 1998), *Inside the Confederate Nation: Essays in Honor of Emory M. Thomas* (Louisiana State University Press, 2005), and *A Broken Regiment: The 16th Connecticut's Civil War* (Louisiana State University Press, 2014). From 2010 to 2015 she was editor of the academic journal *Civil War History*.

Kenneth S. Greenberg is Distinguished Research Professor of History at Suffolk University in Boston. He is the author or editor of numerous works, including *Honor and Slavery: Lies, Duels, Noses, Masks, Dressing as a Woman, Gifts, Strangers, Humanitarianism, Death, Slave Rebellions, the Proslavery Argument, Baseball, Hunting, and Gambling in the Old South* (Princeton University Press, 1996); *Nat Turner: A Slave Rebellion in History and Memory* (Oxford University Press, 2003); *The Confessions of Nat Turner and Related Documents* (Bedford, 1996); and *Masters and Statesmen: The Political Culture of American Slavery* (Johns Hopkins University Press, 1985). Additionally, he cowrote and coproduced *Nat Turner: A Troublesome Property* (2003), which was screened nationally on PBS.

Graham Russell Gao Hodges is the George Dorland Langdon Jr. Professor of History and Africana Studies at Colgate University. He is the author or editor of sixteen books, including his biography *Anna May Wong: From Laundryman's Daughter to Hollywood Legend* (Palgrave Macmillan, 2004).

Matthew Christopher Hulbert teaches American history at Texas A&M University–Kingsville. He is a recipient of the C. Vann Woodward Award and a former Harry Frank Guggenheim Foundation writing fellow whose first book, *The Ghosts of Guerrilla Memory: How Civil War Bushwhackers Became Gunslingers in the American West* (University of Georgia Press, 2016), won the 2017 Wiley-Silver Prize. Proud to have once been labeled a "militant film nerd" by students, he is a sucker for Leone westerns, Lean epics, and Hammer horror pictures.

John C. Inscoe is Alfred B. Saye Professor of History and University Professor at the University of Georgia, where he has taught since 1984. He's taught film courses focused on southern race relations, Appalachia, and American poverty. He is close to completion of a book tentatively titled *Appalachia on Film: History, Hollywood, and the Highland South.*

Ryan W. Keating is associate professor of history at California State University, San Bernardino, where he studies and teaches on the American Civil War, Ireland, and the Irish American experience. He is the author of two books, *Shades of Green: Irish Regiments, American Soldiers, and Local Communities in the Civil War Era* (Fordham University Press, 2017) and *The Greatest Trials I Ever Had: The Civil War Letters of Margaret and Thomas Cahill* (University of Georgia Press, 2017). His love for film came from his father, Mike, and grandfather, Joe, both of whom were passionate about war films and shared that passion with him.

Jacob F. Lee is assistant professor of history at Pennsylvania State University. A specialist in the history of early America and the American West, he is currently writing a social and environmental history of colonialism in the central Mississippi River valley from the fall of Cahokia to Indian Removal. Despite all evidence to the contrary, he continues to believe a great movie can be made about the Rocky Mountain fur trade.

Tom Lee, associate professor of history at East Tennessee State University, has written on Appalachia and the South. Most recently he has turned his attention to agriculture in the Mountain South and especially tobacco. He has great appreciation for the aesthetics of *Cold Mountain* and for its representation of mountain life and people. However, he believes that a number of stories from East Tennessee might be turned into dramatic films and suggests that a drama set in East Tennessee in the midst of the 1861 secession crisis might make for especially compelling cinema.

John F. Marszalek retired in 2002 as Giles Distinguished Professor Emeritus at Mississippi State University. He is currently the executive director and managing editor of the Ulysses S. Grant Association. He is the author or editor of thirteen books and more than 250 articles and book reviews, including *Sherman, A Soldier's Passion for Order* (Free Press, 1993), which was a finalist for the Lincoln Prize. His first book, *Court Martial: A Black Man in America* (Scribner's, 1972), was made into a Showtime motion picture and reissued as a paperback under the new title *Assault at West Point* (Collier, 1984).

Marcus Rediker is Distinguished Professor of Atlantic History at the University of Pittsburgh and senior research fellow at the Collège d'études mondiales in Paris. His books have won numerous awards and been translated into fifteen languages. They include *The Slave Ship: A Human History* (Viking, 2007) and *The Amistad Rebellion: An Atlantic Odyssey of Slavery and Freedom* (Viking, 2012). He is also the producer of the prizewinning documentary film *Ghosts of Amistad: In the Footsteps of the Rebels* (directed by Tony Buba), about the popular memory of the 1839 *Amistad* rebellion in contemporary Sierra Leone. He is currently working as guest curator in the J. M. W. Turner gallery at Tate Britain.

Brian Rouleau is associate professor of history at Texas A&M University. He is the author of one book and several articles on maritime history. More significantly, he once ate dinner in a restaurant while seated one table over from actor Vince Vaughn.

Jonathan D. Sarris is associate professor of history at North Carolina Wesleyan College. A specialist in Civil War history, he is the author of *A Separate Civil War: Communities in Conflict in the Mountain South* (University of Virginia Press, 2006). He is a devotee of the films of John Ford, Billy Wilder, and John Sayles.

John David Smith is the Charles H. Stone Distinguished Professor of American History at the University of North Carolina at Charlotte, where he specializes in the Civil War, southern history, slavery, and the history of racial thought. He is the author, editor, or coeditor of twenty-nine books, including *An Old Creed for the New South: Proslavery Ideology and Historiography, 1865–1918* (Greenwood, 1985); *Black Judas: William Hannibal Thomas and "The American Negro"* (University of Georgia Press, 1999); *Slavery, Race, and American History* (Routledge, 1998); *Lincoln and the U.S. Colored Troops* (Southern Illinois University Press, 2013); and *We Ask Only for Even Handed Justice* (University of Massachusetts Press, 2014). His most recent book is *Dear Delia: The Civil War Letters of Captain Henry F. Young, Seventh Wisconsin Infantry, 1861–1864*, coedited with Micheal J. Larson (forthcoming, 2019).

Diane Miller Sommerville, a member of the History Department at Binghamton University, is the author of *Rape and Race in the Nineteenth-Century South* (University of North Carolina Press, 2004) and, most recently, *Aberration of Mind: Suicide and Suffering in the Civil War Era South* (University of North Carolina Press, 2018). She awaits a Tarantino remake of *Mandingo*.

Matthew E. Stanley is assistant professor of history at Albany State University. He writes on race, region, labor, and collective memory during the Civil War era and the Gilded Age and is the author of *The Loyal West: Civil War and Reunion in Middle America* (University of Illinois Press, 2017). He would like to see Quentin Tarantino commit to his John Brown biopic.

Drew A. Swanson is associate professor of history at Wright State University in Dayton, Ohio. He is the author of three books on the southern environment and agriculture, most recently *Beyond the Mountains: Commodifying Appalachian Environments* (University of Georgia Press, 2018). He's still awaiting a Hollywood epic on nineteenth-century southern soil erosion.

Kevin Waite is assistant professor in American history at Durham University, in the United Kingdom. His book *The Continental South: Slavery, Empire, and the Civil War in the American West* is under contract with the University of North Carolina Press. Chances are, if a film features Clint Eastwood with a six-shooter, he'll probably love it—sometimes against his better judgment.

Stephen J. Whitfield held the Max Richter Chair in American Civilization at Brandeis University, where he taught from 1974 until 2017 and where he also won two teaching awards. He is the author of eight books, including *American*

Space, Jewish Time (Archon Books, 1988); *The Culture of the Cold War* (Johns Hopkins University Press, 1990); and *In Search of American Jewish Culture* (Brandeis University Press, 1999). He served as visiting professor at the Hebrew University of Jerusalem, at the Catholic University of Leuven in Belgium, at the Sorbonne, and at the University of Munich.

INDEX

Hudson, Rock, 240, 245–246
hurricanes, on Sea Islands, 303
Hussein, Sadam, 64
Huston, John, 126

Ibo Landing, 304
In the Heart of the Sea, 23–33
Inarittu, Alejandro G., 44
Indian princesses, 17–21
Indian wars, 251, 254
Indians. *See* Native Americans
Inglourious Basterds, 228, 232, 235–236
interracial marriage, with Native American
    women, 19–21, 39, 42–43
interracial sex, 114–121. *See also*
    miscegenation
Iraq war, 191, 200, 224
Ireland, 265–268
Irish Catholics, in New York City, 182–184,
    186–187
Irish immigration, 265–275
Irish stereotypes, 272–274, 276

Jackson, Andrew, 4, 48–56; films about,
    48–57
Jackson, Rachel, 48, 49–51
Jackson, Samuel L., 229
Jackson, Stonewall, 177
James, Henry, 296
Janney, Caroline, 243
Jarre, Kevin, 162, 167
Jefferson, Thomas, 14–15, 74, 100–101
Jeffersons, The, 116
Jekyll Island, Ga., 165
Jeremiah Johnson, 34–47
Jewish immigration, 289–294, 297
Jews, American, 297
Jezebel, 125–134
Jezebel (Biblical character), 125
Joadson, Theodore, 96, 98–99
Johnson, Andrew, 192, 198–200
Johnson, John ("Liver-Eating"), 37–38
Johnson, Lyndon B., 65
Johnson, Nunnally, 194–195

Johnson, Reverdy, 198
Jones, Howard, 97
Jones County, Miss., 207–216
Journey of August King, The, 73–83
Juarez, Benito, 241
Juaristas, 242

Kane, Carol, 290, 292, 296
Kansas Territory, 137, 141
Katrina (hurricane), 132
Keats, Steven, 290, 296
Kennedy, Jimhi, 164
Kidman, Nicole, 265–266, 274
Killer Angels, The, 172
King, Martin Luther, Jr., 235
King, Perry, 115, 117
King, Rodney, 224, 300
Kingsmont, NC, 279
Kline, Kevin, 196, 199, 201
Knight, Davis, 213–214
Knight, Newt, 207, 210–214
Ku Klux Klan, 1–2, 4, 5, 85, 209

Lawrence, KS, 140
Lazarus, Emma, 297
Lee, Robert E., 5, 141, 143, 174, 177, 239;
    surrender, 192
Leigh, Jennifer Jason, 229
Leigh, Vivien, 126
Lemisch, Jesse, 98
Levin, Henry, 49
Lewis, Meriwether, 13–21
Lewis and Clark expedition, 4, 13–21
Lincoln, 148, 156–159, 209–210
Lincoln, Abraham, 163, 165, 184, 188, 191,
    193, 210, 229–230, 232–233; assassination
    of, 5, 6, 191, 196–197; films about, 148–
    161; on slavery, 151–152, 154, 158
Lincoln, Mary Todd, 150, 152, 154–155,
    156–159
Lincoln, Robert, 156, 159
Lincoln-Douglas debates, 155
Lindsay, Margaret, 129
Little Big Man, 251, 256–261